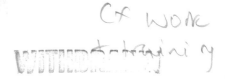

orkin

New Zealand

Fifth edition

Susan James

crimson

D1614457

For Dale, Megan and Clare

Published by **Crimson Publishing**
www.crimsonpublishing.com
4501 Forbes Blvd, Suite 200, Lanham MD 20706
Westminster House, Kew Road, Richmond, Surrey TW9 2ND
Distributed in North America by National Book Network
www.nbnbooks.com
Distributed in the UK by Portfolio Books
www.portfoliobooks.com

A catalogue record for this book is available from the British Library.

ISBN 978 1 85458 392 5

Printed and bound by Colourprint offset, Hong Kong

Acknowledgements

This book is the product of the kind efforts of many people to whom I am greatly indebted. For all her help with research and fact-checking – which always consumes such huge chunks of time and patience – thanks to Clare Kelly. For tracking down contributors willing to share their stories, thanks to Dale Dudman, Megan Kelly and Linda Keown. For their generous contributions and valuable advice, thanks to Michael De Courcy, Dermot Foley, Elizabeth Henderson, Jonathan Hill, Megan Kelly, Sam McLaughlan, James Palmer and Katy Parsons. For all their Christchurch expertise and detailed contributions, and for all the maps, emails, proofreading and corrections as well as their kindness and hospitality, special thanks are due to Marie Jean and Tom Woodhouse. For their photographs, thank you to Justin Cox, Kevin James, Linda Keown and Marie Jean Woodhouse. Special thanks are due to Kevin for his patience and support and for shouldering the whole team's workload so I could spend evenings and weekends writing, and to Nutsy for enduring all those extra hours and late nights behind the laptop.

OVERVIEW**OF**NEW ZEALAND

SOUTH PACIFIC
OCEAN

Paihia
Whangarei

Great Barrier Island

AUCKLAND

NORTH ISLAND

Hamilton

Tauranga

Rotorua

TASMAN SEA

Gisborne

New Plymouth   Lake Taupo

Napier

Cook Strait

Palmerston North

Nelson

WELLINGTON

Greymouth

SOUTH ISLAND

Kaikoura

Harihari

CHRISTCURCH

Mount Cook

Timaru

Milford Sound

Queenstown

Te Anau   Dunedin

SOUTH PACIFIC
OCEAN

Invercargill

Stewart Island

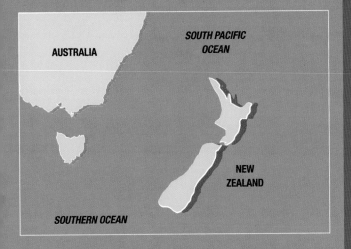

AUSTRALIA

SOUTH PACIFIC OCEAN

NEW ZEALAND

SOUTHERN OCEAN

REGIONS

1 Northland
2 Auckland
3 Waikato
4 Bay of Plenty
5 Gisborne
6 Hawke's Bay
7 Taranaki
8 Manawatu Wanganui
9 Wellington
10 Marlborough
11 Tasman
12 West Coast
13 Canterbury
14 Otago
15 Southland

Contents

Contents

Telephone numbers

Please note that the telephone numbers in this book are written as needed to call that number from inside the country you will probably be calling from. For example, a British removals company to New Zealand will be given as a UK number; a New Zealand removals company from the UK will have its international prefix.

To call another country from New Zealand, dial 00 before the number for the country concerned, then the subscriber's area code minus the first zero, then the subscriber's number.

To call New Zealand from another country dial 00 64 followed by the number minus the first zero.

Exchange rates

Throughout the book, New Zealand dollars have been used. The table below gives an indication of the exchange rates for other countries:

NZ dollar NZ$	British pound £	US dollar $	Euro €	Australian dollar A$
NZ$1	£0.39	$0.76	€0.49	A$0.79
NZ$10	£3.85	$7.58	€4.87	A$7.94
NZ$20	£7.70	$15.15	€9.75	A$15.89
NZ$50	£19.26	$37.89	€24.36	A$39.72
NZ$100	£38.52	$75.76	€48.72	A$79.44
NZ$1,000	£385.20	$757.57	€487.23	A$794.40

(at time of press)

Why Live & Work in New Zealand?

■ ABOUT NEW ZEALAND

New Zealand has a reputation for being an unspoiled 'clean and green' haven in the South Pacific, a diverse landscape filled with uncrowded beaches, mountains, farms and sheep. Although the economy is still largely based on the land, over the last century the proportion of people living in towns and cities has doubled, and the vast majority of people now live in urban areas. Four-fifths of New Zealanders are of European descent, mostly from Britain but also from Germany, the Netherlands, Greece and the former Yugoslavia, as well as other nations. A significant and growing proportion of New Zealanders (one in seven) are descended from the original Maori inhabitants, or are Polynesian or, more recently, immigrants from Asia (the most significant numbers come from China and India). New Zealand's political traditions derive from Britain, but constitutionally it has often been several steps ahead. New Zealand gave women the vote in 1893, 25 years before they were enfranchised in the UK. New Zealand's first woman MP, Elizabeth McCombs, was elected in 1933. In 1938 New Zealand was one the first countries in the world to set up a comprehensive system of social security, from child care benefits through to old-age pensions.

Since European settlement first began in the early 1800s, links with Britain have been close. Early generations of settlers grew up regarding England as 'home'; strangely enough this attitude can sometimes still be found among older, more conservative New Zealanders, some of who have never even set foot outside New Zealand. New Zealand moved from colonial to dominion status in 1907, and in 1947 gained full independence from Britain, making it an independent state within the Commonwealth. New Zealand's foreign policy was basically an extension of British policy and the idea that 'where England leads, we follow', as one New Zealand Prime Minister put it, led New Zealand into a number of wars as a British ally. When Britain joined the European Community in the early 1970s, New Zealand found its own path in the world and its own identity as a Pacific country, rather than an outpost of Europe located in the Antipodes. In general, visitors and immigrants are warmly welcomed. New Zealanders deserve their reputation as some of the friendliest people in the world; when they invite you to come and stay, or to 'drop in any time' it is genuinely meant.

Newcomers will find that while elements of the traditional culture owe something to Europe (the national obsession with sports revolves around cricket and rugby) and New Zealand's youth culture is heavily indebted to America, New Zealand is rapidly and proudly carving its own identity as a Pacific nation. The old ties with Britain have been loosened, and new relationships with neighbours around the Pacific Rim and other Asian countries are of growing importance. Maori and Pacific Island cultures are a strong and growing influence. Auckland has the largest Polynesian population in the world. There are new immigrant communities from various Asian countries and a long-established Chinese

community. The different groups make for an interesting cultural mix, and nearly a third of a million New Zealanders now identify with more than one ethnic group. New immigrants will quickly find that it is important to respect the cultural traditions of various groups, most particularly the Maori as they were the first inhabitants of the islands. The Maori call themselves the *Tangata Whenua*, which means 'the people of the place'.

In many respects New Zealand will seem quite familiar to many immigrants. The main language is English, and the systems of government, schools and healthcare are similar to those in many European countries. A wide selection of art and culture is on offer in the larger cities.

REASONS TO LIVE IN NEW ZEALAND

New Zealand offers many advantages for those considering a change of scenery. The standard of living is high and the exchange rate is favourable, so your savings should go a long way. British and American arrivals will not have to learn a new language and will find the culture reasonably familiar. The climate in most parts of New Zealand is warmer than northern Europe. There are the attractions of living in a less crowded country, with, in general, fewer social problems and a lower crime rate.

With a population of roughly four million and about the same land size as Britain, there is a significant amount of unpopulated land in New Zealand's and in many ways living in a country with such a small population is idyllic. Although traffic can be busy in the main centres, escaping from the cities and getting back to nature is quick and easy.

New Zealand offers families a great lifestyle, with plenty of space and time to spend together and an almost inexhaustible selection of outdoor activities to enjoy together. Children will enjoy growing up with the freedom that New Zealand still offers, and can discover talents for sports and activities such as snowboarding, kayaking and surfing that they might never have had the opportunity to even try at home. The education system is well respected internationally, and most new migrants find that their children thrive in their new environment once the initial homesickness gives way to the excitement of life in a new country.

Most migrants report that they find it easy to get to know New Zealanders, and although new friends are not a substitute for old, you need not fear being isolated for long in your new country – you just need to get out there and meet some new people.

THE PROS AND CONS OF LIVING IN NEW ZEALAND

Despite having a comparatively low gross domestic product (GDP) per capita compared with other developed countries, New Zealanders enjoy a high standard of

In a way, making the decision to leave was the hardest part; once the decision was made it was just a case of getting on with things.
Vita Evans

living. While it is true that income per head of the population compares unfavourably, the upside is that euros, US dollars and pounds sterling go a relatively long way in New Zealand. Other attractions for immigrants are the non-quantifiable factors that make for quality of life: clean air, clean water, miles of unspoiled and accessible beaches and native forest, and some of the most spectacular scenery in the world. If your idea of the good life is a city where 'rush hour' is nowhere near as long as an hour, and the nearest beach is no more than 30 minutes away, then you will enjoy the New Zealand lifestyle.

New Zealanders enjoy a wide range of outdoor activities in their spare time, including camping, climbing, hiking (tramping), swimming, surfing, kayaking and mountain biking (see Time Off on p.341 for more information). Two great attractions of the country are the parks and reserves and the sea. Even New Zealand's biggest cities are within 20 or 30 minutes of hills and forest largely free from human habitation and all the major cities, apart from Hamilton, are on the coast. With a lifestyle revolving around outdoor pursuits, the nightlife in smaller towns is not exactly lively. In the big cities the scene is more interesting. European style cafés and bars have proliferated in the last decade and there is always the traditional Kiwi pub – watering holes more noted for the cheapness of the beer than the social ambience. Licensing laws are liberal and some pubs and cafés in the big cities are open almost 24 hours.

The drawbacks of emigrating have to be considered. You will be far away from friends and family in the northern hemisphere and you may find life a little lonely at first. Many immigrants mention that one of the most diffcult aspects of their new

> Negatives about life so far away from home in the UK include the distance and prohibitive cost of returning to see friends and family, and also the higher cost of living.
> **Katy Parsons**

life is not always being able to afford to return home for all the important family events such as weddings and funerals. New Zealand is 26 hours away from London by plane, and around 13 hours from the USA, and the trip is not cheap. Although doctors do charge for consultations, hospital care is still free for New Zealanders and immigrants from countries with reciprocal social security agreements. But certain types of specialist medical care may be better provided in America, the UK and European countries, simply because New Zealand is too small to have the range of expertise in these areas. In some situations, patients are being sent to Australia for certain types of treatment because of the overcrowded New Zealand waiting lists. Private health insurance is available.

With a smaller population comes a more limited range of choices than you might be used to in terms of shopping, clothes, furniture, holiday options, newspapers and television programmes. The internet does of course offer a great selection of information and shopping, but having things posted from 'back home' may prove more expensive than you might expect, and once you are living on your New Zealand dollars rather than leftover money from home you may well find that the prices of things you used to buy without really thinking about it now seem unjustifiable.

■ Making a permanent move to another country is a very different matter from just visiting it. It may be a good idea therefore to spend a longer period in New Zealand before deciding whether to make a permanent move there.

Look around first

Many people make the decision to move after a visit to New Zealand to see family or friends. If you have a British passport you are entitled to visit New Zealand for up to six months without requiring a visa, and tourists from the USA, Canada and Europe are able to stay for three months without a visa. A visit may be a good opportunity to explore different parts of the country before deciding where you would like to settle. A number of companies arrange coach and train tours with itineraries that cover most of New Zealand in a short period. One such company is Scenic Coach Tours, which arranges custom packaged vacations (www.sceniccoachtours.co.nz). The most popular of their tours lasts 16 days and includes travel around both islands (coach, ferry and train tickets), accommodation, boat sailing in Milford Sound and entrance fees to various attractions. Another great company which will put together an entire package to suit your requirements and needs, with a particular focus on outdoor adventures, is the New Zealand Adventure Company (www.nzadventureco. com). Some companies will also arrange farm and homestay tours, which will enable you to experience the lifestyle of New Zealand families. If you wish to arrange your own homestays throughout the country, contact New Zealand Homestay (www. homestay.co.nz.)

It will also give you a chance to assess the real costs of living in New Zealand. Financial considerations are an important factor when you are living on a fixed income. You can use a visit to assess the property market in order to find out what kind of housing you will be able to afford. In general, if you have sold property in the UK or USA, you should be able to afford a New Zealand house of at least an equivalent if not better standard, particularly if you choose to live outside the main cities.

■ If you are thinking of retiring to New Zealand, rental accommodation is generally easy to find, so you may like to try living in your prospective retirement locality for a while.

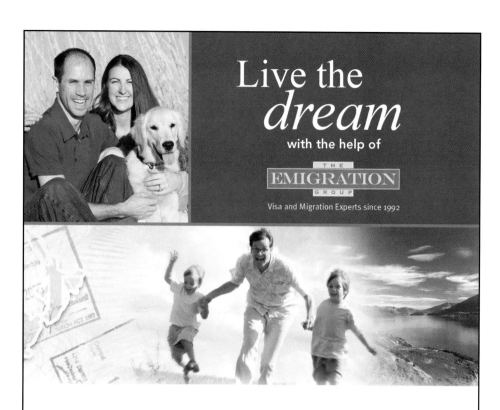

Live the *dream*
with the help of

THE
EMIGRATION
GROUP

Visa and Migration Experts since 1992

If you are seriously thinking about emigrating to New Zealand or have already decided to emigrate, you are probably wondering just how to go about it. Where do you start? What help will you need and from whom? Are you eligible for a Visa? Will you find a job and how will you face the challenge of starting a new life overseas? Well, help is at hand.

The Emigration Group was established in 1992 to provide expert guidance to people wishing to emigrate and to ensure they achieved a happy and prosperous new life overseas. Our successful track record over the years has seen us help more than 10,000 people make a fresh start and enjoy a terrific lifestyle 'Down Under'.

We offer not only a wealth of experience, but full assistance with each aspect of migration: **Visa Preparation and Management; Employment Search; Homes and Resettlement**. How we can help you with each of these vital elements of emigration is covered in the next few pages. As you will see, our complete service provides the essential one point of contact for all your migration needs. Enlisting our expertise to help you 'Live the Dream' assures you of unrivalled personal service in the months ahead as we guide you and your family through one of the most important moves of your lives.

Over the following pages, our client Neill Sperath recalls his experiences of his new life in New Zealand.

A Personal Tale…One Recent Migrant Tells His Story

Neill Sperath, a recent migrant to New Zealand recalls his migration experiences and how New Zealand has had a profound impact on his life.…

Ever since travelling to New Zealand as part of a 'Round the World' trip in 2000, I was fascinated with New Zealand and wanted to live in this beautiful country. Throughout my visit, New Zealand had struck me as a country with a great climate, friendly people and beautiful countryside.

I returned to Germany (where I lived at the time) to begin a well-paid position as Centre Manager for a shopping centre but the possibility of living in New Zealand just didn't leave me. I felt I was right back in the European rat-race and always longed to return to the 'Land of the Long White Cloud'. After a second visit in January 2003 in what seemed to me like a homecoming, I made a firm decision to emigrate. The same day that I returned from this visit I phoned 'The Emigration Group' to find out more about the services they provide. Interestingly, I had picked up their brochure about immigration to New Zealand in 2000 and had kept this for three (!) years.

What impressed me was that they offered a full service to potential immigrants. A service that included professional assistance in the preparation and correct submission of immigration documents to the authorities but also the very important job search aspect of the process. Most emigration consultants offer merely the first but even if an applicant is able to secure a visa without a job; the chance of successfully resettling in New Zealand without a job is almost nil. I will return to the importance of a job offer later.

I have now been in New Zealand for around three years and have earned the nickname 'Mr. New Zealand' from my friends because I surely must be the country's number one fan! I cannot even begin to imagine going back to Europe to live. Why do I like New Zealand so much?

This space is not large enough to write all the reasons why I love this country, but I will identify some of them.…

The incredible natural beauty that New Zealand offers. It is unrivalled anywhere in the world. In one day, you can go tramping through a rainforest in the morning, go skiing in the afternoon and relax on an amazing beach in the evening. No other country in the world offers that diversity.

The locals…Kiwis are a nice, easy-going and friendly people. New Zealand is very culturally diverse, so as an immigrant it is not difficult as in many other countries to fit in and you're made to feel welcome.

Neill and wife Ceillhe show they are really enjoying their life in New Zealand

The pace of life…On any day of the year, I can go to beautiful beaches to relax and enjoy this amazing country. There are also many business opportunities here given the reduced level of bureaucracy, which leads to many small businesses being set up.

The climate…On a normal winter's day in Auckland, the temperature is around 15 degrees Celsius, while in summer it is normally quite consistently in the high twenties – not too hot, not too cold. It is worth noting that average daytime temperatures in winter are the same as many summer days in the UK!

Let me now return to the importance of employment. Trying to find a job from 12,000 miles away is no easy matter. It has to be the right one, one that matches (in the eyes of the NZ Immigration Service) an applicant's qualification and experience. For me this was too important a factor to be left to chance. I had no knowledge of the local labour market and knew that the more help I had the better my prospects would be. Thus, I needed little persuasion to enrol onto the Jobsearch Programme offered by The Emigration Group.

They guided me through the jobsearch process superbly. Having a local specialist to market me was very effective. They arranged a total of seven interviews for me to coincide with my trip to New Zealand to meet potential employers. After an intense selection process, I was in the lucky position to be offered five jobs! I accepted the one as a Marketing manager for a shopping centre in East Auckland.

I have no doubt that this success would never have been possible without expert help from 'The Emigration Group'.

Having the job offer and contract in writing, I could now lodge my visa application. The same day I booked my flight to New Zealand and a week later I was on the plane to Auckland!

The Emigration Group in the UK did not stop assisting me at this point. They continued following up with NZ Immigration, lodging my residency application and handling everything to do with obtaining residence for me. Six months later, I obtained my Residency Visa and was delighted to be allowed to stay permanently in what I consider to be the most beautiful country in the world.

The fresh air, great climate, lovely people and stunning scenery are a combination that is unique in this world. I have certainly not even for a moment regretted my decision to emigrate.

Furthermore, I am very thankful to The Emigration Group for having assisted me so brilliantly in realizing my dreams to live here. I can wholeheartedly recommend them to anyone that really wants to emigrate.

Neill and his wife Ceillhe have recently set up their own business, specialising in personalised tours and other leisure activities in New Zealand, such as kayak fishing and walking tours. For details, visit www.newzealandtours.travel

Live the *dream* with the help of EMIGRATION

advertisement feature

■ PERSONAL CASE HISTORIES

Sam McLaughlan

What brought you to New Zealand?

I only followed the trend by coming to New Zealand, the land of migrants. Everyone came here from somewhere else; there are often jokes about most people's *wakas* being Qantas or Air New Zealand. (A *waka* is a type of canoe that the first Maori arrived in.) Like many New Zealand migrants from centuries past, I was in the process of migrating somewhere but had a bust compass (which I was very content with) and I just needed someone to tell me my destination. In short: I was travelling, I met Linda, she was from New Zealand, there are fewer bureaucrats in New Zealand, the government was not likely to spend my taxes on invading other countries – I am not into supporting collateral damage! Also, house prices are absurd in the UK. I was feeling a little claustrophobic on my own island, so being an adventurous spirit I was more than happy to venture off to another. I am sure there are a large number of 'follow your Kiwi partner home' migrants such as myself here now.

How easy did you find sorting yourself out when you first arrived?

I arrived in New Zealand with just a few contacts and managed to set myself up with a bank account, a house to rent and enrol at myself university within two weeks. I had just come from England where it had taken me six months and too many phone calls to prove I was a part of the system after returning from travelling. They were confused because I had been out of the country for too long and had not voted in the most recent election, so I was consequently blacklisted although I had absolutely no debt. Pretty frustrating, especially as Britain is my home where life should be a breeze for a 'born and bred'.

How did you obtain residency?

I came into New Zealand on a student visa, which was very simple to obtain. I have always found the immigration department here incredibly straightforward, helpful and accessible. Linda and I knew that we would eventually be applying for my residency based on our de facto relationship, so we had kept a file of anything that related to our relationship – from shared amenity bills and joint bank statements, through to hundreds of emails and hastily scribbled and embarrassing love notes and photos of us together madly in love. Our parents and good friends also wrote formal letters as witnesses to our relationship. Towards the end of the first year in New Zealand we sent away my application for residency, along with two big lever-arch files filled to brim with 'evidence' of our relationship. When you apply for a New Zealand residence visa based on your relationship, you are automatically given a work visa for a couple of years (from memory), the idea being you can stay in New Zealand with your partner while the application is being processed.

How did you buy a home and how did your residency status affect the process?

In March of my second year in New Zealand, Linda and I wanted to buy a home. She was pregnant, and we were living on just my income, but the bank wanted my residency confirmed before they would give us a mortgage. Buying a house was a question of scouting around, as you would in the UK or anywhere; we required various assurances, but most importantly I needed confirmation of my residency. This was a real problem and having subsequently talked with others who have been in the same position it has become clear that this is a bit of a Catch-22 for many awaiting residency status. The mortgage companies will not lend you money unless you have residency and a sure way to get residency as a couple is to have joint debt.

The official line from the Immigration Department is that it can take up to two years to process a residency application; however, amazingly, they fast-tracked our application and completed in under a week so that we could buy the house. I'm not quite sure exactly how we managed to pull it off, but I think it was largely down to Linda putting in hours to them on the phone, pleading and playing the 'poor pregnant lady without a house' card! It certainly worked. The whole thing culminated for us in the space of 24 hours; just as we had put down our offer on the house, my folder came to the top of the pile at the Immigration office, and they were really helpful and did everything they could to 'really' fast-track my residency so that we could go ahead and purchase our first home.

I'm really pleased it all came together so smoothly (although it was not without a lot of hard work), but it was expensive, and it feels like the visa process here is designed to earn some good money. While I was studying – although it did not seem directly related to learning how to stop small children throwing chairs at each other – I learnt that New Zealand's second largest income is provided by overseas students, an amount topped only by that brought in through tourism, and that schools are thriving and dependent on it too. The more foreign students' bums you squeeze onto school chairs the more squash courts you can have, apparently.

What differences have you found between New Zealand and the UK?

I love it here; the Kiwis are welcoming and unassuming. They are as friendly as any Canadians or Americans I have met but without what sometimes seems to be an excreted enthusiasm. I used to complain that the water surrounding had a large effect on the UK's attitude, and that the general UK mindset was a little less open than that of its European neighbours... but New Zealand is an island too, so I suppose that reasoning doesn't quite work. Though the New Zealand government may have its fingers in some interesting pies, for the most part it keeps its nose out of other people's business. This is what makes it the laid-back country that it is.

It has taken me two years to feel at home here, and it was the small things that knocked me at first. The difference in town planning and architecture did have a real impact on me as a new arrival, and though I was quite consciously moving away from England, I found that I definitely did miss it. The streets of New Zealand seem empty in comparison, and to a Pom that can be really quite eerie. I think you have to arrive at the right time in your life, as the culture here in provincial New Zealand isn't the most exhilarating. To be fair though, I am so busy with work and a young baby at home I don't get the chance to get out and search for culture very often! What I have seen and been involved with has been interesting – the Maori and Pacific cultural events, arts and music are wonderful. I do miss exhibitions at the Tate Modern, and great music gigs, although even if I were in England right now, I'd be at home with the baby anyway! Ah, the joys of family life – luckily I love it.

Are you enjoying working in New Zealand?

As a teacher I am having a ball here, the education system here seems to suit my personality: it is forward thinking, and focused on helping children learn how to learn as much as it teaches them their times tables. I feel like the New Zealand education system is proactive. Instead of just talking about things, children here are actually putting them in place and trying them out. I like that a lot – just talking as an end in itself is often a waste of time.

The diploma I took in teaching was very intense and did not allow me the time or space to work in an earning job as well. I studied to become a teacher for a variety of reasons, but in terms of migrating it is a global skill that I feel will be constantly in demand, and a New Zealand qualification is recognised by many western countries as well as being relatively easy to transfer, if you can handle paying a few pennies. My teaching course was a safe investment, and there is a definite demand for male teachers here. New Zealand faces the same challenge as the UK in that it is particularly short on male primary school teachers. I invested time in looking at available jobs while I was studying and introducing myself at the schools I was going to apply to. This gave me a distinct advantage I think, and within one day of interviews was offered jobs at two different schools and was able to negotiate my pay; I was very lucky.

How have you found the healthcare system?

I have found healthcare here to be more efficient, but also more costly than in England. The maternity ward here was fantastic and we had outstanding midwife support for our home birth – we doubt this will be so readily available to us in the UK next time round. I have enrolled with my partner's family doctor – with a 'community services card' (income-tested card which entitles you to a discount on healthcare) a visit to the GP costs NZ$25, without the card it would cost around NZ$50 – quite a stinger! I do get an appointment within hours of calling though, and find the service top quality.

What advice do you have for intending migrants?

Migrating is a challenging affair; leaving all that is familiar behind to and come to live in a new land is much more emotionally difficult than you might anticipate. New Zealand has its differences, and it is important to remember that just because it is another western country does not necessarily gurarante a smooth transition for every new arrival.

We live in a sunny, quiet and spacious place near all amenities, the sea and rivers for swimming in are all just 10 minutes away and we manage to live here on one teacher's wage. Could we do that in England with this little hassle and this quality of life? I don't think so. But these things have to be what you are looking for when you come to live in New Zealand because that is what you get. If you want a life somewhere seething and rife with vibrant cultural diversity and creativity don't come and live in provincial New Zealand... not just yet anyway!

Katy Parsons

Despite having no family there, Katy was drawn to New Zealand by the lure of the great outdoors, the promise of less hustle and bustle than the UK and the huge range of outdoor activities available. Katy has not made a full move to New Zealand yet, but is on a working visa based on her profession. She has lived there for eight months now, in Havelock North, which she chose because of the warm and consistent weather, the ease of access to both Auckland and Wellington and importantly because that is where she was offered a job as a physiotherapist, based on her training and experience from the UK.

How did you register to work in your profession in New Zealand?

There is currently an extreme shortage of physiotherapists in New Zealand, but I still had to produce a huge portfolio for the New Zealand Board of Physiotherapists before I was able to register to practise in New Zealand. No more training was required, but because of all the work and documentation required, collating the portfolio itself and presenting it to the Board did work out to be quite expensive.

How would you compare life in New Zealand and the UK?

I find the average cost of living in New Zealand a little more expensive than the same kind of living in the UK, based on the costs of general purchases. However, expenses such as renting a house work out as relatively cheaper than they would in the UK so there are definite differences which probably balance out in the end. Compared to the UK, I enjoy the New Zealand lifestyle more, with a slower pace of life, more relaxed people who are more welcoming and helpful as a rule than people in the UK, less traffic, and of course fewer people in general. Making friends is very easy, as the people are friendly and warm in welcoming newcomers, and I have found joining a sports club to be invaluable in meeting a wide range of new friends. I enjoy a wide range of sports in my spare time, including kickboxing, road biking, running, swimming, mountain-biking, tramping and triathlons. Importantly for me, the weather is more consistent and almost predictable, which allows for a greater number of recreational outdoor opportunities and consequently more activities on offer for free. Negatives about life so far away from home in the UK include the distance and prohibitive cost of returning to see friends and family, and also the higher cost of living.

How do you find the healthcare system in New Zealand compared to the UK?

The healthcare system in New Zealand, with the ACC [Accident Compensation Corporation] feature, is very effective at providing care for most people. There is a self-referral system to health professionals, which is a good idea because this way people don't have to pay or see a GP if they don't want to. For physiotherapy first contact care, there are no waiting lists whereas in the UK you routinely find that patients have had to wait anywhere from 3 to 8 months before they even make it as far as seeing a physio for the very first time.

Have you had any problems with not having a local credit history?

I haven't experienced any problems resulting from not having a local credit history, and my initial transition to New Zealand in terms of arranging bank accounts, credit cards, utility accounts and a mobile phone was possibly smoother than others might experience as my move to New Zealand was work based and first contacts with all these companies were arranged through my new job. Since then, I have found absolutely no problem in being granted credit cards and opening new bank accounts with simple proof of my job and income. All other accounts and providers have proved easy to deal with, and I haven't experienced any problems at all. I plan to stay for another year before thinking seriously about whether to stay on in New Zealand or return to the UK, but at the moment all signs point to staying as I am enjoying life here so much.

Vita Evans

How did you come to live in New Zealand?

I left London in November 2004, and have been living in Auckland ever since. It was a wrench to leave the bright lights and bustle of London, but I was fortunate to have never quite reached that out-and-out loathing for the place before I left it. I had just come to a point in my life where I realised that I needed to make a big change right then or it might never happen, and it suddenly occurred to me one day that my life didn't have to involve so much bad weather and so much time spent commuting. Things like people sniffing and coughing all over me on my way to work every day, and being surrounded for hours every day by people listening to industrial techno at full volume on their tinny iPod headphones had started to really get to me. A big thing I realised about the UK once I started looking at leaving is that people there talk a lot about making changes to their lives – like going to live in the country to farm goats, or getting out of the rat-race and going to knit organic jumpers on an island or harvest olives for a living – but then they just wait for a sign, or a push, or for something to happen. Everything just seems like hard work. It's important to figure out your priorities and decide what you really want, and what you can live without, work out what you love and how you want to live, and then find out where you can do all those things. I wanted to find some space and some peace, to be able to enjoy a house with a garden while still living in a city and enjoying all that city life offers, and to buy a dog and take it for long walks on the beach. I wanted to spend more time doing the things I wanted to do and enjoying the freedom of spontaneity once in a while, and less time running around trying to keep appointments made in my diary three or four months previously.

How did you make the move and decide where in New Zealand to live?

Leaving London in the winter, with all the lead-up to Christmas and trying to get home on the tube crammed up against the spenders with all their millions of pounds worth of pointless shopping, and heading for the sunshine and fresh air was hugely exciting and a great release. In a way, making the decision to leave was the hardest part; once the decision was made it was just a case of getting on with things.

Between deciding to move to New Zealand and actually leaving the UK, I left myself 12 months to arrange everything. I started looking for a job in New Zealand right away, and arranged to go for a 3-week visit in February. During those three weeks, I had a look around Christchurch, Wellington and Auckland, to make a decision about where I wanted to be, and with an eye on the kinds of jobs available in each place. As I am a homeopath and yoga teacher, but also had an earlier career in marketing and publicity, I felt confident that I could find work in any of these cities, but wanted to try and compare the cost of living with the likely income I could expect before making a firm decision. As it turned out, I found Christchurch a little quiet and maybe too sedate for my tastes; although the opportunities for outdoor living and general leisure activities were immense, and there was a fair bit going on in terms of the arts, I just didn't quite get the feeling that I wanted to wake up there every day. Wellington I loved for the gorgeous hilliness, amazing restaurants, the coffee, the wonderful performing arts scene, and the quirky wooden houses nestled everywhere, and I have good friends there, but in the end my decision not to live there was based largely on the weather – the damp, the cold, the rain and the wind would have been too much for me. And after all, I wanted to leave all that behind in England and have a whole new life with lots of open windows and evening G&Ts in the garden – Wellington weather is just too unpredictable. So I settled on the idea of living in Auckland, and immediately narrowed my employment search to fit. Friends introduced me to a few people in my line of work, and it was relatively easy to secure a job and line it up to start when I was due to arrive in November. I sold my flat in Muswell Hill, and converting the profit I made on that into New Zealand dollars certainly plumped it up somewhat. The fact that I had proof of means independent of any income dependent on my job was helpful in securing my visa I think.

How did you settle in when you first arrived? When I arrived, I lived with friends in Epsom for a few weeks before finding a room in a beautiful villa in Ponsonby. From there, I was walking or cycling into town for work every day, and although the working hours are longer than in the UK, the days seemed to have so much more time available because I was cutting out all the darkness and commuting. I worked in the publicity job for a couple of months, but by that point had made enough contacts to be able to set up my own yoga classes and start consulting as a homeopath. I did a few intensive refresher yoga-teaching courses, just to have the New Zealand qualifications, but my experience and qualifications in the UK would have been enough to get started. I joined the New Zealand Council of Homeopaths, as they recognised my qualifications from the British Institute, and that has been invaluable in terms of contacts, information and local information.

How are you enjoying life in New Zealand now?

I am now married to a Kiwi, and we live about an hour north of Auckland. We live right on the coast, looking straight out over the sea, and on a clear night you can see the lights of Auckland city across the water. Twice a week I drive into Auckland for classes and consults, and I use that time to catch up with friends in the city and to do any town-type things that need attending to. The rest of the time, I teach classes and see patients locally, and just generally enjoy life. We spend a lot of time on the beaches, both near our home and over on the West Coast, and we have a very happy dog who enjoys nothing more than playing in the water. There are several lovely vineyards and great cafés near us, with wonderful food and wine – perfect places for a special meal, or even just a coffee with friends. We often go snorkelling during the summer evenings, and have spent a lot of time putting in a big vegetable garden. I just love the peace and quiet of life up here, with all the city has to offer just a drive away, and have never been happier. Moving to New Zealand was the best thing I have ever done, and I've never looked back.

How do you keep in touch with friends and family from the UK?

I have hardly had time to miss family and friends from the UK; we are their top holiday destination, so we see most people a lot more regularly than I thought we would, which makes the daily distance much more bearable. Email and cheap telephone calls shrink the gap as well, as I am in touch with my closest family and friends several times a week now – ironically we are probably closer now than we were when we lived in the same country.

Elizabeth Henderson

What made you decide to live in New Zealand?

I came to New Zealand as my family and I wanted a change from Newark in the UK, although both my husband and I still own houses in the UK. We initially considered both New Zealand and Australia before deciding on New Zealand, where we arrived in October of 2007. We live in Hawkes Bay, which we chose because my husband found work there.

How did you register to work?

As I have been qualified for six years and have worked as a physiotherapist for the duration. I did not have to undertake any further training. Due to my experience, my qualifications were compatible with those required to practise in New Zealand. I had to submit a portfolio to the New Zealand Society of Physiotherapy for registration purposes.

How did you deal with the New Zealand Immigration Service?

My family employed an immigration consultant to fill out all the paperwork that we needed in order to apply for a two-year working visa. We had to undergo medicals and police checks in the UK, which are explained on the New Zealand immigration website. We travelled to New Zealand with just two suitcases each and sent our work things separately by air freight. Using an immigration consultant, although it does cost more than completing all the paperwork ourselves, gave us the peace of mind of knowing that all boxes have been ticked and everything required will be supplied with nothing overlooked.

How would you compare life in the UK and in New Zealand?

We have found some aspects of life in New Zealand relatively cheap in comparison with the UK, however we are currently looking at buying a property there and are surprised at the extremely high interest rate (up to 10% is not uncommon). We are enjoying the differences in New Zealand lifestyle compared to the UK; it is far more active and outdoors-based rather than centred on crowding round the TV. We also find that the people tend to be friendlier than in the UK and everyone that we have met is interested in the UK and where the family comes from.

How have you made new friends?

I have enjoyed settling into a new social life, and have made many new friends, particularly through working with other new immigrants. Joining a gym is the other way that I have met new people and made a lot of new contacts, and I am enjoying keeping fit and cycling to work on a regular basis.

Did you have any problems arising from not having a local credit history?

Opening bank accounts proved relatively easy, as I opened accounts through my bank in the UK prior to arriving in New Zealand. Credit cards proved a little more difficult as I am on a 2-year working visa rather than a permanent resident, but everything was arranged with a face-to-face meeting at the bank, and then I received the two cards I needed, activated and ready to go, within a week. The bank also offered my family a pre-approved mortgage for NZ$400,000 if we could put together a deposit. We have had no problems at all arising from our lack of local credit history.

Is your move to New Zealand a permanent one?

We love the lifestyle, the weather and the sunshine in New Zealand, although of course we miss our extended family in the UK. We are considering making the move to New Zealand a permanent one, but are going to wait until we have lived there for a little longer before making our final decision.

Dermot Foley

Where in New Zealand have you lived and worked?

I returned to New Zealand in November of 2007, having previously lived and worked in both Auckland and Queenstown where I enjoyed the sunshine, the snow in Queenstown, and the nightlife in both places. Finding jobs has been a major drawcard in terms of choosing where to live as well, so I feel fortunate to have landed on my feet in every respect.

Where are you from originally, and what is your line of work?

Originally from Managhan in the Republic of Ireland, I had been living in England for the six years between my first visit to New Zealand and returning there this time. I was a student in Ireland, and then studied and practised physiotherapy in England. I graduated with a BSc (Hons) three-year physiotherapy degree, which I have been able to convert into a NZ Physiotherapy Registration after 6 months spent compiling a portfolio and communicating countless times with the New Zealand Board. I found the whole process very time consuming, but not difficult, and I calculate that it cost in the region of NZ$2,200 to transfer my skills to New Zealand, not including flights and other non-work moving costs of course.

How easy or difficult did you find making the actual move?

Making the move was a fairly easy process for me as I had no property in the UK and I was renting before I left. The visa application process was speeded up by a trip to the New Zealand Embassy in London to discuss and confirm the type of visa I was applying for and to establish what I needed to provide in order to qualify. Although I found the New Zealand immigration website very helpful in terms of answering most of my questions, it gave me more confidence to meet with the relevant people face to face to be sure that I wasn't overlooking anything vital in the application process, and to make sure I was doing everything correctly. I set up my bank accounts once I arrived in New Zealand, by meeting with a bank/accounts manager face to face and explaining my situation. I went armed with my passport, work contract and letter of reference from my employer, and I have found that most banks were more than keen to take control of my money for me!

What differences have you found between life in New Zealand and the UK?

I have noticed a marked rise in the cost of living in New Zealand between living there in 2002 and returning this time, but I have also found that wages have increased so overall they seem to even each other out. I think I can afford most things I need fairly easily, on my salary, with a little left over now and then. Compared to the UK and Ireland, I feel that New Zealand offers a better quality of life in terms of what you can buy for your cash (real income), the availability of sports facilities and of course the weather. I also find Kiwis more approachable and sociable, even though they do curse a lot more than the English! The same differences in views happen both in New Zealand and in the UK. Most mainstream people are tolerant of different cultures and people from different places, although inevitably the few people who behave badly tarnish the overall tolerance of the masses.

What differences do you find in the healthcare system?

I have found both good and bad points to the New Zealand healthcare system. With ACC now covering recent injuries, the accessibility to physiotherapists has improved which means that people can be seen faster without GP referral. I find the wait times for specialist appointments to be very long both in New Zealand and in the UK and believe that both systems could be improved. The New Zealand availability of things like magnetic resource imaging (MRI) and computerised tomography (CT) is better than that in the UK – but again the wait times for these procedures let the system down.

Are you keen to make the move to New Zealand a permanent one?

Overall I have found most Kiwis to be very welcoming and eager help you to settle in. I am loving the weather, the sun, surf and snow, and although I am finding it difficult being so very far away from my family in Ireland and the UK I am already considering making the move a permanent one. I have made good New Zealand friends already and, as a rugby player, am looking forward to meeting more new people with the start of the rugby season. I am enjoying the outdoor lifestyle, and have taken up surfing, wakeboarding and shooting since arriving in New Zealand.

What advice do you have for new arrivals?

My advice to new arrivals is: try not to socialise exclusively with people from your home country, as tempting as it might be to sink into an old familiar routine, and make the effort to get out and join local clubs and teams. Above all else, ask locals for advice and help – they will oblige. As an example – if you're looking to buy a car/move house/buy a surfboard/get the internet – ask someone what they think the best way is to start going about it.

How did you first come to New Zealand?

I spent 6 weeks travelling around New Zealand 5 years ago, and then found work in Queenstown in order to prolong my stay as I found I was smitten with the country. I particularly loved the fact that I could leave my car door or front door unlocked without any real fear of thieves or intruders. I was taken with the fact that New Zealand seemed to be a place without all the problems of violence and crime that so many other societies seem to suffer, and of course the fact that I was offered a job doing what I love didn't hurt either. Being surrounded by so many people who share my passion for rugby is another huge plus.

Fiona Worseley

Where are you from and how did you come to move to New Zealand?

Originally from rural Somerset and thereafter living in Bristol and London in the UK, I met my Kiwi husband in England, and visited New Zealand with him after we had known each other for just two months. We made the decision to move back to New Zealand as my husband was offered a job in Greymouth, and we arrived in April 2007, when I was 30 weeks pregnant.

Where do you live now?

We have since moved from Greymouth, on the West Coast of the South Island, over the Alps to Rangiora in Canterbury to be near my husband's parents. We felt that there were better opportunities for the family on the East Coast, but enjoyed living on the West Coast while we were there.

How are you finding working in New Zealand?

My daughter is now 18 months old, and I am once again working in the pharmaceutical industry as I did in the UK. This time I am working part-time, in order to care for my child as well, and have found the perfect job difficult to track down. I have found the swap from a high-powered job in central London to a part-time role in a small and highly regulated market quite difficult, although my skills were easily transferred. I had two previous part-time jobs; one was in a vineyard, which I loved because of the outdoors work and the people, and the other was in an office, which I did not enjoy at all!

How do you compare quality of life in the UK with life in New Zealand?

In terms of property, we felt that we were priced out of the UK market, and could never have afforded anything we would have wanted to buy. In New Zealand we own our own three-bedroom home on a quarter-acre property, and it seems to us that the average Joe and Josephine can have a much better quality of life here. It is difficult to make a direct comparison of quality of life, as my family's life and situation has changed so much with the arrival of our daughter and my move to part-time work. In London, we lived in a rented flat on two good salaries, and then on just my husband's salary as my pregnancy progressed.

We do find some things in New Zealand very expensive though – particularly baffling is the high price of dairy products since New Zealand is such a major dairy producer. Meat and veg are more expensive than expected, and not always of the best quality in the supermarkets. However, the 'farm gate' and farmers' market options offer choices of considerably better quality foods, in season, for much more reasonable prices. You can often pick your own fruits and vegetables as well, and it doesn't come fresher than that! Other quality-of-life aspects are more space, cleaner air, and the fact that people are nicer to you, strangers smile at you in the street, and I have found the support for new mothers outstanding.

How different do you find the people in New Zealand?

Making new friends with children has been easy, but making time for them in my busy life can be difficult. The politeness drove me mad to start with though. With my 'straight-from-London' mentality, if I asked for something in a shop that was what I wanted, not to be asked how I was. I realised though that they genuinely do want to know! In terms of medical care, I have found that doctors treat you more as an individual and less as a number, and that the Accident Compensation Corporation (ACC) system works well if you need treatment such as physiotherapy. There is also much better access to homeopathy and other 'alternative' health treatments.

Do you have any advice for intending migrants?

The process of moving itself was relatively easy, but we have the following advice for others making the move:

- Carry out careful research into moving companies, and check the small print regarding insurance.
- Allow plenty of time to obtain your visas – aspects like the police check can take quite some time.
- Think really carefully as you are packing – we had many 'treasures' that I absolutely couldn't live without and were lovingly packed for the move. Two years later I have realised that a large proportion of them are now junk, ready to be thrown away.

Did you have any problems not having a local credit history?

With a Kiwi husband, I experienced no problems with things like buying a house, accessing credit, and opening bank and household utility accounts.

Are you enjoying living in New Zealand, and do you plan to stay?

I find that in my experience Kiwi families are a lot more involved, and I am really enjoying the support offered by living near my in-laws. Of course I miss some things about life in the UK, particularly living near my sister, the wonderful hedgerows and the musty old pubs, but the scales dip firmly in New Zealand's favour, and we have plans to live here permanently.

How do exchange rates affect my migration to New Zealand?

When migrating to New Zealand you will need to exchange your money into NZ Dollars. This will involve a currency transaction which exposes you to currency risk. It's essential to buy NZ Dollars at the right time because if you don't pick the ideal exchange rate, you'll arrive with less of your hard earned money than you could have done. Take a look at the following example:

Let's assume you're migrating to New Zealand and have accumulated a net wealth of £150,000 after the sale of your house, car and other assets. Had you exchanged your currency at the end of January 2008, you would have arrived with A$393,255 but had you exchanged one month later, you would have arrived with only A$361,830. That's a **loss of 31,425 Kiwi Dollars in only 4 weeks** – and it's solely due to exchange rate fluctuations.

Exchange your money with expert guidance, patiently delivered

Halo Financial, who regularly feature on industry leading financial television channels CNBC and Bloomberg, is a specialist currency company that combines financial expertise, the latest technology and a round the clock trading presence to ensure they secure the best possible currency deals for you.

So whether you need to make an immediate currency transaction, fix an exchange rate for up to 2 years in advance or make regular currency transfers to or from the United Kingdom – such as pension, mortgage, salary or rental income – Halo Financial can help.

Halo Financial deliver:

- Market leading exchange rates (up to 4% better than the banks)
- 0% commission charges
- Protection against exchange rate volatility (fixed rates up to 2 years forward)
- A prompt, proactive service delivered by your personal currency dealer
- The information you need, when you need it

So contact Halo Financial – the New Zealand Dollar exchange rate can fluctuate greatly so it's never too early to investigate such an important service and have your currency concerns put to rest. 5 minutes of your time today, could save you £'000's before you move to New Zealand.

Tel: 0845 521 2058
Email: help@halofinancial.com
Web: www.halofinancial.com/register

Before You Go

■ VISAS, WORK PERMITS AND CITIZENSHIP

Throughout New Zealand's history, population growth has been boosted at various points by government policies designed to attract immigrants. Britain was the main source of new arrivals for most of the first century of European settlement, and the other major source of European immigrants was the Netherlands. New Zealand missed out on achieving some of the ethnic diversity Australia enjoys by not actively encouraging immigration from other European countries in the post-Second World War period. The last major campaign to attract immigrants was during the 1950s. Those were the days when the New Zealand government paid for immigrants' passage on the condition that they stayed for at least two years. When this scheme ended, a more restrictive immigration policy was introduced, based on occupational quotas. Most potential immigrants were required to have a job waiting for them before they applied for residency.

In 1991 the government changed the occupational quota scheme to a points-based migrant system that is similar to the Canadian and Australian schemes. Applicants for residency are ranked according to the number of points they score for attributes such as age, qualifications, work experience, family and offer of employment. Policy changes in 1995 caused a dramatic downturn in the number of migrants, and from 1995 to 1997, these numbers were down by over 60% due to the difficulty of getting into the country. The Government has since realised that New Zealand needs migrants who will bring new ideas and skills, invest in business, create new opportunities and international contacts, and who will help New Zealand compete on the global stage.

New immigration policies covering entrepreneurs, investors and those on long-term business visas (temporary residence) were introduced in 1998. In November 1999, special provisions were made for IT specialists, and in October 2001 an extra 10,000 visas a year were allocated to the General Skills and Business immigration category. The immigration minister at the time said that this increase reflected the 'desire to ensure that talent tops the list of residence approvals'. An entirely new category – the Talent Visa – allows highly skilled temporary residents to apply for permanent residency. This visa came into effect in April 2002 and in fact provides two options. One allows employers in New Zealand who are accredited by Immigration New Zealand to offer overseas people jobs without the

people in question having to satisfy the long list of usual criteria. After two years of holding a work permit these people can go on to apply for residence. The other version of this visa allows particularly good sportspeople, musicians, writers, artists, and so on, to do the same if they have a sponsoring organisation within *i* **New Zealand Immigration, National Office:** P.O. Box 3705, Wellington; (09) 914 4100 from outside New Zealand; 0508 558 855 from outside Auckland but inside New Zealand; you can submit questions about immigration matters on the Immigration New Zealand (INZ) website: www. immigration.govt.nz

New Zealand. There is information about both of these new types of visa in both the *Self Assessment Guide* and the *Guide to Working* (published online and in hard copy by the New Zealand Immigration Service), or you can visit the website: www.immigration.govt.nz/migrant. For more information, contact the New Zealand Immigration Service. There are offshore branches in Apia, Beijing, Jakarta, Moscow, Suva, London, New Delhi, Shanghai, Washington, Bangkok, Hong Kong, Nuku'alofa, Singapore and Taipei. See the main website for contact details.

■ APPLYING FOR NEW ZEALAND RESIDENCY

If you qualify for permanent New Zealand residency you will be entitled to work in New Zealand without any restrictions. You will be issued a residence visa if you apply outside New Zealand or a residence permit if you apply from within the country. A residence permit will expire if you leave the country; if you wish to leave temporarily after taking up residence, you must apply for a Returning Resident's visa. This visa will be valid for two years if it is your first Returning Resident's visa, or for an indefinite period or 12 months or 14 days, depending on whether it is your second or subsequent such visa.

FACT

■ There are three main streams of immigration, and only a restricted number of applications in each stream will be successful.

Immigration streams

For the 2007/2008 year, the government allocated 45,000 places for people to be granted New Zealand residence under the immigration programme. The General Skills and Business category provides 60% of this total, this category encompassing the Skilled Migrant Category (SMC), closed General Skills category, Work to Residence, Investor, Entrepreneur, and Employees of Relocating Businesses. As a result, 27,000 people will be approved under the Skilled/Business stream as part of the year's immigration programme. Of these, 19,000 people will be under the Skilled Migrant Category (SMC), with the remaining 8,000 from the other subcategories. The Family Sponsored stream will account for 30% including applications under the headings of Partnership, Dependent Child, Parent, Sibling, Adult Child, Family Quota, Family-Sponsored Transitional Policy and closed Humanitarian category. Ten per cent is made up from the International Humanitarian Stream, which includes a Refugee Quota of 750, Refugee Status, a Refugee Family Quota of 250, a Samoan

Quota (1,100), Pacific Access (650), Victims of Domestic Violence, Contingency/ Ministerial Direction, and International Humanitarian Transitional Policy. The main categories are explained below.

Bear in mind that the New Zealand Immigration Service operates from a weighty manual that is over 1,000 pages long, and acceptance criteria are complex to say the very least, so what follows in this section is no more than a rough overview. Contact the New Zealand Immigration Service for the most recent rules, categories, application forms and procedures. If you want to speak directly with an immigration specialist, you will probably need to arrange an appointment.

Immigration refusal criteria

Medical certificates must be no more than three months old at the time that you lodge your application, and must be provided for your partner and all your dependent children, even if you do not have custody of the children. Forms can be downloaded from the New Zealand Immigration website (www.immigration. govt.nz). Chest x-rays are now required for everyone over 11 years old (except pregnant women). If you don't have an acceptable standard of health your application will be declined unless you are granted a medical waiver. The New Zealand Immigration Service (NZIS) will consider a medical waiver if all other requirements of your residence application are met, unless you are suffering from severe haemophilia, medical conditions requiring renal dialysis or active tuberculosis.

In accordance with the Immigration Act of 1987, you will not be accepted if you have ever been convicted of a crime and served a sentence of five years or more, or a sentence of 12 months or more in the last 10 years. You will not be accepted if you are subject to a current New Zealand removal order, or if you have ever been deported from any country. And it goes without saying that you will not be accepted if it is suspected that you constitute a likely danger to New Zealand security or public order, and/or if you are believed to be associated with any group or organisation with criminal objectives. These days, because of the sensitivity of race relations and concerns over the political affiliations of the growing number of South African immigrants, you will also be required to declare that you have never been a member of a white supremacist organisation. Like the American immigration requirement to declare that you have never participated in genocide, the point is not that anyone would declare themselves to be racist but that if you make a false declaration, it is an offence under the Immigration Act and you can be deported forthwith. None of this paperwork comes cheaply. New Zealand is the pioneer of charging for the privilege of filling out official forms, and there are a number of forms you will need to complete. See the table below for costs of the different types of visa application.

Immigration consultants

You may consider employing the services of an immigration consultant. The number of organisations offering advice on emigrating to New Zealand has grown substantially since the new immigration policy was introduced in 1991.

Most consultants offer help with all aspects of the immigration process. They will provide general information about New Zealand to help you decide whether you want to make the move. Some consultancies will organise special tour packages to New Zealand so you can visit the country before deciding whether to emigrate. As emigration is a major life step it is very sensible to consider a reconnaissance trip; you can make an application for permanent residency while in New Zealand on a visitor's visa or permit if you decide you like the place. This is easy enough to arrange for yourself, it is not necessary to rely on an immigration consultant for such a trip unless you are very uncertain about travelling.

Once you have made the decision to move to New Zealand, an immigration consultant will guide you through the daunting maze of paperwork and residency regulations. Some immigration consultants say that candidates maximise their chances of qualifying by using a reputable consultancy, but no company can guarantee that you will be successful. Some consultancies charge a fee for a preliminary assessment, which may save you wasting any further money if you are unlikely to succeed. Their final fees will vary widely depending on the services you require and the application you are making; charges may range from a few hundred to several thousand New Zealand (NZ) dollars. Consultancies can assist with the paperwork and will make sure you do not overlook or omit any vital pieces of information. You should be wary of any consultancy that appears to promise that they have a special relationship with the New Zealand Immigration Service – this is certainly a false claim. All applications are considered equally, regardless of whether a consultant has been involved or not. Another useful service some consultants provide is help with settling in New Zealand. Most good consultants should provide you with assistance in deciding where to live, looking for jobs, finding a house and other aspects of organising your new life. In choosing a consultant, the most important aspects to consider are the practical help they can offer. Do they have a job search branch in New Zealand? Do they have contacts that might be useful for promoting your employment chances? According to the New Zealand Immigration Service, the major consultancies they deal with regularly are all above board. If you are uncertain about whether a consultancy is bona fide, you can contact the Immigration Service to check them out. It is worth doing your research to make sure you get value for money.

Useful resources

Access Immigration New Zealand Limited: 199 Pakuranga Road, Pakuranga, Manukau 2010, New Zealand; Post to: PO Box 38–880, Howick, Manukau 2145, New Zealand; +64 9 577 5895; mobile: +64 027 481 2004 or +64 021 641 941; imigr8@access2nz.com; www.access2nz.com. A private company which provides specialist immigration services to both individuals and companies. The website provides information about the separate services for corporate immigration and individual immigration.

Malcolm Pacific: Level 12, 49 Symonds Street, Auckland, New Zealand; Post to: PO Box 6219, Wellesley Street, Auckland, New Zealand; +64 9 309 4187 or 0808 234 7462 toll free in the UK; akld@malcolmpacific.com; www.malcolmpacific.co.nz. Comprehensive service for all New Zealand immigration matters including residence, work, study, visiting and New Zealand citizenship. Malcolm Pacific also

> " My family employed an immigration consultant to fill out all the paperwork that we needed in order to apply for a 2-year working visa. We had to undergo medicals and police checks in the UK, which are explained on the New Zealand immigration website.
>
> **Elizabeth Henderson** "

TIP

■ The benefit of using a consultant is largely to do with the fact that they make sure you complete all forms correctly and provide all required supporting documentation so that the process is not unnecessarily prolonged or difficult, in much the same way that you might use a mortgage broker to arrange your mortgage.

provides a corporate service to employers by assisting staff in New Zealand with immigration issues or assisting employers recruiting staff from overseas.

Migration Bureau: ODG Ltd, London House, 100 New Kings Road, Chelsea, London SW6 4LX, UK; 020 7348 6066; london@migrationbureau.com; www.migrationbureau.com.uk. Note: You should make an appointment to meet with one of the consultants – John McKenna or Nathan Brennan.

The Emigration Group Ltd.: 7 Heritage Court, Lower Bridge Street, Chester, Cheshire CH1 1RD; offices also in London and Manchester; 0845-2304390; info@TEGltd.co.uk; www.jobfastrack.co.nz. Provides full assistance with applications for residence and/or work visas and has a Resettlement Consultant based in New Zealand. Settlement assistance available includes removals, pet shipments, flights, bank accounts, accommodation, job search, and information about visas and residence. Sister company, Taylor & Associates, (see entry below) matches job seekers with employers. Together they provide an effective and total emigration service.

Taylor & Associates (Migrant Employment Search: 27 Gillies Avenue, PO Box 9600, Newmarket, Auckland. New Zealand; (64) 09 520 5421; nzjobs@jobfastrack.co.nz; www.jobfastrack.co.nz. Taylor & Associates links migrants to the New Zealand and Australian job markets, providing the fast track way to a new job down under. Taylor & Associates also produces a free newsletter (Australian and New Zealand Employment Review) that provides a regular update on the employment scene; copies are available from the Emigration Group office (above).

Useful publications

The New Zealand Immigration and Relocation Report: Written by migrants for migrants, customers pay online and are given immediate access to their instantly downloadable e-book. NuKiwi also offers a range of other publications, and discount for more than one purchase as well as a money-back guarantee; www.nukiwi.com.

New Zealand News UK: Published weekly, and either free or for a price of 35p, depending on where you get your copy. Contains up-to-date immigration news, and also carries information about New Zealand-focused activities for expats and prospective migrants in the UK, mainly in London; www.nznewsuk.co.uk. You can also subscribe to their free weekly electronic report.

New Zealand Outlook: Published monthly by Consyl Publishing Ltd. 13 London Road, Bexhill-on-Sea, East Sussex TN39 3JR; 01424-223111; consylpublishing@btconnect.com; www.consylpublishing.co.uk. Aimed specifically at migrants, this publication is a useful way of keeping up with New Zealand migration policy and entry regulations. In the UK six issues cost £10.00 and 12 issues £15.50; in Europe six issues cost £12.00 and 12 issues £20.00; elsewhere six issues cost £15.00 and 12 cost £26.00. You are automatically issued a free membership discount card with a 12-month subscription, and this will give you 10% discount on any of the maps, books or magazines available within *New Zealand Outlook*. If you just want a single copy of the current issue, or a back issue from the last 12 months, send five first class stamps per issue required to Consyl at the address above, along with a note explaining which issues you would like. A selection of articles from previous issues can be found on the website, by following the New Zealand Outlook Archive link.

■ RESIDENCE CATEGORIES

Skilled migrant category

The Skilled Migrant Category operates as a points system based around education and qualifications, work experience and age, your spouse or partner's qualifications and work experience, family and educational links to New Zealand, and access to sufficient funds to establish yourself. To be considered under this category you need to meet the required standards of good health, be of good character, meet the English language proficiency standards and be no younger than 20 and no older than 55. You will also need to meet the threshold of 100 points to register an Expression of Interest (EOI) – you claim points for skills, experience and a variety of other factors. The points are set out in the table on pages 35–36.

Points are available for skilled employment in New Zealand, work experience, qualifications, age and family support. Bonus points are available for employment, work experience and qualifications in identified areas of growth or skill shortage. Bonus points are also available for employment outside Auckland, and for New Zealand qualifications gained in the country over two years, and also sometimes for your partner's employment and qualifications. If you have claimed 100 or more points on your EOI, it qualifies for entry into the EOI pool. Every fortnight, all EOIs over 140 points are automatically selected for an 'Invitation to Apply'. Once these high-scoring applications are skimmed off the top, lower-scoring EOIs with certain factors, particularly required employment skills, are selected. This ranking system is clearly designed to allow the New Zealand Immigration Service to extend its invitations to apply for residence to those who have the most to offer to New Zealand.

The highest points will be available to qualified, skilled migrants who are already working in skilled employment in New Zealand. The NZIS website (www.immigration.govt.nz) features the most up-to-date information about skills New Zealand currently needs in both the Immediate Skill Shortage List (ISSL) and the Long Term Skill Shortage List (LTSSL). These lists are intended to enhance and streamline the processing of work permits, visas and approvals in principle for work permits or visas where there is a known regional labour market skills shortage. Immigration New Zealand will of course still expect you to meet all other aspects of relevant work policy and the department will need to establish to its own satisfaction that your offer of employment (if you have one) is both genuine and sustainable. NZ will also investigate and determine whether the business offering you employment is able to meet its obligation under New Zealand employment law. For most occupations the NZIS sets out a recommended standard of qualification or experience except in instances where the qualification and skill levels are mandatory.

Although a skilled job offer is not a prerequisite, you can see how important it is to consider ensuring that your skills are actually needed in New Zealand before you uproot your whole life to move there. If you have any doubts, check with the NZIS, and also be careful to check the official fees before handing money to an agent.

The process begins with you completing an initial self-assessment. A Skilled Migrant Quick Check is available on www.immigration.govt.nz and in the NZIS 'Self Assessment Guide for Residence'. This will help you to decide whether it is actually worth you submitting an EOI, ie whether you stand a reasonable chance of being accepted. You will then be able to complete an EOI form and send it in. The NZIS prefers that you fill this form online at www.immigration.govt.nz (this is the less expensive method), but you can also obtain a paper form from an NZIS office. This will provide information about your health, character, age, English language ability, and the factors that will help you to earn points. Once it is submitted, the NZIS will check it to make sure that all relevant information has been supplied.

If your EOI is not selected from the pool the first time, it will remain in the pool for three months. If it is still unsuccessful, the NZIS will tell you that your EOI has been withdrawn from the pool. You may lodge another if you wish to. If you have been successful, you will be sent an official invitation to apply for residence. At this stage you will need to send all the necessary documents to support the claims you made in your EOI, such as passports, qualifications and relevant certificates. The application for residence is now a much shorter form than it used to be, as you will have already supplied all the necessary information with your EOI.

Your application for residence is then assessed against government residence policy, and the NZIS looks closely at your ability to settle successfully and make a real contribution to New Zealand's social and economic development. Further verification of some of the information you provided with your EOI will also be undertaken at this stage. Depending on how you are able to demonstrate your ability to settle in New Zealand successfully, your application can be approved with a residence visa or permit, or a visa or permit which enables you to move from work to residence. It is then up to you to confirm your decision to move to New Zealand. A questionnaire will be sent to you after three months, as a formal follow-up so that the NZIS can use your feedback to help future skilled migrants.

To give you an idea of how the points are allocated under the Skilled Migrant category, see the table on pages 35–36. See www.immigration.govt.nz for more information, definitions of terms and an indication of your potential points score and eligibility under this category.

Skilled migrant quick check

- Are you under 56 years of age?
- Are you, your partner and your children all healthy?
- Are you, your partner and your children free of major criminal convictions and not a security risk?
- Can you competently speak, write and understand English?
- Have you been offered a job in New Zealand?
- Do you have tertiary or trade qualifications?
- Do you have at least two years' work experience?

Skilled migrant category points system

Conditions	Points
Skilled employment	
Current employment in New Zealand for 12 months or more (ongoing)	60
Offer of employment in New Zealand or current employment in New Zealand for less than 12 months (minimum of 3 months)	50
Bonus points for offer of employment or employment in: An identified future growth area	5
Identified cluster area of absolute skills shortage	10
Region outside Auckland	10
Spouse/partner employment or offer of employment	10
Work Experience in Skilled Employment:	
2 years	10
4 years	15
6 years	20
8 years	25
10 years	30
There are additional bonus points if your work experience is in New Zealand:	
2 years	5
4 years	10
6 years or more	15
Additional bonus points for work experience in an identified future growth area, or cluster:	
2 – 5 years	5
6 years or more	10
Additional bonus points for work experience in an area of absolute skills shortage:	
2 – 5 years	10
6 years or more	15
Qualifications	
Recognised basic qualification (eg trade qualification, diploma, bachelor's degree)	50
Recognised postgraduate qualification (eg masters degree, doctorate, etc)	55
Bonus points for: Recognised New Zealand qualification (with at least 2 years study in New Zealand)	10
Qualification in identified future growth area or identified cluster	5

(Continued on following page)

Skilled migrant category points system	
Conditions	**Points**
Qualification in area of absolute skill shortage	10
Partner qualifications	10
Close family support in New Zealand	
Age (20–55 years):	10
20–29 years	30
30–39 years	25
40–44 years	20
45–49 years	10
50–55 years	5

To be confident about filling out an EOI you need to have answered 'yes' to the first four questions above and to at least one of the last three questions.

Remember that you must be no younger than 20 and no older than 55 and must meet the threshold of 100 points to be entitled to register an EOI

Applicants can gain 10 bonus points if they have a close family member who is in New Zealand and is a New Zealand resident, as long as that close family member supports the application.

Points to watch out for

- You can only claim points for your highest qualification.
- You do not have to have a job offer, although you will score more points if you do.
- Years of work experience are rounded down, so if you have nine years and eight months of work experience that will only count as eight years (giving you four points).
- Medical assessment requirements are based on whether or not you would be a danger to public health or a burden on the New Zealand health system. Chronic manageable syndromes such as epilepsy would not disqualify you, but having a terminal disease probably would. Health requirements changed from 4 April 2005; these are outlined in the Health Requirements Leaflet from New Zealand Immigration (Form NZIS 1121).

Most immigration consultants offer a job search service. You should consider visiting New Zealand and jobhunting in person, as most employers prefer to meet someone face to face before they make the offer of a job. Remember you can apply for permanent residency from within New Zealand. You will need enough money to finance your living costs while you are waiting for completion of the Immigration Service process, and this could be around six months. First hand experience of any country is of course the best way to decide whether you want to live there.

TIP

- Finding the extra points to raise you above the pass mark is an area where a good immigration consultant may be able to help.

Long-term skill shortage list residence policy

This is a residence policy for people who were granted a 30-7 month Work Visa or permit to allow them to work for an employer in New Zealand in an occupation on the Long-Term Skill Shortage List (which was formerly known as the Priority Occupations List or POL).

To be approved for residence under this policy you must:

- Have held a Work Visa and Work Permit granted under the Long Term Skill Shortage List Work Policy for a minimum of 24 months; and

- during the duration of that visa or permit, have been employed in New Zealand in an occupation included in the Long Term Skill Shortage List for a period of at least 24 months; and

- currently have employment (see below) with a minimum base salary of NZ$45,000 that is in either:

  - the occupation for which you were granted a Work Permit of Visa under the Long Term Skill Shortage List Work Policy;

    or

  - an occupation which is listed on the Long Term Shortage List at the time your application for residence is made; and

- be aged 55 years or younger; and

- hold a full or provisional registration, if full or provisional registration is required to practise in that occupation in New Zealand; and

- be healthy and of good character.

Your employment must be:

- full-time (on average, at least 30 hours per week); and

- ongoing (permanent or indefinite), or for a stated term of at least 12 months with an option of further terms; and

- genuine; and

- compliant with relevant employment law in force in New Zealand. This includes having a written employment agreement specifying the necessary terms and conditions, and meeting holiday, special leave and occupational health and safety requirements.

 To find out which occupations are included on the current Long Term Shortage List, visit www.immigration.govt.nz.

Business category

In order to apply for a Long-term Business Visa you will need to complete an application for a Long Term Business Visa and Permit (form NZIS 1058).

- You must submit all the required information when you lodge your application. If you do not supply this information, your application may be returned.

- All documents presented must be in their original form or as certified copies.

- Anyone can act as your agent or representative, for example a lawyer, consultant, or any other person (including a friend).

- All documents not presented in English must be accompanied by an official translation, certified by a recognised private or official translation service and on official letterhead which includes the name, address and signature of the translator. If you are considering applying for New Zealand citizenship at a later date, it may be worth having your documents translated by a provider approved by the Department of Internal Affairs. Refer to www.dia.govt.nz.

- First-time applicants or those who have held a work visa and/or permit under the Long-Term Business Visa/Permit category for three years and are applying for a further work visa and/or permit will need to pay a fee unless you are from a country listed under the fee waiver agreement. See the NZIS Guide to Fees (NZIS 1028) or www.immigration.govt.nz for details.

- If you have held a work visa and/or permit under this category for less than three years and are applying for a further visa and/or permit, or are applying for consent to change your business plan, you will not need to pay a fee unless otherwise directed by the NZIS.

- If you are in New Zealand, you must show that you have a current permit. Any dependents must also have current permits.

- If you are separated or divorced and wish to bring children to New Zealand, you must prove that you have custody with either custody papers or a court order.

You will need to complete a business plan, covering general information, an outline of the proposed business and its viability, financial information (cash flow forecasts and financing options), your business experience, and your knowledge of the New Zealand market. The NZIS will assess your business plan, looking at whether you have sufficient funds, realistic financial forecasts, relevant business experience, a sound business record, sound business character, and whether you are registered (if professional or occupational registration in New Zealand is required for the proposed business). You must also supply information about the industry in which your proposed business sits, location of the business, maintenance funds, business status, investment capital, expectations of business achievements, proposed ownership structure, overseas links, benefit to New Zealand, your role, the number of employees and their skills, a marketing strategy, SWOT analysis and a proposed timeline.

If your application is approved, you will be granted and/or issued a 9-month work permit/visa to allow you to establish and commence the operation of your proposed business. Further permits/visas may be granted or issued for the balance of the three-year period if:

- you apply within the validity period.

- you provide satisfactory evidence to demonstrate that your investment capital was transferred to New Zealand through the banking system; and

- you provide satisfactory evidence to demonstrate that you have taken reasonable steps to establish or invest in your proposed business.

If you wish to change your business proposal within the validity period, you must seek the consent of a business immigration specialist. Consent may be given if:

- you have genuine reasons for abandoning your original proposal; and

- you have an acceptable business plan for the proposed new business; and

- your new business proposal requires the same or a greater level of capital investment than your original business proposal; and

- you have access to sufficient capital to finance the proposed new business; and
- you have business experience relevant to the proposed new business.

Your permit may be revoked if you undertake a different business proposal without seeking consent. It is understood that a proposal may undergo some modifications or development once it is put into action, but it is best not to jeopardise your chances of staying in the country. If you are unsure whether a change you are making will require consent, you should contact the business immigration specialist who has been assigned to your case.

Further work permits and/or visas beyond the initial three years will be granted only where a business immigration consultant is satisfied on the following points:

- Any time you spent in New Zealand has been spent setting up and operating your original business proposal.
- If you made a change to your original business proposal, consent was granted for that change by a business immigration specialist.
- You, and any family member accompanying you, have not drawn on the New Zealand welfare system.
- You intend to spend the further period in New Zealand either implementing the original business proposed or a subsequent business proposal (which has been given consent).
- You have, in addition to investment capital, access to sufficient funds for your own maintenance and accommodation and that of any spouse, partner, or dependent child accompanying you.
- You meet health and character requirements.

In the event that your application is approved, you must agree to participate in an evaluation of the Long-Term Business Visa/Permit category for a period of up to five years from the date your application is approved. You must also agree to inform the NZIS of any changes to your postal or contact addresses within five years from the date of approval of your application for the purpose of participating in the evaluation.

Investor category

This stream works along the same lines as the Skilled Migrant Category above; applicants first submit an EOI and are then invited to apply for residence if they meet the minimum criteria. Following the lodging of your EOI you will only be invited to apply for residency if INZ assesses that you:

- are aged 54 or younger;
- are healthy and of good character;
- meet the minimum required standard of Engish;
- have at least five years' business experience; and
- have at least NZ$2 million to invest for a minimum of five years.

You will need to state, on your EOI form, what evidence you have to support these claims, but you will not be required to provide the official forms until you apply for residence. It goes without saying that all funds must have been earned legally, and must be owned either solely by you or jointly by you and your partner, or you and your dependent children. If the funds are owned by both you and your partner, you will need to have been living in a genuine and stable relationship for a minimum of 12 months and meet the minimum requirements for recognition of partnerships for the funds to be acceptable in support of your application.

Provided your application is approved, your permit will have certain conditions imposed on it for five years – the required term of your investment. These conditions will be that you:

■ retain the investment for five years;

■ make New Zealand your main home; and

■ participate in monitoring and evaluation as required by the Department of Labour.

Your funds will be held by the New Zealand government for five years and adjusted for inflation during this time. You cannot choose to invest your funds in any other way. After two years, you may apply to INZ to withdraw up to half your money to invest in a business that will benefit New Zealand. You will be required to submit a business plan and pay a fee. At the end of the five-year period INZ will return your funds to you, adjusted for inflation and tax. Within three months of the end of the five-year period you will have to provide evidence that you have met the conditions imposed on your permit. If you have, INZ will issue you with a new residence permit with the conditions lifted. If not, your permit will be revoked.

Your application for a visa or permit can cover your partner and unmarried children who are aged 19 years or younger. If they are dependent on you, your application can also cover children up to 24. To be successful you will still need to gain enough points for your age, business experience and investment funds to meet the pass mark, which is currently set at 12 points.

Entrepreneur category

To apply under this category, you need to:

■ have successfully established a business in New Zealand that is benefiting New Zealand (see below); and

■ be healthy and of good character; and

■ meet a minimum standard of English; and

■ not have applied for or been granted social welfare benefits in New Zealand.

You have successfully established a business in New Zealand if:

■ you have established or purchased, or made substantial investment (a minimum of 25% of the shareholding of a business) in a business operating in New Zealand; and

■ the business has been established for at least two years; and

■ you have been lawfully working in New Zealand in that business for at least two years.

A business is considered to be benefiting New Zealand if it promotes New Zealand's economic growth through, for example:

■ introducing new or enhancing existing technology, management or technical skills; or

■ introducing new or enhancing existing products, services or export markets; or

■ creating new or expanding existing export markets; or

- creating new job opportunities; or
- revitalising an existing business.

The business must be trading profitably on the date you lodge your application or must clearly have the potential to become profitable within the following 12 months.

Employees of relocating businesses

This category aims to promote New Zealand as a place in which to relocate businesses. To be considered under this category the owner(s) of the relocating business needs to satisfy NZIS that the business will:

- operate in New Zealand; and
- be of benefit to New Zealand; and
- comply with all relevant employment and immigration law in force in New Zealand.

New Zealand Trade and Enterprise must support the relocation of the business. NZIS will consult with New Zealand Trade and Enterprise to determine its support for the relocation of the business.

To be approved under this category you need to:

- be a key employee of a business that is proposing to relocate to New Zealand; and
- not qualify for residence under other residence categories; and
- be healthy and of good character; and
- meet a minimum standard of English.

You are a key employee if the chief executive officer of the relocating business can satisfy the NZIS that you will be essential to the operation of the business in New Zealand.

If your application is approved, NZIS will send you a letter setting out the requirements that apply to you, your partner and children. Under the Employees of Relocating Businesses Category you must also comply with the following requirements:

- you must work in the business for a minimum of 24 months following its relocation to New Zealand; and
- inform NZIS if your address changes within this time; and
- show the NZIS that you have met the first requirement within three months after the initial 24-month period has ended.

Sponsorship under the talent (arts, culture and sports) category

To apply under this category, you must provide a completed Talent (Arts, Culture and Sports) sponsorship form (NZIS 1091) from an organisation of national repute with your application for residence. The organisation must agree to sponsor you for residence and the form must include an undertaking by an eligible personal sponsor to provide you with financial support and accommodation during the first two years of your residence, if this should be necessary. Arts, cultural and sporting organisations that want to know more about sponsoring applicants under this Talent Work Policy should see the sponsorship form (NZIS 1091) for more information.

Family (partnership) category

 You are entitled to apply for residence under this category if you have a partner who is a New Zealand or Australian resident or citizen and who sponsors your application. Spouses, de facto and homosexual partners all qualify, but in the case of de facto or homosexual partners you have to go to greater lengths to convince the Immigration Service that the relationship is 'genuine and stable'. Approval is not automatic for any of these cases including spouses, and the Immigration Service will probably require an interview with both partners. Partners who do not meet character requirement in respect of Partnership policy application, unless granted a character waiver, include any person who has been convicted in the seven years prior to the date the application is made of any offence either of a sexual nature or involving domestic violence. Your sponsor will need to show that New Zealand is their primary place of residence. When your application is made and assessed they should:

- hold a valid New Zealand or Australian passport; or
- hold a New Zealand Residence Permit or Returning Resident's Visa which was issued on the basis of an Australian Permanent Residence Visa or an Australian Resident Return Visa.

Your New Zealand partner will not be eligible to sponsor you if they:

- have previously supported or sponsored more than one other successful principal applicant under the Partnership Policy; or
- have previously supported or sponsored any other successful principal applicant under Partnership Policy in the five years immediately preceding the date the current application is made; or
- do not meet the character requirements for partners supporting Partnership Policy applications; or
- were, in the seven years prior to the date the application is made, the perpetrator of an incident of domestic violence that has resulted in the grant of a Residence Permit to a person under the policy for victims of domestic violence; or
- were a successful principal applicant under Partnership Policy if:
  - less than five years have elapsed since the date they were granted residence under the Partnership Policy; or

they have previously supported or sponsored any other successful principal applicant under Partnership Policy.

Partners who do not meet minimum character requirements in respect of a Partnership Policy application, unless granted a character waiver, include any person who has been convicted in the seven years prior to the date the application was made of any offence of a sexual nature or involving domestic violence.

Recognition of partnerships

To be granted residence in New Zealand you and your partner need to prove that you:

- are living together (and have been for a minimum of 12 months) in a genuine and stable relationship; and
- are both aged 18 years or over (or can provide evidence of parental/guardian/other consent if either of you is 16 or 17 years of age); and
- met each other prior to your application being made; and
- are not close relatives according to Schedule 2 of the Marriage Act 1955 or Schedule 2 of the Civil Union Act 2004. (These Acts can be viewed on the internet at www.legislation.govt.nz.)

Parent policy

This policy is for people who want to live permanently in New Zealand and have an adult child who is a New Zealand citizen or resident. You may be granted residence if:

- your child is 17 years or over and sponsors your application; and
- your family's 'centre of gravity' is in New Zealand.

To sponsor you under this policy your child must:

- be 17 years of age or over; and
- be in New Zealand; and
- be a New Zealand or Australian citizen or the holder of a current Resident Permit that is not subject to requirements under section 18A of the Immigration Act 1987; and
- have been a New Zealand or Australian citizen and/or the holder of a Residence Permit or a Returning Resident's Visa for at least three years immediately before the date your completed application is received by INZ; and
- have spent a total of 184 days or more in New Zealand in each of those three years; and
- meet a minimum income requirement (for sponsors under 65 years old). See below for more details.

NB: Legal guardians and grandparents are also considered to be parents in some situations. See www.immigration.govt.nz for more information.

Your sponsor and/or their partner must meet a minimum income requirement to demonstrate that they are able to financially support you (unless your sponsor is aged 65 years or over). The minimum income requirement must be met by income obtained from:

- sustained paid employment; and/or
- regular self-employment; and/or
- regular investment income.

For the current minimum income figure, please check the NZIS website or contact an NZIS branch office. Your sponsor and/or their partner must provide evidence that they are able to meet the minimum income requirement. Your sponsor must also make a legal declaration that they will provide you with financial support and accommodation (if applicable) for at least the first two years of your residence in New Zealand. NB: Sponsors who obtained residence in New Zealand on the basis of their status as a refugee do not have to meet the minimum income requirement or make the legal declaration.

Centre of gravity

The 'centre of gravity' of your family is in New Zealand if you have:

- no dependent children – all your adult children are living lawfully and permanently outside your home country or you have an equal or greater number of adult children living lawfully and permanently in New Zealand than in any other single country, including your home country; or
- dependent children – you have an equal or greater number of children living lawfully and permanently in New Zealand than in any other single country, including your home country. The number of your dependent children must be the same as, or fewer than, the number of adult children living lawfully and permanently in New Zealand.

Under this policy, your children include:

- your biological and adopted children; and
- your partner's children (whether or not your partner is included in this application) if that child has lived as a part of your family unit for most of the child's life between the time your relationship with your partner began and the time that the child turned 17.

Legal guardians and grandparents

A sponsor's legal guardian and their partner will be considered as parents under the Parent Policy if:

- both the sponsor's parents died before the sponsor turned 20; and
- the legal guardian has custody of the sponsor and the right to control the sponsor's upbringing before the sponsor turned 20.

In the context of the Parent Policy you are a legal guardian if your children include:

- the New Zealand citizen or resident sponsor; and
- all your biological and adopted children; and
- any children for whom you are or were legal guardian(s); and
- any of your partner's children (whether or not the partner is included in the application) if that child has lived as part of your family unit for most of the child's life between the time your relationship with your partner began and the time that the child turned 17.

A sponsor's grandparent and their partner will be considered as parents under the Parent Policy if both the sponsor's parents are dead. Only one grandparent and their partner may be sponsored under the Parent Policy. Under this policy you are a grandparent if your children include:

- the New Zealand citizen or resident sponsor; and
- all your biological and adopted children; and

- any of your partner's children (whether or not the partner is included on the application) if that child has been part of your family unit for most of the child's life between the time your relationship with your partner began and when the child turned 17.

Sibling and adult child policy

You may be granted residence under this policy if you:

- have a New Zealand citizen or resident parent, brother or sister who is living in New Zealand and who is able to sponsor your application; and
- have no other siblings or parent who are living lawfully and permanently in the same country in which you are living lawfully and permanently; and
- have an acceptable offer of employment in New Zealand; and
- are aged 55 years or younger at the time the application is lodged.

Your sponsor must:

- be 17 years of age or over; and
- be living in New Zealand; and
- be a New Zealand or Australian citizen, or the holder of a current Residence Permit that is not subject to requirements under section 18A of the Immigration Act 1987; and
- have been a New Zealand or Australian citizen, and/or the holder of a Residence Permit or Returning Resident's Visa for at least three years immediately before the date you apply; and
- have spent a total of 184 days or more in New Zealand in each of those three years.

Your sponsor must make a legal declaration that they will provide you with financial support and accommodation (if necessary) for at least the first two years of your residence in New Zealand.

To qualify as acceptable offers of employment, job offers must be:

- for ongoing work with a single employer (ie, for a stated term of at least 12 months with an option of further terms); or
- for one or more contract totalling at least six months, if you have provided evidence of having had at least two years of contract work; and
- for full-time employment (averaging at least 30 hours per week); and
- current at the time your application is assessed and at the time you are granted residence, and genuine; and
- for a position that is paid by salary or wages (positions of self-employment, payment by commission and/or retainer are not acceptable); and
- accompanied by evidence of full or provisional registration, if full or provisional registration is required by law to take up the offer; and
- compliant with all relevant employment law in force in New Zealand. This includes having a written employment contract specifying the necessary terms and conditions, and meeting holiday, special leave, minimum wage, and occupational health and safety requirements.

If you have dependent children you will need to show that you will meet a minimum income requirement in New Zealand to ensure that you can support yourself and your dependents if you come to New Zealand. If your partner is included in your application and also has an offer of employment in New Zealand, their wages or salary can be taken into account to assess whether you will meet the minimum income requirement. However, your partner's employment offer can only be taken into account if your partner meets the minimum requirements for recognition of partnerships. Your partner's job offer must also be 'acceptable' but does not have to be for full-time employment.

Gross minimum income requirements for principal applicants with dependent children	
Number of dependent children	Total gross annual family income
1	NZ$30,946
2	NZ$36,493
3	NZ$42,040
4	NZ$47,586

Source: New Zealand Immigration Service

Dependent child policy

This category is for people who are dependent children of a New Zealand citizen or resident and who want to live permanently in New Zealand. You may be considered under this category if:

- you are aged 16 years or younger; and
- you are single; and
- you are totally or substantially reliant on an adult for financial support (whether or not that adult is your parent and whether or not you are living with that adult); and
  - your parent(s) are lawfully and permanently in New Zealand;
    or:
  - you are aged between 17 and 24 years; and
- you are single; and
- you have no children of your own; and
- you are totally or substantially reliant on an adult for financial support (whether or not that adult is your parent and whether or not you are living with that adult); and
- your parent is lawfully and permanently in New Zealand.

You must also:

- have been born or adopted before your parent applied for residence, and been declared on your parents' application for residence; or
- have been born after your parents applied for residence; or
- have been adopted by your parents as a result of a New Zealand adoption or an overseas adoption recognised under New Zealand law.

Your parents are considered to be lawfully and permanently in New Zealand if they are:

- citizen(s) of New Zealand; or
- holder(s) of New Zealand Residence Permits; or
- holder(s) of current New Zealand Returning Resident's Visa(s); or
- citizen(s) of Australia living in New Zealand.

If you are under 16 years of age and you have a parent living outside New Zealand, your parent in New Zealand must provide evidence that custody or visitation rights of the parent living outside New Zealand will not be breached by your coming to live in New Zealand.

You can qualify under family reunification if you have immediate family members who are residents/citizens and live permanently in New Zealand. You must be a dependent child, parent, brother, sister or adult child of the person sponsoring you. Dependent children (includes those aged up to 24 years, but they must be unmarried and childless) may qualify to be reunited with their parents if they were declared on their parents' residence application. Single adults may qualify for reunification with a New Zealand brother, sister or parent. Married and unmarried siblings, and dependent children, may now only apply for sponsorship if they have no other siblings or parents living in their own country and if they have an offer of employment in New Zealand. Under the 'centre of gravity' principle, parents may be reunited with adult children provided all their adult children live outside their country of origin, or, if they do not have dependent children, more of their adult children live in New Zealand than in any other country. If they do have dependent children, they may still apply if they have a greater or equal number of adult children living in New Zealand than in any other country. Children may sponsor parents who are alone in their home country. The definition of 'parents' has now been extended to include grandparents and legal guardians in cases where the parents are deceased.

To qualify under any of these categories you will need to provide evidence of your relationship to your family member and proof that they are New Zealand citizens or residents. The sponsor must undertake to ensure that accommodation and financial support is provided to the applicant for at least the first 24 months of residence in New Zealand. If the applicant is successful, they will be granted a Residence Visa (valid for 12 months from the date of issue), or a Residence Permit (which allows you to live in New Zealand indefinitely but expires when you leave New Zealand). You may need a Returning Resident's Visa to re-enter New Zealand. Your first Returning Resident's Visa is issued when you are granted your Residence Visa or your first Residence Permit in New Zealand, and is valid for two years from the date it is issued.

Family quota

There is now an immigration ballot which currently allows an additional number of family members of New Zealand citizens and residents who are not eligible for residence under any other category. You must register your interest at a particular time each year, and if your registration is drawn from a pool (ie, you are successful) your family will then have the opportunity to apply for a residence visa and permit. You will be notified by NZIS in the month after the draw whether your sponsorship has been successful, and, if so, you must then notify your family. Your family must then apply for a residence visa and permit within the next six months by completing an Application for Residence form (NZIS 1000). New Zealand residents/citizens may sponsor a close family member (parents, grandparents, adult children or adult brothers and sisters and their partners and children). The sponsor must be 17 years of age or over, in New Zealand and a New Zealand or Australian citizen or holder of a current residence permit. The sponsor must have been a New Zealand or Australian citizen (or holder of permit) for at least three years immediately before the date their registration is received by NZIS and, in each of the three 12-month periods within that three-year period, have spent a total of 184 days or more in New Zealand.

■ The quota size is announced each year – see www.immigration.govt.nz for the latest information.

■ Registration takes place every April, and winners are given 6 months to file their residency applications.

■ Normal health, character, and relationship requirements still apply.

■ Applicants must be sponsored by a family member who is a New Zealand resident or citizen living there permanently and who is aged at least 17 years.

International/humanitarian stream

Applicants under this category have to be suffering some kind of persecution in their home country and must have a New Zealand sponsor who is a close family member. This stream accounts for 10% of the New Zealand Residence Programme – amounting to about 4,500 places every year. Included in this category are United Nations mandated refugees who are approved under the annual Refugee Quota and asylum seekers who claim refugee status in New Zealand. The categories in this stream are:

■ Refugee Family Support Category;

■ Pacific Access Category;

■ Samoan Quota Scheme;

■ victims of domestic violence; and

■ various other special policies for specific countries.

For information and advice about applying under this stream, contact INZ directly. For details see the website: www.immigation.govt.nz.

■ THE APPLICATION PROCESS

Download or obtain an application for visa from a New Zealand embassy or high commission and complete it along with the required documentation, then return it to the high commission. If you are applying under the Skilled Migrant Category, remember that you must submit your EOI (as outlined above) before being invited to complete an application. NZIS does prefer that you do this online.

Medical requirements include certain blood tests, and the results for these must be sent in. Once you have sent the correct documents Immigration Service staff will check your eligibility. Processing time is often lengthy; currently applications within New Zealand are taking up to nine months to process, while New Zealand House in London advises that applications submitted to them are taking around four to seven months to process. This is only a rough guide, as every case is different and

> **TIP**
>
> ■ A major cause of delay in processing applications is incorrect or insufficient documentation. Make sure, for example, that you send full birth certificates (not short birth certificates) for all family members included in an application for residency.

more complex cases take longer to process. However, to be on the safe side, you should begin the application process about a year and a half before your intended date of migration.

Fees must be paid by cheque (payable to 'The New Zealand Immigration Service'), building society cheque, money order or acceptable credit or debit card (Visa, Eurocard/MasterCard, Delta, Maestro); cash payments are acceptable if you are paying in person. You must check which currency you should pay fees in with the office you will be making the payment to. Remember, irrespective of outcome, visa fees are non-refundable. Fees, like application forms, change regularly, so check you have the correct fee and current versions of the forms before submitting your application.

To get a residence pack from NZIS, visit the website (www.immigration. govt. nz) or request a coupon to complete, then mail it with the required postage and envelope to the Immigration New Zealand branch or agency at the nearest address listed on the back page. Include a self-addressed envelope that is at least 23cm x 33cm (9 x 12in). Ensure you include enough return postage on the envelope; some branches have specific postage requirements.

Fees

> 66
>
> The visa application process was speeded up by a trip to the New Zealand Embassy in London to discuss and confirm the type of visa I was applying for and to establish what I needed to provide in order to qualify. Although I found the New Zealand immigration website very helpful in terms of answering most of my questions, it gave me more confidence to meet with the relevant people face to face to be sure that I wasn't overlooking anything vital in the application process, and to make sure I was doing everything correctly.
>
> **Dermot Foley**
>
> 99

These fees, unless otherwise indicated, are shown in New Zealand dollars. Although these figures are correct at the time of going to print, applicants should use the fees calculator on the website www.immigration.govt.nz or telephone to establish the correct fee, as the charges are subject to review and alteration at various times. Fees must be paid in the local currency of the country in which your application is to be lodged. Acceptable methods of payment vary from country to country, but are likely to include cash, credit cards and bank cheque/bank draft. Again, this does depend on the rules of the office in question. Fees for EOI under both the Skilled Migrant and Investor Categories lodged on a paper form from outside of New Zealand can be paid by credit card, bank draft or bank cheque in New Zealand dollars. Online EOIs may be paid either by credit card or bank draft. Fees for EOIs under the Skilled Migrant Category can also be paid by bank draft in US dollars. The fees shown below are effective from November 2007, but they are subject to change.

NB: There are further fees for additional services; please check the website (www.immigration.govt.nz) or contact your local branch or office for a fees list.

Citizens of certain countries are not charged for some visas:

Austria: No charge for Residence Visas, Returning Resident's Visas (RRVS), Visitor Visas. Standard fee for Work and Student Visas.

Finland: No charge for any type of visa.

Greece: No charge for Visitor Visas and RRVs. Standard fee for Residence, Work and Student Visas.

Iceland: No charge for any type of visa.

Israel: No charge for Visitor Visas and RRVs. Standard fee for Residence, Work and Student Visas.

Fees

Type of application	Fee (dependent on your location)	
	New Zealand	UK/USA
Expressions of Interest		
Skilled Migrant Category		
Paper form	NZ$500	NZ$500
Online form	NZ$400	NZ$400
General (Active) Investor Category		
Paper form	NZ$460	NZ$460
Residence (visa or permit)		
Skilled Migrant Category	NZ$1400	NZ$1800
General (Active) Investor Category	NZ$3400	NZ$3400
Professional Investor Category	NZ$3400	NZ$3400
Global Investor Category	NZ$3400	NZ$3400
Entrepreneur Category	NZ$2600	NZ$2600
Family Category	NZ$700	NZ$1200
Samoan Quota Scheme	NZ$600	N/A
Pacific Access Category	NZ$650	N/A
Refugee Family Support Category	NZ$490	NZ$690
Residence from Work Category	NZ$700	N/A
Any other residence	NZ$700	NZ$1200
Returning resident's visa	NZ$140	NZ$140
Confirmation of Residence status		
(under regulation 11)	NZ$80	N/A
Visitor (visa or permit)	NZ$130	NZ$130
Group visitor visa, per person		
Beijing, Shanghai, Taipei	N/A	NZ$75

(Continued opposite)

Fees

Type of application	Fee (dependent on your location)	
	New Zealand	UK/USA
Bangkok (Thai citizens only)	N/A	NZ$75
ADS	N/A	NZ$40
Other	NZ$80	NZ$80
Student permit		
Online via education provider	NZ$70	N/A
Other	NZ$200	N/A
Student visa	NZ$200	NZ$200
Work permit		
Work to residence: Talent and Long Term Skill Shortage List	NZ$240	N/A
Work partnership	NZ$280	N/A
Other	NZ$120	NZ$120
Working Holiday Scheme	NZ$120	NZ$120
Long Term Business Visa or Permit	NZ$2600	NZ$2600
Limited Purpose (visa or permit)		
Student visa	NZ$200	NZ$200
Further student permit	NZ$200	N/A
Other	NZ$130	NZ$130
Visa to work for a: recognised seasonal employer	NZ$200	NZ$200
Further permit to work for a recognised seasonal employer	NZ$200	N/A
Temporary: Other Special direction fee	NZ$140	NZ$140
Reconsideration	NZ$140	N/A
Variation of conditions	NZ$120	N/A
Request for approval in principle	NZ$180	N/A
Request for transitioning to recognised seasonal employer (TRSE) approval in principle	NZ$180	N/A
Section 35A permit	NZ$200	N/A

Italy: No charge for RRVs and Visitor Visas. Standard fee for Residence, Work and Student Visas.

Japan: No charge for any type of visa.

Mexico: No charge for Visitor, Work or Student Visas. Standard fee for Residence Visas.

Philippines: No fee for Student and Visitor Visas (for visits not exceeding 59 days).

Russia: No charge for Student Visas when period of stay is less than three months. No charge for Visitor Visas. Standard fees for Work, RRVs and Residence Visas.

Turkey: No charge for Visitor Visas or RRVs. Standard fees for Work, Student and Residence Visas.

USA: No charge for Visitor, Work and Student Visas, Standard fee for RRVs and Residence Visas.

Source: New Zealand Immigration Service

New Zealand citizenship

Residence and citizenship are different. If you are granted residence, you retain your original citizenship. However, after you have lived in New Zealand for a certain period of time you may apply for New Zealand citizenship and the right to hold a New Zealand passport. New requirements for citizenship were introduced in April 2005. Once you have resided legally in New Zealand for five years (previously you only had to reside for three years), you may apply for New Zealand citizenship depending on when you were granted residence. This will entitle you to vote and to carry a New Zealand passport. You will no longer require

I came into New Zealand on a student visa, which was very simple to obtain. I have always found the immigration department here incredibly straightforward, helpful and accessible. Linda and I knew that we would eventually be applying for my residency based on our de facto relationship, so we had kept a file of anything that related to our relationship – from shared amenity bills and joint bank statements, through to hundreds of emails and hastily scribbled and embarrassing love notes and photos of us together madly in love. Our parents and good friends also wrote formal letters as witnesses to our relationship. Towards the end of the first year in New Zealand we sent away my application for residency, along with two big lever-arch files filled to brim with 'evidence' of our relationship. When you apply for a New Zealand residence visa based on your relationship, you are automatically given a work visa for a couple of years (from memory), the idea being you can stay in New Zealand with your partner while the application is being processed.

a returning resident's visa when you travel outside New Zealand. From January 2006 children born in New Zealand will acquire New Zealand citizenship by birth only if at least one of their parents is a New Zealand citizen or has permanent residency. New Zealand allows its citizens to hold multiple citizenships; but some other countries do not allow this. You must check with the authorities of the country or countries for which you currently hold citizenship before applying for New Zealand citizenship.

To apply for New Zealand citizenship, you must first read the application guide carefully to be sure both that you are eligible and that you understand all the requirements. Obtain an application form from the Department of Internal Affairs and fill out the relevant sections. Send the completed form, with the required photographs and appropriate fee, to the citizenship office (details below). Do not send your documents at this point. Your application will be acknowledged in writing once it has been received, and then your application will be allocated to a Case Officer who will write to you again, this time requesting your documents. A prepaid courier pack will be supplied with your letter. Once your application has been assessed, you will receive a letter informing you of its success or failure. Assuming you are granted citizenship and you are over 14 years of age, you will swear or affirm allegiance to the Queen of New Zealand at a public citizenship ceremony where you will receive your New Zealand citizenship certificate.

For more information, see www.citizenship.govt.nz. The Department of Internal Affairs (DIA) Contact Centre should be able to assist you with any citizenship inquiries. Online forms are available through the website.

To make your application, post or deliver your forms, fee and photographs to one of the following offices:

 Department of Internal Affairs: PO Box 10–680, Wellington 6143; Level 3, 47 Boulcott Street, 47 Boulcott Street, Wellington 6011; (04) 474 8123 or 0800 22 51 51 (Freephone NZ only); citizenship@dia.govt.nz; www.dia.govt.nz

Wellington
PO Box 10-680
Wellington 6143
Level 3, Boulcott House
47 Boulcott Street
Wellington 6011
Opening hours: Monday to Friday 8.30am – 5.00pm, except Thursday 9.00am – 5.00pm

Auckland
PO Box 6147
Auckland 1141
Level 6, AA Building
99 Albert Street
Auckland 1010
Opening hours: Monday to Friday 8.30am – 5.00pm, except Wednesday 9.00am – 5.00pm

Manukau	**Christchurch**
PO Box 76-222	PO Box 25-211
Manukau City 2241	Christchurch 8144
Level 1	NZI House
Corner of Amersham Way and	Level 6
Osterley Way	96 Hereford Street
Manukau 2104	Christchurch 8011
Opening hours: Monday to	**Opening hours:** Monday to
Friday 8.30am – 5.00pm, except	Friday 8.30am – 5.00pm, except
Wednesday 9.00am – 5.00pm	Wednesday 9.00am – 5.00pm

In the UK
New Zealand Citizenship Office in
London
New Zealand Passport Office
Department of Internal Affairs
New Zealand House
80 Haymarket
London SW1Y 4TQ
United Kingdom
Tel: 020 7930 8422
Opening hours: Monday to Friday
10.00am – 4.00pm.

Other overseas locations

Email: passports@dia.govt.nz or contact your nearest New Zealand Embassy, High Commission or Consulate (see www.dia.govt.nz for contact details).

■ ENTRY AND WORK PERMITS

If you want to visit New Zealand and you are not a citizen or permanent resident, then you may need a Visitor's Visa or Permit. You should apply for a visa from the New Zealand embassy in your home country before you travel. The initial period of a visa is usually three months but you can extend it by a further six months once you are in New Zealand by applying to local offices of the New Zealand Immigration Service. However, increasing numbers of travellers do not need to obtain visas, as New Zealand has negotiated visa-free agreements with several countries. Tourists from the UK are entitled to stay for up to six months without a visa, and American, Canadian and European tourists can stay for three months without a visa. If you do not require a visa, you simply apply for a Visitor's Permit at the airport. You will be required to show that you have sufficient funds to support yourself while you are in New Zealand and you will need a return or onward ticket. Like the visa, the Visitor's Permit is issued for three months initially and can be renewed by a further six months within New Zealand. If you have a friend or relative prepared to sponsor you, they will need to fill in a Sponsoring a visitor form, which they can get from New Zealand Immigration, and which must be sent to you so you can present it when required.

Australia

Australian citizens are free to travel to New Zealand without a visa and can work in New Zealand without requiring a work visa under the terms of the Closer Economic Relations agreement, which creates a free labour market across the Tasman.

Applying for a longer visa

If you know before you travel that you want to stay for longer than three months it is worth applying for a visa even if you are from a visa-waiver country. You can apply for a maximum of 12 months, and your application must be made before your current permit expires.

Studying in New Zealand

Any person wanting to travel to New Zealand for the principal reason of study or training must have a student visa before they travel. You will need to provide an acceptance letter from the New Zealand educational institution, receipt for the non-New Zealand student course fee, evidence of sufficient funds to support yourself, and an outward airline ticket. If you wish to work over the student holidays (November to February), you can apply for a 'Variation of Conditions' to your student permit. If you wish to work following the completion of your course, you can apply for a Work Permit, which will allow you to work a maximum of two years. Some tertiary students may work up to 15 hours a week while studying. The student must be studying for a degree or diploma that would gain points under the Skilled Migrant immigration category: exchange students are not eligible. You must be studying an approved course and must have sufficient funds to cover your tuition fees and maintenance (see the Education section of the Daily Life chapter for a general idea of the cost of New Zealand courses). Dependents of a work visa holder may be eligible for a student visa without already having a place arranged at a New Zealand school. They may also be exempt from overseas tuition fees.

Working in New Zealand

If you wish to work in New Zealand for a short period and you are not a citizen or resident you will need to apply for a temporary work visa. You can apply for one before you travel if you already have a definite employment offer, or, if you find a job while visiting New Zealand, you can apply for a visa there. Your prospective employer will need to provide details of your job title, responsibilities, qualifications required, conditions and duration of employment and pay, as well as proof that they have unsuccessfully tried to recruit a New Zealander to fill the position. You can apply for a work visa for up to three years if you have a job offer before you arrive in New Zealand. However, if you apply for a work visa in New Zealand, the maximum period you will be granted is nine months. The employer will be required to provide the local Immigration Service with the information outlined above. For further information you should contact the NZIS.

Working holiday visa

New Zealand's working holiday visa scheme allows young people from 22 partner countries to spend time in New Zealand and undertake short-term casual work in the areas of agriculture, horticulture and viticulture (grape-growing). People between the ages of 18 and 30 inclusive can apply for the visa, which will enable them to take casual work without requiring a separate work visa while on holiday in New Zealand. You will not be permitted to apply for this visa if you have any dependent children. The New Zealand government must be satisfied that your main purpose in applying for a New Zealand working holiday visa is to holiday rather than to work in any 'career' sort of job; any work you undertake while on this visa is intended solely to supplement your travel funds. All applications for this visa must be made from outside New Zealand, and you are only ever permitted to have one New Zealand working holiday visa. You must meet basic requirements as well as age, including health and character prerequisites, and you will need to provide evidence of sufficient funds to support yourself during your stay (NZ$4,200 plus airfare) as well as providing evidence of onward travel. Once your visa is issued you will have one year to enter New Zealand; your visa is activated upon entry, and it is possible to leave and re-enter New Zealand multiple times until your visa expires.

Working holiday visas permit you to stay for either 12 months or up to 23 months depending on the arrangements between your country of citizenship and New Zealand. (If you hold a valid British passport you are entitled to stay in New Zealand for up to 23 months on this visa, while Irish passport holders are permitted to work and travel around New Zealand for 12 months.) However, you may work for only a total of 12 months, regardless of which length of working holiday visa you are granted. The visa you receive initially will automatically be for 12 months; if you want to extend this you will be required to undergo medical checks at an additional charge. You may also study or train in New Zealand for up to three months while your visa is valid. Working holidaymakers who are able to show that they have worked in the horticulture or viticulture industries for at least three months may be eligible to apply for an extra three-month stay in New Zealand (this is called the Working Holidaymaker Extension permit). Schemes are available for working holidaymakers from the following countries: Argentina, Belgium, Canada, Chile, Czechoslovakia, Denmark, Estonia, Finland, France, Germany, Hong Kong, Ireland, Italy, Japan, Korea, Malaysia, Malta, The Netherlands, Norway, Singapore, Sweden, Taiwan, Thailand, the UK, the USA and Uruguay.

The Working Holiday Visa Application can be downloaded from the INZ website www.immigration.govt.nz. You must fill this out and then post it to one of the appropriate addresses below along with the correct fee and your passport. You must also supply a stamped self-addressed envelope for the return of your passport. It is also possible to apply online. Application packs can also be obtained by telephoning 0991 100100 (costs £1 per minute) in the UK – this is an automated service. Applications can also be made in person, or through a variety of third party organisations (see websites below).

Useful websites

www.bunac.com
www.ccusa.com
www.councilexchanges.org.uk

Useful resources

CIEE (Council) USA: 7 Custom House Street, 3rd Floor, Portland, ME 04101; tollfree: 1800 40 STUDY or 1 207 53 7600; www.ciee.org. Helps students from the USA study abroad.

New Zealand Information, Immigration and Visa Enquiries in the USA and UK
Department of Internal Affairs Office UK: 2nd Floor, New Zealand House, 80 Haymarket, London, SW1Y 4TQ; 020 7930 8422; passports@dia.govt.nz; www.dia.govt.nz.

New Zealand Ministry of Foreign Affairs and Trade: www.mfat.govt.nz. See the website for a list of New Zealand consulates and embassies around the world.

New Zealand Embassy USA: 37 Observatory Circle NW, Washington DC 20008; 202 328 4800; nz@nzemb.org; www.nzembassy.com.

The New Zealand High Commission UK: New Zealand House, 80 Haymarket, London, SW1Y 4TQ; 020 7930 8422; info@immigration.govt.nz (visas, work permits or residency applications) or: aboutnz@newzealandhc.org.uk; www.nzembassy.com.

The New Zealand Immigration Service UK: 3rd Floor New Zealand House, 80 Haymarket, London, SW1Y 4TQ; 09069 100 100 (calls charged at £1.00 per minute); info@immigration.govt.nz; www.immigration.govt.nz.

Information for British citizens in New Zealand

British High Commission: 44 Hill Street, Thorndon, PO Box 1812, Wellington; (04) 924 2888; PPA.Mailbox@fco.gov.uk, visamail.wellington@fco.gov.uk, passportmail.wellington@fco.gov.uk; www.britain.org.nz.

Information for American citizens in New Zealand

Consulate General of the United States of America: 3rd Floor, Citibank Building, 23 Customs Street (cnr Commerce Street), Private Bag 92022, Auckland; (09) 303 2724.
Embassy of the United States of America: PO Box 1190, Wellington; 29 Fitzherbert Terrace, Thorndon, Wellington; (04) 462 6000.

◼ THE LANGUAGES

The two official languages of New Zealand are Maori and English. English is understood everywhere, and is the day-to-day language of most general communications and transactions. Many government and other official documents and communications are offered in both languages, but an English version will almost always be available. Both Maori and English are used all around the country in different types of broadcasting, and there is a Maori language television station. Each language has to some extent influenced the other in the way it is used and in terms of vocabulary. A number of words have crossed over in both directions; the Maori word for 'car' is *motuka*, and the Maori word *tapu* has its own place in New Zealand English. *Tapu* means 'sacred' or 'prohibited'. If something is *tapu* an ordinary person must respect Maori protocol and not touch it or go there – for example, you should not swim in a lake which is *tapu*. There are many other such examples. Many places in New Zealand have both an English and a Maori name – most people will know both, and will either use one or the other without thinking to supply you with the name in the other language as well. This can be confusing to start with, until you learn these things for yourself, so if you are in any doubt remember there is no harm in asking.

The NZ language

New Zealanders speak their own distinctive version of English. Newcomers may be forgiven for thinking that New Zealanders use only two vowel sounds, although of course Kiwis do not have trouble understanding each other. 'New Zealand' as pronounced by Kiwis may sound like 'Nu Zilind'. As well as the subtle distinctions between vowel sounds, further problems for the newcomer may arise from the rapid pace at which New Zealanders speak. Probably more of an obstacle to understanding New Zealanders than the accent is the use of uniquely Kiwi expressions. A 'dairy' is a corner store (open till late and selling most of the essentials), a 'crib' in the South Island or 'bach' in the North is a holiday home (generally on the coast or beside a lake). To 'bring a plate' to a party means you bring a plate of food along to share with others. BYO stands for 'Bring Your Own' alcohol – either to a party or to a restaurant. BYO restaurants have a licence to serve alcohol, but not to sell it. They are usually cheaper than 'licensed' restaurants, but they will generally charge a corkage fee per bottle (of about NZ$5), or sometimes per person. To 'charge an arm and a leg' is to demand a high price for something. Some of the slang is similar to Australian, for example 'Pommy' for an English person, 'bush' for forest, 'shout' for buying a round in a pub or providing a special morning or afternoon tea for workmates (usually on birthdays or when someone is leaving).

FACT

The Maori language has been part of the New Zealand culture since the first people came to these islands, but it has only been recognised as an official New Zealand language since the Maori Language Act of 1987.

For more New Zealand slang see the table on p.362. Additionally, a number of Maori expressions have become part of everyday New Zealand usage, for example *Pakeha* for a person of European descent. *The New Zealand Oxford Dictionary* (Oxford University Press) might prove useful to save you any confusion. This dictionary has been hailed as a celebration of the New Zealand language, and a revised and updated edition that includes over 10,000 words of New Zealand origin was launched in 2004. So if you want to find out what gumboots, mates' rates, wop-wops, biddy-bids, cheerios, housie, jandals, jafas, Swanndris, tinnies and dungers are, the dictionary could be a good place to start. Another useful dictionary is the latest edition of the *Collins English Dictionary*, which includes a relatively high number of interesting and fairly obscure New Zealand words.

The development of learning and usage of the Maori language and English-Maori bilingualism is the primary objective of *Te Taura Whiri i Te Reo Maori* – the Maori Language Commission. Maori is still not widely used in everyday situations. Official signs are bilingual, as are many government documents. The number of Maori language speakers is growing and there is an active campaign to preserve this language (*Te Reo* in Maori). At least some knowledge of the language is a prerequisite for many jobs, especially those within public service.

Pronunciation of Maori words is not difficult to learn even if at first glance some of the place names seem impossibly long and complex. It is a good skill to master though, as correct pronunciation of Maori is a sign of courtesy and also indicates that, as a newcomer, you are prepared to integrate into the local community. The greeting *kia ora* which extends good health to the other person, may be repeated back with the same words. *Haere mai* means 'welcome' and *Haere ra'* means 'goodbye'. Generally Maori words are spelt phonetically. The language had no written form before European settlement.

Maori vowel sounds

There are five Maori vowel sounds, each of which may be short or long:

short a:	like u in 'but'	long a:	like a in 'father'
short e:	like e in 'pet'	long e:	like ai in 'fairy'
short i:	like i in 'pit'	long i:	like ee in 'meet'
short o:	like or in 'port'	long o:	like ore in 'pore'
short u:	like u in 'put'	long u:	like oo in 'moon'

Diphthongs (double vowel sounds) retain the sound of the second vowel clearly. Consonants are as in English with the following exceptions:
wh is pronounced f; hence 'Whangarei' is pronounced 'Fong-a-ray'
ng is like ng in the middle of 'singer, ie the g is never hard
r is slightly rolled

◼ BANKS AND FINANCE

You can use ATMs (automatic teller machines or cash machines) at any time to transfer money between accounts, and order statements or chequebooks. Your money card, known as an ATM card, also functions as a direct debit card for EFT-POS

TIP

◼ Word stress is rather complicated and you would do better to learn by listening to a Maori speaker. It is worth noting that many *Pakeha* (Europeans) pronounce Maori words, particularly common place names, embarrassingly badly. There is however a general trend towards more accurate pronunciation and, in recent years, the standard has risen dramatically. Incorrect pronunciation is increasingly unacceptable, as it shows a lack of respect. This change has been perhaps most noticeable among radio and TV announcers, and, in general, their pronunciation is a reasonable guide.

transactions, using your PIN. EFT-POS stands for Electronic Funds Transfer at the point of sale, and is the same system as has recently been introduced to the UK as the new 'chip and PIN' system. The amount you are charged is immediately removed from your account, meaning that if there are not sufficient funds available your transaction will be declined. Most retailers offer the EFT-POS service; this has been commonplace in New Zealand for at least 15 years already. Cheques are accepted by a few retailers and companies, particularly for the payment of bills on invoice, but advances in electronic banking are fast rendering them obsolete.

New Zealand banks do not issue cheque guarantee cards. The onus is on the receiver of the cheque to make sure it is not fraudulent. Retailers usually require ID for cheques in the form of a credit or EFT-POS card, and often take your name and address as well. Many retailers now refuse to accept cheques, particularly if you do not have a local address. Credit cards are popular in New Zealand, Mastercard and Visa being the most widely used. Most bills are paid through standing orders (called automatic payment or direct credit) and your wages will probably likewise be paid into your account directly. Most banks now offer telephone banking as a standard service to their clients, for a small charge per call. Telephone banking allows you to check balances, transfer funds, make bill payments, and hear a list of recent transactions, among other options. Online banking is another popular option, as it is in most countries, and generally offers the range of services you would expect, from balance enquiries to setting up automatic payments to applying for loans or opening extra accounts. Some banks offer this service for free as part of your customer plan, while others charge a small fee. If this is an important feature for you, check the differences in fees before you choose your bank.

Banking costs

Account holders pay bank fees for their accounts. There will be a monthly account fee of anywhere between NZ$3 and NZ$15, but exemptions may apply

for students and the elderly. This fee may be waived if you maintain a certain balance in your account. There is also a fee for individual transactions on top of the monthly fee, but some banks exempt the first few entries each month. Electronic and telephone transactions usually cost between 25 and 50c, while manual transactions (carried out at the bank) may cost around 50c to NZ$1. If you have an overdraft, the monthly overdraft management fee is likely to be around 12%, with a minimum charge of NZ$2. The government charges a resident withholding tax, currently 19.5% of your interest. KiwiBank currently offers the most affordable fees.

Bank accounts

The main New Zealand banks are the HSBC (branches only in Auckland), Bank of New Zealand (BNZ), Kiwibank (the only New Zealand-owned bank), the National Bank of New Zealand, Westpac, (which has an online facility for opening an account), TSB and ASB (formerly the Auckland Savings Bank, which now operates nationwide). Branches of foreign banks also operate and some have wide experience of meeting the financial needs of immigrants. RaboPlus Bank is an investment bank offering savings accounts in excess of 7% with a minimum balance of NZ$1.

> I set up my bank accounts once I arrived in New Zealand, by meeting with a bank/accounts manager face to face and explaining my situation. I went armed with my passport, work contract, and letter of reference from my employer, and I have found that most banks were more than keen to take control of my money for me!.
>
> **Dermot Foley**

If you wish to open a bank account in New Zealand, it is recommended that you contact the head office of the bank involved to discuss any requirements before you leave for New Zealand. Your current bank should be able to help you open a New Zealand account. There is a generally a fee for this service and a minimum deposit requirement. Some New Zealand banks now offer a new residents' service, which enables you to open your New Zealand bank account before you leave home. Details about the service offered by ASB to UK citizens may be viewed on their website (www.migrantbanking.co.uk). The National Bank of New Zealand also offers a similar service to help you set up a New Zealand account, and has a specialist New Residents Services team. See the 'Moving to New Zealand' section of the National Bank of New Zealand website (www.nationalbank.co.nz) for more information. You are able to deposit up to NZ$25,000 by International Money Transfer before you arrive. For amounts larger than this, you will need to fill in an application form. The National Bank also offers freephone numbers for 22 different countries. One advantage of opening an account before you arrive in New Zealand is that it solves the problem of transferring money; you simply arrange for a telexed transfer to your new account. The

> Opening bank accounts proved relatively easy, as I opened accounts through my bank in the UK prior to arriving in New Zealand. Credit cards proved a little more difficult as I am on a two-year working visa rather than a permanent resident, but everything was arranged with a face-to-face meeting at the bank, and then I received the two cards I needed, activated and ready to go, within a week.
>
> **Elizabeth Henderson**

alternatives to telexing money directly to a New Zealand bank account are outlined in the section on International Money Transfers below. Opening an account once you arrive in New Zealand does not take long, but there are a few hitches for the new arrival. Some banks require proof of a regular income, such as a signed work contract, before allowing you to open a cheque account, even though you may have deposited money with them. You should be issued immediately with an ATM card, which will allow you to withdraw money from a bank or an ATM.

Useful resources

ANZ: 0800 103 123, or from overseas: +64 4 472 7123; www.anz.com/nz.

ASB: (09) 306 3000 or 0800 803 804; www.asb.co.nz. If you wish to set up an account from the UK, contact Commonwealth Bank, 85 Queen Victoria Street, London EC4V 4HA; 020 7710 3990; www.migrantbanking.co.uk.

BNZ: State Insurance Tower, 1 Willis St, PO Box 1299, Manners Street, Wellington; 0800 275 269 or from overseas: +64 4 931 8209; www.bnz.co.nz.

Kiwibank: 0800 11 3355 in New Zealand; +64 4 473 1133 from overseas. www. kiwibank.co.nz. 100% New Zealand owned and operated, offering low fees. Kiwibank also has no account management or monthly base fees, no fees for deposits under NZ$15,000 per month, no fees for transfers between your Kiwibank accounts, and no transaction fees for personal account customers who are full-time students, under 18 years old, non-profit organisations, Kiwibank Home Loan customers or pensioners who have their New Zealand Super paid into their Kiwibank account. There are also no fees to open an account or to apply for a home loan.

National Bank: 0800 181 818 or from overseas: +64 4 382 9608; www.nationalbank. co.nz. To set up an account before you move to New Zealand, see the website for further information.

Westpac Trust: 0800 400 600 or from overseas: +64 9 912 8000; customer_ support@westpac.co.nz; www.westpactrust.co.nz.

KiwiSaver

KiwiSaver is a voluntary, work-based savings initiative to help New Zealanders with their long-term saving for retirement. You should receive information about KiwiSaver from your employer, and your contributions come directly out of your pay. It is designed to be hassle-free, to help you maintain a regular savings pattern. New Zealand Superannuation may not provide enough income for more than a very basic standard of retirement, and KiwiSaver is designed to complement your New Zealand Superannuation (state pension) payments. It doesn't affect your New Zealand Super eligibility or reduce the amount you are entitled to. There is a range of benefits, including a NZ$1,000 tax-free kick-start, a member tax credit of up to NZ$1,042.86 per year, and subsidised scheme fees. Some members are eligible for help with the deposit for their first home. Since 1 April 2008 members over the age of 18 may also benefit from a compulsory contribution from their employer as well. Employers start by contributing an extra 1% of your gross salary, and raise that by 1% each year until a maximum of 4% is reached by 2011. This does not apply if you already receive an employer contribution into another superannuation scheme. The government provides employers with up to NZ$20 a week to help meet the cost of their contributions, so during the first year it costs your employer nothing assuming you earn under NZ$104,000 annually. If you and your employer agree, up until

March 2010 your contribution can be made up of 2% of your salary and 2% matched by your employer. From April 2010 you will both need to contribute 3%, and then 4% each from April 2011 onwards. To qualify for KiwiSaver, you must demonstrate that you are living or normally living in New Zealand. You must also be a New Zealand citizen or entitled to stay in New Zealand indefinitely, and under the age of eligibility for New Zealand Superannuation (which is currently set at 65).

See: www.kiwisaver.govt.nz to download KiwiSaver forms and guides, and for further information. You can also write to KiwiSaver at Inland Revenue, PO Box 1454, Hamilton 3240, or telephone INFOexpress on 0800 257 773 from within New Zealand.

Banking ombudsman

If you have a complaint about a bank in New Zealand your first step should be to contact the bank involved. If you can't resolve the problem through the bank's processes, you can contact the Banking Ombudsman. The Banking Ombudsman's Office can provide you with advice about how to make a complaint, although it will not hear the complaint until you have first approached the bank involved.

The address is: Banking Ombudsman, PO Box 10573, The Terrace, Wellington; (04) 471 0006 or freephone: 0800 805 950; email help@bankombudsman.org.nz; www.bankombudsman.org.nz.

International money transfers

There are no foreign exchange controls on shifting money out of New Zealand. Getting money to New Zealand is most quickly achieved through a money wire or a telegraphic transfer. You can either do this through a specialist money-wiring company such as American Express or Western Union, through the banks, or through currency brokers. The money-wiring companies cost more but the process is much faster, less than 15 minutes. Through the banks it usually takes a couple of days but the cost is about half the amount charged by wiring companies.

A specialist currency broker can help you to obtain the best rate of exchange. One such broker is HIFXplc.

 HIFXplc: Morgan House, Madeira Walk, Windsor SL4 1EP; 01753 859159; info@hifx.co.uk; www.hifx.co.uk; 250 Montgomery Street, Suite 910, San Francisco, CA 94104; 415 678 2770; info@hifx.com; www.hifx.com; and and PO Box 7646, Wellesley Street, Auckland, 09 306 3705 or freephone from within New Zealand 0800 394 439; info@hifx.co.nz; www.hifx.co.nz

Money

New Zealand has a decimal money system using dollars as the monetary unit, each dollar consisting of 100 cents. The abbreviation for the dollar is NZ$ and c for cents which stand after the numbers. At the time of going to press the exchange rate was €1–NZ$1.90, £1–NZ$2.58 and US$1–NZ$1.29. For the latest exchange rate, perform a conversion on www.xe.com.

■ THE COST OF LIVING

Living costs in New Zealand vary, as they do in every country, depending on where you live and how you spend your money. Not surprisingly, spending on housing contributes the most to total household expenditure, averaging 24 cents in every dollar spent. For information about the price of food shopping, see the Daily Life chapter (p.179).

Household income and expenditure

The average of wages and salaries is NZ$50,235. The latest figures show the average weekly income to be NZ$667, which is a rise of 9.4% from 2006. The average for men was NZ$832 and for women NZ$510. Thirty-two per cent of homes have a mortgage, and spend an average of NZ$271 a week on mortgage payments. Twenty-nine per cent of households rent, and the average weekly amount spent on rent is NZ$220. Average weekly net expenditure per household is NZ$956, with the three largest components of this total being housing and household utilities (23%), food (16%) and transport (14%). Wellington households spend the most in the country on recreation and culture, parting with NZ$120 a week. One-fifth of all households have more than one type of computer (desktop, laptop or hand-held).

■ GETTING THERE

Flights

Most travel agents should be up to date with any discounted or cheaper fares that may be available, although the drawback of these deals is usually that the tickets have restrictions and can be very expensive to change once booked. Some antipodean travel agencies offer other services that may be useful, for example, organising temporary accommodation, onward travel or rental vehicles for when you first arrive. However, internet travel websites increasingly offer the most economical fares and are extremely simple to use. Some will also offer you the option of including stopovers and 'multi-leg' trips, accommodation or car hire in your booking. Even if you do decide to use a 'real' travel agent, it is definitely worth researching fares and options online so that you have a more comprehensive understanding of your options and the prices you are likely to pay.

The cheapest flights from Europe are via London, so if you are travelling from another European destination it may be worth checking if it makes sense to go via Heathrow or Gatwick. From London the trip is about 18,355km, and you can either fly east or west to get to New Zealand, with a refuelling stop in Asia or the USA. From Los Angeles the flight covers 10,450km, from New York you will travel 14,180km and the journey from Vancouver is 11,310km. Tokyo is 8,795km from New Zealand, Hong Kong 9,125km and Singapore is 8,410km. From the West Coast of the United States,

Christchruch Airport on a hot day

a direct flight will take you approximately 12 hours. From other places on the Pacific Rim (such as Tokyo, Hong Kong or Singapore) flights last around 10 hours.

Airlines

Pick your airline carefully, and with an eye on your priorities – if you are looking for the cheapest option above everything else, then airlines such as Korean Air are probably your best bet as long as you are happy to fly through Seoul and don't mind slightly less seating room, less personal space and not having a vegetarian meal option. Sadly, Air New Zealand no longer provides the quality of service it once did, despite the fact that you might think it your first choice because of your destination. Problems and hiccups with your booking are something you really don't want to experience, particularly if they are only brought to your attention at the check-in desk with just two hours to go until your flight as happened to several people we have heard of recently. These days even the most loyal of Kiwis will struggle to find any reason why you should use Air New Zealand over and above all the good quality airlines who offer excellent and stress-free services to the country. If it is good service and a comfortable flight that you are after, the general consensus among frequent travellers is that Emirates, Cathay Pacific and Singapore Airlines provide the best choices. Of course, the earlier you are able to book the greater will be the range of choices regarding prices and travel options available to you.

Baggage

Some airlines are much more generous with their baggage allowances than others. Allowances range from just 15kg up to 60kg, depending on which airline you fly with, and whether you travel economy or business class. You shouldn't have more

> " Compared to the UK and Ireland, I feel that New Zealand offers a better quality of life in terms of what you can buy for your cash (real income), the availability of sports facilities and of course the weather.
>
> **Dermot Foley** "

than two pieces of baggage per passenger (infants will be permitted just one piece). In addition, each piece should not exceed the total dimensions of 158cm (62in.) for length+width+height. Some airlines may be forgiving if your luggage is just a few kilograms overweight, but the tendency is to be quite strict and airlines are liable to charge you a penalty fee. Charges can vary considerably. Some airlines have a set rate per extra kilo. Others base their charges on a percentage of the full one-way economy fare. These rates are typically 1%–1.5% of the fare per extra kilo. On a long-haul flight, this can soon add up to a fairly significant sum. In practice this rarely happens, but you should be prepared for the possibility as these are the rules and airlines are well within their rights to enforce them. Check the small print on your ticket.

If you overstep the baggage limit, there is no guarantee that any additional pieces of luggage will go on the flight with you. If you know in advance that your bags are going to be over the limit, you may be able to send them unaccompanied a week or so before you fly. This will cost around half the price of paying for additional weight to travel with you, and you will be able to collect the extra pieces when you arrive. Most airlines will have a 20kg limit per passenger, but will in all likelihood let you get away with up to 26kg. It seems you are more likely to sneak extra weight onto your flight if you check in with plenty of time to spare. All airlines seem to have different policies (and check-in staff have different levels of 'jobsworthiness') so you should make sure you have accurate information well in advance of your flight. Airlines should display information about their baggage weight limits on their websites, or you will be able to find out from your travel agent or the airline's sales outlet. Once you have your ticket, your hold allowance will be printed on the ticket itself and ticket wallets will contain further additional information about baggage allowances. If you have an e-ticket, allowances are usually specified on the confirmation notice. Bear in mind, if you are using connecting flights, that the baggage allowance will possibly be different for each sector of your flight depending on the airline or even the aircraft itself. Always check before you pack.

Following recent tightening-up of airline rules, passengers departing from UK airports are now permitted only one item of carry-on luggage. The maximum dimensions allowed are 56cm (22in.) x 45cm (17.5in.) x 25cm (9.85in.) including all wheels, handle and side pockets, and it should not weigh more than 7kg. All items of luggage which do not fit in the permitted cabin baggage size must be checked in to be placed in the aircraft hold. Musical instruments which do not fit in the permitted cabin baggage size are allowed as a second item of cabin baggage; they will of course need to be screened and you should check with your airline if special arrangements (such as purchasing an extra seat) for very large instruments will be required. Your purse or briefcase may now count as this one permissible piece – if you need to carry on an overnight-style bag try to leave room for your purse or shoulder bag to squeeze inside it as well. Laptops and other large electrical items (such as large hairdryers, etc.) will need to be removed from cabin baggage and screened separately. A laptop bag will count as your one item that is allowed into the cabin. Pushchairs, walking aids and wheelchairs will be allowed into the cabin, but they will be screened.

As with all air travel, remember not to carry any dangerous, sharp or pointy items in your cabin luggage; these include: scissors, knives, tweezers, toy tools or replica guns (metal or plastic), knitting needles, corkscrews, billiard, snooker or pool cues, razor blades, household cutlery, hypodermic needles (unless for medical reasons), catapults, sporting bats, walking/hiking poles and darts. Other dangerous items which will not be allowed in either cabin or hold luggage include: flammable liquids and solids, organic peroxides, infectious substances, instruments containing magnets, magnetrons, non-safety matches, fire lighters, lighter fuel, poisons, arsenic, cyanide, weedkiller, creosote, quicklime, oiled paper, oxidisers, gas cylinders, wet car cell batteries, instruments containing mercury, fireworks, paints, thinners, acids, corrosive, alkalis, caustic soda and of course radioactive materials. You will not be compensated for any items confiscated at security, and the items will not be returned to you. Do not carry any liquids, lotions, liquid cosmetics, gels, foams, foodstuffs, pastes or creams in containers of more than 100ml capacity in your cabin luggage. These containers must be brought to the airport contained in one single, transparent, re-sealable plastic bag, which itself must not exceed 1 litre in capacity (approximately 20cm x 20cm). The contents of the plastic bag must fit comfortably and the bag must be sealed. In practice, these bags are often on offer at the airport, but it is best to arrive with everything in order. Liquids that cannot be placed inside this re-sealable plastic bag must be packed into your hold luggage to be checked in. 'Liquids' include:

We travelled to New Zealand with just two suitcases each and sent our work things separately by air freight.

Elizabeth Henderson

- all drinks, including water, soup, syrups, soft drinks;
- creams, lotions, oils, perfumes, foundation, mascara, etc.;
- sprays and pressurised containers including shaving foams and spray deodorants;
- pastes, including toothpastes;
- gels, including hair and shower gel;
- any other solutions of items of similar consistency.

Baby foods and essential medicines may be permitted in larger quantities than the 100ml limit, but they will be subject to authentication.

You may carry on board liquid items of any size that are purchased after the security check in the Departure Lounge. Most duty-free purchases will be given to you in a special sealed bag; you must not open this bag until you reach your final destination, and you should retain your proof of purchase throughout your journey as you may be required to present it for inspection at transfer points. Be very careful if you will transit through Australia; currently they have the strictest liquid rules of all. At the time of writing, all the above rules relating to liquids, etc. apply but each individual item is permitted only in a container of no more than 50ml capacity. This includes duty-free purchases, even those still sealed in their airport security plastic bag with proof of purchase. All liquids in containers over 50ml will be confiscated.

Sports equipment

Many airlines offer extra weight allowances for 'sports equipment' and sometimes this can be as much as another 20kg, but you should be sure to check with your airline well in advance to avoid any nasty surprises. Sports equipment will be classed as 'oversized baggage' and most airlines have an extra fee per piece. The fee will vary depending on what you are taking with you and your airline, but will probably be chargeable per item. You should also be prepared for your sports equipment to travel on a different flight from your own as this is subject to the availability of space on the aircraft; passenger luggage within the allocated weight limits takes priority and flights are often quite full. Should you arrive at the airport and discover that you are over the limit, the best option is unaccompanied baggage. Your luggage will go on the next available flight, and usually reaches your destination a couple of days after you do. You will have to clear it through Customs at the other end and there may be storage charges as well.

Jetlag and other effects of long flights

There are ways to minimise the effects of jetlag while on the flight. Drink plenty of cool water, avoid alcohol, eat fresh fruit if it is available and stretch your legs, arms and shoulders every so often. Even if you have chosen not to break your flight with a stopover, any flight to New Zealand will include a transfer of at least about two hours for a refuelling stop. You will not be permitted to remain on the plane during this stop. It is important to walk around as much as possible during this time, tempting as it might be to just sit still and wait for your boarding call. Take the stairs instead of escalators, and walk rather than standing on moving walkways wherever possible. This may sound like boring advice, but the jetlag after a 26-hour flight across 12 time zones can be considerable and may last several days. Avoiding the free airline alcohol is not such a big price to pay for being awake enough to enjoy your first few days in your new country. Another idea is to arrive in plenty of time for your flight, or even pre-allocate your seats through the airline or your travel agent so you can ask for bulkhead or exit row seats, which have extra legroom. Aisle seats are better than window seats as you can get up as much as you want without disturbing others in your row. Many airlines now recommend that you have a check-up with your doctor before you fly, to find out about the risks of deep vein thrombosis (DVT) and for information about suitable precautions such as elasticated flight socks and exercises you can do in your seat.

If you have never experienced jetlag before, it can be quite a strange and disorientating sensation, and the effects may differ from person to person. Typically, you will not feel tired when you initially arrive, as the activity of leaving the plane and the airport and the excitement of being in a new place all help to counteract the fact that you may not have slept for the previous 30 hours (worst case scenario!). It is usually not until several more hours have passed that you begin to suffer the exhaustion and 'heavy leg' feeling that some people report, or the light-headedness and sense of the ground rolling beneath your feet, as though you are on a ship at sea. However jetlag manifests itself, it is usually best to drink a lot of water, eat light, healthy meals at the appropriate times and try to make it through as much of the day as you can until it is closer to the time you would normally go to bed – local time that is! Tempting though it might be, it is best to keep yourself busy with little tasks such as unpacking, having a shower, etc., rather than collapsing in front of the television – staying awake will be much more difficult lying on a comfortable sofa. The sooner your body clock adjusts to functioning at the right time in a new place the better; it can take from several days to as long as a week before you find that you are able to sleep properly through the night.

Useful resources

ABTA (Association of British Travel Agents): 68–71 Newman Street, London W1T 3AH; 020 7637 2444; abta@abta.co.uk, www.abta.com.

ASTA (American Society of Travel Agents): 1101 King Street, Suite 200, Alexandria, VA 22314; 703 739 2782; askasta@astahq.com; www.asta.org.

Austravel (UK): London West End: 61 Conduit Street, London W1S 2GB; 0870 166 2020 (general enquiries) or 0870 166 2021 (flights); 0870 166 2120; westend@ austravel.com; www.austravel.com. London City: 17 Blomfield Street, London EC2M 7AJ; 0870 166 2130; city@austravel.com. Birmingham: 12 The Minories, Temple Court, Birmingham B4 6AG; 0870 166, 2160; birmingham@austravel. com. Bournemouth: 107 Old Christchurch Road, Bournemouth BH1 1EP; 0870 166 2150; bournemouth@austravel.com. Bristol: 125 High Street, Staple Hill, Bristol BS16 5HQ; 0870 166 2110; bristol@austravel.com. Edinburgh: 33 George Street, Edinburgh EH2 2HN; 0870 166 2190; edinburgh@austravel.com. Leeds: 16–18 County Arcade, Victoria Quarter, Leeds LS1 6BN; 0870 166 2180; leeds@austravel. com. Manchester: 3 Barton Arcade, Deansgate, Manchester M3 2BB; 0870 166 2170; manchester@austravel.com.

Cathay Pacific: www.cathaypacific.com

Downunder Direct (USA): 6 W Lancaster Ave, Ardmore, PA 19003; 800 642 6224 (office hours are EST 9am–5pm Monday to Friday and 10am–5pm Saturday) or 800 22 79246 or 610 896 9595; info@downunderdirect.com; www.downunderdirect.com.

Essential Travel: Offers a variety of travel information including flight comparisons and online travel quotes. www.essentialtravel.co.uk.

Experience New Zealand: www.experiencenz.com

Flight Centre: Various local branches, with over 1,200 stores worldwide. From the UK 0870 499 0040; www.flightcentre.co.uk to find your nearest branch.

Singapore Airlines: www.singaporeair.com.

Thai Airways International: A good airline with great food and service, this time travelling through Bangkok with the option of a stopover; www.thaiair.com.

Trailfinders (UK): 194 Kensington High Street, Kensington, London W8 7RG; 020 7938 3939; www.trailfinder.com. There are other Trailfinder offices in Belfast, Birmingham, Bristol, Cambridge, Dublin, Glasgow, Leeds, Nottingham, London (Piccadilly and Covent Garden), Oxford, Manchester and Newcastle – check the website for details. www.trailfinders.com.

United Arab Emirates: www.emirates.com

World Connections Travel (USA): 1818 Independence Square, Suite D, Atlanta, GA 30338; 770-393 8892 or 800 777 8892; wctravel@mindspring.com.

Useful websites

Cheapflights: www.cheapflights.com or www.cheapflights.co.uk. Offers a flight comparison facility, with which you can compare deals from hundreds of different companies.

Ebookers: www.ebookers.com. Has a useful and fairly comprehensive Australasia section.

Expedia: www.expedia.com or www.expedia.co.uk.

Jasons Travel Channel: www.jasons.co.nz/new-zealand-motels.htm. In addition to a huge range of motel and motor-lodge listings, you will also find information about other accommodation, transport, rental vehicles, and free downloadable maps and brochures on useful topics ranging from trams and coaches to travel agents and campgrounds.

New Zealand Information Network: www.newzealandnz.co.nz. For travel information inside New Zealand. It might be worth taking a look at before you leave, to get an idea of what you might need to arrange in terms of travel and accommodation directly from the airport. This website gives unbiased information about travel, accommodation and transportation, includes links to the immigration service and offers an information request service. There is also an automotive section for car hire, and a business economy section for information about real estate or business products and services. It incorporates an extensive links directory, options for hotel and rental car booking, and a range of constantly changing and up-to-the-minute special offers.

Opodo: www.opodo.com, www.opodo.co.uk, www.opodo.de, or www.opodo.fr. Opodo is owned by a group comprised of Aer Lingus, Air France, Alitalia, Austrian Airlines, British Airways, Finnair, Iberia, KLM, Lufthansa and Amadeus, so worth thinking about if you are already signed up for air miles with any of these airlines.

Travelselect: www.travelselect.com. Part of the lastminute.com group, there are often very reasonable fares to be had if you plan carefully and book and pay far enough (ie several months) in advance.

Insurance

Working travellers and those on speculative job searches in New Zealand are advised to take out comprehensive travel insurance. You should be able to purchase travel insurance from the same source as your airline tickets; failing that, there are a number of other possibilities, including numerous online companies, general insurance providers, probably your own bank, the Post Office, and so on – even some supermarkets now sell travel insurance.

Useful resources

Columbus Direct Travel Insurance (UK): www.columbusdirect.com.
DirectLine: www.directline.com.
DownunderDirect (USA): 6 W Lancaster Ave, Ardmore, PA 19003; 800 227 9246, 800 642 6224, or 610 896 9595, www.downunderdirect.com.
Downunder Insurance (UK): This website offers links to a number of insurance websites for quotes, some with the option to buy online. email info@duinsure.com; www.duinsure.co.uk.
SquareMouth: Compare travel insurance online www.squaremouth.com.
TFG Global Travel Insurance (USA and Canada): 216-2438 Marine Drive, West Vancouver, BC, V7V 1L2, Canada; 604 351 5278; or USA toll-free: 800 232 9415; info@tfgglobal.com; www.globaltravelinsurance.com.
Trailfinders (UK): 194 Kensington High Street, Kensington, London W8 7RG; 020 7938 3939; www.trailfinder.com. There are Trailfinder offices in Belfast, Birmingham, Bristol, Cambridge, Dublin, Glasgow, Leeds, Nottingham, London (Piccadilly and Covent Garden), Oxford, Manchester and Newcastle – check the website for details. www.trailfinders.com.

◼ PLANNING AN INTERNATIONAL MOVE

Removals

Packing up your possessions and getting them to the other side of the world is an expensive business. There are basically two ways of shipping your household goods to New Zealand, depending on whether the removal consists of a small or large amount. Smaller removals are usually grouped with other people's small removal lots destined for the same port, so they can be shipped in shared containers. Be aware of this when choosing a mover – if you pick a company that does not regularly handle large numbers of this type of removal, your belongings could be delayed for quite some time while they wait for other consignments to fill up the container. Larger removals are usually shipped as whole container loads, which means that they are packed up and sent off immediately on the first vessel sailing to New Zealand. Transit time can take as long as 12 weeks if you are using a shared container. For a full-container removal it will probably take around 6–8 weeks.

When deciding what to bring, remember that the New Zealand electricity supply will probably be different to what you are used to. New Zealand supplies alternating current at 240 volts, 50 Hertz. Having your existing appliances adapted to suit New Zealand supply may work out more costly than replacing them and not worth the trouble. Your removal company should be able to advise you on these points. On the other hand, good quality household furniture, fine china and glass will generally be worth taking with you.

Most people who are planning to move overseas for the first time make the mistake of assuming that an international move is the same as a domestic one. You should use a specialist international mover. Representatives who will visit you to assess your removal requirements can offer advice regarding items you may be undecided about shifting. If you know of anyone who has shifted their household, ask them about their shipping company or, if you are dealing with an immigration consultancy, find out which companies other emigrants have used successfully. You should check whether they are members of an international removals trade association and if the association offers a payment guarantee scheme if the removals company goes bust while your goods are still in transit. Two well-known associations are the Association of International Removers and the British Association of Removers.

When it comes to comparing quotes from different companies, be sure to get quotes in writing based on the same list of goods. Freighting cost quotes for a shared container will be based on the cubic volume of your goods, so it is essential to make sure the removals estimator knows exactly what you want to take as any last-minute extras will cost more.

In the case of a full-container quote, the price per container is standard, but you should get a quote for the costs of any excess goods in case they do not all fit in one container. Make sure you know the type of container they are quoting, as volumes differ between insulated and non-insulated containers. If the quote is based on a shared container load, make sure it includes an estimate of total volume of your goods. If you have only a small amount of effects to move, it will probably be cheaper to pack them yourself. There are few important points:

- You should pack your possessions in stout containers, using a packing filler material such as polystyrene or paper.
- Most removals companies will provide suitable containers.
- Goods packed with straw or chaff will not pass New Zealand agricultural quarantine regulations.
- You should label baggage carefully, inside and out.

Always wait until you have received and checked a written estimate before booking your removal company. You should have written confirmation of several points, including the following:

- the list of items to be shipped;
- a cubic volume;
- special packing requirements for particular items;
- all door-to-door costs including customs and terminal charges, unloading etc.; and
- delivery instructions showing the name of your destination city or town in New Zealand.

Insurance for the move

Insuring your possessions during the move is critical. Shipping firms will usually offer marine insurance as part of the service but you need to check the small print carefully. The cost of marine insurance may not be included in your initial estimate because this is assessed on the value of your possessions. Make sure that the policy covers all risks and that it covers any storage period either in the UK or in New Zealand. If the insurance company has offices in New Zealand, any claims are likely to be settled much more quickly than if they have no New Zealand base. While rates quoted are often very similar, the level of cover can vary so make sure you obtain a copy of the terms and conditions and compare them carefully. Ask for a copy of the insurance company's proposal form well in advance so that you have plenty of time to ask any questions you may have and also to assess the values that you are planning to declare. If you feel at all uneasy about making the right decision or comparing insurance policies and options, seek professional advice.

Useful resources

Abels International Moving Services: Wimbledon Avenue, Brandon, Suffolk IP27 0NZ; 0800 626 769 (freephone) 1842 816600 (Customer Management Centre); enquiries@abels.co.uk or neilpertoldi@abels.co.uk or suebloomfield@abels.co.uk (for enquiries about storage); www.abels.co.uk.

Air New Zealand Cargo (Vancouver, BC): (604) 244 2209; laxcs@airnz.com; www.ca.airnewzealand.com/aboutus/cargo/.

Air New Zealand Cargo (Calgary, AB): (403) 717 4324; laxcs@airnz.com; www. ca.airnewzealand.com:80/aboutus/cargo/.

Air New Zealand Cargo (Toronto, OT): (905) 676 8928; laxcs@airnz.com; www. ca.airnewzealand.com:80/aboutus/cargo/.

Air New Zealand Cargo (Montreal, QU): (514) 428 4363; laxcs@airnz.com; www. ca.airnewzealand.com:80/aboutus/cargo/.

Air New Zealand Cargo (LA): 5625 West Imperial Highway, Los Angeles, CA 90045; 310 646 9891 or 800 421 5913; fax 310-568 8620; www.us.airnz.com.

Air New Zealand Cargo (Chicago): Building 517, Suite 101, O'Hare International Airport, PO Box 661217; Chicago, IL 60666; (773) 686-9837 or (800) 424 1066; www.us.airnz.com.

Air New Zealand Cargo (New York): Building 77, Cargo Plaza Rm. 206, JFK International Airport, Jamaica, NY 11430; 718 244 1333 or (800) 400 0153; fax 718 244 1334; www.us.airnz.com.

Air New Zealand Cargo (UK): London Heathrow; 020 8751 5000 (hours 9am – 5.30pm, Monday to Friday); www.airnewzealand.co.uk/aboutus/cargo.

Allied International: Worldwide network specialists in international removals, with over 1,000 representatives in 130 countries. Check your local phone directory for an office near you, or find one online at www.alliedintl.com. The New Zealand arm is Allied Pickfords: 8 Lockhart Place, Mt Wellington, Auckland. (09) 259 2160; freecall (within New Zealand) 0800 255 433; ap.corporate@allpick.co.nz; www. allpick.co.nz./nz/.

Anglo Pacific International Plc, 5/9 Willen Road, Park Royal, London NW10 7BQ; 020 8965 1234; info@anglopacific.co.uk; www.anglopacific.co.uk.

Avalon Overseas Movers (Europe): Part of the Team Relocations Group, offering advice and help with all customs and other documentation and carrying out in excess of 30,000 relocations worldwide every year; www.teamrelocations.com. Website offers French, German and Dutch language options.

The Baggage Company (UK): 4 Hannah Close, London, NW10 0UX; freephone 0500 868 500; info@thebaggagecompany.co.uk; www.thebaggagecompany.co.uk.

Crystal International (USA): 1901 Camino Vida Roble Suite 206, Carlsbad, CA 92008; 800 307 8900 or 760 431 0266; info@crystalinternational.com; www. crystalinternational.com.

Excess International Movers (UK): Bases in London (including various train stations and airports), Birmingham, Edinburgh, Glasgow, Leeds, Liverpool and Manchester. Head office: 4 Hannah Close, Great Central Way, London NW10 0UX; National freephone 0800 783 1085; 020 8324 2000; International: 0044 20 8324 2000; sales@excess-baggage.com; www.excess-baggage.com.

Excess International Movers (USA): Toll-free number 1 800 260 8098.

Moving.com: Fill in the form to get an online quote; www.moving.com.

PSS International Removals (UK): Head Office, 1–3 Pegasus Road, Croydon, Surrey CR9 4PS; 020 8686 7733; sales@p-s-s.co.uk; www.pssremovals.com. You can submit a direct online enquiry form.

Unigroup Worldwide UTS (USA): One Worldwide Drive, St Louis, Missouri 63026, 540 898 1831 or toll-free: 1 800 325 3924; logistics@uniworldwide.com; www. unigroupworldwide.com. You can request door-to-door surface shipments quotes online.

Customs regulations

Information regarding the importation of household and personal effects and cars into New Zealand can be found in a series of leaflets from New Zealand customs. New Zealand embassies and high commissions should have copies available, or you can obtain information on the internet (www.customs.govt.nz). The basic principle is that if you are coming to New Zealand to take up permanent residence, you can import your household goods and car duty-free. The goods must be used and not be intended for sale or commercial use. If you are a returning resident, coming back to New Zealand after an absence of more than 21 months, your household goods qualify for the duty-free concession, but in the case of cars, you can only qualify for the duty-free concession on the first occasion you arrive to take up residence. You are also entitled, like any visitor to New Zealand, to bring in personal effects duty-free. The list of prohibited imports includes indecent articles and publications, ivory in any form, anything made from the bone of marine mammals, most weapons and some types of food. You may not bring plant material or fruit into New Zealand. The importation of firearms is strictly controlled and a police permit is required.

Import procedures

You should be careful to thoroughly clean any garden tools or furniture, hiking boots, running shoes, or anything else that may have traces of mud or dirt on it. Your goods will be inspected by the Ministry of Agriculture and Forestry (MAF) before being released to you, and they may require such items to be steam cleaned or fumigated to kill off any potential pests or diseases. MAF inspection charges vary depending on the consignment.

Provided that you qualify for the duty-free exemption outlined above, importing your household goods ought to be straightforward. The complicating factor is that you and your possessions will most likely be travelling separately, you by plane and your worldly goods by sea, a process taking six weeks at minimum. You can either wave goodbye to your possessions well before your departure and hope that their arrival in New Zealand coincides with yours, or send them when you leave and manage without them for your first few weeks in your new country. You should make sure that your insurance policy covers any storage time, either before shipping or following delivery at the other end. If your car and possessions arrive in New Zealand before you do, you can avoid paying port storage charges by arranging for a nominee to clear them through customs for you. The Collector of Customs at the port will require evidence of your nominee's authority to act for you and evidence that you are arriving in New Zealand for the first time to take up permanent residence. In the case of a car, additional documents proving that you have owned it for at least one year prior to departure will be required. Your nominee will be required to pay a deposit equivalent to the cost of duty on the vehicle and/or goods, which will be refunded in full once you arrive.

Whether you are picking up your goods yourself or have authorised a nominee, you need to provide customs with an inventory of your belongings. If you have any queries about what types of goods you can import and the procedures contact the Collector of Customs at the port of destination (see addresses below).

Useful resources

New Zealand Customs: Freephone within New Zealand: 0800 428 786 or from overseas: 0064 9 300 5399; feedback@customs.govt.nz; www.customs.govt.nz.
Auckland: Box 29; (09) 359 6655.
Auckland International Airport: Box 73003, Mangere, Auckland; (09) 275 9059.
Christchurch International Airport: Box 14086; (03) 358 0600.

Dunedin: Private Bag 1928; (03) 477 9251.
Invercargill: Box 840; (03) 218 7329.
Lyttleton: Box 40; (03) 328 7259.
Napier: Box 440; (06) 835 5799.
Nelson: Box 66; (03) 548 1484.
New Plymouth: Box 136; (06) 758 5721.
Tauranga: Box 5014, Mt Maunganui; (07) 575 9699.
Wellington: Box 2218; (04) 473 6099.
Whangarei: Box 4155; 029 250 9305.

Importing pets

New Zealand regulates the importation of live animals to prevent the establishment of pests and diseases that could harm the country's productive resources and biodiversity. Requirements for importing animals into New Zealand are extremely stringent, and nearly all animals except for cats and dogs are prohibited. However, if you fulfil all the pre-flight veterinary requirements, your animals may be able to go home with you when they arrive in New Zealand without requiring a quarantine period. Cats and dogs coming from Australia, UK/Ireland, Sweden, Norway, Hawaii and Singapore do not require quarantine, but they do require certification and will be inspected for ticks upon arrival.

If your cat or dog is coming from a specified country or region where canine rabies is absent or well controlled, such as the USA, you should consult the online Import Health Standards on the MAF website (see below) for the latest information. From other places, the length of the quarantine period required depends on the country of origin, but it will be at least 30 days. This is likely to cost over NZ$1,000. Bear in mind that in New Zealand there are only three MAF-registered quarantine facilities for domestic cats and dogs, and for importations where a post-entry quarantine period is required a Permit to Import will not be issued unless the importer has a letter from a quarantine facility confirming that a space has been booked for the animal.

Dogs must have current vaccinations against:
- Distemper
- Parvo virus
- Canine hepatitis
- Kennel cough (boretella), and
- Leptospirosis

Suitable vaccines are Vanguard Plus 5, Vanguard 5, Coughguard B and Leptoguard.

Cats must have current vaccinations against:
- Feline enteristis
- Feline upper respiratory tract infection 'snuffles'
- Feline chlamydiosis, and
- Feline leukemia

Suitable vaccines are Felocell CVRP, Felocell 4 and Leukocell 2.

■ Getting your pets to New Zealand is going to cost as much as getting yourself there, and require as much paperwork and many more vaccinations.

There are a number of firms that specialise in the air freighting of pets (for names and addresses see below) and some international removal companies also offer this service if they are shipping your household goods for you. As this involves organising an International Air Transport Association (IATA) approved air travel container, which must be sealed by a vet, as well as an examination immediately prior to departure, it is probably best to hand your pets over to the professionals. If you are using the services of a professional firm, it is best to contact them a few months in advance to avoid any unforeseen documentation delays. You will need to organise some of the veterinary procedures yourself, as some vaccinations have to be given six weeks prior to departure. There are a number of compulsory tests and the results of these must travel with the animals. Most firms will suggest that you leave your pets with them for the night prior to departure.

The firm you choose to help you may offer services to acclimatise your pet to air travel before the trip takes place, so that it is not too much of a shock for them. However, most firms advise that pets almost always settle down quickly and sleep for the large part of their journey. Pets are transported in the live animal cargo section of the plane; this is insulated, pressurised and temperature controlled (to the same temperature as in the passenger area of the plane). However, excessive heat or cold can prohibit airline pet transportation, and airlines place 'heat and cold embargoes' on pet transport to prevent illness or death in the height of summer or the depths of winter. Bear this in mind when arranging the time of year you want to travel. Your pet-transporting firm will be able to advise you about the best times for your pet to travel during the winter or summer. Pet Transporter Worldwide advises that this is especially important in the summer months for pug-nosed dogs and snub-nosed cats, which are more susceptible to oxygen deprivation and heat stroke. Pet crates will have enough room for standing up, lying down and turning around, but not much more than this as too much space can be a hazard and cause injuries in the event of turbulence.

Pets and the law

New Zealand has quite strict laws governing the control of pets. The animals must not annoy or injure other people, and any dog found roaming freely may be impounded by the Dog Pound. There are laws to protect pets as well; the SPCA (Society for the Prevention of Cruelty to Animals) can take any person who has been cruel to an animal to court. You must also be aware that there are some areas, particularly near wildlife reserves, which have been designated cat-free zones due to the havoc that domestic cats have been wrecking on native bird populations. At present there are only a few of these areas, and the rules are enforced by general community consensus rather than the long arm of the law, but you should ensure that you do not unwittingly introduce a cat to such an area.

An Import Health Permit Application form should be completed; it can be downloaded from www.maf.govt.nz/quarantine/live-animals/index.htm. Animals may have to undergo Post Entry Quarantine at a MAF Biosecurity New Zealand approved facility. Please note that you should apply for this permit well in advance of the scheduled date of importation.

Useful resources

Airpets Oceanic: Willowslea Farm Kennels, Spout Lane North, Stanwell Moor, Staines, Middlesex, TW19 6BW; 01753 685571 or freephone 0800 371554; export@ airpets.com; www.airpets.com.

MAF Biosecurity New Zealand: PO Box 2526, Wellington, New Zealand; 0064 4 894 0459; imports@maf.govt.nz; www.maf.govt.nz/quarantine.

Independent Pet and Animal Transportation Association International (IPATA): 745 Winding Trail, Holly Lake Ranch, Texas 75775, USA; (903) 769 2267; inquiries@ipata.com; www.ipata.com. You can search online for a pet shipper by location or by business name, you can download a list of pet shippers from the website, or use the Fax-on-Demand facility; dial 1 402 951 5501, request file 176, and a complete list of pet shippers will be faxed to you immediately.

Ladyhaye International Pet Travel Agency: Hare Lane, Blindley Heath, Surrey RH7 6JB, UK; 01342 832 161 (Surrey) or 0161 332 7021 (Manchester); info@ ladyhaye.co.uk; www.ladyhaye.co.uk.

Par Air Livestock Shipping Services: Warren Lane, Stanway, Colchester, Essex CO3 0LN, UK; 01206 330332; parair@btconnect.com; www.parair.co.uk.

PetAir UK: 5–7 Castle Street, Cranbourne, Dorset BH21 5PZ, UK; 01725 551124; enquiries@petairuk.com; www.petairuk.com. Run by fully qualified vets.

Pet Chauffeur (New York City): Toll-free 866 PETRIDE or (718) 752 1767; help@ petride.com; www.petride.com.

Pet Transporter Worldwide: Services include all flight and ground transportation, door-to-door pick-up and delivery, care in between flight connections when necessary, TSA and UDSA documentation, boarding and any other service your pet needs. See the website for a list of location-specific offices and contact numbers in the USA (Arizona, California, Colorado, Connecticut, Florida, Massachusetts, Maine, New York, New York City, North/South Carolina, Virginia and Washington), or 1 800 264 1287. The Netherlands: 020 796 5921. www.pettransporter.com.

Useful websites

- www.jetsetpets.co.uk
- www.nationalpetexpress.co.uk
- www.overhill.co.uk
- www.passportpets.co.uk

Quarantine addresses

Ministry of Agriculture and Forestry: Animal Quarantine Division, Box 2526 Wellington, New Zealand; general enquiries +64 9 256 8547; www.maf.govt.nz/ quarantine/. See the 'Contacts' page of the website for telephone numbers in different areas of New Zealand.

Pussy Cat Lodge: 29 Crowther Street, Avondale, Auckland; (09) 828 3410. Spaces for 24 cats. (MAF registered.)

PetHaven: www.pethavenkennels.co.nz

Qualified Pet Services: 150 Airfield Road, Takanini, Auckland, New Zealand; (09) 299 9539; services@qualifiedpet.co.nz; www.qualifiedpet.co.nz. Spaces for 36 dogs and eight cats. (MAF registered.)

Canterbury Quarantine Services Ltd: Highfield Road, Aylesbury, PO Box 23158, Christchurch, New Zealand; (03) 318 1279; www.canterburyquarantine.co.nz. Spaces for 30 dogs and 15 cats. (MAF registered.)

New Zealand quarantine stations

Auckland Wharf: 23 Quay Street, PO Box 39, Auckland City; (09) 909 3019.

Wellington: Centreport House, Waterloo Quay, Port Wellington, PO Box 3042, Wellington; (04) 894 4213.

Christchurch: 14 Sir William Pickering Drive, Private Bag 4765, Christchurch; (03) 358 1856.

Importing a vehicle

If you are considering importing your car, you will obviously want to consider whether the original value of the car plus the cost of freight, port handling costs and insurance is lower than the replacement cost of the car in New Zealand. In general, European cars cost more to replace in New Zealand than their original value plus shipping costs, assuming the vehicle qualifies for duty-free entry (see below for the conditions). Japanese and Asian cars are cheaper because of the commercial importation of second-hand vehicles from Japan, but there have been some problems with quality assurance so be careful if you are planning this route. As a very rough guide, new cars can be purchased for anywhere between NZ$17,000 and NZ$166,000, and second-hand cars for NZ$5,000–NZ$50,000.

If you are emigrating to New Zealand for the first time, you can import your car into New Zealand free of duty provided you satisfy customs that you are importing the vehicle for your own use, that you have owned it for at least a year prior to your departure, and that you are arriving in New Zealand to take up permanent residence for the first time. You will be required to sign a deed of covenant agreeing that if you sell your car or boat within two years of importing it, you will be retrospectively liable for the duty and sales tax (GST). If your car does not qualify for duty-free entry, duty is levied at 20% of purchase price for UK-made vehicles, and 30% of purchase price for other foreign cars, less depreciation. The exchange rate used in calculating the New Zealand dollar value of your car will be based on the current exchange rate at the time you clear your vehicle. The costs of shipping an average car vary depending on the size of the car and which port in New Zealand it is going to. It usually takes about six weeks. Some companies offer a cheaper option where the vehicle is not shipped in a container, but the risks of damage or theft in transit are higher. You should arrange insurance for your vehicle, whichever option you choose. Premiums are calculated on the New Zealand value of the car. Do not pack personal belongings in the car for the journey. There is a risk of pilferage, particularly if the car is not containerised during the journey, and the contents of the car will have to be declared to customs by the shipping company or you will risk getting a fine.

FACT

■ One source of information on second-hand car prices in New Zealand is the classified section of newspapers. You can order New Zealand motor trade magazines from Destination New Zealand and New Zealand Outlook or from the Automobile Association. Some car shipping companies will also provide lists of recent New Zealand prices for common models of cars.

Procedures for clearing your car through customs in New Zealand are as follows. The vehicle will be given the once-over by the MAF quaratine inspection and border check. A number of details about your car will be recorded and then sent on to the LTSA's Transport Registry Centre for recording on the LANDATA database as part of the vehicle's permanent record. You should allow 48 hours for information to be recorded on the LANDATA system. MAF will invoice the importer a fee to cover the cost of the border check and the quarantine inspection conducted on the wharf. If you don't want to arrange the MAF and New Zealand Customs Services processes yourself, you can contact a customs broker. All used vehicles must be steam cleaned before MAF will pass them. You can have your car commercially steam cleaned before shipping but remember to keep the receipt to show to MAF in New Zealand. Some shipping companies will steam clean your car as part of the service. MAF's objective is to prevent any pests and diseases, which could endanger livestock, being brought into the country and their standards are therefore stringent. If inspectors are not satisfied that your vehicle has been thoroughly and properly cleaned, you will be required to have it done again. Your car will need to comply with New Zealand safety regulations, some of which differ from standards of other countries. The Vehicle Identification Number (VIN) will be issued/decoded by your Entry Certifier. The Entry Certifier verifies that the vehicle met the required standards when manufactured, carries out the vehicle inspection to confirm that it is in good condition, and decides whether the vehicle needs any repairs and/or specialist certification for compliance with legal safety requirements. They then verify entitlement to register and issue form MR2A and Warrant of Fitness.

The next steps are registration and licensing, and then your vehicle can legally be driven on New Zealand roads. Check the appropriate Infosheets and Factsheets on the Land Transport Safety Authority website for more detailed information (www.landtransport.govt.nz/importing/). Left-hand drive vehicles require special import permission. Apply to the LTSA.

 Land Transport Safety Authority: PO Box 2840, Wellington; 0800 699 000 within New Zealand or +64 4 494 8600; fax +64 4 494 8601; info@ltsa. govt.nz; www.ltsa.govt.nz

Next you will need to provide documentary evidence to the Collector of Customs that the car is yours and, if you are applying for a duty-free entry, that you have owned it for at least one year prior to importing it. Such proof can include a dated receipt of purchase showing the date delivery was taken, registration papers, odometer details, evidence of the date on which you gave up the vehicle for shipping to New Zealand and your passport showing verification of permanent residency.

You cannot drive the car legally until it has a vehicle inspection certificate and is registered, so you will need to arrange for it to be transported from the port to the nearest vehicle inspection test centre. The Vehicle Inspection Certificate used to be called the Warrant of Fitness (WOF), and in some places testing centres still advertise them as Warrants. Once your car has passed, you take the certificate to a post office, along with the ownership documents and the importation documents, and obtain a registration certificate, sticker and number plates. All of this is likely to take a couple of days.

TIP

■ Your vehicle must have front and rear seatbelts, and a high mounted rear stop light. It is a good idea to have these fitted before you leave because you will not be able to drive the car in New Zealand until it complies with local safety standards.

Useful resources

All America Auto Transport (USA): 1 800 227 7447 or 1 800 CAR SHIPPING; aaat@aaat.com; www.aaat.com. Will send a free information package on request.

Anglo Pacific International (UK): 0800 633 5454; www.anglopacific.co.uk. Offers a comprehensive car shipping service by groupage or exclusive container service.

Autoshippers UK: 0800 389 0784; www.autoshippers.co.uk.

Autoshipping Co. of America: www.carshipper.com (for a wide range of options).

Land Transport (New Zealand): PO Box 2840, Wellington; 0800 699 000 within New Zealand or +64 4 494 8600; info@landtransport.govt.nz; www.ltsa.govt.nz/importing.

MAF: www.maf.govt.nz

New Zealand Automobile Association (NZAA): www.aa.co.nz.

New Zealand Customs Service: +64 9 300 5399; www.customs.govt.nz.

On Road New Zealand: +64 9 444 6921.

PSS International Removals (UK): 020 8686 7733; www.pssremovals.com. You can submit a direct online enquiry form.

Seabridge International: (410) 633 0550; www.seabrdge.com. You can submit a direct online enquiry form.

TnT AutoTransport: 800 USA TNT1 (1 800 872 8681); www.tnt-inc.com.

Transport Registry Centre: Private Bag, Manawatu Mail Centre, Palmerston North 4442; cnr Ashley and Ferguson Streets; 06 953 6200.

Vehicle Inspection New Zealand (VINZ): 0800 GO VINZ/0800 468 469; www.vinz.co.nz

National Support Office, PO Box 10057, The Terrace, Wellington 6143; (04) 495 2500; www.vtnz.co.nz. You can submit an online enquiry.

Now you are ready to take the plunge and move abroad...

Setting Up Home

■ CHOOSING WHERE TO LIVE

For most people, the decision about where to live is influenced first and foremost by employment prospects. New immigrants are most likely to buy houses in Auckland, Wellington or Christchurch. In all three cities the residential areas are mostly suburban and it is most common for people to commute by car into the city centre to work. Each suburb has its own particular character and prices can also vary considerably between areas for reasons as diverse as mere fashion or, in the case of hilly areas, related to the amount of sunshine that different parts enjoy, or the views they afford. In Auckland, for example, your property is worth more if it has a view of the harbour or Rangitoto Island. It is worth looking at the less fashionable

Sources of information

Typical New Zealand house prices can be ascertained from the property section of some New Zealand newspapers. The main newspapers can be read online, see www.stuff.co.nz for various area options. More detailed advertisements can be found in New Zealand real estate magazines. Information may also be obtained from the Real Estate Institute of New Zealand's website (www.reinz.org.nz).

Immigration consultants may also offer advice on buying properties. The property market in New Zealand's main cities has been a little jerky of late, due to high interest rates and uncertainties about the strength of the economy. This seemed to correct itself in late 2007 though, and prospects for the property market moving forward look positive.

Most New Zealand houses are detached, single storey houses on individual plots of land known as 'sections' (the term 'bungalow' to describe a modern house of this type is not common). The average New Zealand home consists of three bedrooms, a living room and dining room, kitchen, laundry and bathroom. Most homes near cities or towns are built of timber and stand alone. Many are insulated, but most do not have central heating or double glazing. The standard size of the New Zealand section used to be a quarter of an acre, but as urban property prices have risen in recent years, subdivisions have become more common and new houses are being built on much smaller sites. The average size of new houses is now smaller and more compact at just under 170 square metres. Although the vast majority of houses are still separate units, in recent years city apartment living has increased in popularity.

areas, where first homeowners and young families often buy. If you are aiming at the more affordable end of the market, you will get more house for your dollar.

If you have children, your choice may be influenced by proximity to schools. The location, however, does not always make a lot of difference to the standard of education on offer. Inner city schools perform as well as suburban schools on the whole. Rural schools achieve slightly lower academic results than city schools but have the advantage of smaller class sizes and better pastoral care. The best idea is to visit schools in the area and see what you think of the atmosphere. If you do decide you would prefer a particular school, bear in mind that this will have an impact on where you can live as some New Zealand schools do employ zoning policies.

For further information about zoning and how it affects your area and chosen school, see the Ministry of Education dedicated website at http://www.schoolzones. co.nz/enrolmentzones. This site offers searches for schools throughout the whole of the country; you may search by school name or by home address. If searching by home address, the site will present you with a list of all the schools you are zoned for. Many schools do not have enrolment zones. If your address is within 3km of an 'un-zoned' primary school or within 5km of an 'un-zoned' secondary school, these schools will also be shown in your list. You will also be shown a map depicting the location of the schools in relation to your home address and the enrolment zone (if it exists) for each school. Additional school details provided by this website include the name, age range, type of school, controlling body, telephone number, address, email contact and the school's own website details.

How Do New Zealanders Live?

New Zealand has a high level of home ownership, with nearly three-quarters of dwellings being owner-occupied. New Zealanders tend to be quite house-proud, and spend a lot of time on home improvements and gardening. The average standard of housing is high. Household services such as water, electricity and sewerage are almost universal. Over 98% of all homes have colour TVs, most have videos, and around a third have dishwashers.

Of those Kiwis living in rented homes, a quarter live in state houses rented from Housing New Zealand [NHZ], while the majority lease housing from private landlords or companies. Local authorities do not play a major role in providing housing. Rental accommodation is usually provided unfurnished except for ovens, and sometimes fridges and washing machines. Whiteware is easily hired if you prefer not to buy your own, or hire-purchase is a good option if initial outlay is a problem for you and you don't mind spending a little more to pay by installment.

The majority of households are made up of just one family. Amongst Maori and Pacific Island communities, where extended kinship links are important and because average incomes amongst these groups tend to be lower, households are more likely to include more than one family or extended family members. Even amongst Maori and Pacific Island homes though, one-family households are the most common. The average number of occupants per dwelling is 2.7 people.

Levels of second home ownership are also quite high. Many New Zealand families own what is known as a 'bach' (pronounced 'batch' rather than like the composer) or 'crib'. 'Bach' is the North Island term (deriving from the word 'bachelor'), while the word 'crib' is only used in the South Island. The bach is a great New Zealand institution. These mostly unpretentious and comfortable dwellings are often furnished with various items discarded from the family home, and provide the perfect way for families to 'get away from it all' with the minimum of planning. Although a bach is traditionally a small holiday cottage near a lake or by the sea, some wealthier families now have beach homes that border on 'pimp-my-pad' levels of ostentation – these probably would not be referred to as 'the bach' but are more likely to be 'the beach house' or 'holiday home'.

◼ NEIGHBOURHOODS

This section provides an overview of the main residential areas within Auckland City, Wellington City and Christchurch City (as well as a few popular residential areas just outside of Christchurch). The information provided should give you a general idea of the areas you might look at more closely in terms of possible places to live. There is no substitute for having a look for yourself though when it comes to deciding where you want to live; and staying in an area for a while (even renting there before you make the decision to buy) so you have the chance to really get a sense of how well it will work for you and your family is highly recommended. There are some words/ phrases used in this section that might be new to you:

Decile ratings: All state schools are ranked using a socio-economic positioning system – this is calculated using various data, including average salaries in the area, the percentage of local families registered with social welfare, and so on. Decile 1 is the lowest ranking, and decile 10 is the highest; decile 1 schools are the 10% of schools with the highest proportion of students from low socio-economic communities, and decile 10 schools are the 10% of schools with the lowest proportion of these students. Schools with the lower decile ratings receive more government funding than schools with higher decile ratings. Each school should be judged on its own merits however, as rankings within the decile ratings chart are not always the best indicator of results (although they will probably give you a very rough idea). Country schools for example might have a lower decile rating than city schools based on relative family incomes, but they might have smaller class sizes meaning pupils receive more teacher attention and achieve better results. Lists of schools with their decile ratings and contact details can be found by searching 'deciles information' on www.minedu.govt.nz.

Dairy: A small local grocery store or corner shop

Infill housing: Additional housing built into an already established residential area. The classic Kiwi home used to sit on a quarter of an acre of land, but residential gardens are now more and more frequently being divided up and town houses/ separate flats or units built on them and sold off to maximise profit from the property. Building and planning permission is required.

Main residential areas of Auckland City

Central City/Central Business District (CBD)

All price ranges are catered for, but that's not to say that you are guaranteed a penthouse with a harbour view for your pennies. The vast majority of inner city dwellers are European or Asian, and most are renting. Owners in the inner city market are largely property investors, but if you are looking to live in the city your very best find would be a lovely converted loft apartment. These, however, cost a premium. Parking is not always easy or affordable, but some apartments come with secure underground car parking spaces. It's not the greatest place to live with children or teenagers, but a brilliant location if you want to experience apartment living in the country's biggest city. There are a few parks in the city, including Victoria Park, Myers Park and Albert Park.

Living in the central city will never be particularly peaceful, but it is exhilarating, always interesting and perfect if your idea of quality living includes walking to work, not having

Best for: Students and childless professionals, going out
Less good for: Car parking, quiet, homes with gardens
Price factor: NZ$110,000-well over NZ$1million to buy; NZ$280-NZ$500+ per week to rent

> We live right on the coast, looking straight out over the sea, and on a clear night you can see the lights of Auckland city across the water.
> **Vita Evans**

to worry about a car, slipping seamlessly between leaving work in the afternoon and sliding straight into Auckland's diverse nightlife before heading home to crash and then doing it all over again the next day. Almost everything you could need is right on your doorstep – a huge range of restaurants, cafés, nightclubs, bars and shops, the Viaduct, Aotea Square Market on Saturday mornings, K Road, Vulcan Lane, the list goes on.

There are not many schools in the CBD; if you need to get to schools you will need a car or a bus pass. Transport links are the best from downtown Auckland – this is where all the local buses and trains run from. Britomart, downtown, is the central connection point for ferries, rail services and buses.

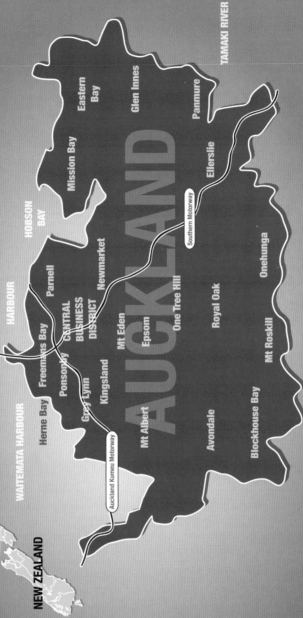

NEW ZEALAND

AUCKLAND

WAITEMATA HARBOUR

HARBOUR

HOBSON BAY

Herne Bay

Freemans Bay

Ponsonby

Grey Lynn

Kingsland

Mt Albert

Mt Eden

CENTRAL BUSINESS DISTRICT

Parnell

Newmarket

Epsom

One Tree Hill

Mission Bay

Eastern Bay

Glen Innes

Ellerslie

Panmure

TAMAKI RIVER

Avondale

Blockhouse Bay

Mt Roskill

Royal Oak

Onehunga

Southern Motorway

Auckland Kumeu Motorway

MANUKAU HARBOUR

AUCKLAND

Downtown Auckland

Herne Bay

Epsom

Central Business District

Avondale

Settlement of this area began in earnest with the completion of the Great North Road in the 1850s. Originally home to potteries, mills, brickyards, tanneries and market gardens, Avondale became increasingly suburban from the 1920s. It was in Avondale that the kiwifruit (or Chinese gooseberry) was developed. Easy access to the city, Unitec and relatively affordable prices make Avondale popular with a wide range of people. This area is filled with young urbanites who can't afford inner city prices, first time buyers, students and families. There is a broad range of house styles here – 100-year-old renovated villas, bungalows from the 1930s and '40s, loads of brick-and-tile units and family homes, townhouses, and infill housing (on subdivided sections).

Best for: Going to the races, state schools, bringing up a young family
Less good for: Boutique shopping
Price factor: NZ$250,000–NZ$600,000+ to buy; NZ$210–NZ$430 per week to rent

The central area has been given a facelift, and there is a strong community spirit here, but the two large shopping malls nearby (only 5–10 minutes away) have had an inevitable impact on quality shopping opportunities.

The college is zoned, and gets consistently good results, so many families move to live in this area simply for the school.

Blockhouse Bay

Situated on the northern coast of the Manukau Harbour, this is an improving area with a good community feel; there are rugby clubs, bowling clubs, tennis courts, parks, an ice skating facility, and a community centre offering a wide range of activities. In the 1920s Blockhouse Bay was a popular holiday resort for city families, accessible only by rough roads but offering summer holidays camping on the beach or in small cottages. These days, chances for a great meal or a coffee in a local café or restaurant are improving and there will be easy access to the north-western motorway once the proposed motorway extension is completed. Regular bus services operate from both Lynfield and Blockhouse Bay. The suburb is about 11km south-west of the city centre. There are nine schools within a 3km area here, with Lynfield College in particular hosting a large number of ESL foreign students. Hilltop School is a private co-ed with small class sizes, and Halsey Drive is a decile nine school which

Best for: Sports facilities, swimming, parks
Less good for: Dining out
Price factor: NZ$350,000–NZ$1million+ to buy; NZ$200–NZ$380+ per week to rent

achieves excellent results. Shopping is varied here – there is a shopping complex at Lynfield with a supermarket, modern shops and fast food places, while the centre at Blockhouse Bay itself is much more 'villagey', and attracts the more traditional residents. Most homes here are bungalows between 30 and 50 years old, but there is also plenty of weatherboard infill housing, as well as apartments and brand new houses springing up here and there.

Eastern Bays

Best for: Strolling around the waterfront, eating out, views
Less good for: Affordable housing
Price factor: NZ$380,000–NZ$3 million+ to buy; NZ$350–NZ$700+ per week to rent

This is a very popular and absolutely gorgeous part of Auckland – beautiful views, wonderful old homes, relative ease of access to the centre of town, and sought-after schools. The schools are good quality, although many children from here attend private schools in other areas, and there are three local secondary schools including Sacred Heart, the Catholic boys' school. There are many older families here, often living in homes that have been passed down through the generations, as well as more aspirational Aucklanders with newer money who want to be proud of their address. There are many different types of housing here, from small strongholds of state housing to apartments, to enormous homes with harbour views dripping in opulent furnishings. The area's tremendous popularity has inevitably caused supply and demand problems, with the result that there is much infill housing already in place. Opportunities for renovation and adding value to homes have largely been exhausted. But this is a wonderful place to live, if you can afford it; all the bays are suitable for swimming and sunbathing, there are many walks, a bird sanctuary, and more reserves and parks than you can shake a stick at. Choices for meals out are greatest at Mission Bay, there is range of good shops in a village-style centre at St Heliers, and there is an historic independent cinema at Mission Bay. Although there are small boutique food shops around, supermarket-style grocery shopping is thin on the ground, but with Newmarket only 15 minutes' drive away this doesn't seem to present locals with too much of an insurmountable problem. The train into central Auckland takes only eight minutes, and the Greenlane interchange is only 20 minutes' drive away. Similar to Oriental Parade in Wellington, sunny weekend afternoons along the waterfront can become quite congested with yummy mummies, cyclists, skateboarders, speedy sugar-high toddlers, ice-cream-lickers, runners, pooch-paraders, roller-bladers and post-prandial strollers – Aucklanders come from all over to enjoy this spot.

Best for: Horse races, bus routes
Less good for: Traffic congestion at busy times
Price factor: NZ$300,000–NZ$1.3million+ to buy; NZ$285–NZ$625+ per week to rent

Ellerslie

Sandwiched between Remuera and Mt Wellington, Ellerslie, along with neighbouring St Johns and Meadowbank, is a very residential, stable, friendly area. The motorway is close, although not near enough to be a nuisance, and the area is only 7km to the south-east of the city centre, close to State Highway 1. Driving to the airport can take as little as 20 minutes. There are train stations at both Ellerslie and Meadowbank (trains into the CBD take about 20 minutes), and regular bus services along main routes. Plenty of supermarkets, retail shops, and smaller specialty shops are located around this area; there is easy access to the beaches and waterfronts, and to the golf club at Remuera, as well as to Auckland Domain and One Tree Hill (unfortunately no longer boasting its essential tree). An enormous new shopping complex can be found in nearby Mount Wellington. There is an expanding netball centre, the university sports centre, and of course the famous Ellerslie Racecourse which is also the venue for Auckland's biggest second-hand car fair every Sunday. Ellerslie also boasts a Rudolph Steiner school, providing for students right through the age range from new entrants to secondary school.

Epsom

Situated behind Mount Eden, and populated by families, Epsom is a great location for schools and this of course contributes to the cost of living here. With the highly regarded Epsom Girls Grammar and Auckland Grammar both operating zoning systems, properties in these zones are in high demand among families. It is estimated that being in the zones for these schools can stack as much as an extra NZ$100,000 on top of already steep house prices. Other schools include St Peter's College and Marcellin

Best for: Schools, tree-lined streets
Less good for: Shops
Price factor: NZ$275,000–NZ$1.7 million+ to buy; NZ$250–NZ$680+ per week to rent

FACT

James Stuart Freeman lived in Freeman's Bay in the 1840s with a woman who was not his wife. He was described as 'the most disgustingly immoral swindling scoundrel in town'.

College as well as several public and private primaries. Sports clubs are abundant, there is a good library and a community centre as well the Lido Cinema, and because of the well-cared-for streets, century-old villas and bungalow-style houses dating from about 1900–1930 Epsom is a lovely place to stroll around.

Apart from a few antique shops and other small shops, there is very little right on Epsom's doorsteps in the way of shopping. It is close to the lovely independent shops and cafés of Mt Eden though, and not far from the mall at St Lukes, so hardly a retail wasteland, and there are several good restaurants around.

Freemans Bay

This is a lovely area with a view of the harbour and the bridge, and across to the North Shore. Freemans Bay is probably named after the secretary of Captain William Hobson, James Stuart Freeman. Historically the Bay was rundown and unfashionable, and used to be home to boat-building yards, an abattoir and the city morgue. In the 1930s the city council formed the Decadent Areas Committee to revamp the area, and large swathes of the area were cleared out with the building of the motorway in the 1950s. Now it is known for its beautiful houses, especially the beautiful old heritage homes which still exist here despite disappearing from many other parts of the city. Some areas experience traffic noise from the motorways, but it is close to little beaches and boasts two parks and the fabulous Pt Erin Baths where you can swim in a pool with a view of the bridge and harbour. A great area for small families, and excellent cafés and restaurants offer a wide range of fancy foods as well as your standard coffees and muffins. Check out the Eon Design Centre, a showroom and retail space that specialises in New Zealand design by New Zealand designers and artists.

Best for: Swimming with a view of the harbour
Less good for: Parking
Price factor: NZ$375,000–NZ$3million+ to buy; NZ$300–NZ$700+ per week to rent

Glen Innes

Glen Innes is 9km east of the central city and on the edge of the Tamaki River. It was traditionally a low-income area of run-down state housing, but many first time buyers and young families have been moving in to take advantage of these solid little houses on their square sections as they come up for sale. The population here is a diverse mix of cultures (Maori, European, Asian, Pacific Islanders, Indian, Arab and Albanian amongst others) and ages, and is traditionally broadly working class with a strong community spirit.

Talbot Park is a new area of higher density housing, introduced recently by the government in an effort to improve the quality of state housing, and is made up largely of apartments. There are three local primary schools, an intermediate and a high school, all within walking distance of most parts of the suburb, as well as Auckland University's Tamaki Campus. Travel to both the airport and the CBD takes about half an hour, and there are good transport links with a train station on the Eastern Line of the Auckland Rail Network and a hub for Auckland Stagecoach buses.

Glen Innes boasts a good sporting complex with a swimming pool, and sports grounds for tennis, cricket, rugby, and football, as well as walking tracks down by the estuary and a bird sanctuary.

Best for: Food shopping and a rich cultural mix
Less good for: Nightlife
Price factor: NZ$210,000–NZ$525,000 to buy; NZ$175–NZ$350 per week to rent

FACT

There used to be a strong Polynesian community in Grey Lynn when rents were lower, but, as prices soared, the lower income families relocated to more affordable areas.

Grey Lynn

Grey Lynn is a lovely area – close to parks and beaches and only 3km from the city, and near enough to enjoy the bars, restaurants and cafés of Ponsonby without having to pay to live in Ponsonby. Transport links are good, with buses running down Richmond Road and Great North Road, but you can actually walk into the central city from here, through Ponsonby. There is a wonderful little cluster of interesting shops on Richmond Road, including Nature Baby, Moa clothes store, Harvest Whole Foods, and lovely delis and restaurants including Delicious. The other groups of Grey Lynn shops, at the intersection of Williamson Avenue and Great North Road includes a great fish and chip shop, upmarket cafés, a launderette and doctor's surgery, pizza takeaways, dairies, Polynesian food shops, video rental stores, and a Foodtown supermarket. Grey Lynn is centred around Grey Lynn Park, which has a free toddler pool. The park hosts the annual Grey Lynn Festival as well as the Lightspeed Festival and is the home ground of the Richmond Rovers rugby league club.

There are currently a large number of new apartments being erected around this area, but the most desirable accommodation choices are the wooden villas with gardens that are packed into Grey Lynn – they can be cold in the winter, but are absolutely glorious for enjoying a gin and tonic on the porch during long summer evenings.

Herne Bay

This is Auckland's most expensive suburb, on track to become New Zealand's very first suburb in which every property is valued above NZ$1 million benchmark, and it is located just to the west of the Auckland Harbour Bridge. Professionals and merchant families built large houses here from the late 19th century onwards, and there are still plenty of traditional large family homes here as well as extremely modern architect-designed houses and brand new apartments.

There are several exquisite boutique clothes shops along Jervois Road, as well as a few great places for culinary adventures such as Andiamo, Fusion, Shahi, the Jervois Steak House and Saloon, Red, Villa d'Vine, and Erawan. There are also beauty salons and complementary health and beauty therapists, a medical centre, and some hilariously overpriced gift and homeware stores. There is no supermarket, but with Grey Lynn Foodtown not far away and the huge New World just down the hill at Victoria Park you are never far from groceries. Herne Bay is only a five-minute drive into the CBD, has great public transport links, nestles just round the corner from more shopping and dining opportunities on Ponsonby Road, and offers easy access to the little beaches of St Mary's Bay directly opposite the classic-Auckland view of yacht-packed Westhaven Marina.

FACT

■ Named for the English seaside resort in Kent popular in the 19th century, Herne Bay developed as a commuter suburb as it became apparent that it was actually quite close to the centre of town by just a short boat trip.

Kingsland

Best for: Fantastic coffee
Less good for: Motorway noise, depending on location
Price factor: NZ$250,000–NZ$750,000 to buy; NZ$220–NZ$450 per week to rent

Kingsland used to be a very rundown, working class area, but gradually the trendy young professionals and small young families who can't quite afford Ponsonby and Grey Lynn anymore made the move across the motorway and the area is now much more desirable. Eden Terrace, just up the road, is much more industrial and commercial although there are significant residential pockets, and provides flats to a number of students. Morningside, also close by, is centred around the shops on New North Road, near St Lukes Shopping Centre, and is largely commercial. Western Springs, just down the road, is dominated by a large park, the location of the popular annual Pasifika Festival. Western Springs regularly hosts pop and rock concerts and stock car racing. The Auckland Zoo is located here as well, and there are plenty of parks, skate bowls, sports grounds and basketball courts. Bond Street still connects Kingsland to Arch Hill and Grey Lynn, and there is a walking path into the central city, but the motorway is a big psychological barrier. The area is not so brilliant for schools – there is a complete lack of primary schools, with the closest in neighbouring Morningside or Grey Lynn, just one intermediate, Kowhai, which has established bilingual Maori and immersion classes, and the nearest secondary schools are Western Springs College and Auckland Girls Grammar at Western Park.

You can find pretty much everything you need here though, in the cluster of shops around the railway station, provided hanging out in bars and cafés forms a large portion of what you are looking for. The Kingslander pub is a favourite, although it is a slick refurbished warehouse job with a gastro menu and big screens rather than an old-man pub, and coffee-experts Atomic and Roasted Addiqtion both roast and retail here. The Atomic café has a more pared-back minimalist feel, while Roasted Addiqtion embraces the well-trodden floorboards and squashy old sofas approach. There are several other great cafés around, and a spoiled-for-choice selection of cafés and restaurants offering menus ranging in influence from South Asian to French. Village shopping is alive and well in this buzzing little place, but although there are two bakeries here, it lacks essentials such as a greengrocer, butcher and fishmonger. Kingsland boasts an eclectic mix of different types of older workers cottages, timber family homes and cooler contemporary properties, and house prices are climbing although it is still more affordable than other areas with a similar vibe. Leisure activities are well catered for around this area, with Eden Park Stadium (home of cricket and rugby) nearby, public rugby grounds, parks, basketball courts and skate bowls.

Mount Albert

Best for: Family activities and schools
Less good for: Boutique shops
Price factor: NZ$290,000–NZ$2 million to buy; NZ$375–NZ$535 per week to rent

Mount Albert is an extinct volcanic peak, one of the city's older cones thrown up somewhere between 50,000–60,000 years ago. The peak itself is 135 metres high, and surrounded by parkland. Unitec (Institute of Technology) is situated towards the northern end of the suburb, and the Mount Albert Research Centre is located here as well and houses the Auckland centre of HortResearch as well as other Crown Research Institutes. There are plenty of family-activity opportunities around this area; the Aquatic Centre in Alberton Avenue is particularly popular with its wave pool, baby pools, waterslide and waterpolo competitions. There is also a golf course, walking tracks, parks and playgrounds, and sports and leisure recreation centres, and Eden Park is close by too. Upmarket apartment blocks are being built in various locations, and homes in the zones for the schools carry a bit of a price extension reflecting the popularity of the schools. Renovated villas and bungalows on the slopes of Mount Albert are highly sought after, and there is a lot of infill housing as well as a number of townhouses and smaller apartments. St Lukes Mall is located in this area, packed with shops and shoppers from all over central Auckland, with a busy food court, a cinema complex and groaning with franchise retail outlets.

There is a vibrant Asian community along New North Road, with cheerful food stores, picture framing, internet cafés, florists, a pharmacy and a library. Good schools are a feature of Mount Albert, including the popular Gladstone Primary (one of the largest in New Zealand), and newly co-ed Mount Albert Grammar as well as Hebron Christian College and the Catholic Girls Marist College.

Mount Eden

Best for: Picturesque villa, quirky cafés, excellent restaurants
Less good for: Living on a shoestring
Price factor: NZ$300,000–NZ$1 million+ to buy; NZ$240–NZ$600 per week to rent

No longer a bohemian haven for students, writers, teachers, lecturers and artists, leafy Mount Eden has now been primped and preened to within an inch of its life and is in a glowing state of plump and smug good health. Mount Eden village is bursting with boutiques packed with gorgeous things, perfectly-renovated villas from the early 20th century and cafés crammed with pushchairs worth the same as second-hand cars and the well-manicured mummies who steer them. Away from the village there is a separate shopping region along Dominion Road, with banks, restaurants, takeaway outlets, video and DVD rentals and Asian grocery shops.

Neighbouring Sandringham has grocers and butchers, and the Three Kings shopping centre has a library and supermarket. Both Three Kings and Sandringham have a greater cultural mix of residents than Mount Eden, and both are home to large numbers of young families. Mount Eden itself (to be fair, more a hill than a mountain, and actually a 200-metre high extinct volcanic cone) is also known by its Maori name Maungawhau and is a public park boasting spectacular views of the city, the harbour, Rangitoto and One Tree Hill.

The CBD is only 2km away, and is easily reachable by public transport. The local train station was established in 1880 and is 2km from Newmarket Junction on the Western Line.

Mount Eden is home to several high decile primary schools, as well as Auckland Normal intermediate school. Although there are no secondary schools located in Mount Eden, Three Kings, Balmoral or Sandringham, there are a few prestigious schools located nearby – St Peter's College, Epsom Girls Grammar, Auckland Grammar School – as well as the Epsom campus of the University of Auckland.

FACT

■ Mount Roskill used to be referred to as 'Auckland's Bible Belt' due to the large number of churches scattered around here – the greatest number of churches per capita in the whole country.

Mount Roskill

Best for: Churches and ethnic diversity
Less good for: Café cruising
Price factor: NZ$360,000–NZ$1.2 million+ to buy; NZ$260–NZ$500 per week to rent

One of Auckland's larger suburbs, Mount Roskill is home to a culturally diverse group of residents – at least 54 different nationalities are represented here – and a considerable immigrant population. There are occasionally problems related to drugs, burglary and gang activity.

Mount Roskill offers the choice of two golf courses, indoor/outdoor swimming pools, bowling greens, parks and tennis courts. The area is 7km south of the CBD (travel time is about half an hour during rush hour, 15 minutes otherwise) and it is surrounded by the neighbouring suburbs of Three Kings, Mount Albert, Wesley, Hillsborough and Sandringham. The Southwestern Motorway (SH20) is being extended through Mount Roskill, and the extension will eventually continue through Avondale to provide alternative routes north and south to State Highway 1 linking the cities of Manukau, Auckland, Waitakere and North Shore. Although the work has of course been disruptive, the development is generally welcomed as it will ease congestion on local roads that are presently shouldering the load of all the traffic moving from State Highway 20 through to the central city and the western suburbs.

The local school is the very popular and Mount Roskill Grammar, and Lynfield College and private Marcellin College also take a considerable number of local students. The Mount Roskill shops are located at the intersection of Mount Albert and Dominion Roads, there is a medical centre at White Swan and Richardson Road intersection and there are also shopping centres at Mount Eden and Royal Oak as well as Lynfield Mall. Local restaurants offer a bewildering array of authentic dining experiences from around the world, such as Indian, Asian, Thai, Italian, Vietnamese, Chinese, British and Malaysian, and there are plenty of takeaway outlets as well.

Newmarket

Newmarket's main strip is called Broadway and, heaving with more than 500 stores, it is overtaking the central city as the top choice for high-end shopping. It boasts an overdraft-stretching collection of clothes shops, notable among them an impressive list of New Zealand designers including Zambesi, Karen Walker, Moochi, Workshop, Kate Sylvester and Annah Stretton, as well as SAKS, Scarpa, The Pyjama Co., Alannah Hill, Drop Dead Gorgeous and Keith Matheson, to name just a few. Mini fashionistas with well-heeled parents are catered for too, by shops such as Bay Bee Cino, Kidliwinks, Oilily, Room Seven, Lily Moon and Trelise Cooper.

More than 100 cafés, bars and restaurants have squeezed in too, offering loads of choices for your much-needed sustenance breaks during a day spent flexing the plastic. Whether you have the taste for a simple flat white, noodles and sake, a deli plate of delicious morsels, or a pie and a pint, you'll find something here to tickle your fancy. A top stop would have to be Zarbo Delicatessan and Café on Morrow Street, with its gastronomically gorgeous eat-in offerings and a huge selection of own-label oils, condiments, coffees and luxury pantry-fillers to pretend you are buying as gifts and then take home for yourself. You can wind down in the evening with a visit to one of the two popular cinema multiplexes that live here – the Rialto and Skycity Cinemas. Newmarket has lost many of its interesting historic buildings in the name of modernisation over the years – the stunning art deco Olympic Swimming Pool for example was recently and drastically 'redeveloped' when the previously open-air pool was covered up with a cinema complex. The Maori Television headquarters are located on the border of Parnell and Newmarket.

The Newmarket Train Station is a hub for Auckland, lying 3.7km from Britomart and whisking commuters into the CBD in between 5–15 minutes. It is on both the Southern and Western train lines of the rail network, and is the second-busiest station in the city after Britomart downtown. All express services stop here, including those to Waitakere and Pukekohe. The station is scheduled for a significant facelift, including the addition of numerous pedestrian access points, sparkly new buildings, and a plaza, as well as an extended concourse that links up with the main street over the existing tunnel.

Housing-wise there is not a huge amount to choose from in Newmarket unless you are looking for an apartment shouldered by offices and shops, although there are a few small cottages tucked away; it's not a good place for family living, but good for childless professionals who enjoy the delights of a purely urban lifestyle.

Onehunga

Between Mount Smart and Royal Oak, for the past few years Onehunga has been a popular choice with first-time buyers and young families looking for affordable properties with renovation opportunities in a community environment as well as easy access to the central city, motorways and the airport. There is a wide range of housing styles to choose from, including classically Auckland villas and bungalows, low-maintenance brick-and-tile units, townhouses, ex-state houses and apartments. The suburb stretches south from Royal Oak towards the north shore of Manukau Harbour – on the southern shore, linked to Onehunga by a bridge, is the suburb of Mangere Bridge. Onehunga was once considered a poorer and less desirable part of Auckland, but due to the influx of buyers and the care they have lavished on improving their homes here the area has been gentrified somewhat and the community itself has enjoyed a surge of economic growth. Maori, Asian and Pacific peoples make up a significant part of the population, along with Europeans. There is schooling for all ages here, including two primary schools, an intermediate, and two high schools. Onehunga has a good library, soccer and sports club, community centre, cafés and restaurants, a swimming pool complex and a gym.

The town's main street, Onehunga mall, runs north to south along the length of the suburb and is home to a variety of shops and businesses, including the recently-extended Dress Smart Complex which is full of specialty stores and designer brand clothing outlets.

One Tree Hill

Despite the loss of its famous tree, One Tree Hill remains one of Auckland's most recognisable landmarks and from the summit you are rewarded with amazing views of the city. The surrounding area includes Greenlane and Royal Oak, and these areas are well-established and leafy with a selection of different types of housing ranging from villas and bungalows to infill units apartments, townhouses and state housing. There are plenty of schools nearby to choose from, but pick your house carefully if you are aiming for the Auckland Grammar or Epsom Girls' Grammar zones.

Cornwall Park comprises 120 hectares of land roamed by sheep and cattle and covered in native trees such as kauri, rimu, nikau palms and pohutakawa. It includes a farm, and barbeque and recreation areas. The Auckland Observatory is found in the One Tree Hill Domain, just off Manukau Road. Mount Smart Stadium, in Penrose, is a large sporting venue that also hosts large scale music concerts and is the home of the exhausting and exhilarating annual Big Day Out music festival.

Panmure

A south-eastern suburb, Panmure is 11km from the city centre. When the old railway workshops and freezing works were closed in the 1980s, the workforce and the landscape of this area inevitably altered. These days home to migrants from all over the world and first-time buyers lured by affordable properties, this suburb is full of family homes. The more luxurious houses are found along the river. There are plenty

Large houses in Parnell

Best for: Families
Less good for: Nightlife
Price factor: NZ$175,000–NZ$1.1 million+ to buy; NZ$200–NZ$345 per week to rent

of sporting facilities here: walking tracks and parks, rugby and soccer fields, cricket pitches and netball, basketball and tennis courts. It can take as long as an hour to drive into the central city, but only a few minutes to join up with the southern motorway and no longer than half and hour to reach the airport.

There are plenty of intermediate and primary schools here, but no secondary schools. New local government growth initiatives focus on creating a technology park at Mount Wellington, and building medium density housing to accommodate the predicted growth. The enormous Sylvia Park mega-mall in Mount Wellington, which was completed in 2007, is the country's largest mall and houses a wide variety of retailers including cinemas, supermarkets, major banks, bookstores, and numerous fashion and homeware retailers. The 2008 stage includes NZ$200 million of new office space in four separate buildings, a train station and a bus terminal. The centre employs roughly 2,500 staff and it is estimated that approximately 12,000 people at a time visit during the weekends.

Parnell

An historic suburb, first settled in 1841, with buildings dating from the 1860s. By the 1950s the suburb was falling into decay, but it was rejuvenated by developers in the 1960s. Parnell Village was created, and this has since become one of the wealthiest areas in Auckland. The shops, restaurants, bars and boutiques are all unashamedly

> **Best for:** Galleries, jewellers and window-licking
> **Less good for:** Tight budgets
> **Price factor:** NZ$230,000–NZ$4 million to buy; NZ$300–NZ$800 per week to rent

upmarket and there are more than a few high-priced galleries, design stores and antique dealers on Parnell Road and Bath Street. Conspicuous consumption is the name of the game here, and high-maintenance haircuts, pricey designer clothes, flashy cars and hilariously expensive cocktails are all part of the Parnell package.

Parnell is in-zone for the best state schools, and close to many high-end private schools. Homes here are pricey but beautiful, and styles range from enormous old family houses to achingly sleek minimalist apartments.

If you need somewhere to exercise or relax, there is an abundance of parks and green spaces nearby, a pool and leisure centre as well as cinemas in neighbouring Newmarket, several tennis clubs, a museum, a library, and the much-loved and architecturally-striking saltwater outdoor pools at Parnell Baths.

Ponsonby

> **Best for:** Seeing and being seen in achingly trendy bars and restaurants
> **Less good for:** Sports facilities
> **Price factor:** NZ$400,000–NZ$1.5 million+ to buy; NZ$400–NZ$1000+ per week to rent

On the western edge of the CBD, Ponsonby sits along a ridge above Freemans Bay. The area used to have a reputation for being less than desirable in the 1950s and 1960s, when Polynesian and Maori workers took advantage of the cheap rents on the rundown cottages and villas here. Gentrification from the 1970s onwards forced these low-income families out, as happened in Freeman's Bay and Grey Lynn as well later on. Ponsonby is now a high-income area, saturated in pricey and fashionable boutiques, homeware stores selling crisp-cornered linen and the very latest Italian kitchen gadgets, and trendy bars, restaurants and cafés open until late.

At the Three Lamps end of Ponsonby Road the unthinkable has occurred and a Starbucks has opened, coinciding with the keenly-felt disappearance of the much-loved eccentric Expresso Love café.

If you head all the way down Ponsonby Road for 2km you will reach Karangahape Road (K Road to the locals). This is home to a diverse and heady mixture of Polynesian, Indian and Maori clubs, crafts, shops, etc., and a range of seedy 'massage parlours'. The nightclubs and cafés along here are fabulous (try the New Zealand-famous Verona and Brazil), and this is the heart of the buzzing gay and lesbian city scene.

There is a great collection of galleries up here as well – Disrupt (featuring New Zealand artists and street art), Illicit, the Michael Lett Glallery, Artspace, and the nearby Whitespace.

Remuera

One of Auckland's most affluent suburbs, located 4km to the south-east of the city centre, Remuera extends from the Orakei Basin to Hobson Bay in the north and

> **FACT**
>
> ■ Ponsonby used to be home to the Gluepot, the iconic old-man-style tavern that became a popular music venue in the 1970s and was a key supporter of many subsequently successful New Zealand bands. It was closed and converted into apartments in the 1990s.

> **FACT**
>
> ■ Remuera has long been regarded as the Chelsea of Auckland – 'SUV's, known as 'Chelsea Tractors' in London are called 'Remuera Tractors' by Aucklanders.

A modern district in Wellington

Best for: Keeping up with the Joneses, neighbours with impressive original art collections
Less good for: Affordable housing, bohemian lifestyle
Price factor: NZ$750,000–NZ$3.5 million+ to buy; NZ$380–NZ$600+ per week to rent

east, and is bordered by Newmarket, Meadowbank, Greenlane and Parnell. It is only 10 minutes' drive from the central city. The train station lies on the Southern Line of the Auckland Railway Network, and the train will also take you into the CBD (Britomart) in about 10 minutes.

Schools here are highly regarded, and many are private. Corran School caters to all levels; primary schools include Dilworth Junior School, Meadowbank, Remuera, St Michaels, Victoria Avenue, Kings Prep School and St Kentigern; Remuera Intermediate and Hobson Middle School cater to the middle age group; and Baradene College as well as Auckland Grammar and Epsom Girls Grammar are available for secondary school students.

Remuera has a slightly snooty reputation as the high-profile stamping ground of the seriously wealthy and status-focused residents stereotypically adorned with all the apparel, accessories and vehicular trappings of those unashamed of their platinum-card status and gardeners. Remuera homes are some of the oldest in Auckland city – gracious, spacious and gorgeous with mature gardens on tree-lined streets. Remuera has some of the best views of the city and out over the Hauraki Gulf to be found, and the suburb's prestigious history extends back generations; many successful Aucklanders have lived here. Remuera boasts reserves and parks galore, numerous green spaces, running and walking tracks, a golf club and plenty of other sports clubs including badminton, squash, gymnasiums, bowling, tennis, cycling, netball, rugby and football.

Hospitals, the library, retirement homes, and medical specialists are all of the highest quality. The main shopping centre is a pretty village-style collection of shops and boutiques elegantly displaying antiques and designer clothes, specialist food and wine suppliers, cafés, restaurants and high-end wine bars. If you're looking for a more intense and sustained retail rush, Newmarket's Broadway is only a few minutes' drive away.

Royal Oak

Best for: Young families
Less good for: Driving on the roundabout
Price factor: NZ$340,000–NZ$2 million to buy; NZ$240–NZ$550 per week to rent

Royal Oak is a small suburb between Onehunga and Epsom. It used to be quite scruffy, but has been coming into its own over the past few years and now there is a real community spirit here with lots of newly-opened restaurants and cafés as well as plenty of shops. Character bungalows and infill housing are the norm, as well as state houses and brick-and-tile units. There is a tennis club here, the 'Action Indoor Sports Stadium', a squash club, gymnasium and swimming pool, health and fitness centres, as well as a Zen Buddhist community. There's plenty to keep you busy. There are regular buses into the CBD. Driving to the city centre will take between 15–30 minutes, and both Newmarket and the airport are only 10 minutes' drive away. Royal Oak Shopping Mall is on the corner of Manukau and Mount Albert Roads, at the intersection of five of Auckland's major suburban roads – the Royal Oak Roundabout. The mall is home to 60 shops and services, including supermarkets, florists, optometrists, fashion stores, a pharmacy, craft shops, framers, hairdressers and beauticians, takeaway outlets, cafés and bookshops.

Main residential areas of Wellington City

Central Wellington/Te Aro

Best for: Young professionals; bars, restaurants, theatres
Less good for: Green space, quiet
Price factor: NZ$282,000–NZ$800,000+ to buy; NZ$390–NZ$500+ per week to rent

Central Wellington is compact and indisputably gorgeous – it sits nestled by the hills and watched over by all the beautiful wooden houses on the Mount Victoria slopes. It is the centre of government for New Zealand, but also the main hub for theatre, arts and 'culture'. The central city throbs with wonderful bars, restaurants, cafés, theatres and music venues, and there are numerous cinemas around town. Fine dining requirements are catered to by restaurants such as Logan Brown, good spots for coffee are too numerous to count, but Pravda on Customhouse Quay is a good

TIP

■ Wellington is regarded by locals (and many others) as New Zealand's coolest city – it's just the weather than lets it down. However, if you can handle unpredictable winds, rain and temperatures, there is much here for the urbanite.

NEW ZEALAND

WELLINGTON

WELLINGTON

SUBURBS

1	Wellington Central	9	Oriental Bay	17	Brooklyn	25	Melrose	33	Moa Point	41	Makara Beach	49	Churton Park
2	Pipitea	10	Roseneath	18	Mount Cook	26	Kilbernie	34	Rongatai	42	Ohariu	50	Glenside
3	Thorndon	11	Kaiwharawhara	19	Newtown	27	Maupuia	35	Lyall Bay	43	Khandallah	51	Grenada Village
4	Wadestown	12	Ngaio	20	Hataitai	28	Karaka Bay	36	Houghton Bay	44	Broadmeadows	52	Woodridge
5	Northland	13	Crofton Downs	21	Vogeltown	29	Miramar	37	Southgate	45	Ngauranga	53	Horokiwi
6	Kelburn	14	Wilton	22	Mornington	30	Seatoun	38	Island Bay	46	Johnsonville	54	Grenada North
7	Te Aro	15	Karori	23	Kingston	31	Breaker Bay	39	Owhiro Bay	47	Newlands	55	Tawa
8	Mount Victoria	16	Highbury	24	Berhampore	32	Strathmore Park	40	Makara	48	Paparangi	56	Takapu Valley

Early evening

A modern district

New Zealand's Parliament building

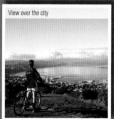
View over the city

place to start your research, and fantastic coffee alongside the best brunch offerings in town can be enjoyed at Fidels on upper Cuba Street. For the best cheap and cheerful Malaysian food, go to Roti Chenai on Victoria Street. Other fabulous cafés include Parade Café along Oriental Parade, and the Lido Café on Victoria Street. For a real treat, rub shoulders with the young professional crowd at the peerless and legendary Matterhorn bar and restaurant in Cuba Mall.

Theatres in the city include Bats, Circa, Downstage, and the St James Theatre and Opera House. The Michael Fowler Centre is one of the country's premier concert halls and home to the New Zealand Symphony Orchestra, as well as other music and dance events. The Wellington Town Hall is another popular venue.

Lambton Quay houses most of the designer fashion boutiques and department stores, and shopping centres here include the Old Bank Arcade and Chambers, Harbour City Centre and the biggest – Capital on the Quay. Willis Street and Cuba Street have their own share of fashion boutiques, cafés and restaurants too. In terms of housing, space is at a premium in the central city, so flats and apartments are the norm and there is significant demand so they are not cheap.

Public transport runs to and from the central city, with buses and trains to various areas and the cable car running up the hill from Lambton Quay to Victoria University, botanic gardens and Kelburn. As with the rest of the country, the public transport is not a strong point. The centre itself is so compact though that it is easy to walk everywhere.

Aro Valley

Best for: Students
Less good for: Avoiding damp
Price factor: NZ$500,000+ to buy; NZ$440–NZ$700 per week to rent

Traditionally a favourite area with students and young bohemian writers, artists and intellectuals, due to the availability of affordable accommodation (often

seemingly kept in a state of deliberate disrepair especially for this low-income market) and the proximity to both the city and the university. Well-maintained wooden houses here are lovely though, and in very high demand because of their character and charm; a significant proportion have been snapped up and renovated by young professionals nostalgic for their student days here, and others have been demolished to make way for new apartments that developers are slapping into place. It really is a valley, between Kelburn and Brooklyn, and properties on the hills probably have a better chance of avoiding the damp in winter and the ants in summer than those directly on the valley floor along Aro Street, but the hills are steep and may severely limit sunlight hours depending on location.

Aro Street runs the full length from Willis Street all the way to Raroa Road leading up to Kelburn. There is a small cluster of shops on Aro Street, where you will find a 'mini-mart', a delicatessen, a small park and community centre, a great video rental store, excellent fish and chip shop, a bakery and cafés. Gradual creeping gentrification seems to be taking hold.

Berhampore

Best for: Sense of community, affordable property
Less good for: Slick luxury bachelor pads
Price factor: NZ$210,000–NZ$500,000+ to buy; NZ$280–NZ$560 per week to rent

Property in Berhampore ranges from cheap apartments to mid-range character period homes in a range of styles – there's something here for everyone. It is an ethnically-diverse area, located around Adelaide Road. Benhampore lies 7km to the south of Wellington City centre and its neighbours include Newtown and Island Bay. The Berhampore Municipal Golf Course has 18 holes and offers a great view of the city and Cook Strait, and the green belt area is ribboned with walking tracks. Other local features include the Chinese Sports and Cultural Centre (a large sports stadium), Wakefield Park (where both soccer and cricket are played) and the Wellington City Nursery (which grows plants used all over the city by the City Council). Liardet Street Park is used for soccer, rugby and touch rugby, and has artificial surfaces too. Martin Luckie Park, on Lavuad Street/Mt Albert Road, is used for rugby, rugby league, softball and tennis. Wellington Hospital is nearby, in Newtown. Berhampore School is a co-ed decile 4 primary school, with a roll of less than 200, and is located on Britomart Street.

Breaker Bay

Best for: The beach
Less good for: Shops and cafés
Price factor: NZ$400,000+ to buy; NZ$300–NZ$600 per week to rent

Breaker Bay is on the East Coast of the Miramar Peninsula, with a view over to Port Nicholson. It sits where the Cook Strait and Wellington Harbour meet, and is fairly sheltered from the northerly winds. This is a very small suburb, with just a commuter bus running during peak hours, Monday to Friday only. This bus is called the Seatoun Express, and it runs from Breaker Bay into Molesworth Street via Kilbirnie Shops, Courtenay Place and Wellington Station twice in the mornings, and then back again twice in the late afternoon/evening. Buses do run to nearby Seatoun shops though, and you can walk from there.

Breaker Bay itself doesn't have any shops or cafés, so Seatoun is your closest stop for provisions and treats. The bay the suburb is named for is the only clothing-optional beach in Wellington (although to be honest getting your kit off doesn't always seem like the most appealing option in Wellington weather); it is located at the far north end, while families tend to use the end nearest the road.

Brooklyn

Best for: Rising above it all
Less good for: Bars and nightclubs
Price factor: NZ$365,000–NZ$500,000+ to buy; NZ$260–NZ$420 per week to rent

Brooklyn is a lofty, self-contained community on the eastern slopes of the hills 3km south of the CBD, near Aro Valley and Mount Cook. Transport links from here are good, and the journey into the city centre takes only 5 minutes on the bus or by car. Brooklyn is home to New Zealand's first wind turbine, which was erected here in 1993 as part of research into wind power generation.

Clubs and facilities here include the Brooklyn Smallbore Rifle Club, the Renouf Tennis Centre, Brooklyn Walkers, the Brooklyn Community Centre (which hosts markets, dance classes and table tennis nights) and Brooklyn Northern United Football Club. The art deco Penthouse Cinema is still on Ohiro Road, where it has been operation since 1939. The cinema also houses the Penthouse Café, which serves meals from brunch through to dinner, as well as coffee. Takeaway choices abound, from the Brooklyn Fish Supply and Brooklyn Café through to a branch of Burger Wisconsin, and Chinese, Indonesian, Thai and Indian food.

Properties here vary in style, from a few remaining old timber cottages and villas, to bungalows, state housing and apartments. This is a popular place to live, and the community is expanding with increasing infill housing as well as new subdivisions. Brooklyn School is a state primary, and St Bernard's School is a Catholic primary; both are co-ed.

FACT

Churton Park and Paparangi

Best for: Young families
Less good for: CBD access
Price factor: NZ$350,000–NZ$480,000+ to buy; NZ$320–NZ$500 per week to rent

A large, affluent, family-oriented area bordered by Johnsonville, Churton Park is one of the northern suburbs of Wellington. Culturally, it is quite diverse. The landscape is fairly hilly with steep hills. Much housing is built on new subdivisions, where dense bush has been cleared to make way for expansion and development. Plans are in

Churton Park is a popular place to live and the suburb is expanding rapidly with the population almost doubling since 2001. Further growth is inevitable, as subdivisions are being built in the western parts of the suburb.

place for work to start on a new shopping centre development.

There are lots of little parks, and walkways. Churton Park itself is a sports and recreation field, and Churton Park Primary School has a good reputation although it is oversubscribed. About 180 families in this suburb are currently outside the zone for the school, and in 2007 plans to build a new school were announced although it is not yet known when this will open. Although there are no schools for older children in the immediate area, intermediate and secondary schools go to nearby Raroa Intermediate, Newlands Intermediate, Onslow College and Newlands College.

Paparangi has a shopping centre, although no supermarkets. Eco-adventure leisure choices locally range from gentle bush walking to high-adrenaline white-water rafting. Paparangi Primary School has a decile 9 rating, and Paparangi Kindergarten is here as well. The children's playground has recently had a major makeover, with new play equipment installed including spin bowls, swings, basketball hoops and a partial court, slides and tunnels.

Crofton Downs

Crofton Downs is part of the greater Ngaio area, and it is served by the Johnsonville branch of the commuter railway that runs from the central city to the north Wellington suburbs. Crofton Downs has expanded significantly with the general spread of greater Wellington, and there are a number of new subdivisions here. Houses here are often weatherboard, but solid, built in the 1960s, and appealing to first time buyers. Crofton Downs offers residents easy access to the city centre by train or car, local parks and reserves, a medical centre, a pharmacy, a hardware store, florists, and zoning for a range of schools including Onslow College and Chartwell School.

Best for: Affordable housing with good city access
Less good for: Café society
Price factor: NZ$300,000–NZ$560,000+ to buy; NZ$320+ per week to rent

Grenada North and Grenada Village

Best for: Sports facilities
Less good for: Cultural groups and activities
Price factor: NZ$400,000–NZ$450,000+ to buy; NZ$340–NZ$500 per week to rent

Grenada residents have a strong sense of community, with an active residents' association. Recreation facilities are excellent, with numerous walkways through native bush and near streams, many public picnic areas, large sports fields and two covered tennis courts. Grenada North Park on Jamaica Drive has artificial surfaces for all-weather soccer and cricket. Seton Nossiter Park is a 30-hectare natural reserve. Housing here is mainly modern, built in the last 15-20 years, and well-maintained.

Hataitai

A great location on the edge of Evans Bay means that this eastern suburb benefits from great sun as well as its own enviable microclimate. Lying between Mount Victoria and the Miramar Peninsula, Hataitai is fairly accessible to central Wellington thanks to the Mount Victoria Tunnel.

Property covers the full spectrum, from simple sections with building permission, and character-rich old timber cottages, through to sleekly impressive view-enhanced pads and low-maintenance townhouses. There are plenty of walking opportunities along the coast, and the green belt, and residents enjoy good transport links to both the city and the airport. Hataitai community groups, include religious groups, a social netball club and a football club, as well as

> **Best for:** Outdoor living
> **Less good for:** Students
> **Price factor:** NZ$400,000–NZ$830,000+ to buy; NZ$250–NZ$500+ per week to rent

several churches and primary schools. The Cycling Velodrome is an outdoor concrete track just above the netball and rugby areas at Hataitai Park. Gluttony options abound, including fish and chips, the ubiquitous Burger Wisconsin, Thai, Chinese and Indian food, Hell pizza, pub delights at The Realm (go round the back for food), quality wraps and kebabs at Lamaso, brunch and coffee at Café Bellagio, and there is a hot bread shop as well to meet your bakery needs.

Highbury

> **Best for:** Views
> **Less good for:** Bars and restaurants
> **Price factor:** NZ$400,000–£750,000+ to buy; NZ$350–NZ$600+ per week to rent

Highbury is a quiet little area behind Kelburn, traditionally favoured by academics needing proximity to the university in critical combination with distance from the students. Transport links are reasonable, with buses running fairly frequently into town and the cable car not too far away, and walking into the central city would take about 30 minutes, while you could walk down the hill to Aro Valley in about 15 minutes.

Housing options, as with so many areas of Wellington, are varied; there are attractive first-time buys here, but also grand family homes from earlier generations. Residents are generally fairly respectable. The area is not as affordable now as it once was, but is still a great place to live in terms of proximity to great cafés, the city and local shops, elevation (which can make all the difference in escaping the dreaded damp) and wonderful views out over Karori in one direction and the city and harbour in another.

Highbury relies on close neighbour Kelburn for such necessities as shops and schools, but Highbury residents are quite definite about not being part of Kelburn.

Houghton Bay

Best for: Surfing and seaside living
Less good for: Local shops
Price factor: NZ$495,000–NZ$585,000+ to buy; NZ$350–NZ$450 per week to rent

Largely residential, Houghton Bay lies south of Wellington city, between Lyall Bay and Island Bay, on the edge of Cook Strait. It takes roughly 10 minutes to drive here from central Wellington, and buses 23 and 32 will carry you into the CBD, although services are limited in the weekends. A good surf spot, despite inconsistency due to winds and the reef break, tiny Houghton Bay is also good for diving and fishing as well as walking. Swimming is not recommended here, due to the strong undertow, but is safer at nearby Princess Bay, and walkers can use the Southern Walkway (which begins at Oriental Parade and covers 11km) and Greenbelt. Buckley Road Reserve and Southern Headlands Reserve are much loved by locals and walkers from surrounding areas as well.

Not far from the beach is the Wind Garden, a garden specially created to withstand the harsh salty winds and other weather fluctuations of this coastal location; you can visit the garden by appointment, or obtain information from here about growing gardens in exposed areas. The Pines is the local venue used by a wide range of community groups, or for private hire and parties; it also hosts cabaret nights. Houghton Valley School is a state co-ed contributing school with a decile 9 rating. There are no cafés or shops here, but the shops and takeaways of Island Bay are only 5 minutes away. Sinclair Park in Houghton Bay is used for soccer games and training.

Island Bay

Best for: Children, close-knit community
Less good for: Finding DIY property projects
Price factor: NZ$500,000+ to buy; NZ$400–NZ$600+ per week to rent

Island Bay, 7km south of central Wellington, is a thriving coastal community and is one of the most popular seaside suburbs. Favourite local activities include beach walking, cycling, kayaking, scuba diving and other watersports, and swimming if you can brave the often-chilly water.

Island Bay is just 10 minutes' drive to the airport and the Miramar Golf Club, and 15–20 minutes' drive into the city. Public transport links to the city are relatively good, with the number 1 bus service running from Island Bay to the Wellington Railway Station every day of the week.

Residents combine in an interesting cultural mix, with a significant proportion of Italian immigrants. Island Bay is packed with cafés, restaurants and small shops – reflecting the tastes and heritage of the residents as well as the seaside location – including The Bach (modern New Zealand food), Brass Monkey Café, and Kai in the Bay (offering authentic Maori fare) as well as a boutique butcher, dairies, a baker, fish-and-chips and other takeaways, and even a hammock store. The supermarket is not very large, so for weekly grocery shopping you will need to visit one of the supermarkets in Kilbirnie.

Public amenities are excellent, with a library, parks and reserves, a medical centre, pharmacy, several churches, Plunket rooms, a community centre, five pre-schools and four primary schools. There is a even a cinema here – the newly-restored Empire Theatre. Shorland Park has children's play equipment and picnic areas, and is just across from the beach. Property here is in demand – as well as flats and apartments, there are plenty of period-style character homes with mature gardens and plenty of space.

Johnsonville

Best for: Suburban living
Less good for: Boutique shopping
Price factor: NZ$390,000–NZ$500,000+ to buy; NZ$280–NZ$525 per week to rent

Close to Lower Hutt and Porirua, Johnsonville is a self-contained suburb in its own right, as well as being only 10 minutes' drive from the Wellington CBD (depending on motorway traffic of course). Johnsonville began as a service centre to surrounding rural areas in the 19th century, and was linked to Wellington City by electric railway in 1938. The suburb rests in a small geographical basin. Housing here is available in a wide range of styles with something to suit every taste, ranging from well-maintained modern housing to early settler timber houses. It has good schools: three primaries, one intermediate and the decile 10 Onslow College.

Jacksonville was the first place in New Zealand to have a shopping mall, which was built in the 1960s. The shopping centre now houses, banks, bookshops, major supermarkets, clothes stores, bakeries, and so on. It serves people from the surrounding middle-class suburbs. There is a wide choice of takeaway outlets as well. Other facilities are excellent, including sports centres, a swimming pool complex, medical centres, retirement homes, and a community centre. Johnsonville is one of Wellington's fastest-growing districts, and there are still further subdivisions planned, so development and population looks set to continue in the foreseeable future.

Kaiwharawhara

Best for: Coastal living
Less good for: Established character properties
Price factor: NZ$450,000–NZ$700,000+ to buy; NZ$280–NZ$350 per week to rent

Another seaside suburb, Kaiwharawhara is north of the city centre on the western shore of Wellington Harbour. The railway station is on the Melling Line, the Hutt

Valley Line and the Paraparaumu Line and all trains go into the central city. There is a specialist organic grocery store and café here, great bush walks and a picnic and barbeque area beside the Kaiwharawhara stream. However, although a number of people do live here, there is not an especially large residential population – the area is more used by commercial and industrial businesses.

Kaiwharawhara is in-zone for several schools including Onslow College, Ngaio School, Northland School. The Kaiwharawhara Stream runs from Karori into Wellington Harbour.

Karori

Best for: Families, cycling, tramping
Less good for: Walking into town
Price factor: NZ$475,000–NZ$700,000+ to buy; NZ$320–NZ$750+ per week to rent

Karori is a beautiful historic area at the western edge of Wellington's urban area, and is New Zealand's largest suburb with a population of roughly 14,000 at the last count. Property here has raced up the popularity ladder over the last few years, with a corresponding startling hike in prices, but it's easy to see why. Karori has everything you will need for self-contained family living. Houses have decent-sized gardens, and properties are relatively flat (by Wellington standards), but as with so many areas in Wellington you must be vigilant against damp and check any property very carefully before committing to a purchase as damp can make life miserable.

You will find different sorts of homes here, ranging from stately colonial villas to modern executive residences. There are supermarkets, and not one but two little clusters of shops, as well as an excellent public library and a much-loved swimming pool complex. Schools here include Karori Normal, one of the oldest surviving primary school in New Zealand, St Teresa's School, Karori West Normal, and the Samuel Marsden Collegiate School (a private girls' school). The Karori Wildlife Sanctuary is the enclosed home to now-rare native birds that were once plentiful in this area. The hills around Karori offer several parks and reserves, and there are plenty of places for dog-walking and mountain-biking; Karori is home to the region's only dedicated mountain-biking park. Public transport runs along Karori Road in the form of a trolley bus which comes all the way from Lyall Bay; the service is extremely frequent compared to other routes around the city.

Kelburn

Best for: University access, cafés
Less good for: On-a-shoestring lifestyles
Price factor: NZ$425,000–NZ$690,000+ to buy; NZ$400–NZ$500+ per week to rent

One of the earliest settled suburbs of Wellington, Kelburn is home to the main campus of Victoria University of Wellington (the law school and other faculties are now based in different parts of the city). There are three other campuses: Pipitea, Karori and Te Aro. Victoria is well-known for programs in humanities, law and some sciences, and is one of only three New Zealand universities offering architecture. Ironically, although the university lives here, very few students can afford to, and hardly any student flats remain. Wellington students tend in general to be less 'scarfie' and rowdy than students at Canterbury, Lincoln, Massey and Otago, and are much more integrated with the city that hosts them; town and gown merge quite comfortably.

Kelburn is a prestigious address, and property prices are high, The cable car is a Wellington landmark, and runs from Lambton Quay up the hill for 800 metres crossing the motorway, with the second to last stop for the university and student residential hostels and the top terminal being close to the Botanic Gardens and the Carter Observatory. There are several entrances to the Botanic Garden, which is open between sunrise and sunset every day and includes rose gardens, plant collections, native forest, park areas, formal gardens, herb gardens and walkways. Kelburn Park on Salamanca Road is used for rugby, cricket, soccer, croquet, tennis and five-a-side; it also has a children's play area. Major roads also run through here, and bus services, as you might expect, and fairly good.

Kelburn village is made up of a cluster of rather good shops and cafés nestled together on Upland Road. There is a lovely old Anglican church here, an antique shop, a small supermarket, a good vet, pharmacy, wine store, butcher, hairdresser, beautician and florist as well as several lovely cafés (Caffe Mode is the locals' favourite), a wine bar, bakery, delicatessens and restaurants.

Best for: Sports and community facilities
Less good for: Property bargains
Price factor: NZ$400,000–NZ$630,000+ to buy; NZ$330–NZ$600+ per week to rent

Khandallah

One of Wellington's more affluent suburbs, Khandallah (meaning 'resting place of god') was named for the old Khandallah Homestead which was built in 1884 by Captain James Andrew after he retired from the Indian Army. Streets in Khandallah sport a high proportion of Indian-origin names. Above Khandallah stands Mount Kaukau, which supports the city's main television transmitter – this can be seen from far and wide. Churches in Khandallah serve Anglicans, Catholics and Presbyterians in the community and schools include Cashmere Avenue School and Khandallah School. Khandallah School accepts children from New Entrants through to Year 6, has about 350 pupils and is rated a decile 10. Children from this school general continue to Raroa Normal Intermediate.

There are many impressive older houses in Khandallah, as well as embassy residences, and many new, well-maintained modern properties. Community groups meet in the Onslow Community Church and the Khandallah Public Hall. The Khandallah Arts Theatre is home to an amateur theatre club which presents several productions every year. Other community facilities include Khandallah Park (with a café, picnic area and playground), the Khandallah Pool, Nairnville Park, the Khandallah Town Hall, scout club, bowling club, Plunket Toy Library, the Onslow

FACT

■ Property in Khandallah is sought-after; this is Wellington's wealthiest northern suburb, and houses frequently offer wonderful city views.

Historical Centre, several heritage building that are open to the public, the Arts and Crafts House, and the Khandallah Tennis and Squash Club.

From Khandallah it is an easy 10 minute drive into central Wellington city, and public transport connections are efficient and frequent.

Kilbirnie

Best for: Sports and fitness
Less good for: Arts and cultural activities
Price factor: NZ$345,000–NZ$445,000+ to buy; NZ$300–NZ$500+ per week to rent

Three km south-east of Wellington city centre, Kilbirnie is bordered by Hataitai, Lyall Bay and Melrose, and separated from Newtown by the town belt. Kilbirnie Recreation Centre is a modern facility for inline- and roller-skaters and skateboarders, as well as cyclists. It is also home to a preschool play space. There is a library here, a tennis club, a karate club, women's gym and the Wellington Region Aquatic Centre with its 50-metre pool.

Kilbirnie Park is the main sports park, used by both rugby and cricket clubs. A new indoor sports centre is planned for Cobham Park, and this will include 12 indoor courts. Local schools include St Patrick's Primary, Evan's Bay Intermediate, Kilbirnie School, and St Patrick's College.

Retailers include a children's bookshop, an organic food store, garden centre, bakery, specialist food suppliers as well as several large supermarkets, and there are also bars, takeaway outlets, cafés and a range of ethnic restaurants. The bigger, more 'retail park' stores for homewares, DIY and electronics etc., can be found in Lyall Bay out behind the airport, or of course in central Wellington.

Lyall Bay

Best for: Coastal living, sports
Less good for: Local shops
Price factor: NZ$425,000–NZ$735,000+ to buy; NZ$400–NZ$600+ per week to rent

Situated on the coast road between Wellington Airport and Island Bay, the Lyall Bay community is focused on the waterfront and there are few shops or amenities here apart from a few small shops and cafés near the beach. However, residents are only three minutes' drive from the comprehensive facilities of Kilbirnie. Wellington Airport is nearby, and noise from the planes can be a problem for some residents although most claim to grow used to it.

Lyall Bay is popular with surfers, windsurfers and kite fliers. Plans are in place to establish an artificial surf reef to increase the good surf here. There is a large zoned area on the beach where dogs are allowed to run off the leash, as well as a dedicated children's play area on the waterfront. Local primary Lyall Bay School is a decile five co-ed primary. Good value property can still be found here, both in the character timber homes on the hill and in the more modern family houses on flatter ground down below.

Makara

> **Best for:** Getting away from it all
> **Less good for:** Public transport
> **Price factor:** NZ$260,000+ to buy; NZ$260–NZ$350 per week to rent

Makara is a small settlement next to the beach on Wellington's south-west coast, often whipped by strong winds, but extremely invigorating. It is easily accessible from both Karori and Johnsonville, and the sea here offers boating, fishing and diving opportunities. The 'nature experience' here is more rugged isolation than manicured perfection, and you can walk for miles over the coastline and the hills around the bays from Makara Beach in both north and south directions. You can walk around the coast to Opau Bay and further, or up the hill past the site of a Maori *pa* towards Fort Opau before heading in across farmland and back towards the coast.

The 'authentically rusted' café at Makara (Ma and Pa's Seaside Café) on the beach offers coffee and wholesome food if you find yourself in need of fortification on the weekends. There is no public transport to Makara, but there is a golf course.

Miramar

> **Best for:** Amenities and affordable family housing
> **Less good for:** Students
> **Price factor:** NZ$420,000+ to buy; NZ$450 per week to rent

South-east of the city centre, this eastern suburb lies on the Miramar Peninsula next to Seatoun and Rongotai. Other suburbs on the Peninsula include Maupuia, Strathmore and The Heights. Try the Chocolate Frog Café (sister business to the Chocolate Fish Café) for great food and coffee. Local schools are Scots College, Miramar Christian School, Seatoun School, Holy Cross School, Strathmore Park School, Worser Bay School, Miramar North, Miramar Central and Miramar South. 'Art for Kids' classes are also held in Miramar, and there is a Kohanga Reo as well as various other preschool facilities.

There are several churches in Miramar, most notably the impressive Church of the Holy Cross on the corner of Miramar Avenue and Hobart Street. It was the first church with a curved roof in New Zealand, and the church bell was brought especially all the way from Limerick in Ireland. Local sports clubs include the Miramar Rangers, Miramar Bowling Club, Miramar Golf Club, Miramar Softball Club and the AFC soccer club.

Miramar enjoys a broad range of shops and services – there are pharmacies, a library, hairdressers, an art gallery and art supply shop, video library, travel agent, car rental, health practitioners such as GPs, chiropractors, podiatrists and dental services. Housing here is for the most part fairly modest, and consists of a large

FACT

■ Peter Jackson's special effects studios, film production and sound facilities and Weta Workshop are in Miramar. Jonah Lomu was another notable resident.

proportion of solid 1930s family homes. As with most areas of the city, house prices are being driven up by increasing demand, and young professionals and developers are looking to this area for investment and first-time buys.

Mount Cook

Best for: Cafés
Less good for: All-day sun
Price factor: NZ$410,000–NZ$665,000+ to buy; NZ$400–NZ$550+ per week to rent

Slightly confusingly not a mountain at all or even a terribly large hill, Mount Cook is to the north of Newtown. You can easily walk from here to the central city, and both Wellington High School and the Wellington campus of Massey University are located here. It is a sunny area in the summer, but watch out for damp especially in the winter. Properties here include lovely little colonial cottages, many of which have now been revamped by proud owners and developers.

Prince of Wales Park, on Salisbury Terrace, is used for rugby games and cricket matches. One of Wellington's most popular cafés, and the wholesaler of some of New Zealand's best coffee, is Caffe L'Affare on College Street. Welcoming and child-friendly, this is the place Wellington young professionals often choose to sip from steaming cups and munch on their Eggs Benedict from behind gently rustling weekend newspapers.

Mount Victoria

Best for: Bars and nightlife; views and sunshine
Less good for: Large gardens
Price factor: NZ$500,000–NZ$1.5 million+ to buy; NZ$285–NZ$600 per week to rent

One of the oldest and most established suburbs in Wellington, Mount Vic is a significant hill to the east of the CBD and home to a large number of residents, as well as business and churches. In the 1950s, this area was the centre of Wellington's Greek community, and in the 1960s a large proportion of residents were Samoan. Then new residents moved in and started renovating and refurbishing much of the housing, beginning the gentrification of the suburb.

Houses here are now priced well above average for the city, and create a wonderful bank of 19th-century façades watching over the harbour when viewed from below. The angle of these homes ensures afternoon sun and spectacular views. These wooden homes are well-loved and often carefully restored, and the image of them seemingly piled on top of each other on the hillside with St Gerard's Catholic church and monastery solidly protective behind is a staple Wellington postcard picture. Local schools include Clyde Quay, Wellington East Girls' College and Wellington College (for boys). Depending on your location in Mount Vic, walking down into the city centre or onto the waterfront takes only a few minutes. The lookout at the top of the hill offers panoramic views of the city and surrounding areas.

The much-loved Paramount Cinema has nestled on Courtenay Place at the foot of Mount Victoria since 1917, and has been substantially renovated in recent years. Most of the major film events for Wellington, such as the Italian Film Festival, Out Takes, and World Cinema Showcase are held here. Courtenay Place itself is crammed with good bars, cafés, restaurants, theatres and nightclubs, and bus transport links are excellent.

Mount Victoria has its own Rotary Club branch and Toastmasters' Society. Favourite local activities – if only to work off excessive enjoyment of all the bars and restaurants an easy stroll from your door – include walking, running and mountain biking.

Newlands

Best for: Schools
Less good for: Cafés and restaurants
Price factor: NZ$378,000–NZ$460,000+ to buy; NZ$360–NZ$500 per week to rent

A well-treed area with wide streets, Newlands is about 8km north of the CBD between Johnsonville and the harbour. Newlands is well served by buses to and from the city and Johnsonville. There are plenty of dairies and takeaway outlets around, there is an excellent new skate park, and Johnsonville shopping centre is only minutes' drive away.

Other local facilities include Newlands shopping mall, a community centre, dental clinics, a squash club, a tennis club, a scout group and several different churches. Newlands Park, on Newlands Road, is used for rugby, soccer, cricket and softball. The most prestigious properties, with stunning views of Wellington Harbour and the Hutt Valley, are to be found in the Dress Circle of the Bellevue Estate – homes here will set you back between NZ$600,000 and NZ$1million. However, other property in Newlands is much more affordable with some of the lowest comparable prices in Wellington, and includes several new housing subdivisions. The schools here and nearby are well-regarded; Newlands Intermediate and Newlands College both have decile 9

Best for: Diverse ethnic community
Less good for: Big chain retailers
Price factor: NZ$425,000–NZ$580,000+ to buy; NZ$300–NZ$580 per week to rent

ratings, and primary schools include Newlands, Rewa Rewa and Bellevue. There is also a choice of kindergartens and other preschool facilities available. Newlands College is now zoned due to increasing demand.

Newtown

Best for: Unpretentious family living
Less good for: Flash bachelor pads
Price factor: NZ$335,000 (section only)–NZ$680,000+ to buy; NZ$200–NZ$410 per week to rent

Newtown is a character-packed area of Wellington, with interesting shops, cafés and restaurants. Property prices are climbing as professionals flood in to take advantage of the area's proximity to the CBD and the popular small timber houses. Along the green belt lies the zoo, and next to this is Newtown Park – a natural amphitheatre with a 400-metre all-weather running track and sports stadium. There is a soccer ground above this. The National Hockey Stadium is also found in Newtown, as is the Wellington School of Medicine and Health Sciences of the University of Otago. Wellington Hospital is on Riddiford Street – this is the city's main hospital and the region's acute care hospital with services ranging from cardiology, intensive care, cancer care and neurosurgery. Private healthcare facilities in Newtown are the Ewart Hospital on Coromandel Street, Southern Cross Hospital on Hanson Street, and Wakefield Hospital on Florence Street.

The Newtown Community Centre is a venue for all sorts of different activities, including dance, martial arts, parties, public meetings and group meetings. It is also home to the Newtown community computing project, and the Newtown Citizen's Advice Bureau, a family budget service, and the Newtown Playcentre. Both the Hurricanes and the Wellington Lions use Rugby League Park, on Hall Street, for training. The New Zealand Drama School and the National Dance and Drama Centre share a purpose-built building on Hutchison Road. Newtown Library is a well-used and friendly facility, located on Constable Street. Nearby Melrose is home to the privately-owned 40-seat Time Cinema.

If you have a taste for Mexican food, try the excellent Mexican Café on Riddiford Street. Converts argue that the Pizzeria at Mediterranean Food Warehouse on Constable Street has the best pizza in the city. For coffee, cakes, breakfast, lunch, dinner and everything in between, sample the homemade delights at the child-friendly Ballroom Café upstairs near the intersection on Riddiford Street – you can't miss its yellow and purple façade and it's a great place to meet friends and relax for a couple of hours.

FACT

■ You could buy a good family home in Ngaio for between NZ$400,000 and NZ$500,000.

Ngaio

Ngaio lies next to Khandallah, and the two suburbs share the Indian influence apparent in their street names. Ngaio enjoys a more down-to-earth reputation than Khandallah, and the close-knit community here includes families and people of varying ages. Other neighbours are Crofton Downs and Wadestown. Facilities are excellent in Ngaio, with residents having use of a community hall, library, pharmacy, dentist, medical centre, Plunket rooms, toy library, churches and Ngaio School – the local co-ed primary. Other good quality schools are nearby, so there is plenty of choice. The small village boasts a popular café and a few shops, and it hosts the Ngaio Community Arts Festival as well.

There are plenty of parks and reserves in Ngaio – Trelissick Park is worth a special mention – as well as a tennis club and several community organisations.

Several buses run to nearby Johnsonville, and the commuter railway travels in and out of the central city from Ngaio Railway Station. The area is only about 10 minutes' drive from downtown Wellington. Ngaio lies on the main road between Johnsonville and Karori, in a small valley.

There is plenty of good quality family housing on offer here, with opportunities for DIY enthusiasts to really get stuck in. Property purchases prices cover a broad stretch, from under NZ$350,000 for a section with permission to build to over NZ$1million for a 'wow'-factor multi-bedroom, multi-bathroom property with swimming pool and spa pool on a huge section.

Northland

Northland lies on the city fringes in between Karori, Kelburn and Wilton. Local children usually attend either Cardinal McKeefry Catholic primary school in Wilton or Northland School on Harbour View Road. Northland's housing is a mix of old and new, conversions and renovations, ranging from big family homes to flats – there's something for everyone – and many properties here offer a view in one direction or another, ie of the harbour and city or the hills. It is a quick drive or bus ride from here down into the CBD, Parliament, the university and the law school, and Northland is a great place for young professionals or more advanced students with busy lifestyles.

On-the-go takeaway outlets are a feature of Northland's small group of shops, including pizza, burgers, fish and chips and other favourites. The Botanical Gardens Café is also nearby, as are the Kelburn shops on Upland Road. Ian Galloway Park, on Curtis Street, has facilities for rugby, cricket, softball, touch rugby, a BMX track and artificial surfaces.

Oriental Bay

Oriental Bay is named for the Oriental, one of the first ships to bring British settlers to the region. A very short drive or walk from the CBD, Oriental Parade along Oriental Bay is most Wellingtonians' favourite spot for a walk. Oriental Parade stretches all the way from the end of Kent Terrace at the foot of Mount Victoria round to Point Jerningham, and then as the road continues round to Kilbirnie it is renamed Evan's Bay.

Like Mission Bay in Auckland, it gets crammed with cyclists, rollerbladers, joggers, prams, dogs, families and general ice-cream-lickers on lovely sunny afternoons. A few years ago the waterfront had a major facelift with the beaches made bigger and sandier and even a whole new beach created near the Band Rotunda thanks to the re-homing of about 27,000 tonnes of golden sand from Takaka near Nelson, so it is now a great place for swimming, sunbathing and sandcastle-building too. There is a new pier and extra (much-needed) car-parking has been added in various spots. You will be spoilt for choice when it comes to looking for a bite to eat around Oriental Bay – try the Manhattan Lounge, the White House, Parade Café and Vista Café for starters – all have good food, great coffee and excellent views. There are a number of hotels along here, as well as a few art deco apartment blocks, modern apartments, and quite a few perfectly renovated and treasured and elegant old character homes as well. Demand is high, and prices are even higher – for a a two-bedroom apartment you might expect to pay a minimum of between NZ$550,000 and NZ$770,000: a family home here could cost you anywhere skywards from NZ$2 million.

Owhiro Bay

Best for: Seaside living
Less good for: Public transport
Price factor: NZ$385,000–NZ$635,000+ to buy; NZ$280+ per week to rent

Owhiro Bay is a fairly isolated spot with unsealed roads leading down to the bay itself. Home to the fur seal colony at Sinclair Head, and the Red Rocks, this is a popular spot for coastal walking. The shore here is barren and rocky, and pounded by the waves from Cook Strait although it is sheltered from the north winds to some extent due to being on the south coast.

Public transport is somewhat limited; a bus service that runs to Happy Valley passes by Owhiro Road, but does not run during weekends. The Owhiro Bay Quarry closed in 2000, when the site was purchased by Wellington City Council for 'restoration and rehabilitation' involving stabilising the slopes here with careful planting to prevent further erosion and water run-off.

Owhiro Bay School is on Happy Valley Road, and is a decile 9 rated co-ed.

Pipitea

Best for: Apartments close to work or law and business school
Less good for: Houses with gardens
Price factor: NZ$282,000–NZ$800,000+ to buy; NZ$390–NZ$550+ per week to rent

An area in the heart of downtown Wellington, Pipitea is home to the Law School Campus of Victoria University as well as the schools of Management, Government, Economics and Finance, Marketing and International Business, and Accounting and Commercial Law. About 6,000 students use this campus. There is a modern marae in Pipitea as well, built in the early 1980s for Wellington's urban Maori population. Transport links, as you might expect, are excellent, with buses, trains, the motorway, the ferries and the cable car all nearby.

This is not an area for family housing, of course, but there are apartments and flats on offer if living super-close to your work or study is important or you need a city crash-pad.

Rongotai

Best for: Access to the airport
Less good for: Nightlife and entertainment
Price factor: NZ$400,000–NZ$465,000+ to buy; NZ$280–NZ$400+ per week to rent

Close to Lyall Bay, Miramar and Kilbirnie, and home to Wellington Airport, Rongotai is one of the eastern suburbs. There is a retail park here, and the inevitable traffic accompanies this. Other shopping is nearby at Miramar and in Kilbirnie. Residentially, Rongotai is a relatively small suburb, and is often lumped in with Evan's Bay or Kilbirnie. Rongotai College is the local co-ed state school. Local sports clubs include the Oriental Rongotai Football Club and the Wellington Aero Club is based in Rongotai.

There are strong community groups and residents' associations around this area, such as the Kilbirnie/Lyall Bay/Rongatai Progressive Association, and they raise and discuss issues such as noise pollution from the airport and proposed council development plans.

For eating out, try Carlton Café on Coutts Street or head to the nearby suburbs with waterfront cafés and restaurants.

Roseneath

Best for: Lofty living with harbour views
Less good for: University access
Price factor: NZ$530,000–NZ$1million+ to buy; NZ$500–NZ$1,500+ per week to rent

Perched on the hill above Oriental Bay, at the northern end of Mount Victoria, Roseneath is a well-established area and a prestigious address which emerged as a small area of Wellington in about 1888. This little inner-city suburb is an easy stroll down the hill to Oriental Bay or Evan's Bay (although slightly more effort is required in the other direction of course), and has a good café called Feast as well as a hairdresser.

Roseneath School is an excellent small co-ed primary with a great reputation, and there is a High Anglican church (St Barnabas) perched on the hill on Maida Vale Road as well. Property here comes in all shapes and sizes – from small character cottages to sleek modern apartments, and there is a selection of carefully maintained large Edwardian and Victorian family villas as well. Many offer fine views across the city or the harbour, and homes here are amongst the most valuable of any real estate in Wellington.

Seatoun and Karaka Bay

Best for: Seaside village living
Less good for: Transport to city
Price factor: NZ$450,000– NZ$1 million+ to buy; NZ$400–NZ$700+ per week to rent

A lovely seaside community with a village atmosphere, Seatoun is a coastal sanctuary 7km southeast of central Wellington city. It is only minutes' drive from the airport, and 15 minutes from town. Property prices here are high; Seatoun Heights boasts some of Wellington's premier houses with extremely grand views. As Seatoun's popularity continues to climb, so homes around here are snapped up despite fairly significant price tags. Windsurfing, kayaking, swimming, fishing, cycling, diving and walking along the shore are all popular activities. Several yacht clubs – including Worser Bay, Evans Bay and Port Nicholson – are within 10km. The Wellington public transport network (Metlink) is currently trialing a new ferry service, which travels from Days Bay to Queens Wharf via Seatoun. If successful, this trial will result in increased services to both Days Bay and Seatoun.

For brunch, lunch, supper and a roaring fire in winter try Solstice restaurant and café on Dundas Street. For a more informal café experience in a gorgeous setting, visit the Chocolate Fish Café opposite the popular sheltered swimming beach at Scorching Bay, along Karaka Bay Road.

Schools in this area include Seatoun School, Strathmore Park School and Worser Bay School (a state primary). Only minutes' drive away you'll find two excellent garden centres, both with in-house cafés, and Miramar Golf Links is easily accessibly from Seatoun.

Strathmore Park

FACT

■ There are significant numbers of Greek and Turkish immigrants in the Strathmore Park community.

Best for: Families and sports
Less good for: A car-free lifestyle
Price factor: NZ$275,000–NZ$445,000+ to buy; NZ$380–NZ$600+ per week to rent

Strathmore Park grew up around Scots College (an independent boys' secondary and preparatory school for day students and weekly boarders) after the private school opened in 1919. From the 1930s it was the site of a state housing development. Strathmore Park Kindergarten is on Strathmore Ave and Strathmore Park School is just across the road from Scots College.

Playing grounds and shopping centres are to be found here, as well as the Strathmore Bakery and Café. Metlink buses 43 and 44 run between Strathmore and Khandallah through central Wellington on weekdays only, and with extra services during rush hour.

There is a Community Health Service here and several excellent cafés in nearby Miramar.

Tawa

Best for: Families
Less good for: Independent shops
Price factor: NZ$339,000–NZ$440,000+ to buy; NZ$280–NZ$350+ per week to rent

Tawa is 15–20 minutes from the CBD with good motorway access. It is also on the main railway line into central Wellington. There is a low- to medium-security women's prison here, but it does not pose any problems for families in the area.

Originally a small farming settlement, the creation of subdivisions for housing and development was begun after 1945. There are good parks and schools here; notable is Tawa College, a decile 9 co-ed state secondary school with the roll of over 1300. The school maintains close contact with the surrounding community and has a good reputation for the arts, particularly singing. Other schools include Greenacres, Hampton Hill, Linden, Redwood, St Francis Xavier, Tawa School and Tawa Intermediate.

The Tawa Recreation Centre offers facilities for clubs, community groups and casual use as well as sports such as badminton, basketball, indoor football, netball, volleyball and table tennis. After-school and holiday programmes for children are held here too, and the centre can be hired for children's birthday parties.

There are a number of churches in Tawa, including the Tawa Gospel Hall, the Union Church, Anglican, Catholic and Salvation Army churches, and the Tawa Samoan Community of God. There are plenty of community groups in Tawa, including health and support groups, groups for senior citizens, youth and children, and sports and recreation clubs. Tawa Plaza and Tawa Mall are the main shopping areas – offerings are, fairly predictably, mainly chain retailers, supermarkets and so on, but you will be able to satisfy your daily household and grocery needs here.

Thorndon

Best for: Proximity to Parliament and CBD
Less good for: Direct sunshine hours
Price factor: NZ$585,000–NZ$1million+ to buy; NZ$450–NZ$700+ per week to rent

Thorndon is only a short work from Parliament, the National Library, government buildings and the CBD, so residents are always close to the best public transport central Wellington has to offer. The Westpac Stadium, an international-class venue for rugby matches and one-day cricket, can be accessed from Thorndon Quay. Bolton Street Cemetery is the final resting place of William Wakefield and other notable early settlers. However many of the graves were damaged or demolished when the motorway ploughed through here in the 1950s.

Wellington Girls' College, a decile 10 secondary with a roll of over 1200, is on Pipitea Street and other local schools include Thorndon Primary School and Queen

123

Margaret College. There is a Taekwon-Do club in Thorndon, as well as the heated outdoor Thorndon Pool.

High-end shops sell antiques and collectables, original art, designer women's clothing and boutique homewares as well as interior decoration desirables. There are some acclaimed restaurants and cafés carefully positioned at the Glenmore Road end of Tinakori Road, a renowned fresh fruit supplier and one of the city's largest central supermarkets. Property is varied – some original workers' cottages remain, as well as large old colonial family homes, and there a modern apartments and townhouses now as well. One thing has not changed however, and that is the prestige factor of a Thorndon address. Along Tinakori Road remain some of the original 19th-century shops and commercial buildings, still in use by retailers, designers, consultants and other small businesses. The Botanic Gardens lie on the hill between Thorndon and Kelburn.

Thorndon was famously the birthplace of author Katherine Mansfield, and the house she lived in has been painstakingly restored and survives as a tourist attraction.

Vogeltown and Mornington

Best for: Golfers
Less good for: Local shops, public transport
Price factor: NZ$385,000–NZ$485,000+ to buy; NZ$360–NZ$500 per week to rent

Vogeltown overlooks Newtown, from the hill to the east of Brooklyn. Mornington is tucked into a sheltered position on the hills behind Brooklyn. The Mornington Golf Club is on Adelaide Road, along with Berhampore Golf Club, close to Wakefield Park. Ridgway School is a co-ed primary with a decile 9 rating and a roll of about 170 pupils; it is located on Mornington Road. There are various community groups in this area, including martial arts groups and an indoor bowling club. Public transport links and shopping facilities are not fantastic, but are better at nearby Brooklyn.

Wadestown and Wilton

Best for: Gardeners
Less good for: Restaurants
Price factor: NZ$450,00–NZ$650,000+ to buy; NZ$280–NZ$600 per week to rent

Wadestown is located on the southern slopes of Ngaio Gorge and Wellington's western hills above Thorndon, only a few minutes' drive from the CBD, and Wilton is north-west of the city centre, behind Wadestown. Both are leafy lovely suburbs, increasingly popular and with excellent bus connections – close enough to the city for easy access, but far enough away to feel you are keeping the hustle and bustle at arm's length. The local shops on Wadestown Road are a gathering point for local residents. Homes here are established and elegant, with decent-sized mature gardens and attractive street presence, and the average resident is relatively affluent. Originally these areas were workers' settlements but now residents are typically professionals and public servants, and/or from the older, more established Wellington families and living in the family homes.

Wilton Park is used for soccer and cricket games, and the Otari-Wilton bush is a great place to get away from it all in 100 hectares of botanic garden dedicated to native plants and forest. For budding botanists, the Wadestown-Wilton Horticultural Society meets and holds events monthly at St Luke's Centre on the corner of Pitt Street and Wadestown Road. The Western Suburbs Junior Rugby Club is based at Ian Galloway Park, there is a Plunket service here.

Cardinal McKeefry is a Catholic primary and intermediate school catering for both boys and girls; Wilton and Wadestown are both in-zone for Onslow College. Other local schools include Wadestown School, Otari School and a Montessori school. The Wilton Playcentre is an early childhood centre on Gloucester Street.

Main residential areas of Christchurch

It is important to note that Christchurch does not have suburbs with precisely delineated or legal boundaries – suburbs are simply references to general areas of the city. For prospective house-buyers, this means you must be extra vigilant with estate agents and property locations, particularly if living in a particular area or being in-zone for a particular school is important to you and your family. Even if you never intend to have a family, zone issues have an important impact on resale value.

Central City

Hagley Park is the best known park in the city, and the largest at 160 hectares. It is a great place for running, walking, tennis, golf, rugby, soccer, hockey and cricket with many sports groups, particularly runners, meeting here. There are large open areas and enormous established oak trees. The central city library is on the corner of Gloucester Street and Oxford Terrace. Alice in Videoland is a wonderful DVD and video library with a tremendous rental collection.

Try Dux de Lux at the corner of Montreal and Hereford Streets; it is a microbrewery and restaurant offering excellent seafood and vegetarian food, and is one of the most popular places in town. There are countless other opportunities for dining, shopping, sports and fitness, coffee, theatre and cinema outings, and all the other delights of an established city.

South of Lichfield Street square is packed with bars, restaurants and apartments, full of young professionals. Accommodation is varied, from period villas and old workers' cottages through to the increasing numbers of inner-city apartments.

Best for: Proximity to bars, cafés and CBD
Less good for: Parking
Price factor: NZ$220,000–NZ$600,000+ to buy; NZ$280–NZ$600+ per week to rent

Addington

Best for: Inner city location
Less good for: Space and gardens
Price factor: NZ$220,000–NZ$400,000+ to buy; NZ$225–380+ per week to rent

Home to the famous Addington Raceway, this suburb grew up around the Addington railway station from the 1860s onwards. The new Christchurch Railway Station was built here in 1994. The journey, measuring 231km, is a popular tourist attraction and is a spectacular experience. Addington is situated close to State Highway 73 (a short motorway) and lies 2.5km south-west of the city centre. This area is still rather industrial, with a variety of warehouses, factories and other businesses, but although it used to be a lower socio-economic area because of its inner city location it is precisely this factor that is giving Addington a hand up onto the 'fashionable property' ladder again.

There is now an interesting mix of light industrial, residential and retail properties here, and Addington is close to a number of sports venues, particularly those in south Hagley Park. Trendy cafés such as the Tea Room and Vanilla Bean reflect the tastes of the new residents now choosing this area for their homes.

You can find authentic old cottages and bungalows around here, and developers have started filling it up with urban-style apartments for buyers keen on the inner city lifestyle. Unsurprisingly, Addington is more popular with childless professionals or student couples than families. Buildings are fairly densely packed, so you are unlikely to find the classic Kiwi quarter-acre here, but for those looking for low-maintenance living with easy access to the city bars, cafés, cinemas and shopping it has a lot to offer.

Aranui

Best for: Affordable housing
Less good for: Safety and schooling
Price factor: NZ$220,000–NZ$280,000+ to buy; NZ$175–NZ$300 per week to rent

North of the Estuary, this working-class and ethnically-mixed suburb was originally a small village built around the tram lines that ran out to New Brighton. It is now served by bus routes numbers 51 and 5. It sits in eastern Christchurch, 5.5 km from the central city. There is a lot of state housing here, mainly built after the Second World War, so mostly mid- to late-20th century houses and units. There are few sections available. Local recreation areas include Cuthbert's Green, Bexley Reserve, Delamane Park, Waionui Park and a few smaller reserves.

There are a few supermarkets, including New World and Pak'n'Save and several independents of the 'corner shop' variety. The main shopping areas are Aranui Shopping Centre and Hampshire Street Shopping Centre.

There is a Seventh-Day Adventist church here, an old people's home and hospital as well as a community learning centre offering classes in everything from gentle fitness to languages and computer skills.

Aranui School is a decile 1 state co-ed with a roll of about 250, and Aranui High School also offers Adult Studies programmes. Other local schools include St James, and Chisnallwood Intermediate.

Avonhead

Best for: Proximity to airport, College of Education
Less good for: Old character properties
Price factor: NZ$180,000–NZ$700,000+ to buy; NZ$360–NZ$400 per week to rent

Avonhead is 7km north-west of central Christchurch, not far from the airport. Christchurch College of Education is only a few minutes away. Local schools include Avonhead School, Russley School, Merrin School and Westburn School. Burnside High, with its excellent reputation as a co-ed school, is also handy. There are plenty of leisure and recreation opportunities, with nearby green spaces including Crosbie Park, Avonhead Park, Burnside Park, Ferrier Park, Hyde Park, and many smaller reserves scattered throughout the area. Burnside Park has playing fields for senior and junior rugby and cricket, and the swimming facilities at Jellie Park are close.

Avonhead Shopping Centre incorporates a large supermarket and a range of

other shops, and the Bush Inn Centre is home to a popular restaurant/bar. Other dining options include the Merrin Street Café, for a la carte dining, as well as a range of takeaway options and small cafés. There are plenty of choices of ethnic restaurants in the nearby Upper Riccarton/Church Corner area. You will be able to serve most of your shopping needs here, but shopping strips in Upper Riccarton and on Waimari Road are very close by.

Housing is largely stand-alone homes built around the 1970s or more recently. Older family houses (from the 1950s) can be found in neighbouring Burnside.

Avonside

Best for: Schools, access to the river
Less good for: Shopping
Price factor: NZ$270,000–NZ$650,000+ to buy; NZ$240–NZ$330 per week to rent

The Avonside area borders the Avon River (as its name might suggest), and it is built on the fertile soils of the river's flood plain. As Christchurch was being developed in the early years, this area had a reputation for being extremely swampy and not particularly conducive to travel. The Avonside parish church was built in 1874, and the original parish (established in 1859) covered much of what now comprises Aranui, Burwood, Linwood, Marshlands, New Brighton North New Brighton, Parklands and part of Phillipstown.

Avonside Girls High School is located here – like a number of other schools, it provides special programmes and support for international students for a price. Avonside is a state school for girls from Years 9–13 and has a role of about 1200. Set in park-like grounds in historic buildings, beside the river, Avonside is a well-regarded school with excellent resources.

Beckenham

Best for: New library
Less good for: Bars and nightlife
Price factor: NZ$250,000–NZ$460,000+ to buy; NZ$250–NZ$320 per week to rent

Located 3km south of the city centre, Beckenham is a peaceful, green and predominantly residential inner suburb built around the Heathcote River. There are several churches in this area, serving Baptists, Anglicans and Methodists. Beckenham School is a state co-ed primary school with a medium-decile rating and a roll of about 450.

For basic but reliable dining out, try Tuskers Bar and Bistro, for pizza go to Filadelfio's, or for large, café-style eats go to Sophie's Café.

The new Christchurch South Library includes a café; it is part of Christchurch's excellent public library system and serves a number of adjoining suburbs.

Bryndwr

Best for: Proximity to bars, cafés and restaurants in surrounding areas
Less good for: Property bargains
Price factor: NZ$270,000–NZ$370,000+ to buy; NZ$335–NZ$420+ per week to rent

Bryndwr is generally considered to be the area around Aorangi and Wairakei Roads. This is one of the very few New Zealand places with a Welsh name – it means 'next to the water'. For the first 100 or so years of European settlement, this area was farmed in manageable blocks devoted to orchards, sheep, cattle and market gardens.

There is a considerable proportion of state housing from the 1950s and 1960s, which mushroomed during the peak in demand after the Second World War, as well as a mix of other types of housing including bigger more established homes and infill housing. There is now very little undeveloped land left around Bryndwr and Burnside, but this area is covered in established trees and parts have a pleasant leafy feel.

The area boasts some fairly fancy neighbours: Merivale, Burnside and Fendalton. Bryndwr is in the Burnside catchment area, and also has an excellent library.

Schools in Bryndwr itself include St Patrick's (a Catholic school for Years 1–8 with a roll of 175) and Aorangi Primary, and it is close to the Burnside schools as well.

Burnside

Best for: Sports activities, schools and parks
Less good for: Neighbourhood cafés
Price factor: NZ$340,000–NZ$700,000+ to buy; NZ$280+ per week to rent

The Burnside area was originally part of a farm with a large homestead owned by William Boag. The area is adjacent to Christchurch International Airport, and Russley Golf Course. Like Bryndwr, Burnside experienced rapid growth as the expansion of Christchurch forced the city outwards. This sprawl only expanded as servicemen returned home from the Second World War and began buying land and building homes for their families. In the 9 years following 1945 approximately 12,000 new homes were built in these areas combined, and there sprang up many new subdivisions. For while in the 1950s and 1960s this area was one of the most rapidly expanding in the whole of the country. Now there is little remaining development potential here, and a significant amount of infill housing, but there are also older houses either in need of a spruce-up or fresh from a sale-enhancing facelift; property prices are therefore correspondingly wide-ranging.

Burnside surrounds a central park called, predictably enough, Burnside Park, as well as Jellie Park, which is smaller. Burnside Park is used for tennis, bowls, soccer, rugby and touch rugby. Aqualand, with its indoor and outdoor pools and aquaslide is in Jellie Park, although it is not currently open as it is being redeveloped.

There are a number of schools here, including Burnside Primary, Burnisde High, Kendal School, Isleworth School, Cobham Intermediate, Roydvale School and Christ the King Primary. The high school is very popular, and this does tend to drive house prices up. There is a bowling club here, a community church in which various events including exercise classes are held, a rugby club, a fitness centre, and as with most of Christchurch there are excellent opportunities for walking and cycling. Residents normally shop in neighbouring suburbs.

Cashmere

Best for: Fabulous views
Less good for: The unfit
Price factor: NZ$385,000–NZ$1 million+ to buy; NZ$380+ per week to rent

Cashmere is the oldest suburb on the lower Port Hills, with the oldest houses dating from the 1890s. It incorporates the areas known in real estate language as Cashmere Hills (some super-swish, ultra-modern pads, with price tags to match) and Cashmere Flats (still aspirational, pricey and much in demand). Property here is fairly established-feeling, with the older homes enjoying long-established and well-cared-for gardens.

It is a fashionable place to live, having always been popular because of the view. It is relatively close to the excellent Christchurch South Library. There are a number of parks and reserves in Cashmere, a tennis club and a bowling club, as well as excellent cafés and bars such as Fava, women's fitness and treatments centre Chillspace, and fashion clothing boutique Lavish.

Cashmere High School is a well-regarded state school with a most recent roll count of about 1,700, making it one of Christchurch's largest.

Fendalton

Best for: Prestigious address
Less good for: Those on a budget
Price factor: NZ$550,000–NZ$2 million+ to buy; NZ$380–NZ$500+ per week to rent

FACT

■ Fendalton is the most expensive of Christchurch's suburbs, and many fashionable properties were built here in the late 19th and early 20th centuries.

A desirable area, with established trees in the gardens of the older homes, roomy period houses full of character, and a distinct 'old money' feel. Property here is very expensive, and if you are thinking of buying here you must be vigilant in monitoring real estate agent claims about area.

Fendalton is zoned for Christchurch Girls' High and Christchurch Boys' High, which are considered the city's most prestigious schools. The surrounding areas do not necessarily fall within these zones; be careful to check exact zoning boundaries and restrictions before you buy as you may pay up to about NZ$70,000 more for a property just to be in the zones. Fendalton School is also located here. Fendalton Library is another of Christchurch's good public libraries.

FACT

Lyttleton is probably the most arty and bohemian area of Christchurch, home to an interesting collection of painters, potters, textile artists and other craftspeople and musicians.

The main route to the airport from the city runs through the centre of Fendalton. There are excellent delicatessans here, cafés, and a great sports and fitness centre.

Ilam

Best for: Proximity to university
Less good for: Restaurants
Price factor: NZ$295,000–NZ$500,000+ to buy; NZ$260–NZ$380 per week to rent

The University of Canterbury, as well as the main campus of the Christchurch College of Education (CCE), is situated in the leafy suburb of Ilam, which is about 5km northwest of the city centre and close to Riccarton. There is a lot of student accommodation here, as you might expect. The university also runs a community education programme which covers a diverse range of topics including languages, writing, business, personal development and so on. Sessions are usually held during the weekend or in the evenings, and courses normally run for one term and are reasonably priced.

Cobham Intermediate is a state co-ed for Years 7 and 8 with a roll of about 740 and a decile 8 rating, and Ilam Primary School is also located in this area, as is Villa Maria College – a Catholic girls' school for Years 7–13. Ilam is home to the Christchurch Science Centre.

Linwood

This large eastern suburb is for the most part working class and lower middle class. Linwood was the home of the original Edmonds baking powder factory that achieved fame and still inspires endless nostalgia in Kiwis around the world with its appearance on the Edmonds Cookbook front cover. In 2007, police named Linwood as one of Christchurch's burglary hotspots; it seems that crime statistics are worse on the Aranui side, and there is a fair bit of graffiti here.

Linwood is home to Eastgate Shopping Centre, a well-used library and schools: Linwood Aveue Primary, Linwood Intermediate and Linwood College. Linwood College is a co-ed secondary school with a culturally diverse roll of over 1,000. It services surrounding communities from Lyttleton and the Bays to Sumner/Redcliffs. There is a sewage treatment plant and oxidisation pond, which is landscaped and renowned for birdlife, near Linwood. The area gets busy at rush hour with commuter traffic passing through on its way between the city and Sumner.

Best for: Affordable housing
Less good for: Going out
Price factor: NZ$215,000–NZ$380,000+ to buy; NZ$200–NZ$300 per week to rent

Lyttleton

Best for: Harbourside community living
Less good for: Access to the CBD
Price factor: NZ$275,000–NZ$850,000+ to buy; NZ$250–NZ$555 per week to rent

Lying about 10km from Cathedral Square in central Christchurch, Lyttleton is built on a hilly harbourside landscape and is built around a working port.

There are plenty of hillside scenic reserves here, as well as Lyttleton playing fields, a recreation centre, a library, the Corsair Bay reserve and lots to do in and around the harbour.

Local shops can be found on 'shopping strips' along London Street, Oxford Street and Norwich Quay, and bus route 28 serves this area. The local schools are Lyttleton Main, Lyttleton West, St Joseph's and Linwood High. There are few sections available for building on and development out here now, but a fairly broad selection of housing styles presents itself. Homes range from mid-19th-century cottages through to large, sleek, modern houses on the upper slopes.

Mairehau

Best for: Family homes
Less good for: Students, renting
Price factor: NZ$239,000–NZ$400,000+ to buy; NZ$235–NZ$420 per week to rent

Mairehau residents enjoy living in a community that is close to central Christchurch, and has good access to public transport, although the area does have something of a reputation for being on the rough side.

Mairehau High School is decile 4 and co-educational, and has a good reputation for basketball. Its catchment area is diverse with contributing schools ranging from decile 1 to 10. Contributing schools range from a primary school with around 70 students to an intermediate school with a roll of over 800. Within the school's catchment are extensive new housing developments and it is anticipated that roll growth will continue for some years yet. The school is also being redeveloped over the next few years.

Merivale

Best for: Luxury delicatessens and boutiques, private schools
Less good for: Real estate bargains
Price factor: NZ$400,000–NZ$1 million+ to buy; NZ$220–NZ$700+ per week to rent

Another inner suburb, Merivale is a trendy and desirable area to live, and property prices reflect this. With living space in demand, there is an increasing amount of infill housing as people cash in on the rush by subdividing their sections to build (and sell on) new homes. There are very few sections available in this area, and housing styles range from brand new to 19th-century buildings, as well as townhouses and units. Bars, cafés and several high-end clothes boutiques are sited in the busy shopping stretch on Papanui Road, as well as local favourite Italian restaurant Tutto Bene.

The upmarket Merivale Mall is packed with shops stocking fashion accessories, clothing, shoes, gifts, homeware, health and beauty products and services and so on.

Just behind the mall on Aikmans Road you will find a clutch of smart bars and restaurants nestled in the courtyard – definitely the place to be seen. Other shopping is on offer on Papanui Road as well as in the Holmwood Shopping Centre. Gourmet takeaways can be found at Traiteur of Merivale, with a weekly-changing menu and a generous range of options. Local amenities include Elmwood Park, Abberley Park and Millbrook Reserve. You can drive to the inner city from Merivale in just five minutes, and a number of bus routes serve this area as well including the Metrostar and routes 10, 11, 12, 13 and 15.

St George's private hospital is located in Merivale, along with a number of medical specialists. St Margaret's College is an independent, decile 10 Anglican girls' school for both boarders and day pupils in Merivale – it achieves excellent results, and is attended by about 145 boarders, with a total roll of 740 or so. Rangi Ruru Girls' School is another independent, and has places for girls from Year 7 to Year 13. St Andrew's College is a decile 10 private co-ed with enrolments from pre-school age through to Year 13. It is the South Island's only co-ed independent primary and secondary school. Other nearby schools include Elmwood Normal, Selwyn House, Ferndale, Heaton Intermediate, Christchurch Girls' High and Christchurch Boys' High.

New Brighton

Best for: Self-contained community feel
Less good for: Immediate access to the CBD
Price factor: NZ$225,000–NZ$400,000+ to buy; NZ$180–NZ$400 per week to rent

New Brighton is a seaside suburb on the beach of Pegasus Bay. Landscape here is flat, and of course coastal, and the area is about 8km from central Christchurch. Named of course for Brighton in England, the community was even given its own pier in 1894 although this was demolished in 1965 and replaced with a new concrete pier. The pier and its building are across the road from the New Brighton Mall, a shopping street containing many shops and food outlets – it was popular in the 1960s as one of the few places where Saturday shopping was permitted. Shops are located on Estuary Road and Caspian Street. New Brighton is a lower socio-economic area, but might be due a renaissance in part because of its coastal location and the lovely beach, and recently land has been subdivided and the Parklands suburb has spread out.

Houses and developments crept south down the Spit since the 1950s, and North Beach (north of New Brighton) used to have its own tram and trolley bus lines into central Christchurch. Now Christchurch City Bus Services run between the city and New Brighton regularly and frequently on route numbers 5, 40, 51 and 60, and the journey takes about 25 minutes. The closest schools are South New Brighton Primary, North New Brighton and Aranui High. Christchurch City Council is currently implementing its 'New Brighton Revitalisation' plan, so the area looks set to increase in popularity. Recreation opportunities here include fishing, swimming, playing with the rugby club, walking on the beach and dunes or along the Pegasus Bay Track and estuary. Amenities include Rawhiti Domain, South New Brighton Park (containing Pleasant Point Domain), South New Brighton Park and Kibblewhite Reserve.

The nearby QEII Sport and Leisure Centre on Travis Road offers a stack of classes and activities, including aerobics, Pilates, yoga, dance, prenatal and mother-and-baby courses, Tai Chi, swimming classes, and hydro-slides. Recreation classes offered by the QEII for pre-school and school age children include gymnastics, jazz and hip-hop dance, fitness, basketball, and general ball skills for hockey, rugby and soccer. Thomson Park is nearby, and the New Brighton Library is situated right on the beach. Cafés to try include the Salt on the Pier and Heller & Hibbs, and good pizza can be found at Spagalimis.

FACT

■ Godwit birds arriving from Siberia and Alaska fly into the reserve at the end of the spit to spend the summers.

Northwood

Best for: New homes
Less good for: Fancy restaurants
Price factor: NZ$370,000–NZ$500,000+ to buy; NZ$330 per week to rent

A new outer subdivision to the north of Christchurch, with facilities including the Northwood Shopping Centre and Northwood Gardens. There is also a supermarket and a pre-school with a créche.

Northwood covers about 77 hectares, and includes 630 houses on 285–1,500 metre-squared lots, as well as a 64-unit retirement village and 40 medium-density terraced houses. The area was developed over a 5-year period, based on a master plan, on a flat river terrace between Styx Mill Reserve, which is a major wetland area, and two state highways.

The area is great for cyclists and pedestrians, with routes possible through reserves as well as along roads and pathways, and public transport is provided by route 12.

TIP

■ There is a great kite shop on Opawa Road.

Opawa

Best for: Established housing
Less good for: Occasional flooding
Price factor: NZ$225,000–NZ$365,000+ to buy; NZ$290–NZ$330 per week to rent

A fashionable southern suburb, and about 2.5km south-east of the city centre, Opawa is next to St Martins and Woolston. Built around the Opawa River, there have been occasions on which flooding has proved a problem for Opawa residents. The area is located alongside Brougham Street, which is one of the city's main arterial routes. Much of this area remained as farmland until well into the 20th century. There is plenty of lovely established housing here, and the Rudolf Steiner school, and the Alpineice Sport and Entertainment Centre (offering ice skating etc.) is located on Brougham St.

Papanui

Best for: Mall shopping
Less good for: Clothing boutiques and independent bohemian cafés
Price factor: NZ$270,000-$500,000+ to buy; NZ$270-$320 per week to rent

Papanui is 5km from the city centre, to the north-west, and is a middling sort of area in terms of typical income, house prices, etc. The Sanitarium Health Food Company is based here, employing a number of locals. Sanitarium produces many New Zealand breakfast cereals as well as So Good Soy Milk, a range of vegetarian products, Marmite and peanut butter.

Papanui is also home to Northlands Shopping Centre, the South Island's largest shopping mall and entertainment centre. It has been here for 36 years, and underwent significant development in 2004. The centre houses a Lonestar restaurant, Hoyts cinema complex, The Warehouse, Farmers, supermarkets, fashion clothing stores, gift and homeware shops, banks and ATMs, food retailers and outlets, travel agents, shoe shops, hairdressers and shops for children's clothes and toys. Buses run from Christchurch city centre to Papanui, and the Orbiter bus runs around a ring of suburbs including Cashmere, Riccarton, Burnside, New Brighton, Linwood and St Martins and also stops at the mall. Papanui High School serves the secondary-age population (Years 9–13) here, and is a mid-decile school with a roll of over 1,400. Several primary and intermediate schools in the area feed into the high school.

Redcliffs

Redcliffs is a very pleasant area with a warm community feel. Barnett Park is the location for the new purpose-built Community Crèche building; the crèche is a not-for-profit organisation originally established 25 years ago by the Sumner Running Club to provide members with somewhere to leave children, giving them time to exercise. Because of its location in the Port Hills, between Lyttleton and Christchurch Harbour, Redcliffs enjoys its own microclimate. It is one of Christchurch's outer coastal suburbs, next to Sumner. Redcliffs School and James Street pre-school are sited in this area.

There are a number of medical services, and retirement and rest homes here. Properties are generally suitable for mid- to high-range budgets. There are plentiful opportunities for running, walking and cycling, and nearby Sumner offers plentiful dining choices. Redcliffs is also close to the estuary, with its leisure opportunities for activities such as yachting and windsurfing.

Riccarton

TIP

■ Riccarton Racecourse hosts a Sunday market for bargain hunters.

Best for: Students; motels
Less good for: Traffic congestion
Price factor: NZ$210,000–NZ$500,000+ to buy; NZ$220–NZ$500 per week to rent

Riccarton is west of the city centre, 3km from Cathedral Square. It is close to Canterbury University in nearby Ilam, and so a popular choice for students. There are a significant number of low-rent student flats here, but there are pockets of other sorts of residential housing around. There are older properties still here, but developers are converting these into flats or knocking them down as they get their hands on them. Very few sections are available to build on. Nevertheless, the range of housing is still fairly large, from 19th-century timber houses through to contemporary homes with many townhouses and flats.

Dining-out options are what you might expect in the cheap-and-cheerful range: noodle houses, buffets and bars, as well as the usual range of takeaway and fast food outlets. There are also fancier choices, particularly along Rotherham Street, which really comes alive with bars, restaurants and nightlife in the evenings. Transport links are good, with regular buses including Orbiter, Metrostar, Routes 3 (Avonhead), 5 (Hornby), 19 (Burnside), 24 (Hyde Park), and 83 (Hei Hei).

Riccarton Road is an oasis for the motel-hunter as they stand almost shoulder-to-should all along the street; the number of unremarkable and 'reasonably priced' choices for a night's accommodation is dizzying.

The closest schools are Wharenui, St Teresa's, Kirkwood Intermediate, Christchurch Girls' High and Christchurch Boys' High. Westfield Mall (formerly called Riccarton Mall) on Riccarton Road, houses a department store, supermarket, and theatre complex. Other amenities include Hagley Park, Riccarton Bush and Wharenui Pool. There is a martial arts school in Riccarton, as well as health and fitness centres, and several different churches. Riccarton House is a heritage site covering almost 12 hectares, with historic buildings set in parkland and gardens, next to a stream

TIP

■ If you are partial to a good curry, treat yourself at Mantra on North Avon Road in the village.

and surrounded by native forest full of wonderful old trees. There is a restaurant and a café here, as well as an outdoor courtyard for refreshments. The western end of Riccarton is understood to be a separate suburb, known as Upper Riccarton.

Richmond

Best for: Transport
Less good for: Shopping
Price factor: NZ$245,000–NZ$540,000 to buy; NZ$230–NZ$320 per week to rent

Located to the inner north-east of Christchurch city centre, Richmond was originally known as Bingsland. Lines for the trams and trolley buses used to pass through here on the way out to North Beach. Property here was originally working-class housing, with small shops and artisans' workshops.

Richmond is home to Richmond School, a small lower-decile school providing for students from Years 1–6. 45% of the students are Maori, and 39% European. Altogether, 22 different cultural groups are represented on the roll. Richmond School was first established in 1873 in the Avonside Sunday School rooms, but has since shifted location.

St Albans

Best for: Proximity to city and fashionable areas
Less good for: Buying a section
Price factor: NZ$225,000–NZ$600,000+ to buy; NZ$250–NZ$450 per week to rent

Just 3.5km from the central city, St Albans is one of Christchurch's largest suburbs and it is flanked by Merivale and Shirley. The Heathcote River runs through this area, and like Opawa there are several tree-lined streets. Originally working class, St Albans is now firmly middle class. Property here is mostly 20th-century. free-standing, with some units, townhouses and some housing for elderly people. Few sections are available anymore. A lot of development is taking place here, with a resulting significant proportion of new-build and architect-designed homes springing up. The best properties for investment are to be found close to the Merivale-Papanui Road end of St Albans, in the area known as St Albans/Merivale between Springfield and Papanui Roads.

The exclusive school zones currently extend back as far as Edgeware shopping centre (although zones are always subject to potential shrinkage or expansion), and properties here are significantly cheaper than those in Fendalton and Merivale. The St Martin's shopping centre is on Wilson Road, and there are corner shops too. The St Albans Cricket Club is home to 11 men's and 10 women's teams. St Albans Catholic School is a small school catering for both boys and girls from Year 0 to Year 6, just 2.5 km from the city centre, and St Albans Primary School is in Sheppard Place. Other schools nearby include St Martin's Primary, Rudolf Steiner, Hillview Christian School and Cashmere High. Recreation areas include St Martin's Park, Hansen's Park, Centaurus Park, Waltham Pool, and the riverside reserves. The Orbiter bus serves the area of St Albans, as do buses on routes 66 and 18.

Houses along a popular road in St Martins

St Martins

Best for: Family homes
Less good for: Youn childless professionals
Price factor: NZ$279,000–NZ$500,000+ to buy; NZ$270 – NZ$320 per week to rent

A good area if you are looking for a family home on a decent-sized section, perhaps even with a swimming pool. This inner suburb is 2km south of the city centre and primarily residential with a small shopping centre on Wilsons Road. There is a croquet park here, and it is close to the river. There are a number of schools here, including St Martins, Rudolf Steiner, and Hillview Christian School. St Martins is just 2km south of the city centre and has a park, a medical centre, a scout group, a tennis club, a library and a veterinary clinic.

Scarborough

Best for: Sun and views
Less good for: Access
Price factor: NZ$1 million+ to buy

Just beyond Sumner, this is one of the country's most sought-after residential areas and land here achieves one of the highest prices per square metre; real estate is hugely expensive. Homes are for the most part in breathtaking coastal locations, and are either striking, spotless, architect-designed temples to sleekness, or luxurious renovations and makeovers of character 1940s bungalows. Scarborough is a very popular place for cycling; it has a challenging single track, which can be rocky in parts, but which leads up over Scarborough Hill into Sumner. This is a popular destination for road cyclists in particular, as they arrive here from the city and Port Hills, and is on the way to the popular surf beach Taylor's Mistake. There is also a great hill walk with spectacular view up the coast.

The nearest community offering things like shops and a school is Sumner.

Shirley

Best for: Affordable housing
Less good for: Character homes
Price factor: NZ$290,000–NZ$470,000+ to buy; NZ$290–NZ$350 per week to rent

This is a decent family area, and home to the Palms Shopping Centre, where you can find a huge range of shopping opportunities, including appliances, jewellery, fashion, accessories, music, books, as well as heath and beauty stores, travel agents and banking services. There is also a cinema multiplex here.

The Shirley Leisure Club is for 'older adults' and offers afternoon tea and company, as well as recreation activities. The Shirley Lodge is a modern hotel complex with outdoor areas and bars. The Christchurch Golf Club is also located in Shirley, and there is a library here as well as Shirley Boys' High School. Shirley is on the north side of Christchurch, and is made up of mostly 1950s–1970s homes, with areas of state housing. This area developed a little later than surrounding areas, resulting in a large proportion of inter-war bungalows as well.

Spreydon

Spreydon is one of the larger southern suburbs, and many bungalows were built here in the years between the wars. Spreydon Library, which was renovated in 2007, is on Barrington Street, and Barrington Park is next to this. The area is close to the CBD, but also handy to the airport.

Best for: Affordable character housing, proximity to city
Less good for: Infill housing
Price factor: NZ$250,000–NZ$380,000+ to buy; NZ$285–NZ$350 per week to rent

Sumner

An interesting little community with a cosy neighbourhood vibe, in a pleasant seaside location. There are a number of new apartments here. There is plenty to do in terms of sports such as surfing, and a collection of exclusive little cafés for whiling away the hours with something delicious. For fantastic pizza and glorious swollen calzone, try the Ruptured Duck Pizzeria and Bar on Wakefield Street, or for the neighbourhood-restaurant

> **Best for:** Living by the sea
> **Less good for:** Overcrowding at the village and beach, especially at the weekends
> **Price factor:** NZ$480,000–NZ$700,000+ to buy; NZ$380–NZ$450 per week to rent

experience go to the Cornershop Bistro. Poisedon Restaurant sits directly on the beach.

At the eastern end of the Port Hills, Sumner sits mainly on the floor of the valley although there are also houses on Clifton Hill and Scarborough Head. From 1888 Sumner had its own tram line from Christchurch and it became a popular resort for Christchurch dwellers escaping the summer heat in the city. The road was opened in 1937.

When the settlers arrived in Lyttleton in 1850 there was no access road to Sumner from Christchurch, so they walked the track over the hills to the Heathcote Valley, carrying everything they needed with them. This public walking track is still in use, and of considerable local and historical interest. Sumner is the end point of the legendary Coast to Coast race, and there is an elaborate walking track system right along Port Hills.

Sydenham

> **Best for:** Picking up a bargain
> **Less good for:** Family living
> **Price factor:** NZ$250,000–NZ$350,000+ to buy; NZ$265–NZ$350 per week to rent

Sydenham is an inner Christchurch suburb, 2km south of the city's centre. Traditionally working class, many early residents were employed in factories along the railway line. In the 19th century, Sydenham had a reputation for political radicalism and movements such as women's suffrage and prohibition had strong core support here.

Like Addington, Sydenham declined into a lower-level inner city area, but is now creeping up the fashion ladder once again. There is plenty of infill housing here, as demand for property is increasing, and a significant variety of other property is on offer including period cottages, as well as bungalows and apartments. This is a very central area, but it is still possible to lay your hands on an 'in need of TLC' doer-upper here. Sydenham is probably more commercial than Addington.

Woolston

> **Best for:** Proximity to sports stadium
> **Less good for:** Shops
> **Price factor:** NZ$200,000–NZ$400,000+ to buy; NZ$230–NZ$325 per week to rent

Woolston is 3km south-east of Christchurch centre, and close to major routes in and out of the city. It is bordered by Linwood, and Opawa. This area was staunchly working class in the 20th century, when it was a centre to the country's rubber industry as well as several other factories. These days the suburb mixes residences with light industrial buildings. There is a real mix of different homes here, ranging from low-key brick-and-tile units to 120-year-old wooden villas with stacks of character to new build family homes and townhouses. Woolston residents have good access to the estuary, river walks along the Heathcote River, buses and schools.

The main sports venue in Christchurch – previously known as Jade Stadium and Lancaster Park and now known as AMI Stadium – is close to the north-western edge of Woolston suburb. This is the main venue for top cricket and rugby matches, offering corporate boxes as well as stadium seating.

Popular residential areas around Christchurch

The following are a few areas around Christchurch that are popular choices for those who commute to work in the CBD, although they are not actually within the Christchurch district itself but in surrounding districts.

Darfield

Best for: Proximity to ski-fields
Less good for: Vehicle-free living
Price factor: from NZ$140,000 (subdivision section only); NZ$320,000 (house)–NZ$385,000+ to buy; NZ$250+ per week to rent

Darfield, 45km west of Christchurch, on State Highway 73, is a township serving the surrounding rural area, on the way to the Southern Alps and ski-fields as you head out of Christchurch. It is also handy to two rivers, Waimakariri and Rakaia, both of which are excellent for jetboating, fishing and kayaking.

Darfield is increasingly popular and its population has almost doubled in size since the 1970s. This is the case for many rural Canterbury towns, as there is currently a boom in dairy farming and related agricultural activities and resulting strong demand for rural labour.

Darfield's popularity is also, to some degree, due to the fact that it is within commuting distance of the city, but the area still offers the desirable space for a rural lifestyle. Grocery shopping can be done in Darfield, but for big supermarkets you will need to drive about half an hour in to Christchurch itself. Darfield does have a cluster of useful little shops such as a small supermarket, a pharmacy, vet, farm supplies stores and dairy as well as a pub, hotel, motel, churches, hairdresser, medical centre, physiotherapists, midwives, chiropractor, gym, cafés, tearooms, takeaways and restaurants.

Local schools are Darfield School, and the co-ed Darfield High for Years 7–13, while Kirwee Model School is in nearby Kirwee. Other areas around Darfield include Glentunnel, Springfield, Sheffield, Hororata and Homebush, and these areas have their own primary schools while older pupils come into Darfield High by bus.

Lincoln

Lincoln township is a rural support service town as well as home to Lincoln University, which is an internationally-renowned agricultural and biotechnology campus. Lincoln is about half an hour (20km) southwest of Christchurch, so forms an outlying suburb,

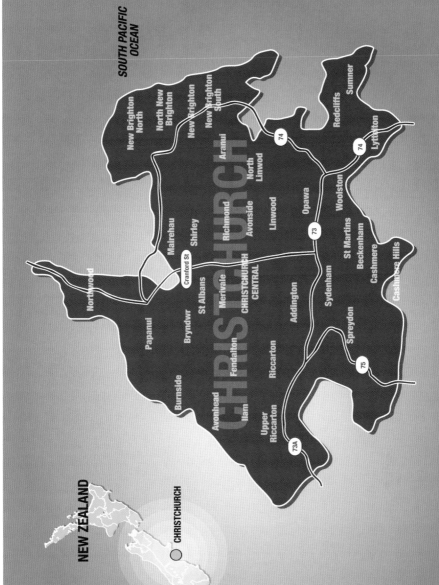

SOUTH PACIFIC
OCEAN

NEW ZEALAND

CHRISTCHURCH

CHRISTCHURCH

New Brighton
North

North New
Brighton

New Brighton

New Brighton
South

Aranui

North
Linwood

Richmond

Mairehau

Shirley

Avonside

Linwood

Northwood

Cranford St

Merivale

CHRISTCHURCH
CENTRAL

Opawa

Woolston

74

Papanui

St Albans

Fendalton

Redcliffs

Sumner

Lyttelton

74

Bryndwr

Addington

St Martins

Beckenham

Burnside

Riccarton

Sydenham

Cashmere

73

Avonhead

Ilam

Cashmere Hills

Upper
Riccarton

Spreydon

73A

75

Christchurch Art Gallery

Christchurch Airport

Sumner Beach

Beckenham

Best for: Agricultural university
Less good for: Restaurants
Price factor: NZ$275,000–NZ$459,000+ to buy; NZ$300–450 per week to rent

with driving time into the city being about 15 minutes. It is only a few minutes from Christchurch International Airport.

The resident population of this small rural township is about 3,000, but another 4,500 or so students come from throughout the country (and overseas) to join these residents during term-time. The university also has about 250 academic staff. Many staff and students commute in from Christchurch.

Local businesses include the local Crown Research Institutes and a number of commercial research facilities. Lincoln High School serves a number of surrounding rural communities on the southern and western borders of Christchurch, including Rolleston, and there is an efficient school bus system in operation.

Property developers are making the most of growth in the township at the moment, and new arrivals are drawn to Lincoln for the village lifestyle, its proximity to Christchurch and the opportunities it offers for education and jobs.

Pegasus Township

Best for: Brand new homes, owner-occupied
Less good for: Character properties
Price factor: start at NZ$162,000+ to buy

A brand new township off State Highway 1 to the north of Christchurch. When completed, it will house 1800 'dwellings' of various sorts, ranging from small family homes to rather more elaborate executive homes. All, of course, will be brand new. Facilities have been carefully planned, and include an aquatic centre, a school, a hot mineral pool complex, a golf and tennis club, an equestrian centre and a yacht club. Leisure activities include cycling, walking, diving, swimming, etc. Other amenities include bars, restaurants and cafés, a central market square, a wine-makers' centre, a hotel, a retirement village, waterfront dining options and boutique shops.

Rangiora

Best for: Semi-rural lifestyle with easy access to the city
Less good for: Students
Price factor: NZ$210,000–NZ$450,000+ to buy; NZ$320–NZ$420 per week to rent

FACT

■ The population of Rangiora has doubled since the 1970s.

An outlying community, about 25 minutes' drive from Christchurch on State Highway 71 at off-peak times, Rangiora is the principal town of North Canterbury and lies 11km northwest of Kaiapoi and 27km north of Christchurch. It is inland from State Highway 1, but lies on the main railway line running north. Rangiora is 20 minutes from the hills and bush-tracks area, 10 minutes from the beach, and provides access to variety of outdoor activities as well as excellent shopping.

Lots of new arrivals to New Zealand, and many other commuters to Christchurch as well, choose to make their homes in this middle to upper-middle socio-economic area with its strong sense of community. Rangiora is semi-rural, and close to beaches. It is a self-contained town offering a variety of properties, some with established gardens, and boasting a sizeable shopping centre with a number of interesting independent shops. Local educational facilities are North Canterbury Community College (including the Equestrian Academy), Rangiora Borough School (the largest primary school), St Joseph's Primary School and Ashgrove Primary School, as well as Rangiora High School (a high-decile, co-ed school, almost 125 years old, with a roll of over 1500). Rangiora High incorporates an associated farm, which provides some pupils with the opportunity to start agricultural training. There are also about three outlying schools around this area. Established as a sawmilling town in the 1850s, Rangiora became the contact and service heart for a large rural area of orchards and farms.

There are some beautiful buildings here, including St John the Baptist Anglican Church which was designed by Benjamin Mountfort and is one of Canterbury's largest and most acclaimed wooden churches. Rangiora is home to the Rangiora Players and Rangiora Brass Band. There is a jazz and ballet school here, a number of churches and community groups, a Toastmasters Club and a speakers' group.

Rolleston

Best for: Rural lifestyle, new-build homes
Less good for: Older character properties
Price factor: start at NZ$375,000–NZ$500,000+ to buy

Being only 20km from Christchurch, this satellite township allows residents to enjoy a well-serviced rural lifestyle, close to a large city. More subdivisions are being created on the edges of the township to satisfy the steady demand from people wanting to build homes in this area. The offices of the Selwyn District Council, which services ratepayers, are located here. Rolleston Square, in the middle of the Rolleston Square Shopping Centre, is used by groups and clubs for displays and performances. Rolleston calls itself 'the Town of the Future' and for the most part has a very 'new feel'.

There are many vineyards in this area, and Rolleston also has a community centre and library, supermarket. There is a low-to-medium male security prison located at Rolleston.

Several churches are located here, as well as dairies, garages, a garden club, a bowls club, a dentist, a medical centre, pharmacy, early learning centre, playcentre, Plunket rooms, a school, and rugby, rugby league, tennis and soccer clubs.

■ RENTING PROPERTY

Most immigrants rent property while they look for a house to buy – this is a very wise idea, if only so you have more breathing space and time to think about where you want to buy eventually, and to see how things like travelling to work and school pan out for you and your family. Renting is also the best solution if you are not

FACT

■ The population of Rolleston has more than doubled in the past 10 years, and is now close to 4,000.

TIP

■ Some travel agents and immigration consultants may also provide assistance in finding a temporary place to stay. This type of arrangement tends to be more expensive than finding a rental house yourself, but it has the advantage of the accommodation being ready and waiting for you as soon as you step off the plane.

> I find the average cost of living in New Zealand a little more expensive than the same kind of living in the UK, based on the costs of general purchases. However, expenses such as renting a house work out as relatively cheaper than they would in the UK so there are definite differences which probably balance out in the end.
>
> **Katy Parsons**

sure yet how long you are going to be staying in New Zealand, or if you are on a limited-period work contract and working visa. A lot of people simply prefer renting to owning their own home – it is certainly a lot less hassle! It is possible to arrange to rent a furnished apartment before you arrive in New Zealand through an immigration consultant or through some of the newspapers for intending migrants: *New Zealand Outlook* and *Destination New Zealand* (see Residence and Entry Regulations for subscription details, or visit www.emigratenz.org online). It will certainly be cheaper than staying in a hotel while you are house hunting.

The cost of rented accommodation is dependent on the area you choose, although of course you can expect to pay more if you want something more than just a typical three-bedroom house. Rental properties are advertised in the daily newspapers – mostly on Saturdays, but some on Wednesdays as well. Real estate agents and websites such as trademe.com are also good places to start looking. Cheaper not-so-well-maintained houses can be hard to find in towns with large student populations. However, many students leave their flats in mid-late November, so this can be a good time to find a bargain. You can also use a Real Estate letting agency, but you may have to pay as much as the equivalent of one month's rent as a fee for them to find you a suitable flat. The majority of privately let houses are unfurnished, although they may contain the odd piece of furniture. If you require a furnished property, it is probably best to go through a real estate agent.

What types of accommodation are available to rent?

All types of accommodation are available to rent; whether they all make financial sense may be another matter, but you will be able to find something suitable providing you are prepared to pay for it. Rental properties are available in all locations, and all price brackets, and, it goes without saying, at all sorts of different levels of quality. Rental prices are dependent on all the practical factors: size of property, location and desirability, condition of the house and its fixtures and fittings, and so on. Of course, you will pay more for a spacious house with a garden that is in a good area, close to well-regarded schools, and boasts a pristine finish than you will for a dark cramped flat with no parking space, stained carpet and peeling paint on the walls.

For the rental market, most homes in New Zealand will be described by real estate agents or their owners as 'townhouses', 'houses', 'units' or 'apartments'. A townhouse will be either detached or semi-detached, probably fairly modern, and may have a small garden or patio area. It is likely to be quite low maintenance. A house will be larger and detached, with a bigger garden, maybe closer to the good old Kiwi classic quarter-acre 'section' with a decent-sized garden, and maybe a garage or carport and a driveway. It is likely to have three or more bedrooms. Units, also called 'flats', are most likely to be in a row of single-storey similar homes, down a shared driveway, either very close to each other or possibly even attached in a 'terrace' sort of arrangement (although they will not look like the terraces you might be used to if you come from the UK). They are often also referred to, sometimes a little disparagingly, as 'brick-and-tile units' – they are usually low maintenance, often rented rather than owned, and will be one of the cheaper rental options. They will usually have some outside space, whether a garden or a patio area. An apartment will usually be in a block, with other apartments next to/above/below it. The vast majority of all sorts of homes available to rent will come unfurnished, although 'unfurnished' still usually includes curtains, a cooker, carpets, and perhaps a fridge. There may also be the possibility of negotiating with the agent/landlord, once you have decided you are interested enough in a property, to include extra furnishings, although as this is an unusual way to rent a house in New Zealand you should not be too put out if they refuse.

Finding accommodation

Local and national papers will be full of rental accommodation available, and real estate agents are another good place to look. Bear in mind that if you rent through an agent there will be an agent's fee to pay, and the property will probably be managed as well so the landlord will be paying a management fee. With this in mind, many landlords in New Zealand prefer to deal directly with their tenants themselves, thus cutting out the middleman. If you find a property through a newspaper, you will save on the agency fees and it may also be possible to negotiate better terms with a private landlord. If you find a property through an agent, you will be expected to pay the fee to them yourself, and this will usually be the equivalent of one or two weeks' rent but could conceivably be as high as the cost of four weeks' rent. Remember to ask about this early in the proceedings so you avoid nasty surprises once you think you have found your dream home. The main property websites offer rental properties as well as properties for sale – some contacts will be through agents and some through private landlords; try www.realestate.co.nz, www.sella.co.nz and www.trademe.co.nz to get you started.

Other good places to look for rental accommodation advertisements include local shops and noticeboards at local libraries, health-food stores, etc. It is worthwhile letting all the locals you meet know that you are searching for a house to rent as well – competition for good rental properties in the right area can be stiff, and you might just land on your feet if you find you know someone who knows someone...

What is involved in renting accommodation?

You may not always require proof of income/employment and/or references from previous landlords in order for a landlord to agree to rent a property to you, but it is best to have these to hand just in case they are required.

Tenancy/rental agreements

There are two main types of contract for rental properties: periodic tenancy and fixed-term tenancy. As the name suggests, a fixed-term tenancy provides an assurance that you can stay in the property for a specified period of time. During the duration of this tenancy, the rent cannot be increased unless there is a clause in the lease – you should of course read any such document carefully before signing it. If a landlord is insistent on a long fixed-term tenancy, you might do best to look for another property; as a new immigrant you might not wish to be tied into living in one place for years at a time. Periodic tenancy agreements are more common, and these have no fixed timescale as such. If you wish to end your tenancy you must give your landlord three weeks' notice, and your landlord must give you six weeks' notice if they require that you vacate the property. Under this type of agreement, the landlord has the power to increase your rent, but must give you 60 days' written notice. If the rent increase is unacceptable to you, you have plenty of time to provide the landlord with notice that you intend to quit the property. It is actually reasonably rare for landlords to increase rental prices dramatically for sitting tenants in the short term at least, and even if it does happen it shouldn't occur more than once every 12 months. If you have concerns or questions about the way a landlord is treating you, approach the Citizens' Advice Bureau to see what they think.

Your residential tenancy agreement form is for landlords and tenants to fill in together before you move into the property. It sets out all the key things that both agree to do, such as paying rent on particular dates, whether pets are allowed, whether the landlord or the tenant is responsible for upkeep of the garden, and so on. It also includes a property inspection section, which both landlord and tenant have to agree to. This section should include an assessment of the condition of the property and any fixtures and fittings that both parties are happy with; it is important, as the return of your bond at the end of your tenancy will be dependent on everything being in the same condition as it was when you moved in.

Resolving problems: the tenancy tribunal

The Tribunal is a special court for resolving problems tenants and landlords are unable to work out between themselves. Any landlord or tenant who wishes to make an application to the tribunal will be charged a fee of NZ$20. The hearing will be public, and it is normal for parties to represent themselves rather than having legal representation. In special cases, a lawyer will be permitted, ie:

■ when the figure in dispute is an amount greater than NZ$3,000;

■ if a solicitor has been managing the affairs of one party due to illness, disability or absence;

■ if the other side agrees or the tribunal allows it. When one party is represented by a lawyer, the tribunal will usually agree to the other side having a lawyer too.

The Tribunal can award compensation or order work up to the value of NZ$12,000. Claims for more than this need to be filed through the District Court. The most common orders made through the Tribunal are possession orders, monetary orders and work orders.

A possession order becomes necessary when the tenant does not fulfil their legal obligations and the situation is serious, and it involves the termination of the tenancy, with the landlord applying to have the tenant evicted from the property. This can happen if the tenant is:

■ more than 21 days behind on their rent;

■ substantially damaging the property or threatening to do so;

■ assaulting the landlord or the landlord's family or agent, other tenants of neighbours, or threatening assault;

■ breaking the tenancy agreement, when the landlord has given at least 10 days' notice to put matters right and the tenant has not.

In cases where a tenant is behind on their rental payments, and the landlord has given 10 working days' notice that the rent needs to be brought up to date, and by the time the case is heard the rent is 21 days or more in arrears, the matter will be treated as a serious breach.

A monetary order forces a landlord or a tenant to pay money to the other party. These payments could be to rectify problems such as:

■ payment of rent arrears or refund of overpaid rent;

■ payment for damage, cleaning, gardening or rubbish removal;

■ reimbursement of costs, such as urgent repairs;

■ payment of exemplary damages (like a fine) for legal breaches such as not paying the bond to the Department of Building and Housing, denying legal access, or seizing a tenants good;

■ payment of compensation for loss of goods or loss of use through poor repair.

A work order may be made or agreed to by the Tenancy Tribunal, and will stipulate that a person must do work to remedy lack of repair, damage or lack of maintenance. If the work order is not complied with by that person, they may be ordered to pay money instead.

For more information, see www.dbh.govt.nz/tenancy-tribunal.

What will renting cost?

Fees

As mentioned above, if you have used an agent to find your rental property, you will be liable for their fee – this could be anywhere between say NZ$250–NZ$1000, but is more likely to be towards the lower end of the scale.

Bond

You will need to pay a bond as a security against damage to the property and to cover the landlord in case of tenant vacating swiftly in the middle of the night without paying their rent. These details will be in your rental agreement. Although you pay your bond directly to the landlord, s/he is legally obliged to deposit the amount with the Bond Centre at the Department of Building and Housing. With your landlord, you should complete a bond lodgement for at the beginning of the tenancy. It will record how much bond money has been collected by the landlord, and will be sent to the Department of Building and Housing to be held until the tenancy is ended and the tenant leaves the property. Further information about tenancy bonds as well as the bond lodgement form can be obtained for free

■ Your landlord is entitled to ask you to pay as much as four weeks' rent as a bond, although it is more common to be asked to pay two weeks' worth.

A typical New Zealand garden – plenty of space for a BBQ

from the Department of Building and Housing. Either download the forms from the website (www.dbh.govt.nz) or telephone 0800 836 262 to receive copies by post.

Insurance when renting

Although the building insurance is the responsibility of the owner, ie the landlord, you should not forget to insure your contents. Contents insurance will cover your belongings when they are at home or temporarily moved elsewhere in the country. Policies generally have a mix of replacement and indemnity cover, meaning that they provide replacement cover for certain items, such as furniture and carpets, with indemnity cover for many other things. Indemnity cover means that if an item is stolen etc. you will receive a cash payment based on the original value minus an amount for depreciation. Often, an overall sum is insured. Most policies have maximum payout limits for specific items like jewellery, cameras, etc. Items over this value must be separately detailed in the policy. Some insurance companies require a valuation certificate for items worth over a certain amount, and it is wise to have valuations done for valuable or rare items.

Prices vary depending on the value of what you insure, the kind of home you live in, your location, and so on. Contact insurance providers such as www.tower.co.nz, www.aainsurance.co.nz or your local bank for more information, or have a look at www.consumer.org.nz to compare the best policies and deals available.

Rent

Rent is usually paid fortnightly and in advance. Your landlord may ask for two weeks' rent in advance. Market rent is described in the Residential Tenancies Act as the amount 'a willing landlord might reasonably expect to receive and a willing tenant might reasonably expect to pay for the tenancy' in comparison with rent levels for other properties of a similar type, size and location in similar areas. if your landlord is trying to charge you significantly higher rent than seems reasonable, the Tenancy Tribunal can order them to reduce it.

Other Costs

Legally, landlords are also entitled to ask for real estate agent's fees and/or solicitor's fees charged for setting up the tenancy. This is fairly unusual however. A landlord may also ask for 'option money', which is basically a holding deposit of no more than one week's rent for holding a house or flat until you make up your mind. If you take the property, the amount must be refunded or put towards your rent. If you don't take the property though, the landlord may keep the money.

Aside from these costs and fees outlined above, there are no other charges that a landlord can legally request from you. In rare instances, dodgy landlords trying to take advantage of potential tenants have been known to demand 'key money', which is basically any payment for giving you the tenancy (aside from rent, bond, or agent's/solicitor's fees). Sometimes this is categorised as a deposit for the key to the house, or a deposit on the washing machine or anything else supplied with the tenancy. This is illegal, and you should refuse to pay it. Such landlords will probably back right off once they realise that you know what you are talking about and are not to be taken advantage of, but if you feel it is necessary you should contact Tenancy Services.

Average Property Market Rental By Area	
Location	Average weekly rent for a two-bedroom house
Kerikeri/Paihia	NZ$197
Whangarei	NZ$177
Auckland – Mt Eden	NZ$380
Auckland – Sandringham	NZ$355
Auckland – Remuera	NZ$420
Hamilton	NZ$200
Tauranga	NZ$215
Gisborne	NZ$160
Napier	NZ$200
New Plymouth	NZ$180
Palmerston North	NZ$160
Wellington – Brooklyn	NZ$302
Wellington – Karori/Kelburn/Northland	NZ$400
Wellington – Thorndon/City	NZ$390

Location	Average weekly rent for a three-bedroom house
Nelson	NZ$220
Christchurch	NZ$230
Queenstown	NZ$260
Dunedin	NZ$180
Kerikeri/Paihia	NZ$270
Whangarei	NZ$250
Auckland - Mt Eden	NZ$465
Auckland - Sandringham	NZ$420
Auckland - Remuera	NZ$500
Hamilton	NZ$270
Tauranga	NZ$285
Gisborne	NZ$220
Napier	NZ$270
New Plymouth	NZ$265
Palmerston North	NZ$230
Wellington - Brooklyn	NZ$390
Wellington - Karori/Kelburn/Northland	NZ$498
Wellington - Thorndon/City	NZ$410
Nelson	NZ$270
Christchurch	NZ$280
Queenstown	NZ$350
Dunedin	NZ$220

Source: Tenancy Services Division, Department of Building and Housing, February 2008

Useful resources

Tenancy Services, Advice/Mediation & Enquiries, Department of Housing and Building: 0800 836 262 or Bond Enquiries 0800 737 666; info@dbh.govt.nz; www.dbh.govt.nz/tenancy-index

Citizens Advice Bureaux (National Office): 0800 367 222 (0800 FOR CAB); www.cab.org.nz. Citizens Advice offers free confidential advice on housing, health, legal and consumer problems, employment and budgeting. There are 87 offices throughout New Zealand, from Kaitaia to Invercargill.

Land Information New Zealand (National Office): Lambton House, 160 Lambton Quay, Private Bag 5501, Wellington; (04) 460 0110; fax (04) 472 2244; info@linz.govt.nz; www.linz.govt.nz. Government department providing land and property information. Website includes government policy, maps, valuation rates, and a searchable database.

Legal Services Agency: Prime Property Tower, 86-90 Lambton Quay, PO Box 5333, Wellington, DX SP22526; (04) 495 5910; fax (04) 495 5911; email info@lsa.govt. nz; www.lsa.govt.nz.
Netlaw: www.netlaw.co.nz.

■ BUYING A HOUSE IN NEW ZEALAND

It is possible for a foreign national to buy a house in New Zealand, but it is important to note that this does not give the purchaser any automatic right to live permanently in New Zealand. If you are a permanent resident, there are no official restrictions on the type of property you can buy in New Zealand. If you have less than permanent residence, however, you are limited to buying a home on less than five hectares (12.5 acres) of land or undeveloped land up to five hectares, provided this land is not on, or next to, a 'sensitive area' (such as an island or a reserve).

The property market

The latest Real Estate Institute reports show that the New Zealand residential property market has rebounded after a few quiet months in late 2007, with higher sales and a new record national median price of NZ$352,000. This eclipses the previous record of NZ$351,000. October saw historically very low sales of just 6,854, the lowest October figure since 2001, but November showed seasonal recovery generally expected in spring, with sales jumping up to 7,837. At the time of writing, the suggestions in the media that the market has turned into a buyer's market and that prices are falling just aren't supported by the figures.

FACT

■ The latest figures show that house sales move relatively quickly in New Zealand. The median number of days it takes a property to sell is 36.

Auckland is the single largest regional market in New Zealand, and the regional median price has risen to NZ$450,000. The Auckland Metropolitan region is now NZ$453,000, and within this the Auckland city sales median is now NZ$487,000. Of the 12 real estate regions, the past year has seen six rises and five falls with just one region, Otago, experiencing an unchanged median. See the table below for the median house prices by region.

Median House Prices By Region	
District	**House Price**
Northland	NZ$307,500
Auckland	NZ$450,000
Auckland City	NZ$487,000
Metropolitan Auckland	NZ$453,000
Hamilton City	NZ$332,125
Tauranga	NZ$392,500
Waikato/Bay of Plenty	NZ$322,750
Taupo	NZ$336,000
Hawke's Bay	NZ$275,000
Napier City	NZ$320,000
Hastings City	NZ$270,100
Manawatu/Wanganui	NZ$228,000
Taranaki	NZ$275,000
Wellington	NZ$395,000
Nelson/Marlborough	NZ$333,000
Canterbury/Westland	NZ$314,000
West Coast	NZ$188,000
Christchurch City	NZ$307,000
Central Otago Lakes	NZ$430,000
Otago	NZ$235,000
Dunedin	NZ$255,000
Southland	NZ$209,025
Invercargill	NZ$207,000
Median selling price	NZ$352,000

Source: REINZ Residential Report 2007.

Lifestyle blocks

Lifestyle blocks vary in size, but are generally between two hectares and 10 hectares in size. Properties of these sizes are also in reasonably close proximity to rural towns, as local government by-laws usually only permit such small size subdivisions near the

townships. Most of the developed blocks have large modern houses of three to four bedrooms. In recent years it has been an attractive alternative to families from large towns to purchase bare land and to build a dwelling to their own design. Many still commute to the nearest city to engage in their main form of employment. However, there are a growing number of job opportunities in the countryside especially in the dairy farm industry, which has seen a massive growth in the last five years.

Subdivision of large farms into lifestyle blocks is an ongoing process. The further from the nearest rural town, the larger the area of the subdivisions ie 20 hectares or in some regions as much as 50 hectares. These larger sizes, however, test both the financial resources and the time available to maintain them, unless the purchaser is prepared to engage in some fairly intensive rural activity such as horticulture. Olives and grapes are becoming increasingly popular in regions with suitable growing conditions for such activities. In these cases the purchaser must be prepared to accept a lengthy gestation period expressed in years before their development efforts begin yielding a return.

Bare land lifestyle blocks range in price depending on the region and also their size and proximity to the nearest rural township and city. Generally the larger sized blocks work out as less expensive per hectare than the smaller blocks. Around Auckland expect to pay between NZ$145,000 and NZ$300,000 per hectare for a very small lifestyle block. Whereas around Christchurch the price for a smaller block would be in the region of NZ$30,000 and NZ$80,000 per hectare. These smaller blocks would be between two and four hectares in size.

The price of lifestyle blocks with large modern dwelling is more problematic. In addition to the size of the land area and its proximity to the nearest large town or city, there is also the size, style, materials of construction of the dwelling and facilities such as tennis court, swimming pool, and stables and other outbuildings. The more recently constructed dwellings usually contain four bedrooms, one of which will have an en suite. Generally it is less expensive to buy bare land and build the dwelling and facilities to your specifications. However those who prefer to avoid the hassles associated with the building process should expect to pay a premium to those who sell after undergoing the travails of construction in the countryside. Prices around the Auckland area for a two-hectare property with a four-bedroom dwelling start at about NZ$600,000. In the rural environs around Christchurch a four-hectare property with a four-bedroom dwelling will range in price between NZ$400,000 and NZ$800,000.

Most lifestyle blocks are generally within 50 km of large urban centres or, expressed in time, usually only one hour's commute to shopping malls, large hospitals and cultural activities and events expected from cities. The travelling distance can become onerous for those with teenage children who crave the social scene and attractions available in the larger cities.

Because there are large numbers of 'lifestylers' there now exist a sound range of support services as well as some very good websites (see end of this section for details) where members can access a wide range of technical advice relating to smaller scale agricultural activities. There are also contractors who are available to undertake such tasks as shearing small mobs of sheep and making hay from these smaller pastures. Rural supplies and support service businesses, known in industry as stock and station agents, as well as professional farmers on large rural properties, are other sources of advice and support when sought.

Many lifestylers run a small number of sheep or a few cattle and/or provide grazing to a nearby larger farm. These are generally ways that they keep their pastures in a tidy state. They cannot be looked on as a significant source of income. Others use the rural hectares as the opportunity to engage in their hobbies such as horse and pony riding or breeding. Some even enjoy running a few poultry and having farm-fresh eggs.

There has been a steady growth in the number of lifestyle blocks over the past 10 years. This suggests that this is a reasonably attractive alternative to those who are seeking the rural experience without cutting their ties with the larger urban areas where they commute to work and enjoy major cultural activities and events.

However for those contemplating lifestyle-block living there is a note of caution. The steady increase in energy costs is likely to make regular commuting from a place in the countryside to the nearest large city an increasingly expensive item in the household budget. At least one vehicle should be four-wheel drive to cope with jobs like moving feed and small numbers of animals if necessary, and off-road driving. Furthermore for those who seek a wider choice of education for their children, especially at the secondary and tertiary levels, there is often the prospect of long days of driving, or the children residing in the city in hostel or other weekday accommodation.

This section was kindly contributed by Tom Woodhouse. For further reading see the Useful references – lifestyle blocks section in the Appendix (p.405).

Useful websites
- www.brittons.co.nz – information on moving housing and other relocatable buildings in the North Island.
- www.koanga.org.nz
- www.lifestyleblock.co.nz
- www.lifestylelivestock.co.nz
- www.shearingworld.com/thebloke.htm; tel 0800 843 256 for the Lifestyle Block Bloke, who is like a rural hire-a-hubby.
- www.smallkiwifarms.co.nz

Purchasing and conveyancing procedures

Buying a property is less complicated in New Zealand than in many other countries. Establishing clear title is generally straightforward because there are fewer complications like cross-leasing and leasehold properties. As a result you do not get chains of prospective buyers waiting for the next person in the chain to organise the sale of their house. Nor are there problems with establishing who actually owns the property in question.

When you wish to buy a property, you need to obtain the free copy of *Real Estate* or *Property Press* magazines published by the combined local real estate firms. This has a photo of each property, relevant information, and details of the estate agents involved. You may attend an 'open home' (which means you turn up at that address at the time specified), or you can arrange a private visit with the estate agent. The agent is working for the seller, and receives a commission for the sale from them, but must present the property fairly to the buyer. It is possible to deal with several agents at once, as many estate agents have sharing arrangements over the commission for the sale.

It is sensible to have a solicitor check the title details when you come to sign the agreement to buy the property. A solicitor would also be useful in terms of arranging to get a Valuer's Report should you need it, or a Land Information Memorandum (LIM) Report. A LIM report establishes the town planning requirements and anything that could affect the property, and is available from the local authority.

Most home-owners in New Zealand have a mortgage from a bank or financial institution. Most commercial and industrial properties are leased, as this provides an annual cost for taxation purposes. Your agreement to purchase a property can be subject to obtaining mortgage finance or the sale of your current New Zealand property. Your solicitor's charge may add around NZ$500–NZ$950 to your expenses, but it could save you from making a costly mistake. The market is not regulated, so you can ask around for a reasonably priced solicitor. A useful place to start might be Lawlink, a network of 17 independent legal firms, which can also be accessed online (www.lawlink.co.nz).

Finding a property

Most people begin either by approaching a local real estate agent or searching in free weekly property newspapers in their desired location. A good paper to try is the *Property Press* which is freely available in inner city areas and has a weekly readership of about 723,000. It is New Zealand's most popular property paper, and is published in many different areas from Auckland to Central Otago. It is produced every week, apart from The Lakes District edition, which is published fortnightly. The real estate sections of your local newspapers are another good place to start, and these will give you a good idea of prices in different areas. Agents will often advertise open homes in the newspaper as well, and these are a great opportunity to look inside a property without feeling pressured. It is also a good way to meet agents who might have other suitable properties on their lists.

Most major real estate agents have websites that you can browse. Links to many of these can be found through www.propertypress.co.nz, or on www.realenz.co.nz and www.realestate.co.nz.

Establish relationships with a number of real estate agents, and make sure that they are aware of your needs and exactly what you are looking for. Remember that the agent is working on behalf of the vendor (seller) and will receive a percentage of the sale price. Take this into account when you are negotiating your purchase price.

There are many types of property on offer, although the variety is not as great as in countries where architecture of many periods co-exists. European-style architecture has only a short history in New Zealand and the typical period house is a wooden Victorian villa. This type is very popular with the do-it-yourself set as a renovation project. Most older houses were made of wood because of the risk of earthquake. The standard New Zealand house of the post-war period is a three-bedroom, brick single-storey building on a large section. Before this, houses were generally built with a northern hemisphere model in mind and thus did not always make the most of the New Zealand climate. Modern houses are designed to capture the sun and to make the most of outdoor living during the summer, with decks and sliding doors to blur the indoor/outdoor distinction. Because of rising inner city land prices, there is a growing trend towards building town houses and apartment blocks. Town houses are compact units, often multi-level, usually built as part of group on one site. In the suburbs, where land is cheaper, you can find modern mansions with swimming pools, en suite bathrooms, separate living rooms and dining rooms, all on a huge site. Often these homes also have separate living areas and bathrooms for the children. At the other end of the budget spectrum, you will find houses advertised as 'the handyman's dream' or 'needing TLC' (tender loving care), which is a real estate euphemism for a dwelling in dire need of repair. This type of property brings a glint to the eye of the home handyman who seems to lurk under the skin of most New Zealand males and quite a few females. If your acquaintance with nails is confined to those on your digits, then you should probably avoid this type of property and look for something a more immediately habitable. On the other hand, lovely old villas in various locations can still be picked up relatively cheaply if you are prepared to spend the money and the time on renovations and, once 'done up', they make very desirable homes.

Keep a note of lists of questions you want the agent to answer about each property you see. Questions to consider might include:

- Have there been any alterations? If so, have these been certified?
- Which chattels will remain (eg carpets, curtain rails, curtains, dishwasher)?
- Where are the boundaries of the property?
- How much are the rates?
- What is the Council Valuation?
- Why is the home for sale? If it has been on the market for a while, why hasn't it sold?

Taking a closer look

Once you find a house you are interested in, you need to take a closer look. Make a list of all the things that are important to you and find out about each of them before you make any purchasing decisions. Here are a few suggestions to get you started:

TIP

- You should look at as many houses as you can to get a good feel for the market. It may be a good idea to keep notes of each house you visit, so that you can compare them later.

- Leaks, dry rot, and borer.
- Storage space in the kitchen, bedrooms, etc.
- Structural defects (check also that any alterations made comply with building codes).
- Electrical wiring – check whether it is old or worn, and check the meter box to make sure there are no tangles of worn wires as this is a bad sign.
- If you are buying an apartment, make sure you know about any service charges or any unusual rules for the building.
- Noise from traffic, industrial areas or aeroplanes.
- Signs of flooding or erosion.
- Zoning restrictions for schools (if this is important to you) and any planned development or building proposals that might affect the property. Check these with the local council.
- Check that the floors are level and the piling structurally sound.
- Water pressure – turn on taps and the shower, and flush the loo.
- Insulation – above the ceiling and under the floors.
- Check the boundaries against the survey plans for the property – just because there is a fence don't assume that this is where the legal boundary lies.
- Potentially troublesome neighbours.
- Subsidence (look for cracks and ill-fitting doors and windows) and damp (mildew and smell).

Remember that repairs can be a major expense, and if it is found that repairs are necessary to a house you would like to buy you should ask the real estate agent to negotiate with the vendor either to have the repairs made or to deduct such necessary costs from the asking price. If you request an LIM report from your local authority, this should outline any alterations and changes that have been made to the house, as well as any plans the local authority may have to make changes to the area or the property. Bear in mind that this report may still not be definitive as the LIM will contain information only about changes and alterations the council is aware of. You must compare your own inspection of the property with the LIM to make sure that there are no discrepancies or 'unauthorised' alterations.

Useful resources

As there are such a large number of real estate agents operating in New Zealand it is impossible to list them all here. All worthwhile companies are listed on the internet. To find one in your area try Harcourts Real Estate (www.harcourts.co.nz or email enquiries@harcourts.co.nz) or L. J. Hooker (www.ljhooker.co.nz or email enquiries@ljhooker.co.nz). Other useful websites for real estate agents include: www.harcourts.co.nz; www.harveys.co.nz; www.barfoot.co.nz; www.leaders.co.nz; www.bayleys.co.nz and www.professionals.co.nz. For general information, have a look at www.realenz.co.nz, www.propertystuff.co.nz and www.consumer.org.nz. Also try the Real Estate Institute of New Zealand online at www.reinz.org.nz. You can contact REINZ at PO Box 9284, Auckland; 0064 9 353 2250; fax 0064 9 353 2251; info@realenz.co.nz.

Other organisations, such as the following, may also be useful when you are doing your research. Overseas Investment Commission, Reserve Bank Building, PO Box 2498, Wellington, New Zealand; 0064 4 471 3838; fax 0064 4 471 3655; oic.

govt.nz; www.oic.govt.nz. Land Information New Zealand, Lambton House, 160 Lambton Quay, Private Box 5501, Wellington; 0064 4 460 0110; fax 0064 4 472 2244; info@linz.govt.nz; www.linz.govt.nz.

Specialist companies such as Orientation New Zealand (address below) exist specifically to offer advice and support to those planning to move to New Zealand.

Where to live in Auckland – Homefinders can help you find a home to buy or rent. This service is run by ex-migrants and specifically tailored to new migrants, and can offer you as much or as little help as your require – from advice and information about suitable suburbs and schools to help with buying a home. +64 9 376 4849; www.aucklandhomefinders.co.nz.

Miscellaneous useful resources

Directmoving.com (USA): 331 4215 7500 or 331 4215 7507; fax 331 4215 7505; expat@directmoving.com; www.directmoving.com/expat.

Orientation New Zealand: PO Box 58473, Greenmount, Auckland; 021 374500; fax 09 448 2266; mandy@orientationnz.co.nz. Specialist advice and support for those planning to settle in New Zealand.

Relocations International: 34 Douglas Street, Auckland; (09) 378 9888; fax (09) 378 8072; gspeed@reloc.co.nz; www.reloc.co.nz. Wellington office: 101–103 Molesworth Street, Wellington; (04) 479 3765; fax (04) 479 3769; julia@reloc-wgtn.co.nz.

Borrowing money to buy a property

Mortgages are the standard method of financing house purchasing in New Zealand. The majority of properties have a mortgage on them. If you wish to apply for a mortgage, or any other finance, it will be helpful to have records from your previous bank showing repayments, pay slips, references showing your work history, evidence of any other property that you own and the equity you hold in it, etc. As with applying for a mortgage in other countries, you will need to supply your mortgage provider with evidence of the amount you have available for a deposit, proof of your salary/income, official information about the value of your equity in any other properties or significant items or investments you own, and at least six months' worth of your most recent bank statements as a standard part of your application. Your solicitor will help and this should be discussed before you make an offer to purchase a property.

Banks are the main lenders, but you should discuss your circumstances and needs with a financial advisor and/or independent mortgage broker to make sure you are getting the very best possible deal. A good place to start is the New Zealand Mortgage Brokers' Association (www.nzmba.co.nz). Building societies used to be separate institutions from banks but since deregulation in the 1980s they have been allowed to provide the same services and most have now converted themselves to banks. The banks have responded to the competition to provide mortgages by offering more flexible repayment terms.

If you are a permanent resident of New Zealand, you will be provided with identical mortgage facilities to those provided to New Zealand citizens. This means that you should be able to borrow as much as 90% (sometimes more) of the value of the property you are buying. If you have a work permit rather than residency, banks

I arrived in New Zealand with just a few contacts and managed to set myself up with a bank account, a house to rent and enrol at myself university within two weeks.
Sam McLaughlan

or lenders will require more commitment from you, although their requirements will vary. Some will require that you fund at least 20% of the purchase price, but other stricter companies will require you to fund at least 50% of the purchase price. If you search thoroughly you should be able to find a loan for 80%, depending of course on your circumstances and the kind of property you are looking to buy. If you are borrowing more than 60% of the purchase price, the bank will require a Valuer's Report.

The maximum amount you may borrow is not always directly related to your salary but you will be expected to provide information about your monthly income as part of a hypothetical budgeting exercise. As a general rule of thumb, your repayments should not be more than 35% of your gross income less any other fixed repayments (eg other loan repayments, credit card repayments, hire purchases, etc.). If for example you and your partner earn a combined gross income of NZ$2,200 each fortnight, 35% of this is NZ$770. If you have fixed payments of, for example, NZ$90 a fortnight, then your surplus available for home loan repayments will be NZ$680 per fortnight.

When considering how much you can borrow, it is important to be realistic about what you can afford in terms of repayments. Remember that interest rates in New Zealand are high. As a very rough guide, if you borrow an amount of NZ$350,000 for 25 years at an interest rate of 9.00% per annum, your repayments will be NZ$1,355 fortnightly or NZ$2,937 monthly. If you borrow NZ$200,000 at 7.50% interest per annum your payments will be NZ$680 fortnightly or NZ$1,480 monthly. The amount you can borrow varies from lender to lender and does depend on where and what you are buying, and fluctuations in both the property and credit markets.

Before you start the hunt for your new home, you should confirm just how much you are able to borrow by obtaining a Home Loan Eligibility Certificate. This will give you virtually the same bargaining power as a cash buyer, by predetermining the amount you can borrow (provided of course the property you choose meets your lender's home loan criteria). Once you have found the home you want, make a conditional offer (subject to arranging finance and other conditions recommended by your solicitor) and contact your lender.

To arrange finance, you will have to decide on the type of mortgage that suits you best, and provide all the necessary documentation and information to your chosen lender so that they can make a decision and the process can move forward. Among others, items you are likely to be required to provide include:

- evidence of savings;
- several different forms of identification;
- bank statements for the most recent six months;
- Evidence of your deposit;
- evidence of income (recent pay slips, letter from employer, or if you are self-employed a copy of your latest financial accounts, GST returns, or a letter from your accountant);
- details of outstanding debts (credit card balances, overdrafts, existing loans, vehicle finance, other mortgages); and
- a registered valuation if you are hoping to borrow more than 90% of the purchase price.

Mortgage and associated costs

Your lender will charge mortgage establishment/application cost of around 1% of the value of the mortgage. The Land Titles Lodgement fees (to change the registered ownership of the property) are payable by cheque if you send your forms by post, although if a lawyer acts on your behalf this fee will come out of general legal disbursements. At the time of going to print, the fee for lodging your land title electronically with an image, or a manual lodgement, is NZ$60. An additional counter fee of NZ$20 applies to manual priority lodgements. Auto-registration, or electronic lodgement with a template costs NZ$37. Standard forms are also obtainable from legal stationers. Conveyancers and lawyers lodge the legal documents (transfers records of sale, discharge mortgages, new mortgages, etc.) and LINZ (Land Information New Zealand) registers the changes to the land title. Since 1 June 2002, titles are generated by and recorded on a computer system called Landonline. Titles are now called 'computer registers' and they are evidenced by the image of the register in Landonline. The landowner can request paper copies of these. New titles will be created once LINZ approves and deposits a survey plan produced by a surveyor. This approval will be granted once LINZ is satisfied that the plan meets its required standards. The underlying title for the land will then be cancelled and overwritten with a new computer register for each new parcel of land on the plan. For more information see www.linz.govt.nz.

Other costs you should budget for include:

■ Solicitor's fees, including 'disbursements' (payments made on your behalf by your solicitor, such as search fees and registration costs (see above), postage, photocopying, etc.

■ Bank fees and service charges.

■ The registered valuer's fee (if applicable).

■ Building inspection (if you choose to have one).

■ Land Information Memorandum (again, if you choose to get one).

■ Your share of the general rates (from the date of settlement) on the property.

■ Home and contents insurance premium.

■ Mortgage protection insurance (more comprehensive and repays the mortgage in the event of your death) or mortgage risk insurance (will pay the mortgage for a fixed period if you lose your regular income). There is no government benefit to help you pay the costs of a mortgage.

■ Power, gas and phone costs from the settlement date onwards.

■ Moving costs.

■ Your share of Body Corporate fees (from the date of settlement) if you are purchasing a Unit Title property.

Repayment conditions

Repayments are usually made on a monthly basis, but can be fortnightly. Fortnightly repayments will reduce the amount of total interest you pay, so are worth considering. The usual term of mortgage used to be 25 years, but it is increasingly common for people to arrange shorter-term mortgages with commensurably higher monthly repayments. Most banks will not approve of a mortgage arrangement that requires you to repay more than one third of your monthly income. Interest rates can be either fixed or floating. There are three main types of mortgage: table, reducing or interest only. In a table mortgage you pay equal monthly (or fortnightly) payments of interest and capital over the whole term of the mortgage. In a reducing mortgage, monthly payments start high because you pay fixed amounts of principal, plus the amount of interest you have accrued that month. At the beginning, there will be a lot of interest to pay off, but this will decrease as the principle is repaid, resulting in decreasing monthly payments. Whether you choose a table or reducing mortgage, you will also be able to choose between a variable or fixed-rate mortgage. Some borrowers take a mixture of variable and fixed-rate mortgages.

The third type is an interest-only mortgage, which is exactly what it sounds like. You pay a higher rate of interest on a monthly basis, which tends to add up to the same sum, more or less, as a repayment mortgage, but at the end of the whole term the original sum borrowed is effectively written off. The banks are quite flexible about changing the repayment conditions once you have entered into the mortgage, for example increasing or decreasing the size of monthly payments or switching to fortnightly payment intervals. You can even alter the type of mortgage or transfer it to another property.

The home loan process

- Obtain a home loan eligibility certificate from your chosen lender.
- Notify your mortgage provider once you have found the home you would like to purchase.
- Lender approves the mortgage.
- Lender sends the documents to your solicitor.
- You meet with your solicitor to sign the documents.

- On the settlement day, providing they have received your solicitor's certificate, your lender will transfer funds to the appropriate account.
- Settlement funds are then transferred to the vendor's solicitor.
- Solicitor 'settles' with the vendors. Solicitor exchanges keys and you take possession of the house.
- Your solicitor then registers the transfer of the title and mortgage with Land Information New Zealand.

Furniture: buy or rent?

Furniture is not cheap, so if you have not brought your own with you it might be worth renting some key pieces for a few months while you settle in. That said, after months of packing and planning and being surrounded by crates before you left you might want nothing more than to start your new life with a houseful of brand new furniture. However, it is probably wise to take some time to make sure that you are comfortable and happy in the house and the area that you have moved to before you make the additional commitment. And if you are renting prior to buying a more permanent home you

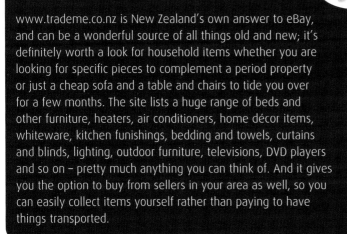

might think it best to wait until you are in your final destination to see which furniture suits is best. For example, if you end up buying a beautiful soaring-ceilinged, honey-floored old villa or a crisp-edged art deco apartment, you will want your furniture to complement the character of your home rather than clashing with it.

Ways of purchasing a property

Offer and negotiation

If not for sale by auction or tender, the property will have an advertised sale or list price or will be sold by negotiation, meaning you can put in an offer through the real estate agent. This is for many the quickest and simplest method of purchasing. You can make your offer when you are ready, and can build in conditions such as obtaining a builder's report which will be met once the offer has been accepted by the vendor. This saves you having to pay for expert help before you even make an offer, as opposed to working with auction and tender in which cases you have to get all this information beforehand. Seek advice from your solicitor about the offer you wish to make.

By tender

Purchasing by tender is a very popular way of selling houses, although it can be a nerve-wracking process for prospective purchasers. It involves making a formal offer to either the vendor or their agent without knowing how much either the vendor is expecting or how much others have offered. You are not able to counter-offer, and for this reason it is advisable to put your best offer forward. To follow this purchasing procedure, first obtain a copy of the tender document. Have the details checked by your solicitor before submitting your offer. Then, once tenders have closed, the vendor will decide whether to accept any of them. If they decide not to, they may decide to negotiate with the highest tenderer. Remember, if your tender is accepted, your offer becomes unconditional and you are legally committed to purchasing the property. Even if your tender is unsuccessful, you must remember that you are still liable for all costs incurred, such as solicitor's fees and valuation.

Auction

This is another relatively popular way of buying a property in New Zealand. You need to have formed a strong opinion of the value of the property, and just how much you are prepared to pay for it. Decide specifically on your maximum bid before the auction begins, and be vigilant against getting swept up in the excitement and bidding more than you can afford. You must also be very careful to carry out thorough research before turning up to bid, as purchases at auction are unconditional of course, meaning that you are legally bound to complete the purchase.

Prepare for an auction purchase by consulting with the real estate agent involved and your solicitor. Remember that a valuation may be required if your bid is successful, but have your finances pre-arranged. Inspect the property thoroughly and commission an independent survey. Be sure you are clear about what is included in the sale price, such as boundaries to the property, etc. Find out about the terms of the auction and make sure that your finances are sorted before the day; you will probably be required to pay a deposit (by debit card or cheque usually, but do check with the auction house first) immediately on acceptance of your bid. Finally, make sure that you know what the required settlement date is, and check whether this suits your plans. If you need this altered, consult your solicitor.

Private sale

An increasing number of people now choose to handle their property sales themselves. Although this approach might mean that the vendor misses out on the breadth of advertising opportunities and thus potential buyers available to a professional real estate agent, it also means that the vendor saves themselves the estate agent fee. If you do choose to buy privately, tread carefully and ensure that you consult your legal advisor or solicitor at each step through the process. It is important when buying privately to pay your deposit to your solicitor rather than directly to the vendor, so that the money is held in a trust account until all the details of the sale are finalised.

Negotiating tips

■ Know what the property is worth.

■ Always remember that the agent is working for the vendor and will be trying to negotiate the highest price possible.

■ Do not rush or procrastinate about your decision.

■ You may find you have increased bargaining power if you can offer a bigger deposit, or you are able to be flexible about the settlement date.

■ Don't be afraid to attempt to bargain down the price of a property you want. You may find that the vendor is prepared to accept less than the asking price.

Building your own house

If you are toying with the idea of building your own place, you should weigh up the advantages of building the house you want in the location of your choice against the potential problems inherent in spending such a lot of time and money to achieve your dream. If you are building in an area designated for new housing, such as a developing subdivision, you should be aware that there will be a significant amount of other building going on around you, and this may continue for years.

When arranging finance to purchase a section with the intention to build, the same basic principles apply as to borrowing to purchase a new home. When planning how much you need to borrow, you should definitely allow for cost over-runs and a contingency fund for materials, labour, and extensions to original time scales. Remember that banks are also aware of this, and will generally lend a little less than you are requesting to allow for it. Your deposit will be used to purchase the land, and the remaining required funds will be determined by a valuation of the building plans. Depending on your bank or lender and their lending criteria, it is likely that they will release funds to you in stages as 'process payments' during different stages of completion.

When choosing your section, make sure you are happy with the size, and that if it is on a slope that you understand how much it will cost to build on and maintain. Check for other things like access, drainage, sunshine and views (check that these won't be compromised by any other building work), other planned building work nearby, services provided to the site (power, sewer, gas, etc.), soil (as digging into rock is much more expensive than working with soil), and residential zoning (which stipulates the size and type of dwelling you will be permitted to build on the section.

Once you have found your section and arranged your finance, you then need to cover the following steps:

- Find an architect, draughtsperson, or design and build company.
- Obtain concept plans and choose materials, fixtures and fittings.
- Prepare final plans and working drawings.
- Choose a builder (either through tender or by comparing detailed quotes obtained from a number of different builders). Builder's quotes should be made for the total cost of building, including both labour and materials. Your architects may be able to recommend a builder they have experience of working with in the past. The building process could either be managed by a builder with a fixed price contract, or you could hire a professional (architect, project manager, etc.) to manage the whole job including hiring subcontractors, buying building materials, etc. You should be very careful before making the decision to manage the project yourself with a 'labour only' contract however, as this could leave you legally liable if anyone is injured on the job and any delays or mistakes could prove very expensive.
- Review your final costs.
- Review and sign your building contract (you must consult with your solicitor before signing this).
- Apply for building consent (and resource consent if required) from the local council.
- Building begins – regular inspections will take place throughout the construction process. Before building commences, you should contact your insurance company to find out whether you need builder's risk insurance. This may in fact be covered by your builder's own insurance, but it is essential that this is established before work begins.

Renovating

Most of the principles that apply to building (above) also apply to renovating. A frequent problem with renovations is that it is very easy to underestimate the size of a renovation job, the length of time it will take and how much it will cost. If you are considering renovating your new house as soon as you purchase it, it is a good idea to include the cost of renovation project in your initial home loan application. Otherwise you can always apply for a top-up to your loan.

Home and contents insurance: your own home

There are different types of insurance cover available. Multi-risk policies (called accidental damage policies) provide blanket cover for all losses unless specifically excluded. Defined risk policies, as the name suggests, list what risks the policy provides cover for. This type of policy is less costly but accidental damage policies are probably a better option. Your house can either be insured for its indemnity value, or replacement value. The indemnity value is the depreciated or current market value of your house, excluding the value of the land. It does not replace with new, nor would it cover the cost of rebuilding, but you should be able to buy a similar house. The replacement value can be open-ended or fixed sum. The difference between this and indemnity value is that there is no deduction for depreciation. Open-ended replacement value means the insurer will pay the full cost of repairing or rebuilding as new. Fixed sum replacement value means that the insurer will pay up to the agreed sum. Typical premiums exclude the value of the land and can be reduced by increasing the excess, or installing burglar and fire alarms. (For more information about insuring contents in a rental home, see the Renting section on p.149.) Premiums are cheaper outside the larger cities, and most expensive in the Auckland and Wellington regions.

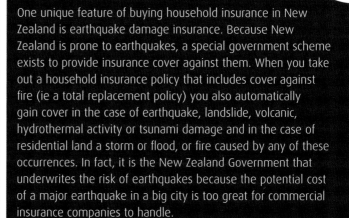
Natural disasters

One unique feature of buying household insurance in New Zealand is earthquake damage insurance. Because New Zealand is prone to earthquakes, a special government scheme exists to provide insurance cover against them. When you take out a household insurance policy that includes cover against fire (ie a total replacement policy) you also automatically gain cover in the case of earthquake, landslide, volcanic, hydrothermal activity or tsunami damage and in the case of residential land a storm or flood, or fire caused by any of these occurrences. In fact, it is the New Zealand Government that underwrites the risk of earthquakes because the potential cost of a major earthquake in a big city is too great for commercial insurance companies to handle.

It makes sense to take out household contents insurance with the same firm as you have your house insurance with (and maybe your car insurance as well). You should get a discount for having both types of insurance with the same company and it will save arguments over who is responsible for a claim. Again you can either get a multi-risk or a defined risk policy for either indemnity or replacement value (for a house of the same size). If you have an accidental damage policy you can sometimes buy an extension to cover your possessions outside of your house, for example, personal sports equipment.

Your insurance company will charge you a compulsory disaster insurance premium which they pass on to the Earthquake Commission's Natural Disaster Fund

 Earthquake Commission, Level 20, Majestic Centre, 100 Willis Street, Wellington; (04) 978 6400; fax (04) 978 6431; claims 0800 652 333; e-mail info@eqc.govt.nz; www.eqc.govt.nz.

EQC was established by the government in 1945 to provide earthquakes and war damage cover for purchasers of fire insurance. Later cover for other natural disasters was included, and then cover for war damage was dropped. The modern EQC is a government-owned Crown Entity. For 60 years it has collected premiums, and has used these to build up the Natural Disaster Fund. The Natural Disaster Fund is currently worth around NZ$5.4billion, and the EQC has its own overseas reinsurance cover as well, in case of catastrophic earthquake. If that is not enough, the government is required to make up any shortfall, and this government guarantee ensures that the EQC will always be able to meet its obligations, regardless of circumstances.

The maximum amount the Commission will pay out is NZ$100,000 (+GST) or the amount for which you have insured your home on a replacement basis, (whichever is lower) and NZ$20,000 (+GST) for personal belongings or the amount for which you have insured them. (Again they will pay out the lower amount). For a claim on a house, the excess is 1% of the amount of the claim, with a minimum of NZ$200 per dwelling. For belongings, the excess is NZ$200 and for land the excess is 10% of the amount of the claim, with a minimum of NZ$500 per dwelling and a maximum of NZ$5,000. The coverage is fairly basic and does not extend, for example, to motor vehicles, trailers, boats, swimming pools, jewellery, securities and documents, or works of art. Nor will the Commission pay for any indirect costs arising out of an earthquake such as, for example, the cost of having to stay in rented accommodation. Top-up cover with an insurance company will cover the items noted above which EQCover does not include, and will also cover you for the value of your house above the NZ$100,000 covered by the government. Earthquakes large enough to cause serious damage are rare.

SERVICES AND UTILITIES

Coping without local references or credit history

Of course, you will need to be prepared for the fact that you are starting out in a country with effectively no history there. Depending on your circumstances,

TIP

■ Before you emigrate, it is a good idea to advise your bank of your intentions, and perhaps request a note from them to the effect that you have been a good customer.

mortgage companies and banks will in all likelihood require extra assurances before they extend you the same rights as privileges as they do their lifelong customers, and it is best to be prepared in terms of your own personal and financial records.

In all likelihood you won't run into any major problems though, especially if you are bringing savings or any other lump sum with you to start your new life. Make sure you have all your bank and credit card statement from the previous 6–12 months, proof of any savings and investments you may have, information about the current value of any properties you own and the amount of equity you have in each as well as a current market valuation and official reports of current rents or any other income payable to you. Your original bank might have ties with a New Zealand bank, or actual branches in New Zealand, which will make things a lot easier. All this said, New Zealand is a country familiar with immigrants and companies you need to deal with should have systems in place to help you.

However, confusing stories about services available to those without a local credit history do arise, such as the surgeon from the UK who was told she was unsuccessful in applying for a New Zealand credit card with a limit of NZ$1,500, but found out the same day that she was eligible for a NZ$475,000 home loan. Different providers have different rules and criteria. Customer service providers will usually go out of their way to help you find a reasonable solution to any obstacles that might be thrown up. If necessary, it might be possible to ask a friend or relative already established in New Zealand to guarantee you as a customer or borrower for a limited time. Consider bringing a written reference from a previous landlord, or a personal reference from a friend or business contact.

Utility companies generally build up a picture of their customers through years of association, so if you are setting up accounts without any previous records in this country, it might be wise to have potentially reassuring records on hand from your home country, either a reference from a utility supplier or mobile phone provider, or bank statements showing regular payments for telephone or electricity services. Another solution to potential problems might be to offer to pay a 'bond' or an advance payment as a credit against your account, or to pay in advance for the basic services (line rental, standard electrical supply etc) at least for the first few months until you build up a history with them.

> I haven't experienced any problems resulting from not having a local credit history, and my initial transition to New Zealand in terms of arranging bank accounts, credit cards, utility accounts and a mobile phone was possibly smoother than others might experience as my move to New Zealand was work-based and first contacts with all these companies were arranged through my new job. Since then, I have found absolutely no problem in being granted credit cards and opening new bank accounts with simple proof of my job and income. All other accounts and providers have proved easy to deal with, and I haven't experienced any problems at all.
> **Katy Parsons**

It might be as well to keep at least one bank account and your credit cards from your country of origin in use, rather than cancelling everything before you leave for New Zealand, especially if you are able to manage your accounts, view statements and make payments and transfers online. This might make your transition a little smoother, and save you some unnecessary stress, especially in light of the inevitable expenses you will likely have during your first few weeks in your new country. It will also be useful if you still have money in the form of refunds or income due to you in your home country. As you become more established in New Zealand, you can gradually phase out your other accounts if you wish to do so.

Local council tax rates

Each local council in New Zealand levies a tax based on the value of your property to fund local amenities and services. Road maintenance, sewage disposal, water supply, libraries, park maintenance and street lighting are all paid for by your council rates. The value of your property and hence the amount of rates you pay is decided by Valuation New Zealand. Rates are included in the rent of rental properties. Ask your local council for further information specific to your home.

Connecting basic utilities

Services such as electricity, telephones, water and sewerage are just about universal in New Zealand. The best options between electricity, reticulated natural gas and LPG cylinders depend on where you live and how much energy you use. Consumer Online investigates annual energy costs in the five main centres, using common combinations of gas and electricity in the home. You can use the survey on the Consumer website (www.consumer.org. nz) as a guide to the savings you might make by choosing the best plan for you and your household. Holiday cottages in some of the remotest areas may not be on mainline electricity and commonly will have a septic tank rather than being on mainline sewerage, but the average family home comes provided with all services. If you are building a new house on a new section you may need to arrange for a supply to be laid in – ask your local council who to contact. People moving into a house or flat need to arrange for the electricity or gas and telephone to be connected.

An agreement for the supply is signed between the supplier and the tenant, as utilities are not the responsibility of the landlord. Credit references from your previous power, gas and telephone companies may be helpful in setting up your New Zealand accounts. Most government departments providing commercial services were turned into State Owned Enterprises (SOEs) in the late 1980s. They were set up like commercial companies, although as the name suggests they remained publicly owned, and were given commercial targets. The change in performance between the new SOEs and the old government departments was dramatic. When telecommunications were run by the Post Office, average installation time was at least 6 weeks. Now it seldom takes more than two days. The creation of SOEs has also brought with it some competition in the utilities marketplace. Rival telephone companies are now offering price wars on toll calls, and a freer market exists for some utilities. Contact your local council to find out which companies supply utilities in your area. Otherwise, ask your landlord, the previous owners of your home, or your neighbours which companies supply local properties. Your local phone book is another place to try, or look online at www.whitepages.co.nz searching by service and relevant area.

Electricity

Most of New Zealand's electricity supply is generated through hydro-electric schemes on the main rivers. Hydro-energy has the advantage of being cheap, clean and renewable. Most of the power is generated in the South Island on the rivers draining the mountains of the Southern Alps. Bills come once a month, and an average monthly bill for a three-bedroom house would be roughly around NZ$210. There is usually an initial administration charge for setting up a new account, which is around NZ$100.

New Zealand supplies alternating current at 240 volts, 50 hertz. Any appliances you bring with you may require new plugs. It is important to also consider the fact that you may not be able to find parts or repair services for certain electrical items if they are uncommon in New Zealand. Leave behind your telephones, faxes and telecommunications equipment – it may not work with the local network, and again you may not be able to find anyone to repair it if something goes wrong. New Zealand is a high-tech nation, and the latest electronic equipment will be readily available there.

There are a number of different electricity suppliers in New Zealand, and your options will of course be limited by the area you live in. Some of the main names are Mercury Energy, Contact Energy, Genesis Power, Mighty River Power and TrustPower.

Gas

Household gas supply is not universally available. Natural gas is available as far north of Auckland as Whangarei, in Wellington and on the East Coast in Gisborne,

Napier and Hastings as well as other towns and cities in the North Island. Bottled LPG is available throughout the country, and natural gas is available everywhere there is a natural gas pipeline. In the South Island most gas is of the bottled variety except in Dunedin and parts of Christchurch. To find out which energy suppliers serve your area, call 0508 GAS LIVING (0508 427 548). Alternatively, your local supply company can be found in the front of the Yellow Pages. Before they will connect your property, the gas company will require you to fill in an application for the supply of gas and to pay a bond of around NZ$100.

Water

New Zealand water is clean and quite drinkable, although it tastes better in some areas of the country than others. Most people seem to put up with it, although the bottled water market has grown. People building homes and renovating kitchens now often have a water filter installed with the kitchen taps – a much more eco-friendly and affordable option than constantly consuming bottled water that has been processed, packaged and transported. Water shortages are not normally a problem, although Canterbury and Auckland have suffered droughts in recent summers, and water conservation is often called for in other areas such as Hawke's Bay and Canterbury depending on the weather situation. Such conservation may take the form of a sprinkler ban or other restrictions on watering gardens.

   In some areas, such as Auckland, local councils charge for the water supply and your supply will be on a meter, in others the cost of water connection and supply is included in your annual rates bill.

TIP

■ In Auckland and Hamilton the water can have an unpleasant chlorine taste.

Rubbish and recycling

Rubbish is disposed of in two ways; the local council collects everyone's rubbish bags once a week and residents can take their rubbish to the local 'tip' (dump). Most local authorities charge for weekly rubbish collection (meaning that only official rubbish bags, or bags bearing a correct sticker, will be collected) and for use of the local rubbish dump (usually depending on the size of the load you want to dispose of). Rubbish bags can be purchased at your local dairy or supermarket. Rubbish in these bags should be left on the footpath outside the home for collection on a specific day each week.

If you live in a rural area, you are responsible for the disposal of your own rubbish. In Auckland there is an inorganic rubbish collection once every month, when large unwanted household items, such as furniture, appliances and any other number of objects will be removed for your convenience. Recycling bins are available in most areas, from the council, and are normally emptied on the same day of the week as your main rubbish collection. Recycling collectors have firm rules regarding the condition of your recycling; all bottles, cans, tins, etc. must be washed and clean, and broken glass is strictly forbidden in some areas. If your green bin has been left untouched after all the others in the street have been emptied, it is likely that you have included something unacceptable and they have decided to leave the whole lot. As a general rule all bottles, jars, tins and cans should be rinsed clean. Cardboard boxes should be flattened, and all plastic items should be washed and squashed. It is not always necessary to remove lids and labels. Some councils will provide/sell you special bins for recycling, and some only accept recycling in plastic bags. Most will not accept plastic coated cardboard containers (Tetrapak) like soymilk and UHT containers (as they also contain a foil lining), polystyrene, glass tableware, containers, mirrors, windows, Pyrex, light bulbs, crystal, ceramics, paint, oil, broken glass, sharp objects, batteries, plastic wrap, plastic shopping and bread bags, grade 3–7 plastics (such as ice cream, margarine and yoghurt containers), aluminium foil, sheets and food trays. If you have large amounts of material for recycling (such as large cardboard boxes or a lot of glass bottles), you should take them to the recycling station at your local dump or landfill. Gardening waste is not generally collected, although you can pay to have it taken away – you should considering composting your garden rubbish and kitchen scraps.

For more information see www.reducerubbish.co.nz and contact your local council to find out about what services they offer and what the rules are.

Telephone and internet

There are a number of different companies offering telecommunications services in New Zealand. These include Telecom, TelstraClear (formed when TelstraSaturn and Clear Communications merged in 2001), Vodafone, Global One, WorldxChange, teamtalk, Compass, Call Plus, City Link, Zip, DigiPlus and Ihug. The main competitive services are international, national and cellular (mobile) calls. Most competitors have interconnection agreements with Telecom, and a number also have interconnection agreements with each other.

In most areas you are obliged to hire your phone line from Telecom as they retain a monopoly on the provision of the network, and basic residential line rental (HomeLine)

Who runs the phones?

Telecom, the SOE that took over running telecommunications from the Post Office, was sold off in 1990 to a consortium of two US phone companies and two local companies. The investment programme was part of the process of revamping the company prior to selling it. As a result, New Zealand's rather antiquated phone system was given a much-needed overhaul. At the same time the industry was deregulated to allow competitors into domestic supply and provision of phone units. Deregulation has led to improvements in customer service.

The downside of telecommunications privatisation is that, despite being a private company, Telecom has an effective monopoly in many areas of telecommunications services, because it owns the network. There is no industry regulator to check that the prices Telecom charges consumers are fair. Despite competition in the long distance calling market, some industry commentators argue that toll calls are still too expensive.

costs around NZ$36–NZ$44 including Good and Services Tax (GST) a month and includes unlimited local calling, home line rental, and your white pages listing. There is a reconnection fee when you open your telephone account – this is NZ$48.99 assuming the house already has a Telecom line. Prices vary if a new Telecom line has to be put in place in order to connect you. Telecom no longer supplies rental telephones, but you can buy a telephone relatively cheaply at any number of retailers.

To get your phone connected, Telecom will require personal identification (a copy of your passport) before they can set up your access. Tel: 0800 010 016; fax 0800 324 897. Telecom offers a dedicated call centre for new customers (dial 123 from any touchtone phone in New Zealand and then choose Option 3). It takes about 48 hours to connect a new number. If an installer is required to do the connection, as opposed to a remote connection, a further visit fee is charged, and the installer will quote this on the day.

You can join TelstraClear online, by filling in and submitting a simple joining form. With TelstraClear, you continue to make toll (long-distance) calls in exactly the same way as before, but your national and international calls automatically go through the TelstraClear network. Your telephone number won't change.

New Zealand's long-distance services usually feature off-peak capped call charges, with unlimited duration. (Off-peak is evenings from 6pm to 8am the following morning, and from 6pm Friday to 8am Monday.) These deals are constantly changing, but as a general rule companies frequently have such offers as cheap capped national calls, NZ$5 capped calls to Australia, and NZ$5–10 capped calls to the USA, Canada, the UK and Ireland. Residential service competition is developing, and users should also be able to get a feature on their service plan allowing them to have capped national calls at peak times at a cost of, for example, NZ$2.50 (up to two hours) or thereabouts. TelstraClear offers a competitive range of services and options to residential and business customers in the Wellington, Hutt Valley and Kapiti areas, as well as parts of Christchurch.

Mobile telephone services are provided by Telecom, TelstraClear and Vodafone. The number of mobile phones (called cellular or 'cell' phones in New Zealand) has skyrocketed in recent years and the vast majority of households now have access to a cellphone.

High-speed internet services are becoming common, and internet protocol telecommunications providers are increasingly available, offering competing national, international and landline to mobile calls. Telecom's Jetstream service uses ADSL technology to send high-speed voice and internet data down one telephone line at the same time, in areas where this technology has been installed. TelstraClear provides high speed internet access via cable modems connected to its co-axial cable television network, but TelstraClear is unable to supply Sky TV or mobile phone services. Ihug's Ultra provides high speed internet downloading via satellite dish anywhere in New Zealand, and through a microwave dish in Auckland. The majority of New Zealand households own or have access to a home computer. There are is a range of options for internet access – these vary considerably in terms of quality, service and price. Free dial-up providers offer a basic level of access at no cost, although of course you are paying by the minute for your internet service itself. High-speed internet connections, ISDN, cable and DSL broadband are available in main cities and major provincial areas. Satellite provides an option in remote or rural areas.

Telephone books (White and Yellow pages) are supplied free by Telecom. There are several versions – each one covers a particular area or region. Most of the country is covered by both analogue and digital mobile communications networks, and almost all New Zealand homes have a telephone.

Telecom has a free call ('freephone') number for businesses with a prefix of 0800. This enables customers to call free from anywhere in New Zealand. Freephone numbers for TelstraClear start with 0508. Local calls are free for residential customers, but there is a 50c charge for telephoning Telecom's directory enquiries on 018. You are entitled to two enquiries per call for this charge, and can be connected to the number you requested by pressing 1 after the number is given (for a 30c charge). International Directory Assistance calls cost NZ$1.50 for up to two enquiries. TelstraClear does not offer a directory enquiries service. For international directory enquiries you can dial 0170 (TelstraClear) (you will be charged for this service), dial Telecom International Directory Assistance Service on 0172 (calls cost NZ$1.50 and you can request two numbers for this price) or see the Infobel World Telephone Directories website, which provides information and services for more than 184 countries (www.infobel.com). Telecom's White Pages (alphabetical residents and companies listings) are on the internet at www.whitepages.co.nz, and the Yellow Pages at www.yellowpages.co.nz.

Useful resources

Telecom New Zealand: PO Box 1473, Christchurch; Telecom Service Express 0800 000 000 (24 hours a day, 7 days a week); (7am to 9pm Monday to Sunday) 123 (from any touchtone phone within New Zealand); 0800 800 070 (Home Business) from a landline; *123 from a mobile; International Roaming service 0800 651 000; Telecom Call Centre for new customers calling from overseas +64-3-374-0253 (7am–9pm NZ time, 7 days a week); email there are a number of email forms, for various kinds of queries (everything from sales and services questions to changing your postal address and ordering a copy of your bill), on the website; www.telecom.co.nz. Remember that while Telecom don't charge you for calls made to its service numbers, other service providers may charge you if your call originates from that service provider's network.

TelstraClear Ltd: (except payments) Private Bag 92 143, Auckland; (payments) Private Bag 92143, Auckland; 0508 888 800; fax 0508 888 801; from outside New Zealand +64 9 913 9150, fax +64 9 912 4442; cable locations information 0508 651 050, fax 0508 651 100; www.telstraclear.co.nz. See the website for complete contact details of all TelstraClear offices (including street and postal addresses).

Vodafone New Zealand Ltd: Private Bag 92161, Auckland 1030 for payments and mobile transfer paperwork. Call free on 777 from a Vodafone mobile or 0800 800 021 from another network. For purchase enquiries call 0800837 8673. www.vodafone.co.nz.

Daily Life

TIP

If you can, make arrangements to be collected from the airport, either by family, friends, or through your hotel.

TIP

Just don't mention the sheep jokes (unless you are aiming them at Australia) and try not to pull out the tired old cliché that 'New Zealand is like England was in the 1950s'. Kiwis won't thank you for that one, and even if they aren't offended by it they're likely to have heard it more than once before.

■ CULTURE SHOCK

Arriving in New Zealand

One thing that everyone arriving in New Zealand (unless they have only come from Australia) will have in common is that they will need time to recover from a long period of travelling. This can be tiring at best, even if you have managed to sleep on your flight, and deeply distressing at worst, especially if you are suffering a combination of jetlag, sleep deprivation and the after-effects of planning, packing, goodbyes and a whirlwind of farewell parties. The best way to alleviate the effects is to make it as easy as you possibly can on yourself from the moment you arrive in the New Zealand airport – most importantly, make sure before you embark on your journey that you have arranged somewhere quiet and calm to stay when you arrive, at least for one night, so that you can go straight there to shower, change, and lie down flat for what might be the first time in more than 30 hours! It is important to have at least one light and nutritious meal on the day you arrive, nothing fatty or too heavy, and to drink plenty of water or herbal tea to help your body and mind recover from your journey. Try to stay away from too much alcohol or heavily caffeinated soft drinks for at least the first day or two (tempting though it might be to have a massive celebration the minute you arrive!), as these can merely prolong the effects of dehydration and jetlag. That said, a glass of wine with your supper can be a good way to wind down and relax yourself into sleeping at what your body will probably think is a very strange time indeed. Eating meals at the appropriate times by the local clock, even if you are not especially hungry (just have a small amount) is a good way to help your body adjust more quickly to its new time zone. If you have the energy, perhaps go for a not-too-challenging walk or at least sit outside to breathe in some fresh air and let your skin absorb some sunlight – this will help you feel more awake, and give you a chance to gently explore of your new surroundings.

Settling in

One of the disconcerting aspects of emigrating to a country where the locals speak the same language is that there is a tendency to underestimate the cultural differences. The New Zealand accent can be difficult to understand for a start, particularly as New Zealanders are not usually particularly expressive when they speak and can be quite tight-lipped. While you will usually find the locals fairly open and welcoming in their attitudes to new arrivals, they become quickly defensive at any perceived slight towards their country.

How quickly you manage to submerge yourself in your new community depends largely on how outgoing and sociable you are. As a rule, it usually takes new arrivals between 6 and 12 months to feel truly settled and at home in a new country; until you have lived through an entire cycle of seasons a lot of things may seem more strange

A different culture

Kiwis are very laid-back in their approach, but don't mistake this for thinking that they don't care because most are deeply and immovably proud of New Zealand. The best way to make new friends and start to feel like a part of your new community is to maintain a positive attitude at all times and try to soak up as much information as you possibly can. Keep an open mind to the different possibilities your new country will offer you – if there is one thing you can count on, it's that your life is about to change in more ways than you can imagine.

> I have enjoyed settling into a new social life, and have made many new friends, particularly through working with other new immigrants. Joining a gym is the other way that I have met new people and made a lot of new contacts, and I am enjoying keeping fit and cycling to work on a regular basis.
> **Elizabeth Henderson**

and difficult than familiar. That said, some people take to their new lives almost immediately, and any preparation you can to ease the transition will be valuable. These preparations might be as simple as reading the local newspapers of your intended destination online months before you move, to familiarise yourself with local issues and areas, and to find out more about the community you are heading for. There are plenty of newspapers and resources for intending migrants, available from Immigration New Zealand and private relocation and immigration specialists, but if these are your main source of information you will maintain that feeling of being an outsider as they are written very much from the outside looking in. Look at New Zealand magazines and papers online (www.stuff.co.nz), and also have a look online at the offerings of real estate agents and at discussion boards aimed at new immigrants (www.emigratenz.org) – you can use these to post any questions you might have to those who have already made the move.

The best approach for fitting in is to concentrate on the similarities between you and your friends and family at home and the people who will make up your new community rather than focusing on the differences. Of course, there will be differences and you will probably feel these most keenly at first, but try to take one day at a time and enjoy each new moment rather than becoming overwhelmed by all the change and unfamiliarity. If you talk too much about somewhere else you might be classified as 'a bit of a whinger' and run into 'you don't have to live here' sorts of comments. Remember, the early days are important for forming first impressions, and if you seem overly judgemental then others may be judging you unkindly as well.

Joining clubs and local groups is an excellent way to meet new friends and to find your way into new social networks – shared interests, attitudes and hobbies are a natural path into new friendships. The notice board at your local library might be a good place to have a look for information about local groups, and the local council might be able to supply you with contact details for sports teams, etc. If you see a team practice in progress, there is nothing to stop you going along to watch and then having a chat with whoever seems to be in charge at the end to find out more about it.

Children are another great icebreaker and, particularly if you have young children, you can't help but meet other parents at school and preschool activities,

TIP

Try to avoid the strong temptation to compare everything to 'home' – although they might not crow about it, Kiwis can be prickly and a little defensive about their country.

through links with childminders, extracurricular activities and hobbies, sports groups, and parent support groups.

Keeping in touch with family and old friends

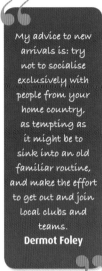

My advice to new arrivals is: try not to socialise exclusively with people from your home country, as tempting as it might be to sink into an old familiar routine, and make the effort to get out and join local clubs and teams.
Dermot Foley

Email and internet, and cheap phone calls, have made keeping in touch with family and friends on the other side of the world infinitely easier than it must have been even ten years ago. Have broadband installed with your home phone, and buy a home computer so the whole family has access to their friends back home – this will be especially important in the early days in your new country, as this is when homesickness is more likely to strike. Your home phone provider should be able to advise you of the best packages available for affordable international phonecalls.

Letters are still a great way to keep in touch with family members as well, particularly with small children and older relatives who may not have access to email. Letters seem to take about a week to arrive (maybe slightly longer at Christmas time). A fax machine at each end might be a good solution as well. Posting items and gifts can prove expensive, depending of course on weight and size, but sending small items is an affordable option. The extensive range of internet shopping options now available means that you can order items online to be delivered to relatives and friends on the other side of the world, and you can also send virtual gift vouchers for online ordering sites offering products such as books, music, DVDs, wine, etc.The postal services generally advises a very early posting date (mid-October for surface mail) to be certain of arrival in time for the festive season, but everything should arrive provided you send it airmail and by the end of November, just to be safe.

I have hardly had time to miss family and friends from the UK; we are their top holiday destination, so we see most people a lot more regularly than I thought we would, which makes the daily distance much more bearable. Email and cheap telephone calls shrink the gap as well, as I am in touch with my closest family and friends several times a week now – ironically we are probably closer now than we were when we lived in the same country.
Vita Evans

■ SHOPS AND SHOPPING

Most types of shops in New Zealand will be familiar to American and UK immigrants, and in some cases even the names are the same. In smaller towns, shops are open from 8.30 or 9am until 5pm or a little later, five days a week, and 8.30 or 9am until midday or later on Saturday.

But things are changing. Sunday shopping began in 1989 and is now well established. Most shops also have one late night when they are open until 8 or

TIP

◾ Posting at Christmas needs to be carefully planned and timed – don't leave it until December to think about, purchase and post overseas Christmas presents.

9pm, usually Thursday or Friday. However, with shops now opening during the weekend, late nights are no longer as important as they once were. In larger towns, many retail shops may be open the same hours on Saturdays as on weekdays, and will probably be open on Sunday as well, although perhaps not for a full day. In some larger towns suburban malls and superstores are drawing foot traffic and business out of the city centre, in favour of convenient parking and one-stop shopping.

In some major cities, councils have made determined efforts to revive the town centres; Christchurch's Cathedral Square, Wellington's Old Bank Chambers, Auckland's Aotea Square and Wanganui's Victoria Avenue are good examples.

Food and drink shopping

Most people buy their weekly groceries from supermarkets. The large supermarkets with the biggest range tend to be out-of-town, which makes access difficult for non-car

> We do find some things in New Zealand very expensive though – particularly baffling is the high price of dairy products since New Zealand is such a major dairy producer. Meat and veg are more expensive than expected, and not always of the best quality in the supermarkets. However, the 'farm gate' and farmer's market options offer choices of considerably better quality foods, in season, for much more reasonable prices. You can often pick your own fruits and vegatbles as well, and it doesn't come fresher than that!
>
> **Fiona Worseley**

owners. If you want to shop without a car at one of these non-central supermarkets, the best way to do it is to catch a bus there and then get a taxi home with all your bags. The major grocery chains are fairly competitive: New World, Foodtown, Pak'N Save, Countdown, Big Fresh and Woolworths (www.woolworths.co.nz).

As in any country, there is a certain hierarchy to the supermarkets, from Pak'N Save at the cheap and cheerful end of the scale through to Woolworths with its more spacious-feeling shopping experience and higher-end products. New World is

Comparing prices

You will find the similar types of food to those you are used to, but most of the stock will be made in New Zealand as imported goods are expensive. Something like halloumi cheese, for example, which is fairly accessible in other countries for a price equivalent of about NZ$4, is both hard to find in New Zealand and heavily marked up with a New Zealand price of about NZ$15. Fruits and vegetables are easily obtainable from supermarkets, but you will get more for your money both in terms of quality and quantity if you can purchase directly from the growers, whether from the small shops or farm-gate stands offered by orchards and farms directly or from farmer's markets. Remember that New Zealand is metric. 1kg = 2.2 pounds. 1 litre = 1.76 UK pints or 2.1 US pints.

What Does Food Cost?

FRUIT AND VEGETABLES (supermarket and greengrocer)

Oranges 1kg	NZ$2.47
Bananas 1kg	NZ$2.40
Apples 1kg	NZ$2.13
Kiwifruit 1kg	NZ$1.97
Sultanas 375g	NZ$1.52
Peaches - canned 410g	NZ$1.65
Lettuce 1kg	NZ$3.23
Broccoli 1kg	NZ$4.38
Cabbage 1 kg	NZ$1.14
Tomatoes 1kg	NZ$9.20
Carrots 1kg	NZ$1.66
Mushrooms 1kg	NZ$8.83
Potatoes 1kg	NZ$1.25
Peas – frozen 1kg	NZ$2.02

MEAT, POULTRY AND FISH (supermarket and butcher)

Beef steak – blade 1kg	NZ$11.69
Beef steak – porterhouse/sirloin 1kg	NZ$21.54
Beef – mince 1kg	NZ$9.53
Pork – loin chops 1kg	NZ$14.32
Lamb – chops 1kg	NZ$10.55
Bacon – middle rashers 1kg	NZ$18.69
Sausages 1kg	NZ$6.06
Tuna – canned 185g	NZ$1.84

GROCERY FOODS (supermarket and convenience stores)

Bread – white sliced loaf 700g	NZ$1.18
Biscuits – chocolate 200g	NZ$2.57
Breakfast biscuits 1kg	NZ$4.85
Flour – white 1.5kg	NZ$1.63
Rice – long grain, white 1kg	NZ$1.77
Milk – standard homogenised 2 litres	NZ$2.90
Yoghurt – six-pack each 150g	NZ$4.27
Cheese – mild cheddar 1kg	NZ$6.93
Eggs – one dozen	NZ$3.19
Butter – salted 500g	NZ$2.01
Sugar – white 1.5kg	NZ$1.95

(Continued on following page)

What Does Food Cost?

FRUIT AND VEGETABLES (supermarket and greengrocer)	
Tomato sauce – canned 575g	NZ$2.46
Chocolate block 250g	NZ$3.35
Potato crisps 190g	NZ$1.98
Spaghetti – canned 420g	NZ$1.15
NON-ALCOHOLIC BEVERAGES (supermarket and convenience stores)	
Coffee – instant 100g	NZ$4.47
Tea bags box of 100	NZ$3.38
Soft drink 1.5 litres	NZ$1.84
Bottled water 750 ml	NZ$1.86
Fruit juice, apple based 1 litre	NZ$1.78
TAKEAWAY FOODS	
Fish and chips – 1 portion	NZ$4.65
Meat pie – hot	NZ$2.86

Source: Average prices obtained from Statistics New Zealand most recent figures

closer to Woolworths than Pak'N Save, with a wide range of good-quality products in stock. The no-frills supermarkets run with minimal overheads. These tend to be large warehouse-style places with high stacked shelves where you pack your own bags and there is not a great range of goods, just all the basics sold very cheaply. Other chains are aiming at the high-income end of the market. They will offer a greater level of customer service, with a range of speciality departments in-store, including a bakery, butcher, delicatessen, seafood counter, etc. but they are comparatively expensive. Most supermarkets are open seven days a week and will usually have at least one late night when they are open until 9 or 10pm.

Local shops

Local shops have not yet disappeared, but they are threatened by the convenience and cheaper prices of supermarket shopping. Most city neighbourhoods have a convenience store (called a dairy). Dairies stock practically everything, from ice cream to batteries, and are usually open late (until 9pm or 10pm), but because they are small they charge higher prices than supermarkets. Some neighbourhoods still have their local butcher, greengrocers and bakery but these are becoming less common.

Delicatessens

Serious foodies will probably miss the range of speciality foods available in the USA, Europe and the UK, but there is a range of excellent and unique small deli-cafés in some places. For example, try Zarbo (www.zarbo.co.nz) in Newmarket, Auckland, or Dixon Street Gourmet Deli (45 Dixon St) in central Wellington. Delicatessens stock a range of imported foods and freshly prepared but at a price. On the other hand, most staple foods are relatively cheap and high-quality fresh foods are abundant.

TIP

To keep abreast of all the delicious eating and drinking options in your new country, and to find out about what's tasty and fresh when and where (and maybe even what to do with it!), pick up a copy of *Cuisine Magazine* from any newsagent or supermarket. (freephone NZ 0800 424 243; email subs@cuisine.co.nz; www.cuisine.co.nz)

The good news is that many New Zealand companies produce European style specialities locally. Many city bakeries now make Italian breads such as foccacia and ciabatta, and fresh pasta can be found in most towns. Olives are grown and pressed in some areas of the country, and local companies also make a variety of tempting cheeses. Pre-prepared meals are more readily available from specialist food stores and delis than they are from New Zealand supermarkets.

New Zealand specialities

New Zealand's varied climate provides suitable conditions for growing a wide range of fruit and vegetables, but you will find that what is available in the shops depends on the season, as it is mostly locally grown. Produce with a short shelf life cannot be imported to cover the off-season because the distances involved are too great. On the other hand you can buy exotic produce common to the area: Pacific Island specialities such as taro (a root vegetable), coconut and plantains are the type of imported produce that is commonly available in the bigger towns. Fresh fish and shellfish are another New Zealand speciality. Green-lipped mussels, Pacific oysters, and local salmon, smoked eel, whitebait and trout are all popular. Because export demand drives up the prices, seafood is not always cheap. The international reputation of New Zealand lamb is well-deserved. The potential of the New Zealand climate is also being well-used by those wanting to grow Mediterranean produce such as avocadoes, which thrive in the north particularly, and new boutique crops such as olives are also thriving.

New Zealand wines

Local wines are generally of excellent quality and a large proportion of Kiwis have a significant wine knowledge and know-how. New Zealand white wines were 'discovered' by international wine writers in the late 1980s, and this had an enormous galvanising effect on the New Zealand industry. The number of vineyards multiplied, and everybody started producing Sauvignon Blanc as that

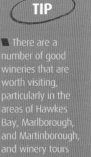

TIP

There are a number of good wineries that are worth visiting, particularly in the areas of Hawkes Bay, Marlborough, and Martinborough, and winery tours make great days out as well as excellent excuses for a holiday.

was in demand. New Zealand wines are not much cheaper at home than they are overseas, but the range is greater and you will find an excellent selection of wines at the larger supermarkets for between NZ$25 and NZ$50 a bottle. There are thousands of labels produced every year. You can buy not just the ubiquitous Sauvignon Blanc but also some seriously good Chardonnay, and some superb red wines – several New Zealand Pinot Noirs, Cabernet Merlots and Cabernet Sauvignons have won international acclaim. Great rose and sparkling wines are now being produced as well.

Other shopping

Most consumer goods are readily available in New Zealand. Imported goods are cheaper than they used to be as a result of tariffs being lowered in the 1980s. However it is probably not the shopping that attracts most visitors or immigrants. There is no equivalent to Regent Street or Fifth Avenue even in the big cities. Department store chains such as Farmers and K-Mart sell most of the essentials from clothing through to household goods and white goods in rather unimaginative surroundings. Basic clothing is comparatively cheap, although design and quality standards are not particularly high in the chain stores. Independent designers flourish in the larger cities selling creative, well-made and unique items of clothing, often through their own boutiques.

Hire purchase

More expensive consumer durables are often available in New Zealand on hire purchase. Once the buyer signs a hire purchase agreement (subject to a credit check) and pays a deposit they can take the goods home to use, and pay the remainder of the price by regular instalments. If the instalment demands are not met, however, the goods can be repossessed.

■ MEDIA AND COMMUNICATIONS

Newspapers

For its size, New Zealand produces a large number of newspapers, but they will not necessarily be of the quality you are used to at home. Regional papers were established last century when provincial government was more powerful than national government and communication networks between the scattered European settlements were poor. These regional papers have all survived and as a result New Zealand has a high number of daily newspapers, but there is no truly national paper. The apparently national *New Zealand Herald* is fairly Auckland-focused and not widely circulated in the South Island. In Wellington, the *Dominion Post* is published Monday to Saturday. Sunday papers, such as the *Sunday Star-Times* are more substantial, but still do not compare favourably in terms of size with their counterparts in either America or Britain. Most of the major papers are of the size and quality of a large provincial paper and betray their provincial loyalties by their selection of news stories. There is only one tabloid style newspaper, *The Truth*, which appears weekly and does not approach the shock, horror, or sheer awful appeal of tabloids in other countries.

Business news is provided by the *Independent Financial Review* and the weekly *National Business Review*, which covers politics and international news as well. A growing trend is giveaway suburban and inner city newspapers, such as *City Voice* and *Capital Times* in Wellington, which includes community news and events, and extensive theatre, performance and exhibition listings and reviews.

Specialist newsagents in the main cities stock overseas newspapers, but they tend to be relatively expensive and usually arrive several days late, particularly European editions. Of course, the internet is probably the quickest and easiest way to access foreign news, with the added bonus that you don't have to wait for the papers to arrive by mail. Links to all the online New Zealand newspapers, from the Aardvark Daily to Xtra News, can be found at www.onlinenewspapers.com/nz. Also see www.stuff.co.nz.

Main newspapers

The *New Zealand Herald*: Conservative in tone and appearance, the Herald was founded well over 100 years ago. It is based in Auckland and the news content reflects this, despite its name. Circulation: 200,309; readership: 547,000; (09) 379 5050; fax (09) 373 6414; www.nzherald.co.nz.

The *Waikato Times*: Advertised as 'As Waikato As It Gets...' and is published in two editions daily. Circulation: 41,083; readership: 94,000; Foreman Road, Private Bag 3086, Te Rapa, Hamilton; (07) 849 6180; fax (07) 849 9554; www.stuff.co.nz/waikatotimes.

The *Dominion Post*: It has a political focus, as might be expected of a newspaper based in the capital city. Published daily in the morning, the Dominion Post is the merger of Wellington icon paper *The Evening Post* and Central NZ daily newspaper *The Dominion*. Used to be a liberal, unpartisan scrutineer of government, but has now become something of a convert to neo-liberal economic dogma. Circulation: 98,251; readership: 254,000; (04) 474 0000; fax (04) 474 0584; www.stuff.co.nz/dominionpost.

The Press: Distributed throughout Canterbury for about 140 years, provides the most comprehensive coverage of news and advertising in the South Island. The Press is published 6 days a week. Good coverage of news from the Canterbury region, less so of national and international stories. The Saturday edition is regularly 130 pages, including the pre-printed feature magazine *The Weekend*. Circulation: 92,465; readership: 233,000; (03) 364 8494; fax (03) 364 8496; www.stuff.co.nz/thepress.

The *Otago Daily Times*: Dunedin based. Circulation: 43,246; readership: 100,000; (03) 477 4760; fax (03) 474 7422; www.odt.co.nz.

The *Sunday Star-Times*: Has the biggest circulation of any New Zealand newspaper at 202,511, with a readership of over 600,000. (09) 302 1300; fax (09) 366 4670; www.stuff.co.nz/sundaystartimes.

The *Sunday News*: The national tabloid newspaper. Circulation: 110,136; readership: 511,000. (09) 302 1300; fax (09) 366 4670; editor@sunday-news.co.nz; www.stuff.co.nz/sundaynews

For information about other New Zealand papers, including readership and circulation statistics and contact details, have a look at the New Zealand Press Association's website: http://nzpa-online.co.nz.

Magazines

Local political comment is provided by the *New Zealand Listener* and the *Political Review*. *The Listener* also carries TV and radio listings, as does the *TV Guide*, which has the biggest circulation of any New Zealand magazine. The most popular business magazine used to be the *National Business Review* (NBR), but the word on the street is that the *Independent Financial Review* now often has the edge. Other very popular magazines are *Next*, *Woman's Day* and the *New Zealand Women's Weekly*, dog-eared stacks of which can be found in nearly every doctor's surgery. *More* magazine is an upmarket women's magazine with interesting and informative articles about a range of issues from health to business, and a no-nonsense practical feminist line. A number of glossy lifestyle magazines have sprung up in the last decade. Of particular note is *Metro*, the Auckland city magazine. Metro's stablemate, aimed at readers in the rest of the country, is *North and South*. Both are liberal on political issues, conservative on social welfare issues and support the economic liberalisation programme launched by the government in the 1980s.

Cuisine is an extremely popular and high-quality publication dedicated to fine food and wine. *New Zealand Geographic* is a good resource if you want to learn more about the country's history, landscapes, people, wildlife, industries and recreational pursuits. There are a surprising number of literary magazines, apparently thriving, despite small circulation. The best established of these is the Otago-based *Landfall*, but the Wellington-based *New Zealand Books* also provides excellent coverage of literary happenings and boasts some pillars of the literary community amongst its regular contributors. Both magazines provide a showcase for fresh writing talent, although *New Zealand Books* is mainly a vehicle for reviews. *Sport* is a magazine of new writing from New Zealand and elsewhere, published annually by the highly-regarded Fergus Barrowman of Victoria University Press. For information about ordering these three literary magazines, ask at a good quality bookshop or see the New Zealand Book Council's website (www.bookcouncil.org.nz).

Magazines exist for just about every sporting pursuit, including boating, horse riding and racing, surfing and skateboarding – *NZ Rugby World*, *Top Gear NZ*, *NZ Fishing News*, *Boating NZ*, *NZ Orienteering*, *NZ Horse & Pony*, *Rugby News* and *New Zealand Classic Car* are all popular. Also among the top 20 most popular magazines are *NZ House & Garden*, *New Zealand Home Trends*, *Your Home & Garden* (NZ), and *NZ Gardener* – see if you can spot a theme there!

You can browse and order online through New Zealand Magazine Superstore – iSubscribe (www.isubscribe.co.nz) – which offers discounts off the cover price for subscriptions. You can order through the NZ Magazine Shop (www.nzmagazineshop.

Consyl Publishing Ltd.:01424 223 111; 24 hour credit card sales 01424 223 161; www.consylpublishing.co.uk

co.nz) – they will also try to track down for you any magazine you are looking for that they don't currently list in their stock. Many New Zealand magazines and newspapers can be ordered through Consyl Publishing Ltd. If you send a self-addressed envelope with five first-class stamps to Consyl at 13 London Road, Bexhill-on-Sea, East Sussex TN39 3JR, they will send you the latest copy of *New Zealand Outlook*, which contains a list of New Zealand publications available. They also sell maps of Auckland City, Hamilton, Napier, Christchurch and Dunedin for £4 each.

Useful websites

New Zealand Listener: www.listener.co.nz
Independent Financial Review: www.stuff.co.nz/ifr/
National Business Review: www.nbr.co.nz
NZ Gardener: www.nzgardener.co.nz
New Zealand Woman's Weekly: www.nzww.co.nz
NZ Rugby World: www.nzrugbyworld.co.nz
Top Gear NZ: www.topgearnz.co.nz
New Zealand Classic Car Magazine: www.classiccar.co.nz

Television

The first thing to say here is that television in New Zealand will almost definitely be quite far below the standard you are used to.

National television channels are operated by the TVNZ Group – TV ONE and TV2. TVNZ also has several subsidiary companies, and has been redesignated as a crown-owned company under special government legislation. According to the TVNZ charter, TVNZ is required to 'inform, educate and entertain all New Zealanders, reflecting and fostering New Zealand's identity and culture'. TV ONE and TV2 broadcast to 98% of the population, and produce over 90% of the most-watched programmes. On TV ONE you can watch New Zealand and overseas drama, news, sport and information programmes. TV2 has a mix of children's and comedy, drama, movies and general entertainment, and is broadly directed at a younger audience. Imported programmes on both channels are mainly from the UK, Australia and the USA. TVNZ Sport Extra is a freeview channel featuring occasional long-form sports coverage. TVNZ 6 is a new general entertainment channel featuring children's, family and mature programming. It is available on freeview only, and is split into three different timeslots called Kidzone, Family, and Showcase. TAB Trackside shows horse racing and is available on all platforms except Freeview.

Maori Television is owned by the Maori Television Service and is a Maori language channel available on all platforms. TV3 Network Services Ltd is a privately-owned free-to-air network. Its focus is general entertainment, especially sport, news, local programming and current affairs. TV3 has exclusive agreements with FOX, Disney, and World Vision, and also sources programming from other international distributors. TV3 also runs C4, which features music and reality TV aimed at the younger, urban

TIP

Don't forget that you can find content from many of the magazines mentioned above online (unless they are published under the ACP Media umbrella, in which case they seem closely guarded in print), so you can browse through and see what suits you best and what tickles your fancy before you subscribe or a buy a copy. Actually, many of the magazines have such excellent online content that you might find everything you need without having to make a purchase.

proportion of the population and is broadcast to more than 70% of the country, 24 hours a day, 7 days a week. About 2.5 million people can access the channel.

SKY Network Television is a pay company with a digital direct broadcast satellite service, which means that virtually all households in the country can receive up to 25 channels. SKY broadcasts SKY sport, SKY movies, CNN, SKY 1, Nickelodeon, Discovery and Trackside.

Prime Television is a free-to-air broadcaster with offices in Auckland, Hamilton, Tauranga, Hastings, Wellington, Christchurch and Dunedin. In 2002, Prime began broadcasting an entertainment-based schedule, following an agreement with the Nine Network from Australia. It had initially been mainly British programming.

TelstraClear operate a cable television network in Wellington, Kapiti and Christchurch. Customers can subscribe to plans incorporating between 25 and 48 channels. Most content is offered on behalf of Sky Network Television, although some channels (such as Discovery Travel and Adventure, TBN and Deutsche welle) are broadcast exclusively through TelstraClear.

There are a number of small regional television services throughout the country, these local services including Family Television Network (Rodney District), Juice TV (Auckland), Alt TV (Auckland). Triangle Television (Auckland), CTV8 (Auckland), Geyser Television (Rotorua), Big TV (Hamilton), Eastland Television (Gisborne), Hawke's Bay Television and Channel 51 (Hawke's Bay), Taranaki Community Television Trust, Channel 7 (Wellington), Triangle Television Wellington, Mainland Television (Nelson), CTV and CHTV (Christchurch) and Mercury Television (Invercargill). In addition, there is a channel called Trackside, which is owned by the TAB and broadcasts live racing, race results and programmes about racing to the whole country.

Television licences

The national broadcasting company, New Zealand On Air, does not charge a household licence fee.

Radio

Radio New Zealand runs a network of local stations, which are funded through advertising revenue and offer a mixed diet of middle of the road popular music, talk back, news and sports. It also runs two non-commercial nationally broadcast stations, National Radio and Concert FM. National Radio's morning news show from 9am to noon, Morning Report, is an excellent source of news and comment on political and economic issues. The Concert Programme broadcasts classical music and information programmes.

There is a large local private radio sector, including student radio, Maori language radio and community access radio. Local and national radio stations in New Zealand broadcast on 110 AM and 332 FM frequencies, so there is a great choice of radio programmes. Radio New Zealand's AM Network broadcasts all sittings of Parliament from transmitters in Auckland, Wellington, Napier, Christchurch and Dunedin. There is also a National Radio Sports Frequency. However many stations, especially FM radio, have a limited range due to the mountainous terrain of the country. An Auckland-based private radio station broadcasts the BBC World Service, with frequencies in Auckland and Wellington. Snippets from the World Service are also broadcast regularly on National Radio. For more information see www.radionz.co.nz.

Typical post boxes in New Zealand

■ POST AND TELEPHONES

Post

Postal services are handled by New Zealand Post, which has a monopoly on letter delivery up to 80 grams in weight. Parcel delivery is also provided by private courier firms. Domestic delivery is once daily, usually mid-morning. There is a network of more than 1,000 Post Offices throughout the country, the majority of which are postal agencies and provide other services as well. Many other outlets also sell stamps, including book and stationery shops, newsagents and dairies.

There are two classes of mail, FastPost, which promises next day delivery anywhere in the country, and Standard Post, which can take 2–3 days. The standard cost of a FastPost letter is NZ$1.00 for a medium envelope (max 120mm x 235mm) or NZ$1.50 for a large envelope (max 260mm x 385mm) and for a Standard Post letter 50c for a medium envelope (max 120mm x 235mm) or NZ$1.00 for a large envelope (max 260mm x 385mm).

International Express is a courier service, tracked and traced from collection in New Zealand to signature delivery overseas, and including compensation for loss or damage up to NZ$2,000. International Air provides Track & Trace on parcels weighing over 2kg and going to Australia, the UK, the USA, and Japan for an additional fee. International

FACT

■ There are three international services for sending items overseas – International Economy, International Air and International Express.

ℹ **New Zealand Post:** Freephone 0800 501 501; www.nzpost.co.nz.

Economy is cheaper, but slower and compensation for loss may be more difficult to obtain. Sending letters by International Air will cost NZ$2 for a medium envelope to the USA or the UK, NZ$3 for large letters and NZ$5 for extra large letters. Official target delivery times for letters are 3–6 working days to Australia (and the South Pacific) by International Air, 13–25 working days to the rest of the world by International Economy and 6–10 working days to the rest of the world by International Air. International Parcel rates will obviously vary depending on the weight of the item you are sending – there is an International Parcel Ratefinder calculator on the New Zealand Post website though, so you can work out what you will have to pay. For customer enquiries and up to date charges. You can also buy stamps and envelopes online, or from your local PostShop.

Post Offices offer a poste restante service for letters and small parcels (up to 2kg) at all locations throughout the country. Redirection service for poste restante within New Zealand costs NZ$7.00; the price of overseas redirection will depend on the service required and the international zone the item is being sent to. There is no storage fee for letters and small packets (under 2kg) for up to 3 months. There will be a small storage fee for parcels over 2kg, which will be held for up to 3 months (the first seven days are free of charge). Any mail uncollected after 3 months will be returned to sender. Note: New Zealand Post is not able to redirect mail to a any hotel, motel, motor-camp or boarding house.

Telephones

For information about having a telephone installed in your house, see the Setting Up Home chapter. New Zealand Telecom has been overhauling the phone system since 1990, introducing standard seven digit numbers throughout the country. There are five area codes for the different regions of the country: 09 for Auckland and northwards; 07 for the Waikato and central North Island area; 06 for the southern half of the North Island; 04 for the Wellington region; and 03 for the South Island. Telecom's toll-free phone numbers start with 0800 and TelstraClear freephone numbers start with 0508. Phone boxes are well distributed but most are now card phones, which can be irritating if you do not have a card handy. Phone cards come in NZ$5, NZ$10, NZ$20, or NZ$50 denominations and can be bought from bookshops, dairies or Post Offices. Local calls from a coin or card phone cost 50c. Very few coin phones can still be found, but you may find original model payphones, which have a button marked A on the front that you should press when the call is connected. In the cities, card and coin phones can usually be found cohabiting, and in some places, credit card phones as well.

■ HEALTH

Healthcare

The health system is made up of public, private and voluntary sectors working together. More than three-quarters of health care is funded by general taxation; treatments are usually free or subsidised and medical treatment is generally very good. You will be entitled to publicly funded healthcare if you are a New Zealand citizen or if you are normally resident in New Zealand.

The provision of health care has been a major political issue of recent years. Major reforms have been undertaken in an attempt to streamline administration and management in the health system. Apart from charges for doctors' fees and some prescription charges, for many years health services were provided free to the user. However, the increasing cost of specialist health services coupled with the reduction in the number of tax-paying workers has brought about a partial user-pays service.

Health spending follows social welfare as a major item of government expenditure. The Ministry of Health, which gives the Government advice on health spending, monitors the Health Funding Authority (HFA). The HFA distributes funding for public health services, personal health and disability support. It also pays for maternity and laboratory services as well as hospital inpatient care. The general pattern of the public health system in New Zealand is that primary health care (GPs, prescriptions, out-patients' visits to hospitals) is paid for by the user, while secondary health care is provided free.

Public healthcare is free for: hospital treatment, including A&E, with some exceptions such as cosmetic surgery; children's immunisations; prescription medicine for children under the age of six; and for people who need more than 20 prescriptions a year (prescriptions are free starting from the 21st prescribed item); prescriptions medicines for public hospital patients; most laboratory tests and x-rays, except at private clinics; and healthcare (including hospital stays) during pregnancy and childbirth for mother and baby. GP referrals to a public hospital for treatment are also free, as is breast-screening for women aged 50-64 and check-ups and basic dental care for schoolchildren.

Healthcare that is subsidised but not free includes: prescription items; visits to GPs; visits to physiotherapists, chiropractors and osteopaths when referred by a GP; and ambulance services.

Over a third of New Zealanders have supplementary private medical insurance to cover the additional costs of private health and surgical care in the public system

> I have found both good and bad points to the New Zealand healthcare system. With ACC now covering recent injuries, the accessibility to physiotherapists has improved which means that people can be seen faster without GP referral. I find the wait times for specialist appointments to be very long both in New Zealand and in the UK and believe that both systems could be improved.
> **Dermot Foley**

TIP

You should enroll with a local doctor or family physician soon after you settle in New Zealand, as ringing around to find a doctor is not something you want to be doing once you or a family member is already ill.

and to enable them to afford the costs of private hospitals. Private health insurance for a couple can cost anything from about NZ$1,450 upwards annually (that amount providing only the most basic cover for hospital and specialist treatment, not including GP visits, prescriptions, or dentists), depending of course on the company and services you choose. Some costs of health care not covered by the state, although they are subsidised.

Finding a doctor

All doctors operate as private practitioners in New Zealand, and you may choose the doctor or medical centre you prefer. Doctors are listed at the front of your local telephone book or by searching online at www.whitepages.co.nz.If necessary, your doctor will refer you on to a specialist for further assessment and diagnosis. As long as you are using the public system by referral you will not be charged if you meet the eligibility criteria. If you choose to go to a private specialist rather than through the public system, you will be charged.

As GPs are private practitioners they can set their own fees. Standard adult consultations (unless the patient is receiving benefits) will cost about NZ$35–NZ$50, as eligible adults between the ages of 25 and 44 pay the full price of visiting the doctor. Other age groups pay less. Children between the ages of six and 17 are charged about NZ$20 if they are eligible for publicly-funded healthcare, taking into account their NZ$15 subsidy, and children under six years old are entitled to a NZ$35 subsidy, meaning that they are not charged. Visits at weekends or nights cost NZ$5 or NZ$10 more. Adults who visit the doctor frequently, or who receive social benefits, receive a NZ$15 subsidy. Prescription charges are a maximum of NZ$15 per item, and optometrists' (opticians) and dentists' charges are from about NZ$70 for a checkup. If you need any work done by the dentist, expect to pay a minimum of NZ$120 on top of your check-up charge. People on low incomes can get a Community Services Card that entitles them to cheaper primary care, but not dental care.

GPs provide most basic health care. It is not necessary to register with just one doctor, although for obvious reasons most people tend to stay with the same doctor. Ambulance services are provided by non-profit, community-based services in most parts of the country. They do not operate as businesses, but make a part-charge of between about NZ$45–NZ$70 to help with running costs.

If you need specialist care, your GP will refer you. Specialist care is free, although there may be substantial waiting time depending on the region you are living in, urgency, and the type of treatment you require. If you opt for a private specialist, you or your medical insurance will be required to cover all fees involved. As a rough guide, the cost of private procedures in New Zealand is:

FACT

To register with a GP, you will need to take your passport and permit/visa.

Cardiac bypass (heart surgery)	NZ$24,000-NZ$28,000
Valve replacement (heart surgery)	NZ$22,000-NZ$34,000
Angiogram (diagnostic test)	NZ$3,000-NZ$3,600
Total hysterectomy	NZ$4,800-NZ$7,400
Laparoscopic hysterectomy (surgery)	NZ$8,000-NZ$10,000
Prostate removal (cancer surgery)	NZ$4,700-NZ$10,800

Radical mastectomy (breast cancer surgery)	NZ$4,200-NZ$6,500
Total hip replacement (surgery)	NZ$12,500-NZ$14,100
Total knee replacement (surgery)	NZ$12,300-NZ$14,800
Cataract removal (eye surgery)	NZ$2,400-NZ$2,900.

Hospitals

New Zealand has 85 public hospitals, including some specialised facilities for the elderly and for people with disabilities. Inpatient treatments, as well as outpatient and day services, are free of charge to all New Zealanders. More services are being provided with user-charges, and waiting lists are growing. Public hospitals still provide no-charge operations but the waiting lists continue to grow and if your condition is non-emergency or life threatening, you will find there is a long wait for surgery. If your case is urgent, you will be put on an urgent waiting list. Additionally, a points system has been introduced so that people of high priority are dealt with first. Cancer control treatment waiting lists in particular are growing, and because of the pressure on oncology resources in New Zealand selected patients are now sent to Australia for radiation treatment. Further and updated information can be accessed on the Ministry of Health website: www.moh.govt.nz. Most of the bigger hospitals will have an interpreter service for patients whose first language is not English.

You are generally less likely than in many other countries to be a victim of medical misadventure at the hands of some young doctor at the end of 100-hour shift. Young doctors went on strike in the late 1980s and successfully negotiated better pay and conditions.

As a result of long waiting lists, a great number of people have taken out medical insurance and elect to go to a private hospital (there are no private beds in public hospitals). Private hospitals cater mainly for elective surgery and for those who prefer a private room and more choice of when they have their operation.

Pre-natal and maternity care

The maternity care system in New Zealand is regarded as one of the best in the world, and offers you a broad range of services and a wide variety of options. You are given the freedom to choose which kind of care is best for you. You choose a Lead Maternity Carer (LMC), who may be a GP (this is becoming less common, and very few GPs attend births anymore), an obstetrician or a midwife, or a group of professionals working together to care for you. Most people are cared for by midwives during their pregnancy, and the midwives in New Zealand take on a lot of the responsibilities that family doctors and GPs in other countries carry out, such as prescribing medication, referral for scans and specialist services, blood samples, and so on.

Government legislation brought in a few years back gave women more choice about what kind of Lead Care they want. The health professional you choose will be responsible for providing all your care or sharing responsibility for your care with another carer during your antenatal period, the birth and during your postnatal period. Independent midwives are qualified to care for women who

> I have enrolled with my partner's family doctor – with a 'community services card' (income-tested card which entitles you to a discount on health care) a visit to the GP costs NZ$25, without the card it would cost around NZ$50 – quite a stinger! I do get an appointment within hours of calling though, and find the service top quality.
> **Sam McLaughlan**

have a normal, complication-free pregnancy and are expected to have a normal birth. This midwife may also be able to make arrangements for the services of a back-up obstetrician if you request this (this will cost you around NZ$1,500). If there are concerns about either your health or that of your baby, your midwife will refer you to an obstetrician for advice or medical care; in this case there will be no associated charges for you to pay. Conditions that would warrant this referral include:

in pregnancy: breech presentation, pre-eclampsia, multiple births, previous caesarean section;

during birth: fetal distress, slow progress in labour; **after birth:** post-partum haemorrhage, major tears, etc.

Obstetricians often provide normal care in pregnancies as well as pregnancies with complications. The care they provide includes antenatal care at their clinics and shared care during labour and birth (with midwives). Midwives will provide the majority of your visits in this situation, although they will refer to the obstetrician as he or she remains the LMC. Obstetricians often share a practice with other obstetricians, so you may on occasion be seen by a colleague instead. Women who choose this type of private care often cite rapid access to private and expert care in case of unforeseen circumstances and complications arising as their main reason for doing so. A midwife will stay with you during labour, with your LMC checking in on your progress from time to time.

Hospital teams may also provide your maternity care – these will be made up of midwives who are employed by District Health Boards and work in teams to provide care for women in the community and in hospital. In pregnancies with complications, your hospital team will probably include obstetricians as well as midwives.

Hospital midwives are not LMCs, but are employed by the District Health Boards to work in the antenatal, post-natal and labour wards. You will be assigned to a particular team of hospital midwives rather than to one individual, and your antenatal visits will normally be at the hospital. One of the midwives from the team will attend your labour at the hospital, but you may have several different midwives throughout if your labour is long.

Independent midwives will see you for antenatal and post-natal visits and will attend the birth. Visits will be either at the midwife's clinic or in your home, and the midwife will stay with you for the whole of your labour. If you choose to have your baby at home, two midwives would normally attend – your usual midwife and one of her colleagues. They can deliver your baby at home, at a maternity hospital or at a base hospital, depending on her contract with local hospitals. Most independents are members of the New Zealand College of Midwives, and their practice is regularly reviewed.

You have three choices of location for your actual labour and birth process: home, maternity hospital, or base hospital. If you have your baby at home or at a maternity hospital the range of drugs on offer to you is limited (you can't have an epidural for example) but there is less chance of intervention with drugs as well. If you choose to have your baby in the maternity ward of a general (base) hospital, they will be fully equipped and qualified to deal with any complications or administer any drugs you may need. If you develop complications in either of the other two locations, you will be referred to a base hospital, and this will be the only place you can have a Caesarean section as well. Your choices will of course depend on your personal preferences, the kind of birth you want for yourself and your baby, where in New Zealand you live and what is available, and who your LMC is.

Antenatal monitoring, screening and diagnostic tests

Monitoring during your pregnancy visits usually includes urine testing, blood pressure checks, weight checks, listening to your baby's heartbeat and checking your baby's growth. Blood tests are recommended two or three times during pregnancy. Other tests may include: ultrasound scans; glucose tolerance testing and polycose testing where diabetes is suspected; maternal serum screening and genetic screening tests such as amniocentesis. Antenatal screening and diagnostic tests are available in New Zealand to try and predict and diagnose the possibility of any structural or chromosomal abnormalities. These tests are always optional, and some parents are 100% certain that they would not request termination of the pregnancy regardless of any abnormality found. However, your LMC should discuss these tests with you so that you can make an informed decision about whether you want them or not.

Aftercare

New Zealand residents are entitled to free midwifery care after a home birth, or after leaving the hospital. Independent and hospital-based midwives are available for 5–10 home visits depending on the health of you and your baby. More home visits are available if you need them. You are also entitled to Plunket visits once your LMC is satisfied all is well and has handed you over to Well Child Services. Visits by a Plunket nurse to your home or by you to a Plunket nurse at one of the Plunket Family Care Centres will provide you with further health checks for your baby as well as support and breastfeeding. There are additional services such as home help and child care, as well as nappy service, although there may be a charge for these services – check what is available with your LMC.

If your baby is premature, has special needs, or is unwell they may be seen by a paediatrician. If you visit the duty paediatrician at a general hospital there will be no charge. However, if you prefer to choose your own paediatrician you will have to cover the costs yourself.

Costs

All maternity care provided by midwives and GPs is free for residents (unless you want an obstetrician), as is staying in a public hospital or birth centre, and referral to an obstetrician in the public sector by your midwife or GP for advice. However, there may be charges for:

- a negative pregnancy urine test
- care and births provided by a private maternity hospital;
- some tests, such as ultrasounds, depending on the policies and funding available through your District Health Board;
- some tests in a private laboratory;
- childbirth education classes (although sometimes these are free);

> " The maternity ward here was fantastic and we had outstanding midwife support for our home birth – we doubt this will be so readily available to us in the UK next time round.
> **Sam McLaughlan**

TIP

Support groups exist for women with special needs such as recovering from a caesarean section, breastfeeding problems, multiple births, children with disabilities and postnatal distress. Ask your LMC for information about how to contact any of these groups.

- all pregnancy, labour and birth care in public hospitals, etc., for non-New Zealand residents;
- transfer from home to hospital or from one hospital to another in an ambulance;
- antenatal visits for advice to private obstetricians (these may cost in the region of NZ$100–150 per visit);
- LMC care from a private obstetrician (costs between NZ$2500–NZ$4000 depending on where you live);
- elective caesarean section with a private obstetrician in a public hospital (costs around NZ$1,800).

Eligibility for publicly funded maternity care

Free maternity care is available to women who are New Zealand citizens or have permanent residency. Women who are not eligible may be charged for antenatal, labour, birth and postnatal services provided to them. Women who are lawfully in New Zealand and the partner or spouse of a New Zealand citizen or permanent resident are eligible. It is important to note that ectopic pregnancy, miscarriage and termination of pregnancy are classified as gynaecology and not maternity. If you are up to 20 weeks pregnant and are referred to a hospital for any of these services you can expect to be charged.

Your rights during pregnancy and birth

You have the right:
- to be treated with dignity, cultural sensitivity and respect at all times;
- to choose your place of birth;
- to choose your caregiver/s, and to change your caregiver/s at any time;
- to choose who will be present at your birth and to ask others to leave;
- to ask about any side effects or potential risks to yourself or your baby before agreeing to any procedures or being given any drug, medication or test. You can accept or refuse any treatments;
- to choose how you will give birth and to feel free to follow your feeling and instincts during birth;
- if transferred to a large maternity hospital, to be accompanied by your primary caregiver and support people of your choice;
- to refuse to allow your baby to be fed infant milk formula if you choose to breastfeed;
- not to be separated from your baby;
- to make a complaint and to receive satisfactory explanations from your caregiver and others involved in your care; and
- to refuse to allow student health professionals to provide care for you or your baby.

Useful websites
- www.ohbaby.co.nz
- www.babywebnz.org.nz
- www.plunket.org.nz – Not-for-profit organisation providing health checks for babies and children under the age of five, advice for parents, and a great car seat rental scheme.

- www.parentscentre.org.nz – 52 centres across the country providing one of the largest parenting networks for parents with children up to the age of six. Provides Childbirth Education and antenatal support.
- www.birthcare.co.nz – maternity and birth services in Auckland Huntly.
- www.lalacheleague.org.nz – advice and information about breastfeeding.
- www.midwife.org.nz – New Zealand College of Midwives.
- www.kidspot.co.nz – Parenting and Pregnancy Resource.
- www.maternity.org.nz – The Maternity Services Consumer Council.
- www.moh.govt.nz/maternity –the Ministry of Health maternity homepage. The 'Information for Pregnant Women' page provides a list of all the District Health Boards in the country and the providers and maternity services available to women in their area.

Early childhood healthcare

All New Zealand children under the age of five are entitled to free healthcare and prescription medicines. The service includes twelve free healthcare checks for children during their first five years and on-call help from the government-provided healthcare service WellChild. Continuing support is also provided, and this can range from routine advice and information about parenting and child development to home help, counselling and specialist help if you find yourselves in difficulty. Care is managed in different ways in different areas; it may be provided by a GP, Plunket nurse, or Practice Nurse – the choice of provider is up to you. Most parents use WellChild services alongside their GP services.

Postnatal WellChild health checks are done at birth, after 24 hours, at five days, and at two to four weeks. Further health checks are carried out at six weeks, then at three, five, nine and 15 months, and at two, three and five years.

Doctor's visits for children under six are subsidised by NZ$35. Fees for children under six vary, but are usually between NZ$10–NZ$15. However many doctors will waive this fee altogether and not charge for the service. Most doctors will make a house call in an emergency, but this will involve an additional fee.

Prescription medicines

Most medicines on prescription are government subsidised for children under six years of age. Common medicines such as antibiotics and paracetamol for children are included.

Immunisations

Immunisation against serious diseases is available free of charge for all children in New Zealand. You can receive all free immunisations at your local medical centre. Your GP will do a general health check of your child at their first round of immunisations. The vaccines are administered by a nurse as injections in the thigh for young babies and in the arm for older children. The government immunisation programme is designed to protect against a range of contagious diseases and provide protection throughout the child's life. You will be advised of any possible side-effects and what to do if problems develop, and after the immunisations you will be asked to wait in the clinic for about 20 minutes so that the nurse can be sure there are no adverse reactions. This is perfectly standard and nothing at all to worry about. First immunisations are generally given when a child is 6 weeks old, and your nurse will advise you when booster shots are required. There is no strict rule about when shots should be given though – it is your choice. Likewise, although encouraging immunisation is government policy, it is not compulsory and some parents choose to go without. As with the other services, it is up to you whether to immunise your child against any particular disease or not. Free immunisation is available for:

■ Hepatitis B

■ Diptheria, Pertussis (whooping cough)

■ Measles

■ Mumps

■ Rubella

■ Tetanus

■ Polio.

The meningococcal B vaccine is also available.

If your child is at increased risk of contracting tuberculosis, immunisation against this is also offered.

For more information about immunisation, see: www.immune.org.nz. For information on child health and safety, child illnesses and free services for parents in New Zealand, see: www.kidshealth.org.nz and www.healthed.govt.nz.

Plunket

Plunket provides free health care checks and advice for all New Zealand children under the age of five. Your community will have a local Plunket nurse who operates out of rooms or a centre in your area. You can choose a Plunket nurse to be your primary WellChild carer if you wish. You will visit the Plunket rooms for checks at different stages in your child's development. Plunket also runs free parent education programmes on topics such as starting solids, caring for children's teeth and toilet training. In some areas Plunket also runs a car seat rental scheme for infants and children.

 Plunket: Freephone: 0800 933 922; www.plunket.org.nz

Dental care

Dental care for adults is not subsidised by the government but is provided free for all primary school children through the school dental system. Most New Zealand primary schools will have a dental clinic on the premises. It is recommended that children have a dental check up at least once a year – school dental clinics provide free check-ups and basic dental treatment for all children including pre-schoolers. If your child requires more complex dental treatment your school service will refer you to a specialist, which will probably incur a cost. Although the school dental service is free, many people still choose to take their child to their private family dentist. Dental fees vary widely, so be sure to look around before choosing a dentist. Also, some dentists will not see very young children. Private dental clinics always charge a fee; this is likely to start at around NZ$50 for a basic check up including a dental examination, clean and x-ray.

Abortion

Abortion is legal under certain strictly defined conditions. The rate is about the same per 1,000 of the population as the UK and roughly half that of the USA. Early diagnosis of a pregnancy is very important, as early abortion is safer and there are more choices available. Abortion is not allowed after 20 weeks of pregnancy under any circumstances, except to save the mother's life. You should consult with a doctor as early as possible – you should request a double appointment time. The doctor will need to confirm and accurately date the pregnancy, and you should speak with them about your decision.

A doctor can refuse to refer a patient for an abortion, but they have a legal obligation to refer the patient to another doctor who will arrange an abortion. You may ask to be referred as many times as necessary to find a doctor who will refer you for abortion services. To obtain an abortion a woman must have certificates from two doctors who are certifying consultants. One of these must be classed as a specialist in obstetrics. These doctors must decide whether the patient's situation meets the legal criteria for abortion, ie if the continuation of the pregnancy would result in serious danger to the life or mental or physical health of the woman, or there is substantial risk that the child would be born with severe disabilities. Abortions can only be performed in a licensed clinic/hospital, and different licences are required for terminations in the first and second trimesters. You should be offered counselling – and if you are not, you may request it. You will be medically assessed and examined. Every clinic will have its own operating procedure for performing abortions, and you should contact the clinic beforehand to ask for information – in some clinics the counselling and the operation may be provided on the same day, in other clinics this will be a two-stage process.

Different procedures are used: D&C, which is a surgical operation, or medical abortion, which uses pills rather than surgery. For more information see www.abortion.gen.nz.

Reciprocal health agreements

New Zealand has reciprocal health care agreements with most Commonwealth countries, including the UK. Visitors from these countries are entitled to access to the New Zealand health care system on the same basis as New Zealand citizens and residents. Visitors from other countries will have to pay full price for health services. For further information see the Ministry of Health website at www.moh.govt.nz.

Health insurance

Private medical insurance

The main reasons for buying private insurance seem to be to cover the additional costs of using the public system, such as doctors' fees and prescription charges, and

FACT

About 75% of New Zealanders have private medical insurance.

to cover the costs of private hospital care. Getting insurance just to cover the costs of primary care is unlikely to be cost effective. The average annual costs for doctors' visits and prescriptions charges may be less than the premiums even for a budget insurance deal that only covers primary care.

There are different plan types that are likely to suit people in different circumstances. Almost all plans will cover surgical hospitalisation. Many also cover costs associated with specialist visits and high-costs diagnostics. Some plans provide cover for day-to-day treatment with options for dental and optical cover. Some health insurance plans are modular, which means that you can build a plan around the type of treatment you want cover for. The main advantages of private hospital care are greater choice over the timing of an operation, and private rooms. You can get hospital-only cover, which is usually cheaper than a comprehensive policy. The public healthcare system should work for you if your condition is acute or life threatening, but for other procedures you will probably find yourself on a waiting list. Ministry of Health waiting lists show that many patients wait more than six months just for their first specialist appointment through the public system.

The number of New Zealanders covered by health insurance jumped by 17,000 in 2007, following an increase of 15,500 people in 2006. The majority of policies (63.4%) are for elective surgical and specialist cover, and people with health insurance are going some way towards relieving pressure from an increasingly stressed public system.

Remember, though, that the public hospital system still provides the full range of care. The advantages of having private insurance are mostly the convenience factor. It is not yet necessary to have private medical insurance in New Zealand. Check that there is a repatriation clause in your policy if this is important to you.

For more information, contact a health insurance provider such as Southern Cross Health Insurance (www.southerncross.co.nz), Sovereign (www.sovereign.co.nz) or Tower (www.tower.co.nz).

The Accident Compensation Corporation (ACC)

New Zealand has a unique system of state protection in the case of personal injury or accident, known as ACC. ACC provides personal injury cover for all New Zealand citizens, residents and temporary visitors to New Zealand, providing no-fault accident insurance cover for anyone who is injured due to accidents in the workplace, at home or on the sports field, for medical misadventure or certain behaviours for which otherwise criminal proceedings might be brought in other countries. Consequently, people do not have the right to sue for personal injury other than for exemplary damages.

Money for ACC comes from levies on vehicle owners, employers, the self-employed, workers and general taxes. This is another area of welfare provision that has suffered from retrenchment in recent years, and the original 1972 ACC system has been reduced. Lump-sum compensation according to a fixed scale depending on the injury has been abolished, and all assistance is made on a case-by-case basis. However assistance is available for a wide variety of costs including medical treatment, private hospital treatment, loss of earnings, loss of potential earnings, home help and child care, house modification in the case of permanent disability and training for independent living. The ACC places great emphasis on aiding people back to the workforce with rehabilitation treatment. The cost of non-work related

In terms of medical care, I have found that doctors treat you more as an individual and less as a number, and that the Accident Compensation Corporation (ACC) system works well if you need treatment such as physiotherapy. There is also much better access to homeopathy and other 'alternative' health treatments.
Fiona Worseley

accidents is met through the earner's premium, which is collected through the tax system, and the cost for work related accidents is collected through the employer's premium or levy. Firms are now allowed to take out accident insurance for their employees through private firms instead of ACC, if they wish.

ACC also covers visitors to New Zealand for certain personal accident injuries. Claims are started when you go to the doctor or hospital, and ACC contributes towards treatment costs, transport (getting to the treatment) costs, and rehabilitation assistance. Visitors may only get this assistance while in New Zealand. For further information, see www.acc.co.nz.

The healthcare system in New Zealand, with the ACC feature, is very effective at providing care for most people.
Katy Parsons

Emergency services

The New Zealand emergency services are police, fire and ambulance. You should dial 111 and your call will be answered by a Telecom operator who will connect your call to the appropriate emergency service organisation. If you use TTY, dial 0800 16 16 16 and your call will be answered by the police, who will alert the appropriate service.

You should call 111 when:

- someone is badly injured or in danger;
- there's a serious risk to life or property;
- a crime is being committed and the offenders are still there or have just left;
- you have come across a major public inconvenience, like trees blocking a motorway;
- if any of the above things is happening now or has just happened.

If you can't decide whether it is a real emergency and you are still worried, call 111 and ask – the operator will help you decide what to do. Some situations will require more than one emergency service, a serious car crash for example. You should ask for the service most urgently needed. Police, fire and ambulance all have links with each other, so the first service to receive the call will tell all the others needed.

If it is not an emergency, phone your local police station. To find the address and telephone number for your local police station, see: www.police.govt.nz/district/phonebook.

It is free to call 111 from mobile phones, landlines and telephone boxes. In an emergency you can still call 111 even if you have run out of money on your cell phone.

> *i* 111 is the number to call in emergencies.

What happens when you call 111?

- The operator will answer, and ask you which service you require – police, ambulance or fire.
- You will be put through to the relevant emergency service communicator. They will ask you for the information they need to send the police to help you – they need to know exactly where you are.
- The communicator passes information to the dispatcher who coordinates the emergency service response and passes on the information you have provided.

FACT

- 90% of emergency calls in New Zealand are answered within 10 seconds.

The police, fire engine or ambulance will find you using their mapping technology and what you tell them about your location.

Police often ask callers to stay on the phone, depending on the nature of the emergency. You should be prepared to help them as their ears and eyes, for example if you saw a robbery in progress you may be able to provide descriptions of the offenders and information about how they left the scene and in which direction. The police communicators will often ask you many questions; they are trying to determine what is happening and how many officers are likely to be required.

You cannot text 111 because texts can't be prioritized by mobile networks, so there is a risk that transmission will be delayed. The operator will also need to know where you are and exactly what is happening, and the quickest to gather this information quickly and accurately is to speak to you directly. In an emergency you should always call 111.

Reporting traffic issues

*555 is the number you should call from your mobile phone to report poor driver behaviour, non-urgent traffic incidents, and road hazards. The Police Communications Centres answer about 320,000 *555 calls every year. However, if something dangerous is happening on the road, call 111.

> *i* **Emergency services**
> **Police:** www.police.govt.nz/generalinfo/calling111
> **Fire:** www.fire.org.nz
> **Ambulance:** www.stjohn.org.nz

◼ EDUCATION

Schools

The New Zealand education system is dominated by the state sector, which educates the vast majority of the population. Schooling is compulsory from ages six through to sixteen and is provided free by the state, although most New Zealand children start school at the age of five and many stay until they are around eighteen. New Zealand qualifications are internationally recognised, and the New Zealand educational system has an excellent international reputation. Increasing numbers of students, particularly Asians, come from overseas specifically to study in New Zealand.

Terms and fees

Most schooling is government-funded. Each state school is given a grant for operating costs and then it is the responsibility of the board of trustees to see that it is properly maintained. However, many state schools are beginning to charge 'optional' fees to cover development and maintenance of school property, and parents are still responsible for the purchase of textbooks, stationery and uniforms if required. Private schools of course charge fees, and these vary tremendously depending on the school.

FACT

◼ New Zealand has high levels of educational achievement – one third of New Zealanders have a tertiary qualification, and another 40% have secondary school qualifications.

Uniforms

Most school pupils are required to wear a uniform, although at some schools pupils are allowed to attend in clothing of their choice (within limits) in the last two years of secondary school. At more progressive or small rural schools pupils are less likely to be required to wear uniform. At a uniformed school, there may still be certain days on which pupils are not required to wear uniform – at some schools these days are known as 'Mufti Days', 'mufti' being understood to mean 'your own clothes'. The school should provide parents with a list of uniform requirements, as well as an indication of where items can be purchased.

School lunches

There is no system of school lunches in New Zealand state schools. Children usually bring packed lunches to school, consisting of sandwiches, fruit and snacks. Many school also have canteens where children can also buy lunch if they want to; in primary schools parents select what foods they want their children to have. Just like any other meal, school lunches need to be well balanced and nourishing rather than full of processed foods. For information and ideas see: www.kiwifamilies.co.nz/Topics/Back+to+School/School+Lunches.

There is no tradition of streaming into academic and not-so-academic schools. Most schools have good cultural, academic and sporting facilities. Even inner city schools usually have extensive playing fields. There is a strong tradition of team sports, and not just rugby, although soccer used to be banned at some particularly strong rugby schools lest the boys be lured away from chasing the oval ball to 'inferior' versions of football. Many state schools offer outdoor activity programmes where pupils learn abseiling, canoeing, kayaking, orienteering and go tramping (hiking) in national parks.

In general, New Zealand state schools are safe and well-disciplined learning environments. Nevertheless, some parents choose alternatives to the state system for their children. Private schools are owned and run by independent boards, but they must meet certain standards. Integrated schools are those that used to be private and are now state schools. They follow the state curriculum, but usually have their own individual beliefs, whether religious or ethical. They charge fees,

> **FACT**
>
> ■ The school year has four terms, beginning in late January and running through to mid-December with holidays in April and July.

Diversity in schools

Like New Zealand society, its schools are becoming ethnically more diverse, particularly in Auckland with its significant and growing Pacific Island and Asian population. Japanese and other Asian languages are replacing European language instruction, which used to be predominantly in French and German. This reflects New Zealand's shift in trade focus, as Pacific Rim countries are now New Zealand's most important trading partners. The language of instruction, except in a few Maori language immersion schools, remains English.

but these are not as expensive as private schools. Like many private schools, integrated schools often offer boarding facilities. It is also possible to board at some state schools. Usually these are rural schools whose students come from a widely dispersed population so boarding is the only practical way of overcoming the problem of huge distances between home and school. However, not all state boarding schools are in the country. Nelson College and Christchurch Boys are city schools with a long tradition of providing a state boarding school education. As state schools, their boarding fees tend to be cheaper than the private sector.

The early childhood education sector includes a range of services; in some cases services are teacher-led, and in others parents and *whanau* (extended family) provide care and attention. A strategy has been introduced to bring consistency in teacher quality to this sector; all persons responsible in licensed and chartered services, and co-ordinators in home-based services, now need to hold a qualification recognised by the New Zealand Teacher's Council, such as a degree or diploma in early childhood teaching. By 2012 all teachers in teacher-led early childhood services will need to be qualified and registered. Primary school rolls peaked in 2002, and are beginning to decrease in most areas as students move on to secondary schools. The exception is Auckland, where primary rolls are still growing and there is still demand for primary teachers. A department has been created in the Ministry of Education for teachers wanting to come to New Zealand to work, and TeachNZ holds information seminars in England, Wales and Scotland. Contact TeachNZ for more information.

i **TeachNZ:** Ministry of Education, PO Box 1666, Wellington;): 0800 832 246; National Office 04 463 8000; TeachNZ.admin@minedu.govt.nz; www. TeachNZ.govt.nz

The structure of the education system

Early childhood

This includes childcare centres, playgroups, playcentres (which are usually run by volunteer groups of parents and cater for children from a young age), kindergartens (usually for the over-twos), home-based care, *Kohanga Reo* (Maori language and culture immersion), Pacific Islands language groups and private crèches. Kindergartens used to be free, but now often have a small weekly charge, and there is also a small charge for playcentres. Crèches, on the other hand, can be quite expensive, although the government subsidises the running costs of all registered childcare centres with qualified staff. The majority of four-year-olds are in some kind of preschool programme.

Learning Maori

A growing number of children, not just Maori, attend *Kohanga Reo* (Maori language 'nests') where they learn *Taha Maori* (Maori language and culture). *Kohanga Reo* use Maori methods of teaching, based on a Maori world view. They have developed their own curriculum and *kaupapa* (guiding principles), and the growth and success of *Kohanga Reo* is a component in the Maori cultural renaissance in New Zealand.

Primary

Full primary schools cater for children aged from five to 12 years old (Year 0 to Year 8). Contributing primary schools offer education for children from Year 0 to Year 6. These children usually then move on to an intermediate school. The primary curriculum includes reading, writing, science, mathematics, and social studies. Children are usually based in one classroom and each teacher covers all areas of the curriculum.

Intermediate

Most children spend two years (Years 7 and 8) at intermediate school between primary and secondary (high) school. Intermediate schools were originally thought to provide a buffer zone to ease the transition between small primary schools and large secondary schools. However, some primary schools are beginning to keep their senior students for a further two years, as the interlude is now considered by some to be disruptive rather than helpful. In rural areas, state composite schools ('area'

TIP

■ Teaching standards are high. The teaching of reading skills is particularly strong and New Zealand reading programmes are copied in British and North American schools.

schools) have always included Years 6 and 7. At intermediate school, some pupils begin studying languages other than English (traditionally French, now increasingly Maori), and move between specialist teachers in different classrooms rather than being taught every subject by one teacher.

Secondary

Secondary education covers Years 9 through to 13. In pre-recession New Zealand, when jobs were easy to come by, it was quite common for students to leave school as soon as it was legal, at age 15. Since then, however, retention rates have improved. The core curriculum consists of seven essential learning areas: language and languages, mathematics, science, technology, social sciences, the arts and health and physical well being. Secondary school teachers have at least one specialist teaching area. Achievement objectives are based on a national curriculum statement for each area. All secondary school pupils work towards a National Certificate of Educational Achievement (NCEA), which was implemented in all New Zealand schools in 2002. The first level takes the place of School Certificate (at the end of the third year of secondary education – Year 11), while the higher levels (two and three) replace Sixth Form Certificate (Year 12) and the University Bursary exams (Year 13). NCEA will include a wider range of subjects and skills than did the earlier qualifications, and students will build on their achievements over the three year levels. Candidates for NCEA can also work towards other qualifications and national certificates. For online information about NCEA see the Ministry of Education website (www.minedu.govt.nz).

Foreign students at New Zealand secondary schools will probably have to pay fees of around NZ$10,000 per year. This covers enrolment, orientation, tuition, textbooks (on loan), English for Speakers of Other Languages (ESOL) classes and any government levies. See www.tki.org.nz for more information about schools and the New Zealand curriculum.

Further education

Further education is divided into three main areas: universities, polytechnics and colleges of education (teacher training colleges). Tertiary education is partly subsidized by the state. The Student Loan scheme allows students to borrow money to pay for tertiary education, and allowances from the state help to pay the living costs for students from low-income families.

Universities

University education was established in New Zealand in 1870, and the country now has eight universities, which offer degree programmes in a range of subjects. Most Bachelor degrees are three-year courses with an option of taking a four-year Honours programme. The universities are: the University of Auckland, the Auckland University of Technology, the University of Waikato (Hamilton and Tauranga), Massey University (Palmerston North, Albany and Wellington), Victoria University of Wellington, the University of Canterbury (Christchurch), Lincoln University (Christchurch) and the University of Otago (Dunedin).

Standards are uniform, and each university has its own specialist subjects, such as medicine at Auckland and Otago, and veterinary science at Palmerston North. Students looking for a campus environment head to Otago or Waikato. Teaching in arts subjects is mostly done in large lecture streams with weekly tutorials of about a dozen students. Admission procedures vary depending on the institution and the specific course. Some high-demand courses, such as medicine, law and business administration, have restricted entry usually based on University Bursary results. Other courses are open to anyone who meets the general university entrance requirement. See the websites of the individual universities (below) for more information, links and contact details.

University of Auckland: www.auckland.ac.nz

Auckland University of Technology: www.aut.ac.nz

University of Canterbury: www.canterbury.ac.nz

Lincoln University: www.lincoln.ac.nz

Massey University: www.massey.ac.nz

University of Otago: www.otago.ac.nz

Victoria University of Wellington: www.vuw.ac.nz

University of Waikato: www.waikato.ac.nz

Polytechnics

There are 19 polytechnics in New Zealand including the Open Polytechnic, and some of these have several campuses in different locations. They offer a wide range of vocational, academic and professional courses. There is increasing crossover with universities in subject areas, although some programmes (such as business studies, marketing and accounting) can be studied either in a polytechnic (for a certificate or diploma) or in a longer degree programme at university. Many polytechnic students either study part-time while working or are on short full-time courses. See the websites of the individual polytechnics (below) or see www.itpnz.ac.nz for more information, links and contact details.

Aoraki Polytechnic: www.aoraki.ac.nz

Bay of Plenty Polytechnic: www.boppoly.ac.nz

Christchurch Polytechnic Institute of Technology: www.cpit.ac.nz

Eastern Institute of Technology Hawke's Bay: www.eit.ac.nz

Manukau Institute of Technology: www.manukau.ac.nz

Nelson Marlborough Institute of Technology: www.nmit.ac.nz

Northland Polytechnic: www.northland.ac.nz

Otago Polytechnic: www.tekotago.ac.nz

Southern Institute of Technology: www.sit.ac.nz

Tai Poutini Polytechnic: www.taipoutini.ac.nz

Tairawhiti Polytechnic: www.tairawhiti.ac.nz

Telford Rural Polytechnic: www.telford.ac.nz

The Open Polytechnic of New Zealand: www.openpolytechnic.ac.nz

Waiariki Institute of Technology: www.waiariki.ac.nz

Waikato Institute of Technology: www.wintec.ac.nz

Whanganui Universal College of Learning: www.ucol.ac.nz

Wellington Institute of Technology: www.weltec.ac.nz

Western Institute of Technology at Taranaki: www.witt.ac.nz

Whititreia Community Polytechnic: www.whititreia.ac.nz

Colleges of education

There are four colleges of education across the country, in Auckland, Wellington, Christchurch and Dunedin. See the Colleges of Education websites (below) for more information, links and contact details.

Auckland: www.educaton.auckland.ac.nz

Wellington: www.victoria.ac.nz/education/

Christchurch: www.education.canterbury.ac.nz

Dunedin: www.otago.ac.nz/education/

International schools

There are no schools in New Zealand specifically set up for international students. However some secondary schools offer senior students preparation for the International Baccalaureate, which is an entrance qualification for most European universities. To find out more, contact New Zealand Trade and Enterprise (see above) or the Ministry of Education National Office.

 Ministry of Education: 45–47 Pipitea Street, Thorndon, PO Box 1666, Wellington; (04) 463 8000; fax (04) 463 8001; www.minedu.govt.nz

Student fees

New Zealand students now contribute 25% of the cost of their tertiary education. Tuition fees differ depending on college or institution, and on which courses are chosen. For specific information you will need to contact the university or college directly. Tuition, which used to be free, now costs New Zealand students between roughly NZ$3,700–NZ$5,700 for a full-time year of undergraduate study, depending on the course and the institution. Fees for courses such as dentistry, veterinary science or medicine are substantially higher. Reductions are available for New Zealand students from low-income families. Fees increase every year, and many students are taking more time to complete their tertiary education as they work to support themselves.

Fees for foreign students are considerably higher, undergraduate course costs will be around NZ$16,450–NZ$25,000 per year for tertiary study, depending on your course. Again, courses such as medicine, dentistry, aviation and veterinary sciences will cost you a good chunk more. Postgraduate courses cost up to NZ$40,000. This includes GST (tax), registration and enrolment, student health and counselling, language support and use of most campus facilities. See also Foreigners at New Zealand Universities below. You will need to pay in advance, as proof of payment is usually required for your visa or permit application. You can pay by credit card, telegraphic funds transfer, bank draft or bank cheque. If you cancel before your course starts, for instance because your visa or visa extension is not granted, or you are transferring to another institution, most or all of your tuition fee will be refunded, except for the registration and administration fees. For more information see www.mynzed.com or www.ted.govt.nz.

Student allowances

Full time domestic students from low-income families are eligible for means-tested student maintenance grants, called student allowances. Students must be permanent residents to be eligible. For single students, the rate of allowance is dependent on age, whether the student lives at home with their parents, and taxable parental income for the last financial year (if the student is under 25). The StudyLink website offers a parental income calculator so you can work out whether you are eligible – and, if so, for what amount – quickly and easily. Students aged 25 and over are not subject to the family means test. There are different rates for those married to another student, and those with a dependent spouse and/or children. Allowances are now administered through StudyLink. To get Student Allowances you must apply within 60 days of your course start date or within 60 days of the day you qualify to get an allowance (if that is later).

 Studylink: 0800 88 99 00 (0064 4 917 3107 from overseas); www. studylink.govt.nz

Student loans

Permanent resident students who do not qualify for allowances may borrow money through the government-run student loans scheme to pay for living costs, course-related costs and fees. Students must be New Zealand citizens, permanent residents or refugees. Each year eligible students may borrow the amount (or part of the amount) of their compulsory fees payable at enrolment, plus an amount for course-related costs (up to NZ$1,000) and another amount for living costs (up to NZ$150 a week). Your compulsory fees are paid directly to your education provider. The amount of loan living costs you can borrow reduces by the amount of Student Allowance you receive after tax (not counting the Accommodation Benefit or Bursary payment). For example, if you get a Student Allowance of NZ$50 a week after tax, you will only be entitled to borrow NZ$100 a week for living costs.

Following a recent change in loan policy, students studying part-time part-year courses may now apply for a loan. The living costs component used to be accessible as a lump sum, but is now paid out weekly over the course of the year. Part-time students may borrow the amount of their compulsory fees plus the proportion of the NZ$1,000 course costs (the length of their course as a proportion of a full-time course). Applications are made through the institution at which the student will be enrolling. All loans incur a NZ$50 administration fee each year. You can pay the loan back at any stage until you earn NZ$16,172 (before tax) per annum, at which time repayment of the loan becomes compulsory as calculated instalments deducted from wages in the same manner as taxes are paid. Interest is currently charged at 6.8% regardless of whether the borrower earns over the repayment threshold or not. However, any Student Loan borrower who has been in New Zealand for 183 or more consecutive days is now eligible for an interest-free student loan. Interest charged will still show on your StudyLink statement, but will automatically be written off by Inland Revenue at the end of the year. You will be sent a statement in May confirming that your interest has been written off if you are eligible. Check your eligibility with Inland Revenue, as rules are subject to change.

Foreigners at New Zealand universities

Foreign students (that is, non-New Zealand residents) get hit even harder in the wallet than New Zealand students, as they have to pay full fees. Fees vary across courses and by university, from NZ$16,450–NZ$25,000 per annum for an undergraduate arts, science or humanities course, to between NZ$18,750–NZ$55,000 annually for medicine or dentistry. For more information see Student Fees above. For specific information on studying at New Zealand universities or polytechnics as a foreign student, contact your chosen institution directly (see web addresses above).

◼ SOCIAL SECURITY

Work and Income New Zealand (WINZ) is the agency which combines employment and income support roles. It has offices throughout the country. Access to the social welfare system in New Zealand does not depend upon establishing a contribution record; benefits are available to all those who meet the residency and income criteria. Although entitlement criteria are generous, benefit rates are not: most benefits are worth considerably less than 50% of the average weekly wage. Increasingly prospective claimants face income and asset tests, for example high-income earners who become unemployed may face a stand-down period before they are entitled to an unemployment benefit and they may have to demonstrate that they have used up their own savings before qualifying for state aid.

Benefits are available to those who fit the criteria and are legal residents of New Zealand, but in some cases applicants must have lived there for several years. There is a reciprocal social security agreement with the UK which entitles UK residents who move to New Zealand to qualify for New Zealand benefits under the same criteria as New Zealanders. Some UK benefits are payable in New Zealand and in some circumstances it may be advisable to keep paying British National Insurance contributions. Immigrants from other countries will have to satisfy residence criteria before they become eligible.

Most benefits are taxed before payment and the net amount is paid to the beneficiary, usually directly into a bank account. For more information see: www.workandincome.govt.nz.

Benefits

Unemployment benefit

Payments are not related to previous earnings and the weekly rate is very low. The single rate currently ranges from NZ$118.98–NZ$255.65 per week after tax, and for married couples, approximately NZ$148.73 each per week, whether or not they have children. Sole parents receive NZ$255.65 per week. Anyone under 25 years old is paid a lower rate, and people under 20 years old are paid a lower rate again. The unemployment benefit is payable to New Zealand citizens and residents only, and there are various factors that may affect entitlement, including the reason you left your last job, whether you previously earned a high income, and so on. The applicant must be actively looking and ready for work, or be involved in a training course. WINZ also helps people with finding work experience and seasonal jobs.

Such work is usually in the tourist business, or in the farming, fishing, or horticulture industries.

Invalid's benefit

Available to people aged sixteen or over who are terminally ill (and not expected to live more than two years, and unable to work 15 hours or more a week), permanently blind, or unable to regularly work 15 hours or more a week because of a sickness, injury or disability which is expected to last at least two years. Generally this is not available to those who have enough money from other means to support themselves. Your partner may be included in your Invalids Benefit, but may need to enter into a Job Seeker Agreement with Work and Income, depending on your family situation. Partners who are pregnant, ill, caring for a special needs child or someone who needs full-time care, or home schooling their child can apply for an exemption. The rates range from NZ$180.54–NZ$293.08 per week, depending on circumstances.

Sickness benefit

This is available to those who can't work temporarily because of sickness, injury, pregnancy or disability. In order to qualify you must be 18 or over, or 16–17 and living with a partner and children you support. You must also have a job but have had to reduce your hours and income due to sickness, injury or pregnancy, or be unemployed or working part-time but unable to look for or do full-time work. You must be a New Zealand citizen or permanent resident. You will need a medical certificate in order to apply, and then regular medical certificates from your doctor, dentist or midwife.

If you are pregnant you will be eligible from your 27th week, or earlier if you have complications. Your payments can continue for up to 13 weeks after the birth if you are caring for the child. The amount you are paid in Sickness Benefit depends on your personal situation, whether you have dependents and so on, but it is likely to be between NZ$118.98–NZ$255.65 per week. It usually takes about two or three weeks for payments to start. You may have to wait longer if you have been working and you got holiday pay or some other payment at the end of your job, had a high income in your last 26 weeks at work, or are getting sick pay from your employer. Payments will be made direct into your bank account.

Domestic purposes benefit (DPB)

The DPB is available to a single woman (NZ$185.92 per week) and to a sole parent caring for a child (under 16). The parent must be over 18 years of age, (16 if legally married) and have a dependent child under 18 who lives with them. For a single parent the rate is NZ$255.65 weekly after tax. People over 16 caring for someone sick or frail who would ordinarily need hospital care can also be eligible for the DPB. Caregivers who are also sole parents may be paid up to NZ$293.08 weekly. The amount that someone receives depends on age and if they are married or have a partner, the number of children living with them and how much other income they have. Payments are made weekly.

Widows benefit

This is for women whose partners have died and who have dependent children living with them, were married at least 15 years and had children, or had dependent children for at least 15 years while married or widowed or were married at least five years and widowed over the age of 50. There are various other criteria, but these can be a little complicated so you should check carefully if you think you might be eligible for this benefit. You can call Work and Income on 0800 559 009 to talk about this. If you don't have dependent children, you and your partner must have been living in New Zealand when he died and for the three years before that (or continuously for five years at another time). You can only get this benefit if you have never remarried or found a new partner. Payments are made weekly, and range from NZ$185.92 to NZ$255.65 depending on your circumstances.

Family support

Family support is cash assistance for low income families. The IRD (New Zealand Inland Revenue) calculates the amount due, based on the applicant's income and the number and age of children in the family. Family Support is paid to the main caregiver of the children, and children can be counted up to the age of 18.

Child support

Parents who are not living with their children make payments to support those children through the Child Support Agency, a division of the IRD. The amount paid in child support is based on the income of the parent paying support. The IRD passes on the payment made to the parent or caregiver with whom the children are living.

For more details on any of these benefits, or to find out about any others you may be eligible for, enquire at the local Income Support Service office or call the Head Office (freephone 0800 559 009). For residents on low and middle incomes, Income Support provides a Community Services Card, which reduces the costs of health care. Permanent legal residents can apply to the National Community Services Card Centre. Application forms can be downloaded from the Work and Income website (www.workandincome.govt.nz), and they are also available from most medical centres and Work and Income Service Centres.

 National Community Services Card Centre: PO Box 5054, Wellington; freephone 0800 999 999

■ CARS AND MOTORING

Unless you are planning on living smack-bang in the centre of Auckland, Wellington, Christchurch or Dunedin in a city apartment and never leaving that one place, the truth is that you will need a car in New Zealand. Cycling to work is popular in Christchurch and Wellington, but households tend to have at least one car as well. The public transport system, while continuing to improve under public pressure and with a lot of work and funding devoted to it, is still going to be considerably less useful than wherever you are arriving from, and aside from commuters in Wellington virtually no-one else relies on public transport as their primary means of getting around on a daily basis. Unfortunately the infrastructure is just not in place yet, and the services are not widespread, interlinked, efficient or frequent enough to make the habitual use of public transport a reality for more than a very small proportion of New Zealanders. One of the truly great pleasures of life in New Zealand is heading

FACT

To relieve problems associated with rush hour, many larger firms operate on 'glide time', which means that, within reason, employees' daily work hours start when they arrive, rather than at an exact set time.

out to the beach after work in the summer, or leaping into the car first thing on a hot Saturday morning and zooming out of the city for a great Kiwi weekend road trip. You can't do that without a car. And if you are planning on hauling things like mountain bikes, surfboards and wetsuits, hiking boots, picnic gear, children and dogs along with you, well, you get the picture...

It is common to see older model cars in New Zealand, this is a hangover from the days when new cars were very expensive so people drove their old car for a long time. Most of the older cars are British or American makes. Modern cars tend to be Japanese makes. Because of the absence of heavy traffic there is not much of a network of multi-lane motorways. Most state highways are single carriageways and as a general rule there are no tolls. Multi-lane motorways carry traffic into and out of the four main cities and through parts of Auckland and Wellington. Congestion on these stretches during rush hour is often a problem, but nothing compared to traffic jams in European or North American cities.

Driving traits

New Zealand drivers have a reputation for being fast and rather aggressive, but the advent of speed cameras and other traffic safety programmes are tending to change this attitude. It is easy to see why you might be tempted to drive well over the speed limit when there is no other traffic in sight, let alone any sign of the law. City drivers are not particularly considerate. It is rare for people to give way to allow cars from side roads to join the main stream of traffic, again perhaps because there are usually fewer congestion problems. Nor do New Zealand drivers willingly move over into the slow lane to let faster traffic past.

Driving outside the main cities is usually a pleasant experience. The roads are uncluttered and the scenery superb. The weather often provides more of an obstacle to reaching your destination than other drivers do. Flooding or heavy snowfalls only occasionally block main routes, particularly the roads through the volcanic plateau in the central North Island and the cross-alpine routes in South Island. There are signs at the start of tricky stretches of road indicating which routes are open. In general the signs indicating distances and routes on the highway system are less frequent than in other countries (although to be fair there is usually only one main route to any destination). Junctions are not as well designed, and roundabouts are less common and tend to be poorly sign posted. But then, there is less traffic on the roads.

Unfortunately driving in New Zealand is not very safe. It has one of the worst accident records per head of population in the developed world. About 500 people die on the roads each year, and the 'road toll' often appears on the national TV news.

The government is trying to improve the statistics by targeting the worst-offending group, specifically young men who drink and drive, so be aware that the blood-alcohol limits are strictly enforced. Increasingly there are official random roadblocks, particularly around the festive season, in which every passing driver may be stopped and breath-tested.

Driving regulations

The maximum speed on highways and motorways is 100km, and in built up areas 50km. Speed cameras are being introduced at various places in cities and on country roads. New Zealanders drive on the left-hand side of the road, and the rules of the road are similar to British driving regulations.

However, there are several important differences:

- At crossroads traffic turning left must give way to on-coming vehicles turning right.
- It is illegal to park facing the wrong way, and safety belts must be worn by the driver and all passengers.
- Traffic lights change straight from red to green, then amber followed by red again.
- Standard international road signs are being introduced.
- One sign that may be unfamiliar is LSZ enclosed by a red circle, indicating a Limited Speed Zone in which the motorist should slow down to allow for children, pedestrians or other traffic. This is frequently used when state highways pass through small towns

As noted above, drink-driving regulations are strictly enforced. The limit is 80mls per 100mls of blood – less than two pints of beer for the average adult male. Drivers under 20 years-old have a lower limit: 30mls per 100mls of blood. Police officers are able to stop motorists at random and breath-test them. The maximum penalty is a NZ$1,500 fine and 6 months in prison. Repeat offenders can lose their license.

Seat belts must be worn in the front of cars and in the back if they are fitted. Helmets are compulsory for motorcyclists as well as bicycle riders.

You can find the New Zealand Road Code online at www.ltsa.govt.nz.

Basic road rules

The following is a summary of the most important information from the New Zealand Road Code.

Keep left

Traffic travels on the left-hand side of the road.

Seatbelts

All modern vehicles are fitted with seatbelts for both the front and back seats, and wearing them is compulsory. If you fail to do so and are caught you will be charged a NZ$150 fine.

Speed limits

Whatever speed you are travelling, always be sure you are leaving enough room between you and the vehicle in front to allow you to stop safely within half the length of clear road you can see in front of you. This should enable you to avoid collision if you have to stop suddenly.

Speed limits are in kilometres per hour, never in miles. Check the road code to familiarise yourself with the relevant signage. There is normally a limit of 50 km/hour within built-up areas. When you are on the open road, speed limits are as follows: 100 km/hour for cars, vans and motorcycles; 90 km/hour for heavy motor vehicles and; 80 km/hour for a vehicle towing a trailer or a caravan. Where you see signs for a Limited Speed Zone (LSZ) you should stick to 50 km/hour whenever any of the following are likely to make a higher speed unsafe: bad weather; poor visibility; the presence of children, pedestrians or cyclists; heavy traffic or; slippery road surfaces. Providing that none of these potential hazards are present, you can assume that the open road speed limit (100 km/hour) applies here. When passing or approaching a school bus, you are required to slow your speed to 20 km/hour.

Overtaking

You should always overtake on the right, unless you are directed otherwise by a police officer, or in situations where there are two or more lanes on your side and you can safely overtake on the left. You must not overtake near a pedestrian crossing, a railway crossing, an intersection, a blind bend, the crest of a hill, or anywhere else that you are unable to see a minimum of 100 metres ahead clearly. A 'no passing line' area will be indicated by a solid yellow line in the centre of the road, on your side. Warning that these are coming up will often be given by a broken yellow line. If you are using passing lanes, you should move into the left-hand lane unless you are overtaking. Always begin indicating at least three seconds before you intend to start overtaking.

Roundabouts

You must signal at a roundabout if you wish to turn on the roundabout rather than heading straight through it. You must give way to traffic on the right, and always turn left into a roundabout. Signal when leaving a roundabout.

Pedestrian crossings

Slow down and prepare to stop as you approach a pedestrian crossing. Never overtake near a crossing and always give way to any pedestrians on both sides of the crossing.

Motorways

Keep to the left-hand lane unless overtaking, and always indicate at least three seconds before changing lanes. If you are travelling on a motorway, it is prohibited to make a U turn, walk or cycle, or stop your vehicle.

Road signs

Stop: You must stop completely then give way to all traffic. There will be two yellow lines on the road to show you the correct place to stop.

Give way: Slow down in readiness to stop. Give way to all traffic not controlled by stop or give way signs. There will be white lines on the road.

Intersections

Slow down and check in all directions, ready to stop. If you are about to turn, you must give way to all traffic not turning and all right-turning traffic coming from your right. Always obey both traffic signals and signs, as well as directions marked on the road using arrows or shown by words written on the road.

If you need to change lanes, make sure that it is first safe for you to move, and signal for three seconds or longer before you change lanes. When travelling straight through an intersection, give way to vehicles approaching on your right.

When turning right, give way to traffic travelling straight through in either direction. If two vehicles are both turning to the right, you are required to give way to the traffic on your right. When turning left, give way to traffic travelling straight through and to traffic turning right into the road you wish to take.

Breakdowns: the AA

Members can call the New Zealand Automobile Association (AA) at any time to assist with mechanical difficulties or breakdowns. Members can also qualify for discounted car maintenance and repair services, free technical and legal advice, discounted Warrant of Fitness services and discounted insurance policies. For membership enquiries, email membership@aa.co.nz or call 0800 500 333. Annual membership costs NZ$89 (Auckland residents only) or NZ$77; the second year costs NZ$80.10 (Auckland residents) or NZ$69.30 (elsewhere in New Zealand) as you get a 10% discount, years three and

 New Zealand Automobile Association (AA): Freephone 0800 500 222; aaroadservice@aa.co.nz

four entitle you to a 20% discount (NZ$71.20 Auckland, NZ$61.60 elsewhere) and during years five through to 24 as a member you will be entitled to a 25% discount, so NZ$66.75 for Aucklanders and NZ$57.75 for everyone else. Associate, business and youth memberships are also available. For more information, visit the website at www. aa.co.nz (you can apply for membership online). The website also offers information about buying, selling and maintaining your car, vehicle finance and insurance, driver training courses, defensive driving courses, and so on.

Accidents

If you are involved in a car accident, the AA advises the following steps:

- Stop and help.
- Do not admit liability.
- Obtain names, addresses and insurance companies of all other parties involved and the registration numbers of any vehicles involved.
- Report details to your insurance company within 24 hours and complete an accident report.
- If someone is hurt report to the nearest police station within 24 hours.
- If no one is hurt, but property is damaged, you must give your name and address to the property owner within 48 hours, and if the owner cannot be located you must give your details to a police officer no later than 60 hours after the crash.

Driving licences

New Zealand's driver licensing system is a three-step process. The first step is a learner's driving licence, which is awarded once you pass the initial theory test required before you are allowed to learn to drive. To apply for this licence, you must be 15 years of age or older, study the New Zealand Road Code, and sit and pass a 35-question theory test at your nearest AA Centre, AA Driver and Vehicle Licensing Agent or Rural Mobile Unit.

To sit the test, you must pay a NZ$79 fee, pass an eyesight test, have your photo taken at the centre, and supply both your proof of identity and proof of address (bank statement or utility bill, etc.). Once you have passed this test, you will be given a temporary driver's licence, which is valid for 21 days, during which time your photo licence should arrive by post. You can then buy learner plates, and practice driving with either a registered driving instructor or a supervising driver who has held a full licence for at least two years and must sit in the front passenger seat at all times while you are driving.

After holding your learner's licence for six months, you can sit your restricted licence test. If you are unsuccessful in passing your learner's licence test, you can re-sit the test an unlimited number of times; you simply need to return to the centre with your proof of identity and a NZ$39.70 fee each time you wish to re-sit the test.

To sit your restricted driver's licence test you must book an appointment at one of the Centres or Agents as mentioned above. This booking must be made in person, as it is not possible to make these appointments over the phone or internet. You need to present proof of identity, proof of address, pay a fee of NZ$88.20, and pass another eyesight test as well as having your photograph taken. This is a practical test, and will take roughly 30 minutes. You need to provide a car to use during the test, and this car must of course have working indicator and brake lights as well as a current registration and Warrant of Fitness. It must also display L plates. Once you have passed this test, you may remove the L plates from your car, and you are now licensed to drive on your own between 5am and 10pm. Between 10pm and 5am you may only drive if you are carrying a fully licensed passenger. If you are under 25 you may sit your full driver's licence after 18 months on a restricted licence, or you can pass a Defensive Driving Course after holding your restricted license for at least 6 months and this entitles you to sit your full licence after just 12 months. If you are over 25 years old you are entitled to sit your full licence after just 6months, or pass a Defensive Driving Course and sit your full licence after just 3 months.

If you don't pass your restricted test, you can re-sit any number of times, as with the learner's licence. You will have to bring proof of identity and pay a NZ$48.90 re-sit fee each time. For more detailed information about applying for licenses, and for a study guide, see www.landtransport.govt.nz.

The full licence is your final step in the licensing system, and includes a practical in-car driving test. The full license driving test takes around one hour, and the car you use for the test must comply with all the same regulations as a car used for the restricted test, apart from the L plates of course. Again, you will need to take your proof of identity and address, and you will need to have an eyesight test and your photo taken. The fee this time will be NZ$115.50. If you pass, you are entitled to drive anytime, during the day or night, and you may carry passengers with you in the car. If you fail, you are able to re-sit the test an unlimited number of times, provided that each time you bring with you your identification and a re-sit fee of NZ$70.80.

If you have a full, clean licence in your home country, and you are over 18 years of age, you can apply for an international driving permit (IDP). This is valid for a 12-month period from the date of issue, and can be used in New Zealand. The AA is the only place in New Zealand where you can apply for one of these. You can't use the IDP as a permanent licence – it is intended really for touring purposes only. Alternatively, you

can use your UK Driving Licence for a period of 12 months from your original arrival date. You must be careful not to let this lapse without making arrangements for your New Zealand licence, as your insurance will be invalidated if you are driving without a current and correct licence. At the end of the 12-month IDP period, you must apply for a New Zealand Photo Driving License, which involves sitting a written and oral test, and then an interview with a police officer to obtain exemption from taking the practical test. Your original license must still be valid in order to apply. Drivers under the age of twenty are eligible only for a restricted licence and are not allowed to drive after dark. If your licence is lost or stolen, you simply apply to the Land Transport Safety Authority (LTSA) to have it reissued. See the LTSA website (www.landtransport.govt.nz) or contact the New Zealand AA (www.aa.co.nz) for more information.

If you need to prove that you are a licensed New Zealand driver, you can request a Certificate of Particulars. This sets out all the relevant details. To apply, fax or email the LTSA Transport Registry Centre (fax 0064 6 953 6367; email info@landtransport. govt.nz) with your name, date of birth and address, and the method by which you want to receive the certificate (fax, email, post, etc.).

Car registration

Cars must be registered with the Post Office and have a current Vehicle Inspection Certificate (VIC) also known as a Warrant of Fitness (WOF). Vehicles first registered anywhere less than 6years ago must have a WoF inspection every 12 months. All other vehicles must have WoF inspections every six months. Cars must also have a Vehicle Identification Number (VIN), an identification scheme to try and cut down on vehicle theft. At the time of writing, the cost of registering an ordinary motorcar was between NZ$323.42 and NZ$452.04 per year. Cars can be registered at any Post Office shop. Re-registration forms are sent out automatically.

Most garages offer VIC testing, which takes about 25 minutes and will cost you roughly NZ$50. The fee for registering change of ownership papers is NZ$9.20, and this must be done within seven days of buying the vehicle. The LTSA should supply you with a 'change of ownership' card to prove that you have advised them of the change. For a small charge, you can apply to have an LTSA agent check that a vehicle isn't reported stolen, and is properly registered and licensed. Further information may be obtained from the Land Transport Safety Authority Motor Vehicle Registration Helpdesk (Freephone: 0800 699 000; email info@landtransport.govt. nz). Of course, the price of car insurance varies depending on the value of the car, the area you live in and the age and driving record of the driver.

Car insurance

You are not legally required to get insurance in New Zealand, however it is sensible to get at least third party coverage. If you are involved in an accident and cause harm to another driver, you will not be personally liable for the injuries you cause them because of the no-faults compensation for personal injury provided by the Government through the Accident Compensation Corporation. But if you write off their car and you have no insurance then, like anywhere else in the world, you will be paying the bill.

The premiums for full insurance coverage vary according to your age (under-25s pay a lot more), gender (some firms offer females a discount because they are

statistically less likely to have accidents) and driving history. A no-claims record entitles you to discounted premiums. You should bring evidence of your claims record with you because a claim-free insurance record may qualify you for the bonus. As a very rough indication, insurance on a car valued at between NZ$35,000–NZ$50-000 will cost you somewhere in the region of NZ$300 a year. Some firms may not be prepared to insure you until you have a New Zealand driver's licence (see above for requirements).

Useful resources

Land Transport Safety Authority Head Office: Level 4, New Zealand Post House, 7 Waterloo Quay, PO Box 2840, Wellington 6140. (04) 931 8700; fax (04) 931 8701. For information on vehicle warranties and vehicle and driver licensing, call freephone 0800 699 000 or visit the website: www.landtransport.govt.nz.

AA Car Insurance: 0800 500 444; www.aa.co.nz/insurance or www.aainsurance. co.nz.

AMI: 0800 100 200; www.ami.co.nz.

AMP: 0800 808 267 or from overseas +64 4 498 8000; www.amp.co.nz.

New Zealand Insurance (NZI): 0800 800 800; www.newzealandinsurance.co.nz.

State Insurance: 0800 80 24 24; www.state.co.nz.

Buying a car

Having researched the cost of importing your car to New Zealand you may decide that the best option is to leave it behind. New cars are comparatively expensive but

 Personal Property Security Register: 0508 PPSR INFO/0508 777 746; www.ppsr.govt.nz

the second-hand market in Japanese and Asian cars is competitive. European cars tend to be quite pricey and parts can be difficult to obtain, as well as ridiculously expensive. Familiar models may go under slightly different names in New Zealand. There is no domestically owned brand, but most cars are locally assembled. The government is reducing tariffs resulting in fewer locally assembled cars and more new and second-hand imported vehicles. Two motor industry websites may be useful: www.autonet.co.nz and www.autovillage.co.nz.

Second-hand cars

Buying second-hand is a viable option. Cars have to be sold warranted as roadworthy. A second-hand vehicle dealer is required by law to inform the buyer honestly about the vehicle and its history, and the car must be of the model, year, and odometer mileage displayed. The Fair Trading Act operates to protect buyers, and under the Act it is not necessary to prove that a certain individual had been misled, only that a typical consumer could have been deceived. There are a number of companies offering pre-purchase vehicle checks, including the AA who will check a car without charge if you are a member.

A second-hand vehicle can be repossessed if its previous owner used it as security for a loan, and the loan was not repaid. The Motor Vehicles Security Register (which now comes under the umbrella of the Personal Property Security Register) can be used to check whether there is any money owing on your car, and to determine whether a security interest is registered against a particular vehicle.

Car hire

If you want to organise car hire before you arrive, your travel agency may arrange rental for you through a New Zealand firm. It is also possible to arrange your rental in advance through an international rental firm, such as Avis (www.avis.com), Hertz (www.hertz.com) or Budget (www.budget.co.nz). You could also try www.vroomvroomvroom.co.nz. Hirers in New Zealand must be at least 21 years of age and will need a current international, UK or New Zealand driving licence.

■ OTHER TRANSPORT

Air travel

As the major population centres are many miles apart, getting between cities by road or rail is fairly time consuming. It can take around 10 hours to drive from Wellington to Auckland, and about four hours between Christchurch and Dunedin. Air travel is a popular alternative. New Zealand's national airline is the state-owned Air New Zealand. It operates out of sites in the main cities. Air New Zealand has expanded its services and now operates a 'no-frills, value-based' domestic service using subsidiary airline Freedom Air (www.freedomair.com). No meals are provided, and the cost of travel documentation is reduced by ticketless travel. Freedom Air began flying the main routes between Auckland, Wellington and Christchurch in May 2001, and now flies to Dunedin, Hamilton and Palmerston North as well as several Australian destinations.

Through its 'GrabASeat' promotions Air New Zealand offers super-low internet-only fares on the main routes – you have to be quick, but there are some excellent prices if you can snap these tickets up (sometimes as low as NZ$59). They are for sale for one day only, or until sold out; in reality they sell out pretty speedily so you need to log on early in the morning! There are also special deals on late night flights or flights during off-peak hours. Holders of the International Student Identity Card (ISIC) can get a 50% discount on standby travel. On the major routes this may entail waiting around in the

airport until a flight has spare seats, but it rarely involves more than a couple of hours delay unless it is a particularly busy period such as the start of the school holidays or the festive season.

Auckland International Airport handles the majority of New Zealand's international arrivals and departures. The website addresses for the three main airports are: www.auckland-airport.co.nz, www.wellington-airport.co.nz and www. christchurch-airport.co.nz.

Trains

The train network is not exactly comprehensive and is largely geared towards the tourist market; there are only a few trains to most major destinations each day. TranzMetro (www.tranzmetro.co.nz) operates commuter-style train services in Wellington (from Johnsonville, Paraparaumu and Wairarapa into the central city). MAXX operates trains in Auckland, as well as buses and ferries (www. maxx.co.nz for timetables and ticketing information). Trains cost more than the

 Tranz Scenic: 0800 872 467, or from overseas +64 4 495 0775 or fax +64 4 472 8903; bookings@tranzscenic.co.nz; www.tranzscenic.co.nz

equivalent journey by bus, although there are some faster services that are more expensive. Many of the routes are chiefly designed with tourists in mind; Tranz Scenic trains offer services such as the Tranzalpine Express from Christchurch to Greymouth across the Southern Alps, and the Overlander (from Auckland to Wellington). Other train lines are Capital Connection (a popular commuter train between Palmerston North and Wellington), and the TranzCoastal (from Picton to Christchurch). Reservations are advisable during the summer on popular tourist routes, and booking well in advance often enables you to buy tickets at reduced prices. (Tranz Scenic may be made by credit card and students are entitled to a discount off the standard adult fare (with ID). Tranz Scenic trains also have a service called Throughfares, which combines your train service with your Interislander ferry booking, so that you only have to make one reservation for your whole trip.

Coaches

Buses (usually called coaches) between major cities provide much more frequent services than the trains. There are three main companies: Newmans, Scenic, and InterCity. Newmans operates in the North Island from Auckland to Wellington, and in the South Island from Christchurch through to Queenstown and Milford Sound. Scenic is located in Auckland, Rotorua, Christchurch and Queenstown. InterCity provides the most comprehensive and economical service, running 120 services a day between 600 towns and cities across the country all the way from Kaitaia down to Invercargill. InterCity often has special limited fares available if you book in advance. Check www. intercity.co.nz for fare information. InterCity also offers the Flexi-Pass, which is valid for most New Zealand coach transport for 12 months and works something like a pre-paid phone card – the more hours you buy the better value you get. Passes are sold in blocks of time (from 15 hours for NZ$164.00 through to 60 hours of travel for NZ$585.00), you can get on and off buses as you please and the pass is valid for any of InterCity's scheduled services. See the website for more detailed information: www.flexipass.co.nz.

Coach reservations can be made by telephone or over the internet.

 Scenic Coachlines: (09) 636 9000; mahunga@scenic.co.nz; Newmans Coachlines : (09) 623 1504; www.newmanscoach.co.nz; and InterCity: (09) 913 6100; www.intercity.co.nz.; https://reservations.coachbookings. co.nz/; info@intercitygroup.co.nz if you wish to book more than six months in advance.

City transport

FACT

■ There is no underground or metro system anywhere in New Zealand.

Public transport in most of the major cities does not provide a sufficiently comprehensive network to replace the private car as the major method of getting to work. Because urban population densities are low by world standards this does not yet produce enormous pollution and congestion problems, although it is best to avoid driving in central Auckland and Wellington during rush hour if at all possible. Inner city parking can be extremely expensive, both in metered street parks and in parking buildings, and parking wardens are vigilant. In Auckland and Wellington, commuter rail and bus networks replace the car for a small percentage of the working population, but services (especially in Wellington) are not always frequent or reliable.

Taxis

Taxis in New Zealand can be found at taxi stands or ordered by phone (check the Yellow Pages for local phone numbers). They do not drive around waiting to be hired, so there is no point trying to flag one down even if it looks empty. The fares are all metered so you do not need to agree a price with the driver before setting off.

In many cities, mini-vans called 'airport shuttles' run a taxi service from the airport into any destination in the central city. Usually there is a flat fee per person for the ride. For an individual, this is almost always a cheaper option than a taxi, although slightly less convenient as you may not be the first person to be dropped off. If you need a shuttle to take you from the city to the airport, try to book at least one day early rather than just ten minutes before you would like to be collected. Because shuttles make more than one 'pick-up', the drivers need to plan their routes to the airport according to stops they have to make along the way. Company listings can be found in the Yellow Pages. Airport shuttles have their own stands outside terminals at most major airports.

The inter-island ferries

There are three types of ferry which cross Cook Strait to carry passengers between the North and South Islands: the Interislander ferry, the Bluebridge ferry and a fast ferry called The Lynx. Combined, these ferries offer about seven crossings in each direction daily, with a roll-on, roll-off service for cars. The trip takes about three hours on the Interislander and 135 minutes on The Lynx. All vessels carry both passengers and vehicles. The standard cost for a small family car is between NZ$130–NZ$255, although there are specials and discounts (between 15%–50%) available for travel during the off peak season (non-holiday periods) and for non-refundable tickets booked well in advance (Ultra Saver fares). Cheaper fares can be had on the Bluebridge service, with crossings with a vehicle from about NZ$130 each way, but crossings are less frequent. The fare for adult foot passengers is NZ$52–NZ$72 standard one way. To check what special fares are available, visit the website at www.interislander.co.nz. The North Island departure point is the Ferry Terminal on Aotea Quay in Wellington, and in the South Island the Picton Ferry Terminal.

The ferries include such amenities as movie theatres, bars, smoking areas, workstations, outdoor observation decks, a nursery (with cots and changing facilities), children's play areas and caféterias. There are also onboard shops and information centres. If the crossing is bad though, food will probably be the last thing on your mind. The Cook Strait can be a particularly rough stretch of water, and travel may be delayed or cancelled during especially bad weather. On the upside however, the scenery as you enter the Sounds is spectacular and you may see dolphins swimming alongside or in front of the ferry.

Useful resources

Air New Zealand: Air NZ Contact Centre, Private Bag 93537, Takapuna, North Shore City 0740; Bookings and enquiries: 0800 737 000; online booking help: 0800352 266; www.airnz.co.nz.

Bluebridge Cook Strait Ferry: 0800 844 844 (NZ only) 0064 4 471 6188 (from overseas); bookings@bluebridge.co.nz; www.bluebridge.co.nz.

Freedom Air: www.freedomair.co.nz. For help, email Freedom Air through the facility on its website.

InterCity Coachlines: CPO Box 3625, Auckland; 0800 468 372, or (09) 639 0500; fax (09) 639 0503; www.intercity.co.nz.

The Interislander and The Lynx: 0800 802 802 or (04) 498 3302; fax (04) 498 3090 or Freefax 0800 101 525; from overseas: tel 0064 4 498 3302; info@interislander.co.nz; www.interislander.co.nz.

Newmans Coachlines: 09 623 1504; www.newmanscoach.co.nz.

Tranz Scenic: 0800 872 467; www.tranzscenic.co.nz.

■ TAX

The taxation system was extensively reformed as part of the economic liberalisation in the 1980s. A goods and services tax was introduced, called GST (a value-added tax), and the philosophy of a 'user pays' policy resulted in a reduction in personal tax rates. GST and income tax are the main New Zealand taxes. Through the 'user pays' policy, government subsidies have been reduced for certain services like university education, and some medical costs. Some government departments have been sold off to become State Owned Enterprises (SOE), and these SOEs also charge out the cost of their services.

The Inland Revenue Department (IRD) is the government agency responsible for implementing and enforcing New Zealand's tax policy, and there are IRD branches in all the cities and major towns. The income tax year runs from 1st April to 31st March of the following year.

Income tax

Personal tax rates	
Annual Income	**Tax Rate**
NZ$0–NZ$38,000	19.5 cents per dollar
NZ$38,001–NZ$60,000	33 cents per dollar
over NZ$60,000	39 cents per dollar
No declaration	45 cents per dollar

NB. Employers are legally required to use the no-declaration rate when an employee does not fully complete their Tax Code Declaration (IR330). A completed form must include name, IRD number, and tax code, and must be signed.

All employees must pay an ACC earners' levy to cover the cost of non-work-related injuries. It is collected by Inland Revenue on behalf of ACC (the Accident Compensation Corporation). Employers deduct this levy from employee's wages, and it is included as a component of Pay As You Earn (PAYE) deductions. It is charged at a flat rate each year – the current rate is 1.3%.

Most people who work for an employer in New Zealand are paid a wage or salary directly into a bank account on a weekly, fortnightly or monthly basis.

Employers usually deduct income tax from employee wages and send the tax payment to the IRD.

There is a rebate system which means that low-income earners may pay about 5% tax. It is then graduated up to 19.5% for NZ$38,000 per annum. Most salary and wage earners have income tax automatically deducted from their wages under PAYE. The employer pays the PAYE monthly to the Inland Revenue. Those who are PAYE and paying Resident Withholding Tax (on dividends or interest from a bank account) do not need to file a tax return. Self-employed individuals, or those with income from a trust or rents, pay three tax instalments throughout the financial year. They receive an IR3 form at the end of the tax year, which they may complete by 7th July, but even this is not compulsory.

Banks charge a Resident Withholding Tax of 19.5% on interest and dividends as they are earned, which is deducted by the financial institution before they send your payment. When you invest, you are required to provide your IRD number to the firm.

If you have a second job, you are taxed at a higher rate (called a secondary rate or SEC). An overall adjustment will take place when you file your annual return. For taxation purposes, a person is a New Zealand resident if they have a permanent place of abode in New Zealand, are personally present in New Zealand for more than 183 days in total in any 12-month period or are absent from New Zealand in the service of the New Zealand government. You cease to be a tax resident is you are absent from New Zealand for 325 days in any 12-month period and at no time in that period maintain a permanent place of abode in New Zealand.

An IRD number is your unique identifying number you will use for all your contacts with Inland Revenue; you will need an IRD number before you start a job or open a bank account. If you do not have an IRD number, your employer or bank will deduct tax from your salary at the 'no declaration' rate (45 cents per dollar). To apply for your IRD number you need to complete the appropriate application form (IR595), which can be downloaded from the IRD website, and return it to the Inland Revenue along with the appropriate identification (such as a copy of your birth certificate or passport).

Inland Revenue Department: PO Box 39010, Wellington Mail Centre, Lower Hutt 5045; (04) 978 0779; www.ird.govt.nz

The IRD will help people complete their tax return at no cost, but the individual must provide all the necessary documents. Tax accountants charge a fee, but this fee can be deducted as an expense on the following year's return. All social security and health spending is financed through general taxation. For further details contact your local Inland Revenue Office or the National Office. If you have IRD queries you need answered before you arrive in New Zealand, contact the Non-Residents Centre. Otherwise consult a New Zealand tax advisor.

Inland Revenue Department Non-Residents Centre: Private Bag 1932, Dunedin, New Zealand; 0064 3 951 2020; fax 0064 3 951 2216; nonres@ird.govt.nz

Because most of your income is taxed at the source, some people no longer file tax returns. It is prudent to make your calculations, though, as you may be due a refund.

Local tax

Local authorities finance their activities by levying rates on land and property. Some local authorities charge separately for services such as rubbish collection and water supply. Rates are levied on the value of your land plus improvements (that is, the house). Rates vary around the country and depend on the value of the land and improvements. Valuation New Zealand revalues property every 5 years.

Goods and services tax (GST)

GST is an indirect tax on most goods and services, uniformly applied at 12.5%. It is borne by the ultimate consumer but is payable at every stage of producing goods or services. GST is almost always included in the display price. It applies to most commodities, but exemptions include rental accommodation, donated goods and services and financial services. Exports are zero rated. Businesses with a net turnover of greater than NZ$40,000 per annum must be GST registered and must complete a GST return every six months. They can claim back the GST content of the goods and services they purchase. However, visitors cannot claim a refund on this tax.

Other taxes

- There is no capital gains tax as such, or death duties in New Zealand. However, capital gains from disposal of personal property are taxed where:
- the property is acquired for resale;
- the taxpayer's business involves dealing in such property; or
- there is an undertaking or scheme with the aim of making a profit.

Gift duty

Gift duty is a charge on gifts worth over NZ$27,000 made in any 12-month period which one person makes to another. However, any person making gifts with a combined total value of over NZ$12,000 in any 12-month period must complete a Gift Statement and forward it to Inland Revenue. The Gift Statement is form IR196, and this form may be downloaded from the IRD website (www.ird.govt.nz). The person who gives the gift is liable to pay any duty when nothing is received in return, or the value of whatever is given in return is less in value than the gift. If something of lesser value is given in return for a gift, the value of the gift, for Gift Duty purposes, is the difference between the two values. The following items would all be classified as gifts for Gift Duty purposes: transfers of any items (eg, company shares or land); any form of payment; creation of a trust; a forgiveness or reduction of debt; and allowing a debt to remain outstanding so that it can't be collected by normal legal action. Subject to certain exemptions, duty is charged on a scale of 5% of the value of a gift worth NZ$27,000–NZ$36,000, NZ$450+10% of amount over NZ$36,000 for gifts worth NZ$36,001–NZ$54,000, NZ$2,250+20% of amount over NZ$54,000 for gifts worth NZ$54,001–NZ$72,000 and to NZ$5,850 plus 25% for an amount over NZ$72,000. Any Gift Duty must be paid within 6months of the date of the gift, even if you have not received an assessment from the IRD. For a comprehensive guide to Gift Duty, download the form IR 195 from the IRD website.

THE LEGAL SYSTEM, COURTS, THE POLICE AND WILLS

The legal system

The New Zealand legal system is based on the English system, and comes from two main sources: the common law, and statute law.

There are three branches of government:

- The Legislature is made up of Parliament, the Governor General, Members of Parliament and Select Committees. They examine, debate and vote on Bills, which are then assented to by the Governor General and become Acts (statutes). In this way the Legislature makes the law

- The Executive is made up of Cabinet Ministers and the public sector. They decide policy, draft bills, enforce and administer Act. The Executive initiates and administers the law.

Parliament building, Wellington

- The Judiciary is made up of the judges, who hear and decide cases by applying relevant law to facts and circumstances, and review decisions made by administrative bodies. In this way the Judiciary applies the law.

Power is separated between these three different branches, and this ensures that no one branch can act in an unconstitutional fashion. Each branch has a different role, but their separation is not absolute and their responsibilities and roles are inevitably intertwined.

The Legislature

New Zealand's Parliament is the highest law-making body in the country; it has developed from the British parliamentary system. Parliament has two parts: the Head of State and the House of Representatives.

Head of State

The Head of State is Queen Elizabeth II, and she is represented in New Zealand by the Governor-General, who is appointed on the Prime Minister's recommendation for a term of five years. The Governor-General invites the leader of the majority party to form a government, is able to make regulations, and his or her assent is required for all Bills passed by the House of Representatives before they can become law. The Governor-General also holds the figurehead position of Commander-in-Chief of the armed forces. Constitutional convention requires that the Governor-General follow the advice of ministers.

The House of Representatives

The New Zealand Parliament has just one chamber, the House of Representatives. Members of Parliament are elected to the House of Representatives for a three-year term, and they meet in the parliamentary buildings in Wellington. New Zealanders aged 18 or over vote in elections to elect Members of Parliament. The House debates and passes legislation, provides government, supervises governmental administration by requiring explanation of policies and actions, supplies money, and represents the view of the people. It has a number of Select Committees which examine proposed legislation (Bills) in detail, often hearing submissions from interested members of the public.

The Executive

Made up of the Prime Minister, Cabinet and the public sector, the Executive conducts the government, decides policy and administers legislation. Cabinet makes or agrees to all important government policy decisions, and co-ordinates the work of Ministers. Cabinet Ministers are advised by public servants.

The Judiciary

Freedom from political interference is an important feature of the judiciary's position. A judgment may be criticised, but personal attacks or attempts to influence a judge's decision are strictly prohibited. The proper course of action in a case where an MP is unhappy with a judge's decision is to introduce a Bill to change the law in question. Judges apply the law to the cases that comes before them, but also develop the law by deciding what Parliamentary legislation means as they interpret it. Judicial review is a growing area of judicial responsibility, examining acts of government and the actions of private administrative bodies. Judges are appointed by the Governor-General, and all judges are lawyers with a minimum of seven years experience.

There are two main divisions of New Zealand law – civil law and criminal law. Civil law covers disputes between individuals, companies, sometimes local or central government, and usually doesn't involve the police. Disputes usually involve money, and include such cases as disputes over business contracts, wills, tax, land and property, family matters such as division of matrimonial property and custody of children, etc. Many civil cases are settled out of court, with all parties agreeing a solution. Criminal law usually involves the police investigating crimes such as theft, murder, etc. Trials are often reported in the media. The accused has the right to be represented by a lawyer and to have evidence against them heard in an open court and tested by cross-examination. If convicted of a crime, a person will be sentenced according to the law and has the right to appeal against conviction and sentence. Criminal prosecutions are usually brought by the police, but also by others such as Local Authorities, Inland Revenue and the Ministry of Transport.

The courts

In the District Court and High Court the Judge sits alone or with a jury. The jury is made up of 12 ordinary people selected at random from the jury roll (based on

the electoral roll), and it decides questions of fact. Questions of law are decided by the Judge, who also directs the jury on aspects of the law as necessary. The Judge plays the role of a neutral referee while each party presents their evidence and arguments to support their own cases. The verdict is given once all evidence and arguments have been heard. In cases without a jury, the Judge decides the verdict. Most New Zealand lawyers are both solicitors and barristers, so they are able to appear in court and deal direct with the public.

The police

The New Zealand Police is a decentralised organisation divided into 12 districts, a national headquarters and service centres. Each district has a central station from which subsidiary and suburban stations are managed. The Hon. Annette King is the current Minister of Police. The Police operate land, sea and air services and as well as responding to crime they run crime prevention programmes and community programmes including Youth Education and Youth Aid services. They enforce both criminal and traffic laws and undertake search and rescue missions as well.

For all emergencies, you should contact the Police by dialling 111 and asking for the Police. In non-urgent situations, contact your nearest Police Station using the number provided in the telephone book or on www.whitepages.co.nz.

Statistics New Zealand now provides a facility for you to gather detailed crime information about your local areas through Police statistics. To explore these figures for yourself, visit www.police.govt.nz/services/statistics/. Information about recruitment and what it takes to be a police officer can be found at www.newcops.co.nz. For more information about the Police see www.police.govt.nz.

Neighbourhood support

Neighbourhood Support is a community-based programme promoted by the police. It encourages standard precautions against neighbourhood crime and general crime prevention awareness around the home and in your local community. It also encourages the fostering of community groups amongst neighbours who all look out for each other and stay aware of each others' homes and properties, particularly in the owner's absence. Most communities have Neighbourhood Support groups, and you should ask about these when you move into your new home. More information can be found on the Neighbourhood Support website www.ns.org.nz.

Wills

If at the time of your death you have a permanent place of residence in New Zealand or you are living in New Zealand for more than half the year, you are considered by New Zealand law to be a resident. This means that any property you own in New Zealand is subject to New Zealand laws if you die intestate. It makes sense therefore to make a will after you have bought a house. If you are retaining assets in your home country, you should check with your solicitor to see that your New Zealand will is recognised there. Property in other countries is normally subject to the inheritance laws of those countries.

New Zealand Guardian Trust: 0800 371 471; email info@guardiantrust. co.nz; www.nzgt.co.nz

You do not have to use a lawyer or trustee company to draw up a will in New Zealand but it does not cost much and may save problems later. Certain procedures must be followed for a will to be valid, and the testator must sign it in the presence of two non-beneficiary witnesses. Trustee companies will draw up a will for around NZ$85. Try the New Zealand Guardian Trust. Offices can be found in Auckland, Whangarei, Hamilton, Rotorua, Takapuna, Tauranga, Napier, Palmerston North, Wellington, New Plymouth, Nelson, Christchurch and Dunedin.

GUNNA GOTTA
Grade 4

Working in New Zealand

▨ THE EMPLOYMENT MARKET

FACT

▨ Small population size and the country's relative isolation mean that New Zealand will always need migrants to fill the gaps in its economy.

Although New Zealand is a small country, it is a modern economy with a growing range of employment and business opportunities. With less than 0.1% of the world's population, New Zealand is never likely to compete with top international salary levels in the world's biggest businesses; however, the lifestyle attracts many skilled workers every year. The Kiwi tradition of 20-somethings leaving the country for a couple of years overseas experience in places like London means that demand for employees often exceeds supply, and at the moment the new high-growth industries (software, wine, education services, etc.) offer a great number of employment opportunities to new migrants with the right skills. Demand for specific talent often leads employers to recruit overseas workers. British and Canadian people in particular are often recruited by the legal and health sectors, and many skilled people come from parts of Asia to work in the New Zealand IT industry every year.

In the past, the country enjoyed very low unemployment with the average level in the 1970s being less than 2%. However, throughout the 1980s unemployment increased rapidly. A large number of jobs were lost in manufacturing industries during the radical economic reforms of the 1980s. Some of the job losses were attributed to long-term trends in the labour market and reflected the same kinds of changes have occurred in other western countries where manufacturing industries were unable to compete with cheaper labour costs in the newly industrialised countries of Asia. There has been a shift in New Zealand's industrial structure from manufacturing to service industries.Other job losses could be traced to the lowering of tariff barriers as a result of New Zealand's conversion to neo-liberal economic policies. Tight monetary policy aimed at squeezing inflationary pressures out of the economy also contributed to the economic downturn.

The latest Employment Survey shows continued demand from businesses for labour, with full-time employee numbers increasing 3.3% driven by a 3.5% increase in full-time employment and a 2.2% increase in part-time employment. The increase was driven by the manufacturing, property and business services, accommodation, cafés and restaurant industries, as well as the wholesale trade, education and construction industries. Annual increases in total gross earnings continue to be stronger than the annual increase in total paid hours with an increase of 7.0%, resulting in a 4.1% increase in average total hourly earnings. Salary and wage rates including overtime have recently increased by 3.4%. Total paid hours increased by 2.8% in the last year, driven largely by the construction and wholesale trade industries. Total weekly paid hours decreased by 0.5% over the year, to 37.96 hours.

The short-term Department of Labour forecast is that the labour market will remain tight, with increased employment, low unemployment and continuing high labour force participation. In the medium term employment growth is expected to ease slightly, but unemployment will remain relatively low. Pressure is expected to continue on some aspects of the labour market including wages, skills and the supply of labour. Recent economic growth has been strong, and is expected to continue through 2008 before easing a little in 2009. Employment growth is expected to remain positive over the next year, but low compared to the last five years. It is expected to ease to about 1% in 2009. Positive labour productivity growth of about 1% is expected to continue for the next two years, with the tight labour market. Also having an impact are recent increased wage costs and the recent period of sustained investment in plant and machinery. Wage growth is set to remain strong with the demand for labour, shortage of skilled labour and the very low unemployment rate.

Unemployment

In September 1991, unemployment reached 10.9%, following a recession and the period of restructuring in the public sector. However, aside from a brief period of increase during the Asian crisis, unemployment has fallen steadily over the last ten years. The number of unemployed is currently around 79,000, with about two-thirds of this number actively seeking work. The country is enjoying the second highest level of employment in the last 20 years, with about 2,150,000 people currently employed. Businesses are straining to increase the labour pool, by encouraging people to return from maternity leave, and even retirement, and encouraging part-timers to work full-time and full-timers to take on even longer hours. There is stronger growth in full-time employment relative to part-time employment over the last year.

Unemployment has dropped by nearly half in the last decade, and continues to decline slowly but steadily; in 2007 it declined a further 2.1% and has been below 4% for the past three years. New Zealand has the fifth lowest unemployment rate in the Organisation for Economic Development (OECD) and is the only country in the OECD to achieve such a low unemployment rate over such an extensive period, according to Ruth Dyson, Social Development and Employment Minister. Employers continue to have positive hiring intentions in all industries, with the most robust being the services industry sector.

Over the next two years, unemployment is expected to rise slightly due to more modest employment growth. The unemployment rate is still expected to remain low on a historical basis though, staying below 4.0%.

FACT

■ At 3.5%, unemployment is currently the lowest it has been in 23 years.

Residence and work regulations

New Zealand requires that foreign nationals working in New Zealand, whether for local or foreign companies, obtain work permits for the period of employment. In most cases this may not exceed three years. Permission from the New Zealand Immigration Service must be sought prior to arrival and it must be shown that the worker has skills not readily available in New Zealand.

If you are visiting New Zealand and have found a job, you may apply for a work permit within the country, but the maximum period for which it will be granted is 9 months. The same restrictions regarding skills apply. Certain groups of individuals can be subject to limitation on period of work visa/permit, ie fiancé(e)s of New Zealand citizens or residents are eligible only for a 9 month work visa/permit in the first instance.

Skills

Due to demand for specific skills in certain areas of the country, the New Zealand Immigration Service has developed Long Term and Immediate Skills Shortage Lists. These are designed to streamline the processing of work permits and approvals in

principle for work permits or visas where there is a known regional labour shortage, but remember that you will still have to meet all other aspects of relevant work policy. You can download a printable PDF version from the Toolbox right-hand menu of the Immigration Service website (www.immigration.govt.nz/migrant/) or from Worksite.

 Worksite: info@worksite.govt.nz; www.worksite.govt.nz

Qualifications

In general, American and British qualifications are recognised and well regarded in New Zealand. New Zealand's university education system derives its structure from British, particularly Scottish, universities so the types of qualifications available from universities are similar in title and content to UK ones. Trade and vocational qualifications have different titles. You can apply to the New Zealand Qualifications Authority ((NZQA – the government agency that oversees the qualifications system) to have your qualifications assessed before you arrive in New Zealand. They will be assessed in comparison with current New Zealand qualifications. There is a fee for this service. For detailed information and application forms see the Qualifications Evaluation Service website (www.nzqa.govt.nz/for-international/qual-eval/). In some cases you may be required to have your qualifications evaluated as part of your application for residency. The necessary forms can also be obtained from the New Zealand Immigration Service (www.immigration.govt.nz), or you can contact the Qualifications Authority directly. The NZQA call centre is open for business between 8am and 5pm, Monday to Friday.

 New Zealand Qualifications Authority: PO Box 160, Wellington; +64 4 802 3000; fax +64 4 802 3112; helpdesk@nzqa.govt.nz; www.nzqa.govt.nz

NZQA has a website called KiwiQuals. The site lists every quality-assured qualification in New Zealand of 40 credits and above, and it allows you to compare them. It is searchable in various ways, including by qualification type, subject, organisation and level of study (see www.kiwiquals.govt.nz). For work, training and careers information see www.kiwicareers.govt.nz.

It is best to obtain details of entry requirements for New Zealand universities from the universities themselves, to be sure that you have the most accurate and up-to-date specific information.

Professional qualifications

The relevant professional bodies regulate professional employment in New Zealand. In order to work in these areas you must register with the appropriate organisations. In most cases this will involve an assessment of qualifications and experience and you may be required to take further examinations as well as paying a fee. In some professions you can arrange to sit these exams in your own country. As an example of the type of procedure you have to go through, the following are the requirements for foreign lawyers intending to practise in New Zealand. Legal practitioners seeking assessment should write to the New Zealand Law Society.

TIP

It is important to contact the relevant professional body in good time because they usually take several months to consider applications and qualifying exams are held only once or twice a year in foreign countries.

i New Zealand Law Society: The Executive Director, Attn: Secretary, Admissions and Credentials Committee; PO Box 5041, Wellington; +64 4 472 7837; fax +64 4 915 1284; admissions@lawyers.org.nz; www.nz-lawsoc.org.nz

You will be required to include the following information:

- Documentary evidence of tertiary educational standing and attainment, including original academic and admission records, showing courses completed and grades.
- Documentary evidence of admission as a lawyer in your own country.
- A curriculum vitae resumé giving names, dates, and places of practice.
- A copy of your law school's handbook showing the structure of the degree and the content and length of each course.
- A statutory declaration verifying identity and certifying the accuracy of the above information.
- Where applicable, a demonstration of proficiency in the English language.
- Proof of identity (certified copy of pages from your passport).
- A statutory declaration or affidavit verifying identity and certifying the accuracy and completeness of the above information.
- Two bank drafts (in NZ$) in payment of application fees: one for NZ$100 payable to the New Zealand Law Society and one for NZ$885 payable to the New Zealand Council for Legal Education. If you are applying from inside New Zealand, the bank drafts must be increased by 12.5% to cover the Goods and Services Tax, so should be NZ$112.50 and NZ$995.65 (NB. Prices are subject to change so check before filing your application). Applications normally take two or three months to consider.

Not all professional bodies have such complex registration procedures. Membership of the New Zealand Society of Accountants is automatically granted to any member of the three British Associations of Chartered Accountants, that is, the Institute of Chartered Accountants of England and Wales, the Institute of Chartered Accountants of Scotland, and the Chartered Association of Certified Accountants. However, any person in New Zealand is able to call themselves 'an accountant'. It is only when they want to call themselves 'chartered' that they will need to join the New Zealand body.

Teachers have to register with the New Zealand Teachers Council after assessment of qualifications by NZQA if they wish to work in the state sector.

Addresses of professional bodies

New Zealand Institute of Architects: Suite 1.5, 72 Dominion Road, Mt Eden, PO Box 2516, Auckland; (09) 623 6080; fax (09) 623 6081; info@nzia.co.nz; www.nzia.co.nz.

Institute of Chartered Accountants of New Zealand: Level 2, Cigna House, 40 Mercer Street, Wellington; PO Box 11-342, Wellington 6034; (04) 474 7840 or (04) 460 0606 (Registry Helpdesk); fax (04) 473 6303; registry@nzica.co.nz; www.nzica.co.nz. See the website for contact details for national and international branches.

The Dental Council of New Zealand: Level 8, 108 The Terrace, PO Box 10448, Wellington; (04) 4 499 4820; fax (04) 499 1668; inquiries@dcnz.org.nz; www.dentalcouncil.org.nz.

Horticulture and Food Research Institute of New Zealand Ltd (HortResearch): enquiries@hortresearch.co.nz; www.hortresearch.co.nz.

Hospitality Association of New Zealand: Level 2, Radio Network House, cnr Abel Smith and Taranaki Streets, PO Box 503, Wellington; (04) 385 1369; fax (04) 384 8044; nsc@hanz.org.nz; www.hanz.org.nz.

Institute of Professional Engineers NZ: 158 The Terrace, Wellington, PO Box 12 241, Wellington; (04) 473 9444; fax (04) 474 8933; ipenz@ipenz.org.nz or membership@ipenz.co.nz; www.ipenz.org.nz.

The Medical Council of New Zealand: Level 13, Mid City Tower, 139–143 Willis Street, Wellington; PO Box 11–649, Wellington; (04) 384 7635 or freephone 0800 286 801; fax (04) 385 8902; mcnz@mcnz.org.nz or registration@mcnz.org.nz; www.mcnz.org.nz.

New Zealand Law Society: 26 Waring Taylor Street, PO Box 5041, Wellington 6145 (DX SP202020); +64 4 472 7837; fax +64 4 473 7909; inquiries@lawyers.org.nz; www.nz-lawsoc.org.nz.

The Nursing Council: PO Box 9644, Wellington; (04) 385 9589; fax (04) 801 8502; oseas@nursingcouncil.org.nz or nzreg@nursingcouncil.org.nz; www.nursingcouncil.org.nz.

Physiotherapy Board of New Zealand: Level 8, 108 The Terrace, PO Box 10 734, Wellington; (04) 471 2610; fax (04) 471 2613; physio@physioboard.org.nz; www.physioboard.org.nz.

New Zealand Teachers' Council: Level 7, 93 The Terrace, PO Box 5326, Wellington; (04) 471 0852; fax (04) 471 0870; inquiries@teacherscouncil.govt.nz; www.teacherscouncil.govt.nz.

New Zealand Veterinary Association: PO Box 11 212, Manners Street, Wellington; (04) 471 0484; fax (04) 471 0494; nzva@vets.org.uk; www.vets.org.nz.

■ FINDING A JOB

Getting a job in New Zealand straight away may be a challenge if you have not been able to arrange work before arriving. Your chance of finding a position will be better the more skills, experience and qualifications you have to offer. But it is not unlikely for even well-qualified and highly experienced migrants to take 6 months, or perhaps even longer, to find suitable employment. It is extremely common for highly qualified migrants to end up accepting more junior positions than they held in their home countries. Rather than seeing this as a blow to the ego, it is best to view it as an opportunity to get the invaluable New Zealand work experience that most employers will require, and as a chance to adjust to your new life without too much initial work stress. You will also have the chance to learn about how New Zealand workplaces operate, and there might be opportunities for promotion if you prove yourself competent and professional in this first role. Difficulties tend to diminish as time goes on and you become more settled, but it is important to ensure you are prepared for a period of adjustment, at least during your first year living and working in a new country.

TIP

■ For a list of employers especially interested in hearing from qualified and experienced people from the UK, see: www.workingin-newzealand.com/profiled_employers.php

Further information

There are several useful websites containing up to date information about current employment trends and predictions, including those of the New Zealand Institute of Economic Research (www.nzier.org.nz), The Department of Labour (www.dol.govt.nz), Statistics New Zealand (www.stats.govt.nz), TradeNZ (www.tradenz.govt.nz) and the Immigration Service (www.business-migrants.govt.nz and www.immigration.govt.nz). An annual guide to the employment environment, employer profiles, professional education and training, and work opportunities in New Zealand, entitled Working In New Zealand Magazine, is available from Working In Ltd for NZ$30 plus shipping costs +64 9 302 0977; fax +64 9 302 0976; www.workingin-newzealand.com).

> Between deciding to move to New Zealand and actually leaving the UK, I left myself 12 months to arrange everything. I started looking for a job in New Zealand right away, and arranged to go for a three-week visit in February. During the three weeks, I had a look around Christchurch, Wellington and Auckland, to make a decision about where I wanted to be, and with an eye on the kinds of jobs available in each place.
> **Vita Evans**

Sources of jobs

Newspapers

Many New Zealand jobs are advertised in newspapers, most of which have a daily Situations Vacant section that tends to be more extensive on Monday, Wednesday and Saturday. Job vacancies are listed in most professional journals. For further information, check the websites listed in Addresses of Professional Bodies. Executive and professional management positions are usually handled by private recruitment agencies. Most international recruitment agencies are represented in New Zealand. The Government's social security agency, Work and Income, provides free job-seeking services for unemployed residents.

The starting place for your job-hunt should be the major New Zealand newspapers and comprehensive employment websites such as www.seek.co.nz. A small number of jobs are specifically advertised overseas. The types of jobs that tend to be advertised directly are in areas where there is a shortage of skills locally, for example in computers and information technology, teaching, medicine or accountancy.

The major daily newspapers, and their Situations Vacant sections, can be read online, or at your local New Zealand Embassy or High Commission (remember though that these papers will be a few days out of date, due to having travelled from New Zealand, and the internet is always going to be the most complete and up-to-the-minute source). New Zealand Herald (www.nzherald.co.nz) mainly advertises jobs in the Auckland area, or take a look at the Stuff website (www.stuff.co.nz), which contains links to major regional papers. Consyl Publishing Ltd in the UK can obtain New Zealand newspapers as well as magazines (01424-223111 or 01424-223161 for 24-hour credit card sales).

Main New Zealand newspapers

Sunday Star-Times: www.stuff.co.nz/sundaystartimes

The Sunday News: Sunday Star-Times' sister publication. www.stuff.co.nz/sunday news

The New Zealand Herald: Auckland-based paper distributed throughout the North Island. www.nzherald.co.nz

The Dominion Post: The second largest daily paper in the country, based in Wellington. www.dompost.co.nz

The Waikato Times: www.stuff.co.nz/waikatotimes

The Press: Distributed in Canterbury and Nelson/Tasman region. www.stuff.co.nz/thepress

The Otago Daily Times: Distributed in lower South Island. www.odt.co.nz

Specialist publications

Some types of jobs tend to be advertised in specialist magazines. These publications are also useful sources of information about the current job scene in their particular field. It might be worthwhile placing an employment-wanted advertisement with them. Many New Zealand magazines can be purchased online from the New Zealand Magazine Shop (www.nzmagazineshop.co.nz).

Useful publications

AdMedia: Profile Publishing Limited, PO Box 5544, Wellesley Street, Auckland; (09) 630 8940; admedia@magazzino.co.nz; www.admedia.co.nz.

Architecture New Zealand and the annual Directory of NZIA Practices: PO Box 2516, Auckland; info@nzia.co.nz; www.nzia.co.nz.

Commercial Horticulture Magazine: The Reference Publishing Company, PO Box 26269, Epsom, Auckland; fax (09) 358 2714; www.nursery.net.nz. Covers nursery industry news, views, features from New Zealand and around the world. You can also order NZ Native Plants Register, NZ Nursery Register, and back issues.

Horticulture News: order from www.nzmagazineshop.co.nz.

Hospitality Magazine: PO Box 9595, Newmarket, Auckland; (09) 529 3000; fax (09) 529 3001; info@tplmedia.co.nz; www.tplmedia.co.nz.

New Zealand Management (The Leaders' Magazine): 3media Group, PO Box 5544, Wellesley Street, Auckland; (09) 909 8400; www.management.co.nz.

Manufacturers Federation Magazine: Published by the New Zealand Manufacturers Federation Inc., PO Box 1925, Wellington; (04) 496 6555; fax (04) 496 6550; admin@businessnz.org.nz; www.businessnz.org.nz.

Marketing Magazine: 3media Group, PO Box5544, Wellesley Street, Auckland; (09) 909 8400; www.marketingmag.co.nz.

Mercantile Gazette: Freepost 5003, PO Box 20 034, Bishopdale, Christchurch; (03) 358 3219; fax (03) 358 4490; subscriptions@mgpublications.co.nz; www.mgpublications.co.nz.

National Business Review: PO Box 1734, Auckland; (09) 307 1629; fax (09) 307 5129; customerservices@nbr.co.nz; www.nbr.co.nz.

New Zealand Forest Industries: Neilson Publishing Ltd, PO Box 75 167, Manurewa, Auckland; (09) 269 4531; fax (09) 2694562; info@npl.net.nz; www.inwoodmag.com.

OnFilm: 3media Group, PO Box5544, Wellesley Street, Auckland; (09) 909 8400; www.onfilm.co.nz.

The Southern Doctor: Provides information about medical jobs in New Zealand and Australia; postmaster@southerndoctor.co.nz; www.southerndoctor.co.nz.

Professional associations

Many professional vacancies are carried in specialist magazines, which are usually published by the relevant professional associations. In some cases all vacancies appear in these publications, for example all permanent teaching jobs are advertised in the *Education Gazette*. They will also usually carry employment wanted adverts. Sometimes it is possible to subscribe just to the employment wanted pages. You can contact the professional bodies listed below for further information. Jobs in the New Zealand State sector appear on the internet at (www.jobs.govt.nz). The Association of Commonwealth Universities advertises positions at New Zealand universities on the Worldwide Vacancies section of its website (www.acu.ac.uk/adverts/jobs).

Useful resources

Chartered Accountants Journal of New Zealand: PO Box 11 342, Wellington 6034; (04) 474 7840; fax (04) 473 6303; registry@nzica.co.nz; www.nzica.co.nz.

Education Gazette: PO Box 249, Wellington; direct-subscribe@list.tki.org.nz; www.edgazette.govt.nz. You can subscribe to receive an email copy for free by emailing: gazettedirect@edgazette.govt.nz. There is also a free vacancy alert email service, to send you vacancies posted in the last 24 hours that match your search criteria. You can subscribe on the website.

Law Talk: New Zealand Law Society, PO Box 5041, Wellington; (04) 472 7837; fax (04) 473 7909; inquiries@lawyers.org.nz; www.nz-lawsoc.org.nz and follow the Lawtalk link.

New Zealand Engineering (e.nz magazine): (04) 474 8941;scornwell@ipenz.org.nz; http://e.nz-magazine.co.nz/main.htm or www.ipenz.org.nz/ipenz/publications for the full range of publications from IPENZ.

The New Zealand Medical Journal: The New Zealand Medical Association, NZMA National Office, 26 The Terrace, PO Box 156, Wellington; (04) 472 4741; fax (04) 471 0838; nzma@nzma.org.nz; www.nzma.org.nz/journal.

Trades and skilled craftspeople

As is the case with the professional associations, in order to work in New Zealand as a trades or craftsperson, you must join the relevant association or society. If you have qualifications and experience in your own country you will not normally be required to fulfil any additional training requirements although you may be required to provide proof of your experience and expertise. You should contact the organisations listed below for further details. Most of these organisations publish a trade magazine, which may be a useful source of information about job prospects. The New Zealand Trades Directory provides online access to contact details for many trade associations on its website (http://nztrades.com).

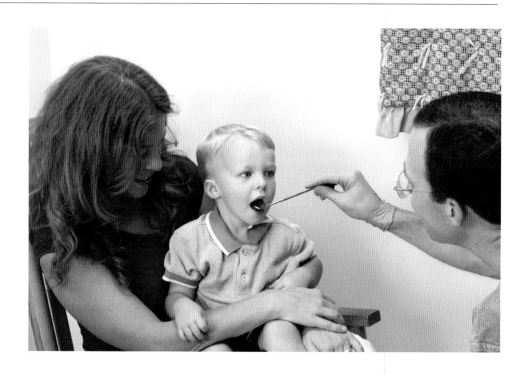

In New Zealand registration is required by law in order to undertake employment as one of the following:

Architect
Barrister or solicitor
Chiropractor
Clinical dental technician
Dental technician
Dentist
Dietician
Dispensing optician
Electrician
Electrical service technician
Enrolled nurse
Line mechanic
Medical laboratory technologist
Medical practitioner

Medical radiation technologist
Nurses and midwives
Occupational therapist
Optometrist
Pharmacist
Physiotherapist
Plumber, gasfitter and drainlayer
Podiatrist
Psychologist
Real estate agent
Cadastral (Land Title) Surveyor
Teacher
Veterinarian

Useful resources

Master Plumbers, Gasfitters and Drainlayers Inc: asharie@masterplumbers.org. nz; www.masterplumbers.org.nz. Also publishes NZ *Plumbers Journal* (subscribe online via main website).

Plumbers, Gasfitters and Drainlayers Board: contact Colleen Singleton, 9th Floor, 70 The Terrace, PO Box 10655, Wellington; (04) 494 2970; fax (04) 494 2975; registrar@pgdb.co.nz; www.pgdb.co.nz.

Registered Master Builders Federation: Level 6, 234 Wakefield Street, PO Box 1796, Wellington; (04) 385 8999 or 0800 269 119; fax (04) 385 8995; MBF@ masterbuilder.org.nz; www.masterbuilder.org.nz.

New Zealand Institute of Building Surveyors: Registered Office Box 1283, Dunedin; 0800 11 34 00; www.buildingsurveyors.co.nz.

New Zealand Institute of Quantity Surveyors: Level 7, 108 The Terrace, PO Box 10 469, Wellington; (04) 473 5521; fax (04) 473 2918; office@nziqs.co.nz; www. nziqs.co.nz.

Master Painters New Zealand Association Inc: Level 5, iPayroll House, 93 Boulcott Street, Wellington, PO Box 25 135, Panama Street, Wellington; (04) 472 5879 or free phone from within New Zealand 0800 724 686; fax (04) 472 5870; nationaloffice@ masterpainters.org.nz; www.masterpainters.co.nz.

New Zealand Property Institute: Westbrook House, 181 Willis Street, Level 5, PO Box 27 340, Wellington; (04) 384 7094; fax (04) 384 8473; national@property.org. nz; www.property.org.nz. Also publishes the *Property Journal* (phone/fax as above; Property Business ((09) 846 4068; subs@agm.co.nz).

International newspapers, directories and websites

Only a small percentage of New Zealand jobs are advertised directly overseas, perhaps because of the obvious difficulties with labour mobility to such a remote country. By far your best option when hunting for work is to search online. In many cases, your first port of call should probably be the website www.seek.co.nz, which features a daily-updated and comprehensive range of vacancies and also allows you the option of posting your CV online where it is available for viewing by potential employers. Another excellent website is www.kiwicareers.govt.nz; it breaks down vacancy links into various sectors, including education, IT, health, the armed forces, creative, manufacturing, engineering and industrial jobs as well as a general job vacancy section and a link to various recruitment agents. For work in the State sector, see www.jobs.govt.nz. Another useful site is EscapeArtist (www. escapeartist.com/Live_In_New_Zealand/Jobs_In_New_Zealand/), which will direct you to the New Zealand segments of a number of worldwide job-search sites as well as taking you straight to some of the best and most up to date New Zealand-specific recruitment sites. For a series of vacancies grouped by category and aimed at the new migrant, see www.workingin-newzealand.com, which has a facility allowing you to submit your CV directly to featured employers online. There are two newspapers available for intending migrants to New Zealand, *Destination New Zealand* and *New Zealand Outlook*. These occasionally carry advertisements for jobs and usually carry advertisements for overseas job-search agencies that will help you look in New Zealand. The weekly paper for New Zealanders in London, *New Zealand News UK*, is a good source of job advertisements for positions in New Zealand. *New Zealand News UK* is distributed free in London outside central city tube stations and all three papers are available from New Zealand House in London, or can be obtained on subscription from the addresses below.

Useful resources

Emigrate New Zealand: a monthly magazine created for 'all would-be Kiwis'. Subscriptions from £1.75 per month. Register online for a free emigration starter pack at www.emigrate2.co.uk – follow the links to New Zealand information.

New Zealand News UK: published weekly, and either free or for a price of 35p, depending on where you get your copy. Contains up-to-date immigration news, and also carries information about New Zealand-focused activities for expats and prospective migrants in the UK, mainly in London. www.nznewsuk.co.uk.

New Zealand Outlook: Consyl Publishing Ltd, 13 London Road, Bexhill-on-Sea, East Sussex TN39 3JR; 01424-223111; consylpublishing@btconnect.com; www.consylpublishing.co.uk. Published monthly.

TNT Magazine: 14–15 Child's Place, Earls Court, London SW5 9RX; 0207 373 3377; fax 0207 341 6600; enquiries@tntmag.co.uk; www.tntmagazine.com. Another free weekly distributed throughout London; contains some New Zealand information, but probably of more use to people interested in Australia.

Useful websites

www.seek.co.nz – Search for jobs or browse through categories.

www.emigrate2.co.nz – Source of emigration information including a searchable database of links to potential employers in different regions and cities around the country.

www.nzrecruitme.co.nz – A service for people who are outside New Zealand. You can register as a jobseeker and put your CV/resume online for New Zealand Employers to browse.

www.newkiwis.co.nz – A service for new workers and residents in New Zealand. You can register as a jobseeker, put your CV/resume online or book a free 'Kiwi Career Success' course to learn about what New Zealand employers look for and how to write a kiwi style CV.

www.anyworkanywhere.com – Information on working holidays in New Zealand.

www.job.co.nz – This portal lists jobs in all areas, with legal and job hunting advice.

www.jobstuff.co.nz – Search jobs by region, industry or agency.

www.jobzone.co.nz – Jobs of all kinds, including casual and holiday work.

Approaching employers direct

Advertising and screening applicants is lengthy and expensive. A well-written CV which lands on the personnel manager's desk at the right time could save them time and money, and find you the type of job you want. It is also worthwhile asking friends, people in the community and also in job centres if they know of any jobs in your field. English language skills are obviously very important, and the biggest hindrance for immigrants in New Zealand trying to find employment, so the fact that you speak English is a good start. You can begin your research by finding contact details for New Zealand companies working in your area of expertise. One place to start is the Yellow Pages, which you can consult at the New Zealand Embassies and High Commissions, or over the internet (www.yellowpages.co.nz). The Information Office on the Second Floor of New Zealand House in London has business directories but is not a job search service. You can obtain a copy of

FACT

■ It is estimated that around 70% of jobs in New Zealand are filled without actually being advertised, so it is worth researching companies and contacting employers that interest you, whether or not they are currently advertising vacancies.

Working In New Zealand from New Zealand high commissions or from the internet (www.workingin.com). There is a list of major New Zealand employers at the end of this chapter.

Chambers of Commerce & professional institutes

Chambers of Commerce operate to promote the interests of their members, local businesses, not as job search agencies, but they are usually prepared to help with information. Local chambers of commerce should provide you with a list of their members for a small fee. A list of Chambers of Commerce in the main cities can be found in the Regional Employment Guide below. Other organisations that will have details of member companies are the professional institutes. Also listed below are the Australia/New Zealand/UK Chamber of Commerce and the American Chamber of Commerce, which publish directories of British and American companies respectively with branches, affiliates or subsidiaries in New Zealand.

Chambers of Commerce

American Chamber of Commerce in New Zealand: PO Box 106 002, Auckland; (09) 309 9140; fax (09) 309 1090; amcham@amcham.co.nz; www.amcham. co.nz.

New Zealand Chambers of Commerce: Level 9, 109 Featherston Street, Wellington; (04) 914 6500; fax (04) 914 6524; info@wgtn-chamber.co.nz; www.chamber.co.nz (Auckland) or www.nzchamber.co.nz.

Australia New Zealand American Chambers of Commerce (ANZACC) Washington DC: c/- Embassy of Australia, 1601 Massachusetts Avenue, N.W., Washington, D.C. 20036; (202) 797 3028; fax (202) 797 3457; info@anzacc-national.org; www. austemb.org.

Professional institutes and registration bodies

New Zealand Registered Architects Board: New Zealand Registered Architects Board: Level 3, The Dominion Building, 78 Victoria Street, PO Box 11106, Manners Street, Wellington; (04) 471 1336; fax (04) 472 5352; info@nzrab.org.nz; www. nzrab.org.nz.

Australia and New Zealand Institute of Insurance and Finance: Level 1, 143 Nelson Street, PO Box 344, Auckland; 0800 103 675 or (09) 379 7128; fax (09) 367 0639; anabranch@theinstitute.com.au (NZ branch); www.theinstitute.com.au.

Electrical Contractors Association of New Zealand: Metro Thorndon Building, 220 Thorndon Quay, PO Box 12 434, Wellington; (04) 494 1540; fax (04) 494 1549; www.ecanz.org.nz.

Engineers Registration Board: Molesworth House, 101 Molesworth St, PO Box 12241, Wellington; (04) 473 9444; fax (04) 474 8933; membership@ipenz.org.nz; www.ipenz.org.nz.

Medical Council of New Zealand: Level 13; Mid City Tower, 139-143 Willis St, PO Box 11-649, Wellington; (04) 384 7635 or free phone within NZ 0800 286 801; fax (04) 385 8902; info@mcnz.org.nz; www.mcnz.org.nz.

New Zealand Bankers Association: Level 12, Grand Arcade Building, 16 Willis St, PO Box 3043, Wellington; (04) 472 8838; fax (04) 473 1698; nzba@nzba.org.nz; www.nzba.org.nz.

New Zealand Institute of Management: Level 9 Lumley House, 3–11 Hunter Street, Wellington; PO Box 67, Wellington; (04) 495 8303; fax (04) 495 8302; national_office@nzim.co.nz; www.nzim.co.nz. See the website for your local office, or to complete an online enquiry form.

New Zealand Teachers Council: 93 The Terrace, PO Box 5326, Wellington; (04) 471 0852; fax (04) 471 0870; inquiries@teacherscouncil.govt.nz; www.teacherscouncil.govt.nz.

Nursing Council of New Zealand: PO Box 9644, Wellington; (04) 385 9589; fax (04) 801 8502; oseas@nursingcouncil.org.nz or nzreg@nursingcouncil.org.nz or admin@nursingcouncil.org.nz; www.nursingcouncil.org.nz.

Pharmaceutical Society of New Zealand: 124 Dixon Street, PO Box 11640, Wellington; (04) 802 0030; fax (04) 382 9297; p.society@psnz.org.nz or enquiries@pharmacycouncil.org.nz; www.psnz.org.nz.

Plumbers, Gasfitters and Drainlayers Board: 9th Floor, 70 The Terrace, PO Box 1065, Wellington; (04) 494 2970; registrar@pgdb.co.nz; www.pgdb.co.nz (go to the website to download the Migrant's Application form).

Real Estate Agents Licensing Board: 29 Gillies Avenue, Epsom, Auckland; (09) 520 6949.

Real Estate Institute of New Zealand: PO Box 5663, Auckland, (09) 356 1755; fax (09) 379 8471; reinz@reinz.co.nz; www.reinz.org.nz.

Veterinary Council of New Zealand: PO Box 10 563, Wellington; (04) 473 9600; fax (04) 473 8869; vet@vetcouncil.org.nz; www.vetcouncil.org.nz.

Placing employment wanted adverts

Another approach is placing an employment wanted advert with the newspapers and specialist publications listed above. You can contact the newspaper and magazine publishers directly for current advertising rates.

Employment agencies

International organisations

There are a number of organisations that can help you find a job in New Zealand. Taylor & Associates specialises in finding jobs for intending migrants, others recruit on behalf of employers and sometimes have New Zealand assignments. The latter type operate on behalf of employers and do not search on behalf of prospective workers, however they will fill some vacancies from people they have on their books so it may be worthwhile sending them a CV and a speculative application. As has been mentioned elsewhere, help with job seeking is one of the services immigration consultancies usually provide.

Recruitment and job search agencies

Adecco: Level 9, Qantas House, 191 Queen Street, Auckland; (09) 309 7572; fax (09) 309 4197; auckland@adecco.co.nz; www.adecco.co.nz.

Geneva Health International: 40–42 Parker Street, London WC2B 5PQ; 020-7600 0859; fax 020-7600 0944; janec@genevahealth.co.uk; www.genevahealth.

com. NZ: PO Box 106 339, Auckland; (09) 916 0200; fax (09) 916 0201; info@
genevahealth.com.

Global Career Link: International recruitment specialists in finance, accounting,
banking, IT, law, HR and sales and marketing. email nz@globalcareerlink.com;
www.globalcareerlink.com/go/nz.

Hudson: Level 6, State Insurance Tower, 1 Willis Street, PO Box 2186, Wellington;
(04) 473 4073; Level 6, 137–147 Quay Street, Princes Wharf, PO Box 579, Auckland;
(09) 367 9000; www.hudson.com

JobCafé International: www.jobcafe.co.nz/.

Parker Bridge Recruitment Ltd: New Zealand offices in Auckland (09) 377 3727;
fax (09) 303 1496) and Wellington (04) 472 4380; fax (04) 472 4379); info@
parkerbridge.co.nz; www.parkerbridge.co.nz or see the Parker Bridge listings on
www.seek.co.nz.Prime Recruitment Contracts: 37 Locks Heath Centre, Locks
Heath, Southampton, SO31 6DX; 01489-559 090; fax 01489-559995; contracts@
prime-recruitment.co.uk; www.prime-recruitment.co.uk.

Psych Recruitment: email enquiry@psych-recruitment.com; www.psych-recruitment.
com. Psychologists recruitment agency.

Taylor & Associates: PO Box 1401, Chester CH1 1FF; nzjobs@jobfastrack.co.nz;
www.jobfastrack.co.nz. Initial enquiries are best addressed to the UK representative
office; 0845 230 2526; info@TEGltd.co.uk.

TMP Worldwide Inc: Visit the website to complete an online 'Contact' form; www.
tmp.com. Advertising and communications, and directional marketing. The website
has pages specifically for those from the USA, Australia, Belgium, France, Germany,
Hong Kong, Ireland, Italy, Malaysia, the Netherlands, New Zealand, Singapore, Spain
and the United Kingdom.

◼ Useful websites

For job listings try: www.job.co.nz, http://jobs.search4.co.uk, www.nzjobs.co.nz,
www.kiwicareers.govt.nz; www.monster.com, www.netcheck.co.nz, www.seek.co.nz
and www.workingin-newzealand.com. Bear in mind though that these do not
necessarily represent the entire job market, particularly towards the senior executive
end. For the latest information about the employment scene, see: www.nzherald.
co.nz/employment/.

WorkSite: The New Zealand Employment Service

The Department of Labour in New Zealand provides job-search assistance through
WorkSite, a national network of offices advertising local vacancies. They carry a
wide range of vacancies for casual, skilled and unskilled work, and offer advice
and information on training for job seekers. It also provides a service specifically
for linking the skills of new migrants with the needs of New Zealand employers
(newkiwis@chamber.co.nz; www.newkiwis.co.nz), which allows you to enter your
details and CV on a database to be searched by potential employers. There is no fee
to use WorkSite or NewKiwis, but you have to be a New Zealand resident or citizen.
Contact WorkSite (info@worksite.govt.nz) for an office near you. The New Zealand
Department of Labour website may also prove useful (www.dol.govt.nz).

Employment agencies in New Zealand

There are a large number of private employment agencies in New Zealand, and
they tend to be generalist rather than specialist by nature. Most cover all sectors of

FACT

◼ Increasingly,
the global talent
shortage means that
employers rely on
agency databases
to supplement
responses to
their vacancy
advertisements.

the economy, both public and private. Within the consultancies, however, there are often specialists who focus on specific areas. These agencies charge the employer when they make a successful placement and are usually free for the job seeker, although they will offer other services such as career assessment and advice on preparation of CVs for which there may be a charge.

🔳 Computing/Information Technology

Candle IT&T Recruitment: Level 10, 3-11 Hunter Street, Wellington; (04) 473 9149; fax (04) 460 8676; equiry.wgtn@candle.co.nz; Level 16, 1 Queen Street, HSBC Building, Auckland; (09) 309 6534; fax (09) 309 3525; enquiry@candle.co.nz; www.candle.co.nz.

Enterprise Staff Consultants Ltd: 3rd Floor, Ferry Building, 99 Quay Street, Auckland, PO Box 1799, Auckland; (09) 306 2160; fax (09) 307 1285; auckland@enterprise.co.nz; www.enterprise.co.nz.

Icon: Level 9, Qantas House, 1 Queen Street, PO Box 5151, Wellesley Street, Auckland; (09) 377 3848; fax (09) 377 8685; Level 3 Johnston St, Wellington (04) 472 1566; fax (04) 472 1562; www.iconrec.co.nz.

Information Technology Recruitment (ITEC): PO Box 6798, Wellesley Street, Auckland; (09) 302 5304; fax (09) 373 2968; Suzan@itec.co.nz (permanent) or Richard@itec.co.nz (contracting); www.itec.co.nz.

Mercury Consulting Group: Level 3, Optimation House, 1 Grey Street, PO Box 10–605, Wellington; (04) 499 2624; fax (04) 499 6880; MercuryRegister@mercuryrecruit.co.nz; www.mercuryrecruit.co.nz.

Beyond Recruitment: Level 12, SAP Building, 67 Symonds Street, PO Box 68–611, Newton, Auckland; (09) 309 3105; fax (09) 377 1512; info@beyondrecruitment.co.nz; www.beyondrecruitment.co.nz.

🔳 Engineering

Career Engineer: PO Box 331 330, Takapuna, Auckland; (09) 489 0820 or 021 666 821; enquiry@careerengineer.co.nz; www.careerengineer.co.nz.

Chandler Macleod: Level 5 Lumley House, 3–11 Hunter Street, Wellington; (04) 473 7693; fax (04) 498 8969; www.chandlermacleod.co.nz

Engineering and Technical Personnel: www.engineerjobs.co.nz.

Rob Law Consulting Group: PO Box 10080, Wellington; (04) 499 8800; fax (04) 499 0955. PO Box 8934, 22 Burleigh St, Eden Terrace, Auckland; (09) 309 9555; fax (09) 309 0008, wellington@roblaw.co.nz or Auckland@roblaw.co.nz; www.roblaw.co.nz.

Technical Recruitment Solutions Ltd: www.trs.co.nz. Offices in Auckland, Wellington and Christchurch.

🔳 Farming

Agfirst Consultants NZ Ltd: PO Box 1261, Hastings; (06) 876 9200; fax (06) 876 9225; www.agfirst.co.nz. More than 20 consultants in 12 locations throughout New Zealand: Bay of Plenty (admin@agfirstbop.co.nz), Central Otago (agfirst@ibbotsoncooney.co.nz), Gisborne (gisborne@agfirst.co.nz), Hawkes Bay (hawkesbay@agfirst.co.nz), Lincoln (alan.street@agfirst.co.nz), Motueka (motueka@agfirst.co.nz), Nelson (bealing@agfirst.co.nz), Rotorua (centralr@agfirst.co.nz), Waikato (john_hall@clear.net.nz and jamesallen@clear,net.nz), Wairoa (ag1@xtra.co.nz) and Whakatane (mark.mac@agrist.co.nz).

Fegan&Co: PO Box 428, Cambridge; (07) 823 0105; fax (07) 823 0107; enquiries@fegan.co.nz; www.fegan.co.nz.

The oil refinery at Marsden Point

Fencepost: fencepost@fonterra.com; www.fencepost.com.
Marvin Farm Services: 95 Awara Street, PO Box 248, Matamata, Waikato; (07) 888 6025; fax (07) 888 6023; info@marvinfarms.co.nz; www.marvinfarms.co.nz.

■ Finance, accounting and banking

Chandler Macleod Group (Recruitment Solutions): Chandler Macleod: Level 5 Lumley House, 3–11 Hunter Street, Wellington; (04) 473 7693; fax (04) 498 8969; Level 5, HSBC Building, 290 Queen St, Auckland; (09) 379 8771; fax (09) 379 8772; www.chandlermacleod.co.nz.
Clayton Ford Recruitment: PO Box 10 083, Wellington; (04) 473 6223; fax (04) 471 2100; wnweb@claytonford.co.nz; PO Box 7697, Auckland; (09) 379 9924; fax (09) 379 7785; support.akl@claytonford.co.nz; www.claytonford.co.nz.
DG&A Recruitment Consultants: PO Box 4006, Auckland; (09) 358 0888; fax (09) 303 0254; debbie.graham@dgal.co.nz; www.debbiegraham.co.nz.
Hays Specialist Recruitment: Unit 4C, 63 Apollo Drive, Mairangi Bay, North Shore 1311; (09) 917 8824; fax (09) 966 6850; accy.auckland@hays-hps.co.nz; www.hays-hps.co.nz

■ Food technology

McFoodies Ltd: PO Box 272 1297, Papakura, Auckland; (09) 294 8088 or 021 293 2190; cathy@mcfoodies.co.nz; www.mcfoodies.co.nz.

■ Hotel/catering

Bravo Hospitality Recruitment: PO Box 68–809 Newton, Auckland 1032; (09) 360 9333; fax (09) 360 9330; 4info@bravogroup.co.nz; www.bravogroup.co.nz. Member of the Restaurant Association of New Zealand.
HHES Hospitality Recruitment: PO Box 90198 AMSC, Level 2/139, Wellesley Street West, Auckland; (09) 379 7532; fax (09) 379 4966; info@hhes.co.nz; www.hhes.co.nz.
Spectrum International Hospitality Services: PO Box 91 083, Auckland Mail Centre; (09) 357 6442; fax (09) 358 0474; info@spectrum-international.co.nz; www.spectrum-international.com.

◼ Medical/health
Auckland Medical Bureau: PO Box 37 753, Parnell, Auckland; (09) 377 5903; fax (09) 377 5902; doctors-amb.nz@xtra.co.nz; www.doctorjobs.co.nz.

Clinical One: Level 13, 120 Albert Street, PO Box 7697 Auckland; (09) 300 4315; fax (09) 379 7785; admin@clinicalone.co.nz; www.clinicalone.co.nz

eNZed Paramedical: 65 MacDonald Road, Glenview, Hamilton 2001; (07) 843 0080; fax (07) 843 0081; info@enzedparamedical.co.nz; www.enzedparamedical.co.nz.

Health.career.co.nz: http://health.career.co.nz.Adcorp New Zealand, Level 1, 21 Allen Street, Wellington; 0800 523 267; health.career@adcorp.co.nz.

Health Recruitment International: Level 9, BNZ Trust Towers, 50 Manners Street, PO Box 11933, Wellington; (04) 496 9262; fax (04) 499 0082; health@recruitment.com; www.healthrecruitment.com.

Medical Staffing International: 35 Kesteven Avenue, Glendowie, PO Box 25-172, St Heliers, Auckland; (09) 575 4258; fax (09) 575 4259; info@medicalstaffing.co.nz; www.medicalstaffing.co.nz.

Medlink International Recruitment Centre Ltd: Recruit specialist physicians. PO Box 337, Wanganui; (06) 348 7664; fax (06) 348 7665; info@medlink.co.nz; www.medlink.co.nz.

◼ Professional/managerial/general
Aacorn International Management Systems: PO Box 101-890, North Shore Mail Centre, Auckland; (09) 357 5090; aacorn@aacorn.co.nz; www.aacorn.co.nz.

Advanced Personnel: 829 Colombo Street, Christchurch; 0800 365 4322; fax (03) 365 7356; Auckland (09) 263 4322; www.advancedpersonnel.co.nz. Also has branches in Invercargill and Nelson.

Drake International: www.drake.co.nz.

IDPE Consulting Group: Level 5, Forsyth Barr House, 165-169 Lambton Quay; PO Box 5288, Wellington; (04) 472 2212; fax (04) 472 2211; info@idpe-consulting.co.nz; www.idpe-consulting.co.nz.

Wheeler Campbell: PO Box 205, Wellington; (04) 499 1500; fax (04) 499 1600; Box 191, Shortland Street, Auckland; (09) 303 4500; fax (09) 303 4501; info@wheelercampbell.co.nz; www.wheelercampbell.co.nz.

Job applications

A typical job application will comprise of a letter of application or covering letter and a CV/resumé. Companies shortlist on the basis of CVs and interview the selected candidates before making a decision. Depending on the level of job you are applying for, and the company, you may be asked to attend more than one interview.

Application letters and CVs

If you are sending off speculative letters it is worth taking the time to telephone the company and ask for the name of the personnel or relevant department manager. A personally addressed letter is much more effective than one which is clearly a copy of something sent to a dozen other companies.

Tips for effective job applications:

◼ Letters, whether applying for a specific vacancy or inquiring about possible future vacancies, should be formal in tone, brief (one side of an A4 sheet), and should outline why you are particularly qualified to work for the company.

■ Your CV should provide a concise summary of your contact details, residence status (ie permanent residence, work visa, etc.) education, qualifications and computer skills, professional/trade skills, work experience and achievements, professional goals and referees. In New Zealand CVs list jobs and qualifications in reverse chronological order, ie the most recent job first and the earliest last.

■ Try to keep your CV brief – somewhere between two and four pages is best – and make sure it is clearly laid out. This is particularly important if you are faxing applications to New Zealand as fax machines blur copy slightly and, if the typeface on your CV is too small, some important details may be lost.

■ These days, most companies prefer you to email your CV to them if you are applying from overseas, so make the effort to ensure that any files you send are well-formatted, clearly laid out, and can be opened in standard programs with a minimum of fuss. Emailing compressed PDF files is probably the safest and most efficient way to do this, but take the time to contact prospective employers and ask them in what format they prefer to receive CVs.

■ It is worthwhile getting some professional advice on the preparation of your CV; services that assist with CVs can be found under Employment Agencies in the Yellow Pages. Do not send original documents with applications.

Your skills and qualifications

Some employers require you to have professional registration even if this is not a legal requirement. This means that the status of your professional training and qualifications is extremely important. Although you may be professionally qualified in your home country and even have a number of years experience, this does not mean your experience and qualifications will automatically be recognised in New Zealand. The New Zealand Qualifications Authority (NZQA) evaluates professional and academic qualifications. This is done as a comparison with similar qualifications obtainable in New Zealand, and is designed to determine whether or not qualifications from overseas meet the same standards as are applied in New Zealand. If your qualifications do not meet New Zealand standards, you may have to undertake retraining or extra study to secure the kind of job you want. Bear in mind that, although NZQA evaluations are official assessments, they are not binding on employers, professional bodies or educational institutions.

It is a good idea to contact the NZQA before you set out for New Zealand. You should ensure that you bring original or certified copies of all certificates, diplomas, degrees and professional qualifications with you when you move, as prospective employers may well need to see these for themselves.

References

Some advertisements will ask that you send a covering letter, CV and references. This does not usually mean a list of people for prospective employers to contact, although your usual list of verbal references should still accompany your application. In New Zealand it is customary for each employer you work for to provide you with a reference (you still need to request this though) when you leave a job. Bearing this in mind, it is worthwhile at least asking your most recent employer for a written reference before you leave home. If references and academic/professional certificates are not requested with the application itself, they will be requested later

for review during the job selection process. Make sure that you either deliver these personally or by courier, and that they are returned to you once the job selection is completed.

Interview procedure

If you are applying for a job in New Zealand from overseas, and a company wishes to interview you, in most cases they will not be prepared to pay your travel costs. Some companies will arrange interviews by video link or telephone. Another option to consider is arranging a number of job interviews to coincide with a visit to New Zealand, or your arrival if your residency has been approved. There are international job search companies that specialise in lining up job interviews before you set off for New Zealand. If you are using an agency to assist you with your residency application, they may have an employment-search facility or should at least be able to point you in the right direction by recommending recruitment agencies in your field.

Job interviews in New Zealand tend to be quite formal and you should dress appropriately for a work situation. If you are concerned about brushing up your job search and interview skills, most bookshops stock 'how to' guides for finding work. It is illegal for employers to discriminate on the basis of gender, race, colour, marital status or sexual orientation. Firms will usually have an Equal Employment Opportunity (EEO) policy in their Mission Statement and will have a quota set of the proportion of their workers who are from minority groups.

◼ SHORT-TERM EMPLOYMENT

Short-term employment prospects are improving as the economy continues to grow. However, as already noted in the *Before you go* chapter unless you are a New Zealander or have residency you will have to get a work visa to work while in New Zealand, even for a short period. One of the conditions of these visas is that you are doing jobs for which there are no appropriately qualified New Zealanders. Given that the types of jobs most people obtain while travelling are unskilled labouring jobs, your chances of working legitimately are not great. There is a lot of paperwork for your employer to get through just to hire a fruit picker.

Alternatively, if you are a British, Dutch, French, German or Irish citizen aged between 18 and 30 you can apply for a working holiday visa before you leave for New Zealand (see the Moving to New Zealand: Before you go chapter for details). If you do not have a work permit, some farmers may not be too concerned if they have short-term jobs, particularly seasonal jobs in rural areas, and cannot find locals interested in doing them. Under these circumstances you may find that employers are more interested in whether you are hard working than legal. But be careful, because in recent years the Immigration Service has been doing sweeps of picking gangs in remote areas to check whether they have work permits.

For short-term temporary work, your best opportunities will be within the areas of agriculture, horticulture or viticulture (grape-growing). If you are on a working holidaymaker visa and you are able to prove that you have worked in the horticulture or viticulture industries for at least you may be eligible for a further three-month extension on your stay in New Zealand. There are also working holiday

TIP

◼ You may endanger your chances of staying in New Zealand if you try to bend the rules on working.

schemes in New Zealand for travellers from Argentina, Belgium, Canada, Chile, the Czech Republic, Denmark, Estonia, Finland, France, Germany, Hong Kong, Ireland, Italy, Japan, Korea, Malaysia, Malta, the Netherlands, Norway, Singapore, Sweden, Taiwan, Thailand, the UK, the USA and Uruguay. See www.immigration.govt.nz for further details. For help with planning your travel, getting around the country and finding temporary work, try these websites:

www.backpackerboard.co.nz – Plan and discuss your trip, look up activities and advice, and learn about the requirements for a working holiday.

www.bunac.com – This international organisation offers working holidays for young people and students and provides support and advice throughout the holiday

www.gobeyond.co.nz – Beyond Backpackers lets you book a bed or get information on travel and work.

www.travellersnz.com – Travellers Contact Point New Zealand provides services for backpackers.

www.hottraveller.com – Jobs, accommodation, activities, tours and working holiday maker journals and blogs.

www.fourcorners.co.nz/new-zealand/working-holidays – Information on travel and visa requirements, including tips on working with your employer during the process.

www.jasons.com – Travel, accommodation and activity information for the South Pacific.

Horticulture and agriculture

There are many opportunities for keen workers in orchards, even if you have little or no experience. However, since the work is unskilled you will find that pay rates are far from high. Fruit picking tends to be paid at what is called piece rates (rates per kilo or per bin filled). Obviously as you get better at the work your pay rates will improve, but it can be discouraging at first, as well as backbreaking depending on the crop; asparagus picking is reputed to be the worst. It is possible to follow the different harvests around the country as each type of produce comes into season and to find work virtually year-round. In the main horticultural areas during the harvest, work will not be hard to find. Farmers advertise locally, sometimes contacting local youth hostels or backpackers' accommodation, or simply putting a sign up at the gate. There is occasionally accommodation available, albeit of a rather basic kind, and you may be provided with some food, such as fresh fruit and vegetables or dairy products. Generally the remoter the area, the more difficulty the farmers have in attracting local labour, so the better your chances. However this is no guarantee that they will be able to pay more, they are just more likely to provide non-wage perks such as accommodation or food in order to get the workers. For details of the timing and locations of various harvests see *Work Your Way Around the World* by Susan Griffith, available from Crimson Publishing. Alternatively, see the website www.seasonalwork.co.nz for different kinds of jobs all around the country, or email Janine@seasonalwork.co.nz.

Unlike fruit picking, working on farms usually requires some experience. For example, you will see almost daily advertisements in the Waikato papers for milkers, but they require people who are already skilled. Some unskilled work is available in shearing sheds, for example the job of rousie (the person who picks up the shorn fleeces), which does not require much beyond a strong pair of arms. If

There are over 48 million sheep in New Zealand

you have some practical farming experience under your belt and want work on a New Zealand farm, you can look for vacancies on the Farm News website (www.farmnews.co.nz) or advertise your skills on the AgriSupport Online website (www.agrisupportonline.com). Another useful contact might be FRENZ International, which specialises in permanent and temporary placement for dairy farm workers. You can use an online application form to apply.

 FRENZ: PO Box 7582, Wellesley Street, Auckland 1141; Auckland (09) 361 2658; Ashburton (03) 307 7172; Hamilton (07) 974 9022; info@frenz.co.nz; www.frenz.co.nz

Wine production is one of New Zealand's fastest growing industries. Innovative sustainable and environmentally friendly vineyard and industry practices are ensuring that New Zealand meets the international demand for wine produced in a 'clean, green' environment. Further expansion is expected as the number of vineyards continues to increase. Often there is casual work available on vineyards tying up the vines, and also during the grape harvest, particularly in the Marlborough and Hawke's Bay regions. The Wine Industry jobsite might be a useful place to start looking (www.wineindustryjobs.com.au). For general information about seasonal work see the WINZ website (www.winz.govt.nz). For further help and information, try the websites listed over:

Agricultural

www.fres.co.nz – Farm Relief Employment Services specialises in matching workers to dairy farming positions.

www.canstaff.co.nz – Canstaff are recruitment specialists on New Zealand's South Island.

Horticultural

www.jobscentral.co.nz – Seasonal Solutions provides advice and opportunities on the full process of finding work in Central Otago.

www.picknz.co.nz – PickNZ helps you find horticultural jobs in the major growing regions of New Zealand

www.adeccopicknplay.com – Pick'n'Play takes the guesswork out of making your stay last longer by fixing you up with temporary fruit picking work close to the fun things you want to do plus well handle work permits and even accommodation.

www.seasonalwork.co.nz – A hub with thousands of jobs listed and links to adventure tourism, harvest trails and English courses.

www.winejobsonline.com – This wine industry site allows both job seekers and employers to make contact over a wide range or jobs, including vineyard work.

www.wwoof.co.nz – Willing Workers on Organic Farms allows members to work on the hundreds of participating farms through New Zealand.

www.nzkgi.org.nz/seasonal-labour – NZ Kiwifruit Growers Inc offers information and fruitpicking jobs in the Bay of Plenty region.

www.hortnz.co.nz/activityareas/seasonalwork.html – Links and information about fruitpicking in NZ.

www.coolstore.co.nz – Offers seasonal work opportunities for fruitpickers.

www.workinnz.co.nz – Mr Apple NZ Ltd have jobs and accommodation for fruitpickers.

www.eastpack.co.nz – Offers seasonal work opportunities. Post harvest kiwifruit operator with 3 sites in Bay of Plenty - Te Puke, Edgecumbe and Opotiki.

Early years and childcare

With the growing number of training courses available (and required) to work in the childcare field in New Zealand, you stand a better chance at these jobs if you actually have a childcare qualification. There is a government-led strategic plan in place to ensure that all providers of early childhood education are qualified and registered by 2012. The PORSE Nanny Network is a good organisation to contact about qualifications required, as they offer appropriate training. This includes the National Certificate in Early Childhood Education and Care accredited by NZQA, as well as free workplace training for in-home educators, nannies and people wanting to explore a career in early childhood care. Posts are advertised in the daily papers or on community notice boards. There are several specialist agencies that can be found in the Yellow Pages or on the internet. Wages are quite low, but such jobs sometimes involve 'living in', so you may avoid food and accommodation expenses. See: www.childcarecareers.gov.uk for more information.

FACT

■ There is increasing demand for childcarers in New Zealand, and this is an expanding and dynamic sector.

Useful resources

Babysitters4U: A childcare directory for both childcarers and parents. Level 4, 315 Manchester St, Christchurch; 027 4638 389; info@babysitters4u.co.nz; www. babysitters4u.co.nz.

Childcare Online: www.childcareonline.co.nz.

Early Childhood Education: Part of the Ministry of Education website; www.ecd. govt.nz.

NZ Childcare Association: www.nzca.ac.nz

NZ Nanny Support Service: (for preschoolers) PO Box 10126, Bayfair, Tauranga 3152; 0508 445 437; www.nanny.co.nz.

PORSE Nanny Childcare Network: In-home childcare services for babies and young children. Offices in Auckland, Rotorua, Johnsonville/Tawa and Upper Hutt, Lower Hutt, Hastings, Wellington, Howick, Napier, Hamilton, Tauranga, Papamoa, New Plymouth, Palmerston North, Christchurch; see the website for location-specific contact details: www.porsenz.com.

Teaching English

The English teaching industry is well structured, with reasonable salaries and working conditions. This is a popular choice of job for young people in New Zealand on working holiday visas from places such as the UK, Australia, Ireland and Canada. The busiest periods for ESL/EFL teaching are February–March and July–October. As an employment prospect you will need the appropriate TEFL or ESL qualifications or experience in order to get a work permit, because as has already been noted above, the Immigration Service has to be satisfied that you have skills not possessed by New Zealand job seekers. Speaking English as your first language is not enough to qualify you. There are many public and private English-language schools, mainly based in Auckland, Wellington and Christchurch.

FACT

New Zealand is a popular destination for Asian students wanting to learn English, because of its reputation as a safe and friendly country.

Useful resources

The Campbell Institute: Level 1, 104 Dixon Street, Wellington; PO Box 24–300, Wellington; (04) 803 3434; fax (04) 803 3435; info@campbell.ac.nz; www.campbell.ac.nz.

Dominion English Schools: 67 Customs St, Auckland, PO Box 4217, Auckland; (09) 377 3280; fax (09) 377 3473; 4th Floor, 116 Worcester Street, PO Box 3908, Christchurch; (03) 365 3370; english@dominion.co.nz; www.dominion.school.nz.

Garden City English School: Level 2 Vero House, Hereford Street, PO Box 2851, Christchurch; (03) 377 0091; fax (03) 377 1251; info@EnglishLanguage.school.nz; www.EnglishLanguage.school.nz .

Languages International: PO Box 5293, Auckland 1036; (09) 309 0615; fax (09) 377 2806; info@languages.ac.nz; www.langsint.co.nz.

Seafield School of English: 71 Beresford St, PO Box 18516, New Brighton, Christchurch; (03) 388 3850; www.seafield.co.nz.

Southern English Schools: 69 Worcester Blvd, PO Box 1300, Christchurch; (03) 365 6022; fax (03) 365 6133; info@ses.co.nz; www.ses.ac.nz.

Tourism/hospitality

There are a lot of opportunities for casual workers in the tourist regions. Tourist destinations are a good place to start looking for hotel, café bar and catering staff positions. Kitchen hand and table waiting jobs are often advertised in local newspapers by the restaurants of large hotels. Working hours are long and the pay relatively low, but on the other hand, the location may make up for the working conditions and it's a good way to make some new friends. Tourists tip better than locals do, as New Zealanders traditionally do not tip serving staff.

If you can ski and have the relevant qualification, there are many opportunities on New Zealand ski fields for ski instructors or ski patrol personnel. Other types of skills that

TIP

It is usually easy to find café work in the main cities, and knowing your way around an espresso machine gives you a definite advantage as Kiwis can be picky about their coffee.

Tourists at Geyser

may help you find employment include aquatic sports skills such as scuba diving, water skiing, or life-saving skills. New Zealand beaches are patrolled mostly by volunteer surf life savers who are well trained and experienced in rescuing people from the often turbulent and dangerous waters, so you are more likely to find employment looking after hotel or private pools. Qualified aerobics instructors, yoga teachers and personal trainers should find opportunities at the many private gyms around the country. Word-of-mouth or being in the right place at the right time is often key to securing these kinds of positions, so don't be shy about walking in and enquiring as to whether there are any vacancies, or leave your CV, and let the people you meet locally know what you are looking for as well. Sometimes it's not what you know, it's who you know!

Useful websites

www.hhes.co.nz – Post your resume and search for jobs. Work throughout the hospitality industry, including temporary positions.

www.hospo.com – An international hospitality recruitment network. Jobs at all levels.

FACT

▧ The most well-known voluntary scheme goes under the name of WWOOF, which stands for Willing Workers On Organic Farms.

Voluntary work

If you want to avoid work permit hassles and still be legal, there are voluntary schemes whereby you can work in exchange for food and lodgings. There are many organic farms in New Zealand so there is the possibility that you could see quite a lot of the country without actually paying for your own keep. Usually you do about half a day's work in exchange for board. The work can be quite varied and you will usually be supplied with strictly vegetarian rations. You should contact Jane and Andrew Strange directly in New Zealand to join for a fee of US$30/CAD$38/£16/24 Euro. See the WWOOF websites for further information (www.wwoof.co.nz and www.organicvolunteers.com).

 WWOOF: PO Box 1172, Nelson; tel/fax (03) 544 9890; support@wwoof.co.nz

Some members of the BioDynamic Farming and Gardening Association (NZ) Inc offer food and board in exchange for work at certain times of the year. For further information and a list of members, see the website (www.organicpathways.co.nz). The New Zealand Trust for Conservation Volunteers is another organisation that offers volunteer work. Projects include such activities as beach clean-ups and planting native forest. Lists of upcoming projects, and contact details for organisers, can be found on the website (www.conservationvolunteers.org.nz). Project lengths vary, and so does the provision of accommodation and food depending on where, when and for how long you will be going.

LONGER-TERM WORK

Executive employment prospects

Prospects are good for executive employment as the local labour market is unable to provide enough suitably skilled applicants for the growing demand. However, the

executive vacancies are for people with a high level of technical and interpersonal skills and the interview process can be rigorous.

Information Technology

New Zealanders qualified in IT and programming tend to be attracted overseas by the comparatively higher salaries, for a time at least. As a result, 'IT Specialists' is a constantly recurring entry on the Long Term and Immediate Shortage Lists (the Long Term Skill Shortage List was formerly known as the Priority Occupations List). There are a few rules of course – you will need a Bachelor of Science, with majors in computer science or information science, and you must be qualified, which, in this case, means a minimum of three years full-time work experience with at least 12 months work experience in the past 18 months in at least one of the specifications on the Information Technology Skills List. Specific IT and ICT workers currently in demand include the following: systems analysts, computer application engineers, systems managers, management and project management staff, policy planning and research staff, systems development staff, technical advice and consultancy staff, senior test analysts, programmers and solutions architects.

In-Demand IT Specialisations	
Databses (DBMS)	Data warehousing
	MS SQL Server
	Oracle
	Sybase SQL Server
Application Development	C
	C#
	C#.net
	C++
	Embedded C
	Java
	Oracle Forms
	.net
	OO.net
	Visual Basic
	Visual Basic.net
	Visual C++
	XML
Web Development	JSP
	Vignette
Application Design	UML
	Rational Rose

Networking Technologies	CCNA (Cisco Certified Network Admin)
	CCNE (Cisco Certifed Network Engineer)
	CGI
	Cisco Firewall/Internet Security
	IPX
	Network Design
	Novell Netware
OS	HP/UX
	SUN OS
	Sun Solaris
	Unix

Medical

Doctors

The numbers of foreign doctors registering with the Medical Council has increased in recent years and there is some concern that this may lead to an oversupply of medical personnel. The increase in numbers seems to be the result of an increase in numbers of skilled immigrants, particularly from South Africa, which has resulted in a reverse 'brain-drain'. The situation in New Zealand has usually been the opposite with trained New Zealanders going abroad leaving opportunities for qualified migrants. You should contact the Medical Council for an accurate assessment of employment opportunities. As has been noted already you must register with the Medical Council in order to practice as a doctor in New Zealand. Doctors from Australia, Britain, Ireland and South Africa, who have been registered in their own country, are usually accepted for registration without requiring further qualifications. Doctors from other countries will usually have to sit registration exams.

Nurses

Nurses must apply to be registered with the Nursing Council of New Zealand.

Teaching

There are excellent work opportunities within the New Zealand education system for well-qualified and experienced teachers. Teachers of children with special needs are also needed in early childhood services, and primary and secondary schools. Qualified, experienced teachers of children with learning or behavioural issues, those working with children with physical disabilities and teachers of English to speakers of other languages are sought-after at present. The majority of overseas-trained teachers appointed to New Zealand schools come from the UK, Ireland, Australia, Canada and South Africa. Across the board, there is such demand that registered teachers originally from New Zealand who have gone overseas to work are being offered a financial incentive to return home to work. Contact TeachNZ for more information.

> My teaching course was a safe investment, and there is a definite demand for male teachers here. New Zealand faces the same challenge as the UK in that it is particularly short on male primary school teachers.
> **Sam McLaughlan**

As noted earlier in this section, immigrants intending to teach must have their qualifications verified and checked for comparability with New Zealand qualifications

i TeachNZ: Ministry of Education, PO Box 1666, Wellington; www.teachnz. govt.nz

by the New Zealand Qualifications Authority. Teacher registration is compulsory for all teachers in the state sector in New Zealand.

If you are a registered early childhood, primary or secondary teacher, you might want to consider working as a supply teacher (called 'relief' teaching) while on a Working Holiday Visa, to get an idea of the work and the country before you commit to longer-term employment. Once you have obtained a Working Holiday Visa, you need to have your qualifications assessed by the New Zealand Qualifications authority, then get registered with the Teachers' Council and find yourself a teaching job. There are costs involved in being assessed and registered, but you will receive a higher salary and, depending on the length of your first job in New Zealand, you may also be able to apply for an International Relocation Grant. For more information and to electronically request the relevant forms, visit the TeachNZ website (www.teachnz.govt.nz). The site has links to other information, including current vacancies.

Population growth in New Zealand has been greater in Auckland than in other areas of New Zealand, and this has caused resulting pressures on teacher supply in all sectors – primary, secondary and early childhood. Vacancies for supply (relief) as well as permanent teachers can be found through the Ministry of Education's TeachNZ website. It is also perfectly admissible to contact schools or early childhood centres directly.

The *Education Gazette* is published fortnightly and advertises all permanent teaching positions in state and independent schools. You can read the Gazette online, where it is constantly updated (www.edgazette.govt.nz), or by subscribing directly to PO Box 249, Wellington; ((04) 917 3990; fax (04) 917 3991;direct-subscribe@list. tki.org.nz). Teaching positions in universities and polytechnics are usually advertised on the institutions' own websites.

Early childhood education

There are new government requirements for all early childhood teachers to be registered by 2012; this means that early childhood education (ECE) teachers are currently under pressure to upgrade their qualifications to meet these requirements. It can be difficult at the moment for centres to meet staff-number requirements; this means that suitably qualified teachers are in demand as supply (relief) teachers right now. At this point, there are no UK ECE qualifications that are equivalent to the New Zealand three-year diploma or degree.

Primary education

The job market is not as buoyant for primary teachers in most areas of New Zealand, although demand is still high in Auckland. The recent Government announcement regarding increased primary staffing levels will create more employment opportunities for primary teachers in the near future. Primary teachers with a minimum of three years relevant teaching experience are now listed on Immigration New Zealand's Immediate Skill Shortage list for work permits or residency.

Secondary education
Demand for secondary teachers is strong throughout the country, particularly in Auckland. In special demand are teachers of physics, mathematics, chemistry, and technology.

For further information, you can contact Irene Lynch, National Manager, TeachNZ.

 Irene Lynch, National Manager, TeachNZ: Irene.Lynch@minedu.govt.nz

Contact the Ministry of Education for Scholarship, Training and Employment information.

 Ministry of Education:0800 TeachNZ (0800 832 246); +64 4 463 8454 or 0800 165 225; TeachNZ@minedu.govt.nz; www.TeachNZ.govt.nz

Company or organisation transfers

One alternative to finding work straight away in New Zealand is to find work with a company with prospects of being transferred to New Zealand. Unfortunately few companies recruit staff with the promise of being posted to a particular country, however if you choose a New Zealand company to work for, your chances are obviously greater. Still this process is likely to be a long-term and rather round-about route into the country. The British/New Zealand Trade Council publishes a trade directory of member companies, which might be useful if you are looking for New Zealand companies in the UK. The American Chamber of Commerce in New Zealand publishes a directory of American companies operating in New Zealand (see: www.amcham.co.nz). The big multinationals also have subsidiaries in New Zealand, sometimes under different names.

 British/New Zealand Trade Council :Private Bag 92014, Auckland; (09) 303 2973; fax (09)303 1868; www.brittrade.org.nz

■ ASPECTS OF EMPLOYMENT

Salary

Salaries in New Zealand are lower than those for equivalent positions in the USA, the UK and Europe. In some areas, living costs are lower as well, although many new migrants report surprise at the costs involved in living in Auckland and Wellington, in particular.

TIP

■ You should not expect a New Zealand salary to be the same as a salary in your home country once the exchange rate is taken into account.

City variations

Salaries are considerably higher in Wellington and Auckland than they are in the rest of the country; this reflects the higher living costs in these cities as well as the higher stress and greater responsibility routinely associated with these positions. Salaries in the rest of the country might be up to 20%lower, but it is difficult to find exactly equivalent jobs to make precise comparisons as industries and work pressures vary so markedly.

It is difficult to make a direct comparison of living standards because so many factors are difficult to compare. For example, going overseas for an annual holiday becomes very expensive when the nearest country is three hours away by plane, and that is only Australia. On the other hand, you have easy access to great beaches and can enjoy much better climate than northern Europeans, year-round. As a generalisation, it would be fair to say that living standards are roughly equivalent for most middle–income earners.

Job advertisements infrequently include the exact salary the employer is offering for a position, instead you will see the words 'salary up to' and 'salary negotiable' featured frequently. When the words 'up to' are used, the figure given will be the absolute maximum an employer is willing to pay for the most perfect and best-experienced of possible applicants – a mere mortal will be lucky to attain it. However, if your experience and skills are in high demand there is always the chance of actually negotiating an even higher salary. Professional and executive salaries are considerably lower than those paid in other developed countries, with an average salary for a top general manager or company boss being around NZ$250,000. Executive packages however are much more likely to include bonuses, fringe benefits such as company cars and health insurance, superannuation schemes, etc. At this level employees are also more likely to enjoy greater and more structured (likely performance-based) productivity bonuses and profit sharing.

A national minimum wage applies in New Zealand – currently this is NZ$9.50 an hour unless the worker is under 18, in which case the Youth Minimum Wage of NZ$7.60 applies.

Recent growth in total gross earnings is driven mainly by the increased contribution of the manufacturing, construction and wholesale trade sector. Stronger growth in total gross earnings than in total paid hours resulted in a 4.1% increase to average total hourly earnings over the last year. Private sector average total gross earnings – driven by the manufacturing, construction, wholesale trade industries – increased 3.9% over the last year. Public sector average total hourly earnings increased 5% over the last year, driven by increased contributions from government administration and defence as well as personal and other services, health and community services industries.

FACT

■ Statistics New Zealand figures show that roughly 40,000 adult employees receive less than the legal minimum wage but that most people earn at least 30% more than the minimum wage.

Average Hourly Earnings	
Average:	NZ$23.32
Private sector:	NZ$21.73
Public sector:	NZ$29.49
Males	NZ$24.68
Females	NZ$21.59
Accommodation/cafés/restaurants:	NZ$15.03
Retail:	NZ$16.12
Construction:	NZ$21.28
Personal Services:	NZ$22.79
Transport, storage and communications:	NZ$22.65
Manufacturing:	NZ$21.84
Health and community services:	NZ$24.58
Wholesale trade:	NZ$23.99
Cultural and recreational activities:	NZ$24.18
Forestry and mining:	NZ$24.72
Property and business services:	NZ$26.43
Education:	NZ$28.14
Government administration and defence:	NZ$30.76
Electricity, gas and water:	NZ$33.29
Finance and insurance:	NZ$31.50

Source: Statistics New Zealand Employment Survey 2007.

Working life

As you might expect for a relatively lightly populated country, typical New Zealand businesses are small compared to those in other countries. However, many large multinational businesses have offices in New Zealand, and there is a strong government sector, particularly in Wellington. The job market varies widely from one region to another, and obviously most of the government jobs and positions within large organisations are based in the bigger cities. Depending on your chosen occupation though, there may well be exciting opportunities in regional centres as well.

Working hours

The traditional standard working week is five days, 40 hours, although many people do put in extra hours and overtime. A working day is typically 8.30 am to 5pm, with half an hour for lunch, although many salaried employees work significantly longer hours than this. Depending on where you work, arriving as close as possible to 'official start time' and leaving at 5pm on the dot might earn you an unshakeable reputation as a 'shirker'. Employers and employees are now

TIP

■ It is a good time to look at working in New Zealand, providing you accept that working life there may be quite different to working in your home country.

Changes in work

There have been dramatic changes in employment trends in many industries over the last 10 to 15 years, and the changes are ongoing. Similar changes are occurring in most developed (Organisation for Economic Development (OECD)) nations. As the workforce is growing older and there has been a big drop in the birth rate, there aren't so many young people to replace those who retire. An increasing number of people from other countries are working in New Zealand, so the workforce is becoming more multi-ethnic. Another change is the types of jobs that people are working in – more employers have introduced flexible working hours as people become less willing to sacrifice their lifestyle and family life for their work. That's not to say that they aren't still looking for a good salary though!

free to set the length of their working week and their start and finish times. Workers in some large factories for example now work four 10-hour shifts spread over seven days. Workers would generally expect to have Saturdays and Sundays off, apart from those working in retail, service, etc. Many employers no longer pay extra for overtime, although you can usually expect to be given time off in lieu of hours worked if you are required to put in a significant amounts of extra time. You should not assume this to be the case in every workplace though. Overtime was traditionally paid at time and a half. In areas such as retail you may be paid overtime if you are required to work a public holiday. Longer working hours are also becoming a feature of many industries.

Holiday provision is still protected by law under the Holidays Act. After 12 months' continuous employment, the employee is entitled to four weeks paid leave. In addition, there are 11 paid public holidays annually. Employees do not have to work on public holidays unless they agree or their contract provides for this. Remember that these will only be paid holidays if they actually fall on a day on which you would normally work. There is no compulsory retirement age anymore, although entitlement to National Superannuation is assessed from the age of 65.

Professionals on salaries can expect to work quite long hours, particularly at the start of their careers.

TIP

You should take your cue regarding working hours from your workmates rather than from your contract if you want to be accepted as part of the team.

> When I arrived, I lived with friends in Epsom for a few weeks before finding a room in a beautiful villa in Ponsonby. From there, I was walking or cycling into town for work every day, and although the working hours are longer and harder than in the UK, the days seemed to have so much more time available because I was cutting out all the darkness and commuting.
> **Vita Evans**

Are conditions declining?

Wage workers used to enjoy a high level of employment protection; national pay rates and conditions were set down in awards, legal documents which bound employers. Unions at a national level did most of the bargaining. Employment protection has been considerably weakened over the last decade and a half, and in some areas of the labour market (particularly casual work in catering, horticulture and agriculture) pay rates and conditions can be very poor. The social security system, once relatively generous, has also been trimmed back. On the other hand personal tax rates on high incomes are lower than in many European countries; there is no capital gains tax, GST (Goods and Services Tax) is 12.5% and the highest income tax rate is 39% (for incomes over NZ$60,001 per annum).

Parental leave

The minimum legislative rights to Parental Leave are laid out in the Parental Leave and Employment Protection Act 1987. Employees adopting a child under six years old are also entitled to parental leave. It is not automatic, you must apply for it. The period of leave is the same for adoptive parents, but there are differences in the advanced notice you are required to give. There are different entitlements for leave, depending on whether the employee has worked for the same employer for an average of at least 10 hours per week for either the immediately preceding six months or the immediately preceding 12 months before the expected due date or adoption of a child. To be eligible, you must have worked at least an average of 10 hours each week, including at least one hour a week or 40 hours per month, for the same employer for 12 months before the expected due date or adoption. The types of leave are as follows:

Special Leave: Up to 10 days during pregnancy for women to have antenatal appointments or classes.

Maternity Leave: Up to 14 continuous weeks for the mother, which can start up to six weeks before the expected date of birth or adoption. Maternity leave may be commenced up to six weeks before the date of birth or adoption.

Partner's/Paternity Leave: Up to 2 continuous weeks for the father around the expected date of birth or adoption. The mother may transfer the entitlement to parental leave payments to her partner, in which case the period of the partner's/paternity leave is extended to match the length of time the payment is received by the partner.

Extended Leave: Up to 52 continuous weeks, excluding any maternity leave taken in the 12 months after the birth. Extended leave may be shared by both parents but may not exceed 52 weeks in total.

All leave must be taken in the first year after the birth or adoption. You will not be eligible for another period of parental leave unless the expected date of delivery or adoption of subsequent children is at least 12 months after your return to work from a previous parental leave. Each partner must take any period of extended leave in a continuous period. The leave can be taken at the same time or separately, to suit the needs of the parents and the child. You are required to give three weeks notice of your intention to either return or not return to work. In the case of miscarriage, stillbirth, death or adoption, you may return to work early, but are still required to give 21 days notice.

Job protection

If you take less than four weeks parental leave, your job must be kept open. If you take more than four weeks, the employer may decide that the job cannot be kept open, but you have a right to challenge that decision. If you accept this decision then you are entitled to a preference period of six months when the employer must offer you a job substantially similar to the one you have left. In the small number of cases where an employer does not have to keep the job open, the employee is still entitled to 13 weeks paid leave. You may not be dismissed for becoming pregnant or for applying for parental leave. Your employment contract may contain special provisions. For further information, contact the Employment Relations Service.

 Employment Relations service: 0800 800 863; www.ers.dol.govt.nz

Trade unions

Prior to the Employment Contracts Act of 1991, New Zealand unions enjoyed a monopoly over workplace representation and union membership in many industries was compulsory. The resulting system of wage determination was highly centralised and inflexible. If unions and employers negotiating in each industry at a national level could not agree, the dispute would be settled through compulsory arbitration by a tribunal made up of members from both sides. As a result of this system,

Negotiating contracts

The Employment Contracts Act of 1991 removed union monopolies over bargaining in the workplace, abolished compulsory membership, and the Arbitration Tribunals. Wage fixing is now in theory completely decentralised, although some of the bigger unions still negotiate at national level. Employers and employees negotiate employment contracts, which may be either collective or individual. Employees may nominate someone to act as their bargaining agent. Employers are obliged to recognise whomever an employee nominates as their bargaining agent, although this does not mean they must negotiate or settle with that agent.

employment conditions were guaranteed at some minimum level in just about all industries, and the disparity between the high paid and the low paid was not very great.

Trade unions no longer have a protected legal status, and total membership fell from approximately 683,000 in 1985 to approximately 339,000 in 1996. Following an even sharper decrease in the following years, which saw membership fall to less than 200,000, union membership has increased every year for the last seven years. Membership of unions lifted by 5,000 in 2006 alone, and there are 80,000 more workers in unions today than there were at the end of 1999. The number of employees on collective agreements has also fallen sharply; the majority of the workforce is now employed on individual contracts.

Flexibility has brought benefits to some employees and industries but has weakened the position of others. Part-time workers, those in workplaces with only a few employees and the service sector generally all have less job security, fewer employment protections and in some cases have seen a real reduction in pay.

The Employment Relations Act (2000) inserts into all collective agreements a requirement to deduct union fees where the employee consents. Unions and employers may vary these arrangements in a collective agreement. Employers must allow union representatives to come into the workplace and union officials must exercise their access rights in a reasonable way. Union members are entitled to attend two union meetings (of up to two hours each) each year. Employers must pay union members who attend these meetings during their normal working hours. Under this Act, any group of employees can set up and register as a union, provided they first become an incorporated society (under the Incorporated Societies Act, 1908) and then register as a union under the 2000 Act. Such groups must have a minimum of fifteen members, be independent of employers, and have a set of union rules.

Most New Zealand unions belong to the national body, The New Zealand Council of Trade Unions (NZCTU). See the website for a list of useful email addresses. The NZCTU publishes a comprehensive directory of all trade unions in the country. The Employment Relations Service can also provide information (0800 800 863; www.ers.dol.govt.nz).

 The New Zealand Council of Trade Unions: Level 7 West Block, Education House, 178 Willis Street, Wellingon; PO Box 6645, Wellington; (04) 385 1334; fax (04) 385 6051; www.union.org.nz or www.ctu.org.nz

Employment contracts

At the beginning of your employment you will negotiate an employment contract with your employer. You can be covered under an existing collective contract if it provides for new workers to join and if your employer agrees. Otherwise you will negotiate an individual contract. Individual contracts can be either written or oral but it is desirable to have a written contract. If you wish to have a bargaining agent represent you, you have a choice between joining a union or employing a private bargaining agent. Remember that though your employer must recognise your bargaining agent they are not obliged to settle with them. An employment contract must by law have certain provisions. There must be an effective personal grievance procedure and disputes procedure. The minimum conditions outlined above – wages and holiday provision and the parental leave provisions – cannot be overridden, although they can be improved upon.

A good checklist for individual employment contracts can be obtained from the magazine published by a network of independent legal firms called Lawlink (09) 300 5470), or found on their website (www.lawlink.co.nz).

Employment tribunal and employment court

Two institutions for resolving disputes were set up under the Employment Relations Act 2000 – the Tribunal, which mostly mediates in disputes, either personal disputes or grievances arising from breach of employment contracts, and the Employment Court which deals with matters referred on by the Tribunal, and more serious issues such as disputes involving strikes and lockouts. There is no right to strike while an employment contract is still current.

Women in work

This number of employed women in New Zealand has been steadily increasing since the 1960s, although it seems to have reached a plateau in recent years after it dropped off slightly in the late 1980s. The participation rates for women are considerably lower than the corresponding figures for men across all age groups, and particularly in the 25–34 age group, reflecting the fact that women are still the primary care givers for children.

Despite still bearing more family responsibilities than men, New Zealand women are moving into previously male dominated areas, particularly the professions. Female students outnumber men in areas such as medicine and law, although this is a recent development and men still dominate at senior levels in these professions.

Equal pay for the same work was established under the Equal Pay Act of 1972, and other forms of discrimination in the workplace based on gender, race or any

 Ministry of Women's Affairs: PO Box 10 049, Wellington; (04) 915 7112; fax (04) 916 1604; mwa@mwa.govt.nz; www.mwa.govt.nz

FACT

■ Over 70% of New Zealand women (over the age of 15) work in either full- or part-time paid employment.

other non-relevant factor is illegal under the Human Rights Commission Act of 1972. If you believe you have been discriminated against unlawfully, you can either use the personal grievance procedures in your employment contract or you can make a complaint to the Human Rights Commission. Between 1987 and 2003 there was a substantial reduction in the gender pay gap; the average hourly earnings of women rose during that time from 79% to 88% of men's average hourly earnings. However, there is still a significant difference in income levels between men and women. Women are still concentrated in a narrower range of occupations, which, in general, pay less well. Equal pay claims are also harder to establish in the new environment of individual contracts. Discrimination in individual cases is much harder to prove than in a situation where everyone receives the same rate of pay for a job. However, the attitude towards women in employment in New Zealand is generally positive. Childcare is becoming more affordable now that the government subsidises pre-school care centres. Some of these advances have been achieved through the efforts of women politicians.

For more information about women in New Zealand contact the Ministry of Women's Affairs or the National Advisory Council on the Employment of Women (NACEW).

i NACEW, c/- Department of Labour, PO Box 3705, Wellington; (04) 915 4059; fax (04) 915 4710; NACEW@dol.govt.nz; www.nacew.govt.nz

■ WORKING CULTURE AND ETIQUETTE

Relationships and communication

- New Zealanders can be somewhat reserved, especially with people they do not know.
- Once New Zealanders develop a personal relationship, they are friendly, outgoing and social.
- Do not appear too forward or overly friendly; be sensitive to the professionalism, comfort zones and restraint of others.
- They respect people who are honest, direct, and demonstrate a sense of humour.
- They trust people until they are given a reason not to. If this happens in business the breach will be difficult to repair and business dealings may cease or become more difficult.

Business meeting etiquette

- Appointments are usually necessary and should be made at least one week in advance by telephone or email.
- It is generally easy to schedule meetings with senior level managers if you are coming from another country if the meeting is planned well in advance.
- Arrive at meetings on time or even a few minutes early.
- If you do not arrive on time, your behaviour may be interpreted as indicating that you are unreliable or that you think your time is more important than the person with whom you are meeting.
- Meetings are generally relaxed; however, they are serious events and you should never assume informality.
- Expect a brief amount of small talk before getting down to the matter at hand.
- If you make a presentation, avoid hype, exaggerated claims, hyperbole, and bells and whistles. New Zealanders are interested in what people 'can do' not what they say they can do.

FACT

Women have a high profile in New Zealand public life. A third of the members of parliament are women and Helen Clark is New Zealand's second female Prime Minister.

FACT

It can be difficult to schedule meetings in December and January since these are the prime months for summer vacation.

- Present your business case with facts and figures. Emotions and feelings are not important in the New Zealand business climate.
- Maintain eye contact and a few feet of personal space.

Negotiations

- The negotiating process takes time.
- Do not attempt high-pressure sales tactics.
- Demonstrate the benefits of your services or products rather than only talking about them.
- Keep any presentations short, snappy and most importantly memorable (in a good way).
- Start your negotiations with a realistic figure. Since this is not a bargaining culture, New Zealanders do not expect to haggle over price.
- Kiwis look for value for their money.
- Do not make promises you cannot keep or offer unrealistic proposals. Kiwis do not generally trust people who have to oversell, and there is a general acceptance of the wisdom that anything that sounds too good to be true probably is.
- Kiwis are quite direct and expect the same in return. They appreciate brevity and are not impressed by more detail than is required.
- Agreements and proposals must state all points clearly. All terms and conditions should be explained in detail.
- Stick to the point while speaking.
- Kiwis are not generally overly demonstrative or dramatically enthusiastic – you should not take this to mean however that they are unreceptive to you or lacking passion about what they do.
- Kiwis appreciate honesty and directness in business dealings.

BUSINESS AND INDUSTRY REPORT

Of course, opportunities vary depending on your location, so the following is a fairly general guide and you should have a closer look into industries you are interested in once you decide where you want to settle. See also the Regional Employment Guide and the Directory of Major Employers.

FACT

Industries expected to grow the most over the next couple of years are business services, health and social services, retail, engineering, and teaching.

Agriculture and forestry

The New Zealand dollar reached a high against the US dollar in 2007, and this has had adverse effects on exporters' returns. High international dairy prices have offset the effects of this exchange rate, but there have been problems for other areas of the forestry and agriculture sectors. Diary prices have rocketed since October 2006, and the Ministry of Agriculture and Fisheries (MAF) predicts payouts of NZ$5–NZ$5.50 per kg for milk solids over the next three seasons. Although forestry prices have provided some difficulties in recent years, log prices have now risen and this is expected to be the beginning of a sustained rise. However, several timber mills have recently been forced to close by the combined effects of the high exchange rate, the weak US timber market, and rising log prices. Recovery will be slow as the US housing market is not expected to bounce back quickly. Lamb prices have also been poor, to some degree due to the high value of the New Zealand dollar and static international prices. However, there are expectations that this will improve as breeding ewe numbers in Europe are declining.

Beef prices have been strong, in part due to strong returns in South Korea and Japan. Returns for farmers are expected to improve as the New Zealand dollar 'softens'. It is forecast that international commodity prices will be stronger over the next three years than they have been recently. Major exports from this sector include meat, dairy products, wool, wood products and horticultural products, as well as a number of specialised products for international niche markets. International dairy prices are expected to remain high, and horticulture crop producers' focus on maintaining and improving already high-quality products is expect to sustain prices and demand for New Zealand products. Returns on beef have been higher than for lamb recently, although it is forecast that they will decline gradually.

FACT

■ New Zealand's first shipment of frozen meat left for England in 1882.

Quality is a key component in the success of the horticulture and arable industries, and international prices for New Zealand kiwifruit, apples and grapes are expected to remain steady. Prices for arable crops have risen and are expected to remain strong because of the drought in Australia. Kiwifruit production is expected to expand and apple orchardists are expected to focus on upgrading varieties.

New Zealand wine has successfully maintained a competitive advantage over the last 10 years, and wine prices should remain fairly stable in international currencies, supported by the perception of New Zealand wine as a high-quality, unique and desirable product. Wine exports are forecast to increase significantly into 2009 and then continue to increase, although at a slower rate, through to 2011.

Across eastern districts, in places such as Marlborough, Central Otago and Waipara pastoral farms and orchards have been converted into vineyards, as returns are high compared to sheep farming. Conversions look set to continue, and forest land has also seen a drop in replanting and an increase in conversion for other uses such as dairy and intensive beef and sheep farming. In Southland and South Canterbury large numbers of sheep farms have been converted to dairy farms, and with the forecast for strong returns on dairy products conversions look set to continue despite the fact that dairy farming does bring additional irrigation demands and so not all land is suitable for conversion. Overall, forecasts are positive, with anticipated growth in agricultural income.

FACT

■ Wine is expected to overtake kiwifruit in terms of export earnings between 2009 and 2011.

For further information, see www.maf.govt.nz, www.fedfarm.org.nz, www.organicsnewzealand.org.nz, and www.nzwine.com.

Agritech and life sciences

These sectors are adding significant value and high tech innovation to New Zealand's oldest foundation industries. The agritech sector is a major contributor to New Zealand's economic wealth.This sector is diverse, but covers all pre-harvest inputs for agriculture including fertilisers and grass seeds, breeding genetics and animal remedies, equipment, and also agricultural tourism. The equine industry is another land-based sector that has thrived in New Zealand, achieving exports of around NZ$150 million and a world-class success record. The natural products sector is a fast-growing export industry for New Zealand, and includes 'nutraceuticals', health products and health foods. Biotechnology is another important facet of the life sciences sector and will be discussed further below. The government has recently highlighted this area as one integral to the long-term future economic growth of New Zealand. International business development is a priority, with particular emphasis on high-growth markets in North America, Europe and North Asia.

Biotechnology

The biotechnology sector plays an important role in New Zealand's economy. Expenditure on this sector has increased dramatically over the past few years and now totals more than NZ$640 million. Export revenue continues to grow, and biotechnology contributes NZ$300–NZ$400 million per year to the New Zealand economy through the primary sector. The majority of growth has come from the private sector. Ten biotechnology companies are listed on the New Zealand Stock Exchange, and four more are listed on the Australian Stock Exchange. New Zealand's strong international position in the areas of dairy, sheep, forestry and horticulture is reflected in its biotechnology industry; agricultural biotechnology accounts for 41% of expenditure and 35% of overall industry employment. Industrial applications represent 19% of expenditure and 14% of employment, medical devices and diagnostics represent 23% of expenditure and 28% of employment, and human health applications (such as nutraceuticals and functional foods) represent 17% of expenditure and 23% of employment. The Australia New Zealand Biotechnology Partnership Fund is intended to accelerate growth in the sector through joint activities in development, marketing and manufacturing. For more information see: www.nzbio.org,nz.

Business services

The largest regional employer in Auckland and Wellington, the business services sector is constantly reinventing itself and upgrading to match the latest developments in IT and communications, which are of course vital to competitive businesses. Staffing, HR in-house training and data processing services are in increasing demand, and companies are ever on the lookout for employees with more advanced skills and extensive experience. Jobs in this sector vary enormously in terms of type and level, and as a result so do experience and qualification requirements; that said, the most up-to-date communications and IT experience will always be valuable if you are looking for employment in this area.

Finance and insurance

Finance includes activities such as banking, accounting, sharebroking, financial planning, and business administration. Most of the large companies and banks in New Zealand are internationally owned companies operating globally, and competition for market share has resulted in many mergers and takeovers as well as regular reshuffling over the last few years. The Taranaki Savings Bank (TSB) and

Kiwibank are the only New Zealand-owned banks. As a result of the dominance of multinational companies, smaller businesses have to diversify and offer extra services in order to attract clients. In recent years some of the foreign owned large companies have shut their doors in New Zealand and now base their Australasian operations in Australia. Most insurance companies operating in New Zealand are also part of large multinational firms.

Although there are many insurance companies registered in New Zealand, the most dominant companies in the general insurance field are State and New Zealand Insurance (NZI). For life insurance, some of the largest companies are AMP, AXA and Sovereign. The main area of growth in insurance work has been in customer service and call centre roles. The increase in call centre work is linked to centralisation, as call centres allow nationwide queries to be handled in one location.

Businesses have become more accountable to their shareholders, and to government authorities, which means that insurance companies have more constraints placed on them through general laws (such as the Privacy Act and the Consumer Guarantees Act), and, because of this increased accountability, businesses are taking out more liability insurance, so demand is growing in that area. Most finance and insurance companies are now centralised (although at one time many of these companies would have had branches nationwide), and Auckland and Wellington provide the largest number of employees to this sector.

The second stage of deregulation in the financial sector occurred in the late 1980s. The regulations governing the supervision and registration of banks was relaxed under the Reserve Bank of New Zealand Act of 1986, and as result most building societies registered as banks and a number of foreign banks established New Zealand subsidiaries. Two further acts in 1987 and 1988 further removed distinctions

Growth of the sector

The fast growth in employment in the finance sector between 1986 and 1991 was, in part, due to deregulation of the financial sector as part of the programme of economic reform instituted by the Labour government in the 1980s. As a result of deregulation there was a rapid growth in money market activity, particularly in the areas of foreign exchange, where all restrictions over transfers were lifted. New Zealand's relatively undeveloped financial industry enjoyed a boom. A range of new financial instruments was introduced such as forward contracts, options and exchange rate futures and secondary markets such as in government securities grew. The share market soared due to the increase in money supply resulting from deregulation. The boom was short-lived however and the inevitable collapse came in October 1987 when the main share price index, the Barclays share index, dropped to below its 1984 level.

between trading banks, trustee banks and building societies. The increase in the number of financial institutions and the range of activities they were involved in resulted in a rapid growth of employment in this area. More recently, technology such as e-commerce and internet communication has had a major impact on the way that many financial institutes and business service providers operate. It has also meant an increase in demand for insurance cover against electronic risks, most particularly related to e-commerce.

The outlook for this sector is not overly positive for the next two years, with some industry experts believing that the finance company industry may shrink by half or more over this time. The market has been damaged by the collapse of 14 finance companies in the last 18 months – victims of a lack of investor confidence and the fallout from the US sub-prime mortgage crisis, which has knocked international credit and equity markets. In future money will need to be sourced from different places and also lent out differently. The non-bank finance sector has suffered from a rise in bad loans and increased reluctance by investors to lend. There are strict new rules including mandatory capital levels and credit ratings under the supervision of the central bank, and it is thought that these will force consolidation.

For more information, see www.icnz.org.nz, www.icanz.co.nz, www.nzier.org.nz and www.nzx.co.nz. See also: www.businesstechnologynewsnow.com

Construction

After a downturn over the past few years, confidence in this area of industry is now lifting. Indirectly, as well as construction workers the industry employs thousands of other people in support jobs related to manufacturing, material supplies and transport services. The highest proportion of building construction enterprises is in Auckland, Wellington and Christchurch. There are three main parts to the industry – residential (homes), non-residential (offices, etc.) and civil construction (bridges, roads, hospitals, etc.). The outlook for the industry is good. While there is a reduced demand for residential building due to factors such as falling migration, the commercial and

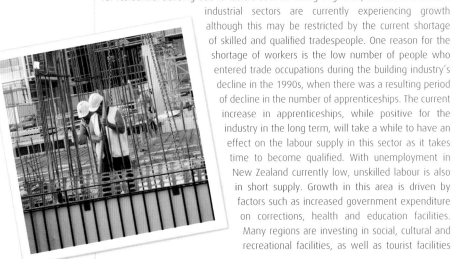

industrial sectors are currently experiencing growth although this may be restricted by the current shortage of skilled and qualified tradespeople. One reason for the shortage of workers is the low number of people who entered trade occupations during the building industry's decline in the 1990s, when there was a resulting period of decline in the number of apprenticeships. The current increase in apprenticeships, while positive for the industry in the long term, will take a while to have an effect on the labour supply in this sector as it takes time to become qualified. With unemployment in New Zealand currently low, unskilled labour is also in short supply. Growth in this area is driven by factors such as increased government expenditure on corrections, health and education facilities. Many regions are investing in social, cultural and recreational facilities, as well as tourist facilities and hotels. Money is also being invested in industrial building such as sawmills and dairy processing plants.

For more information, see www.nzcic.co.nz, www.bcito.org.nz and www.careers.govt.nz.

Creative industries

Creative industries form a key sector in New Zealand's economy, both because of their potential for growth and their ability to enable innovation and improved productivity within other sectors. Growth in this sector is currently 9%, and it contributes 3.1% (NZ$2.86billion) to the total GDP. The sector is diverse, and includes music, television, screen production, fashion, design, textiles and digital content. New Zealand has a competitive advantage in some areas, such as screen production and post production, and has a growing reputation in areas such as fashion and design.

Energy

New Zealand's electricity needs have traditionally been supplied by historic investment in large scale hydro schemes which today provide the country with up to 70% of its total electricity needs. The remainder has largely been provided from abundant natural gas from the giant Maui gas field which was discovered off the Taranaki coast in the 1960s, and from New Zealand's strong geothermal resources in the central North Island.

However, New Zealand's energy environment is now changing fast, as a result of significantly higher gas prices due to the decline of the Maui field, increasing electricity demand of around 2% per annum and new Government climate change policy which seeks for 90% of New Zealand's electricity to be generated from renewable sources by 2025.

The government is also implementing an emissions trading scheme which will set a market based price on carbon dioxide emissions. New Zealand is a signatory to the Kyoto Protocol.

New Zealand has a very strong wind resource, and recently there has been investment in wind farms. Around 3% three per cent of the country's electricity is now generated through wind farms, with a number of large wind projects currently under development. The Tararua Wind Farm is one of the largest electricity generating wind farms in the southern hemisphere. Located on the Tararua and Ruahine Ranges, the Wind Farm has 134 turbines which provide an installed capacity of 160 MW and an annual average output of 620 GWh.

There are five main electricity generating companies in New Zealand:

- Meridian Energy, a State Owned Enterprise, operates a chain of hydro power stations mainly in the lower South Island and is actively developing more hydro and wind projects.
- Genesis Energy, a State Owned Enterprise, operates New Zealand's largest power station, the 1,000 MW Huntly thermal power station, and the Tongariro and Waikaremoana hydropower schemes. The Huntly power station is New Zealand's only coal-fired power station and is the country's single largest emitter of carbon dioxide.

FACT

Experienced carpenters, bricklayers, builders and building control officers, plumbers, gas-fitters and joiners have all recently been included on New Zealand's skills shortages lists.

FACT

New Zealand electricity is based on hydroelectric generation supplemented by thermal and geothermal power plants. There are no nuclear power plants. The country faces declining hydrocarbon resources. With growing industrial, commercial and domestic demand for energy of all types, establishing alternative and sustainable energy sources is a priority.

- Mighty River Power generates primarily from the chain of hydrostations on the Waikato River, and some geothermal production from the central plateau around Taupo.
- Contact Energy is one of New Zealand's largest publicly listed companies and generates from large hydroschemes in Central Otago, three geothermal power stations in the Taupo region, and from large combined-cycle gas-fired power stations at Stratford and Auckland.
- Trustpower is another publicly listed generator, producing electricity from a combination of hydropower plants and wind farms.

All of these companies have multi-billion dollar investment plans in renewable hydro, geothermal and wind generation projects. The Labour Government has recently introduced a new bill into Parliament placing a moratorium on the building of any new baseload thermal generation plants.

Electricity generated by these five main companies is transported by a national transmission grid which runs the length of the country, connecting the North and South Islands. The national grid is owned and operated by the State owned company, Transpower. From the grid electricity is distributed to end users through a network of around 28 regional electricity lines companies.

New Zealand imports the vast majority of all of its oil, which is processed at the country's only refinery at Marsden Point near Whangarei before being shipped and trucked to fuel storage terminals across the country.

Coal deposits exist throughout New Zealand, and South Island commercial coal varies from lignite to bitumous, with North Island coal being mainly sub-bitumous. The west coast of the South Island is the biggest source of bitumous coal – with the most production from mines near Westport and Greymouth – along with Waikato. Most of the coal is exported to Japan, India and China. The quality of New Zealand coal makes it ideal for use in the chemical and steel industries. Industrial usage consumes nearly three-quarters of the remaining production. With the decline of the large Maui gas field off the Taranaki coast, prices for natural gas have been increasing rapidly, helping to encourage the development of new renewable generation options. Gas is produced entirely in the Taranaki region. Other smaller but significant gas fields include Kapuni (operated by Shell Todd Oil Services Ltd), Pohokura, Turangi-1 and Kupe. Although only the Taranaki basin has had commercial petroleum extraction so far, there is petroleum potential in sedimentary basins straddling much of New Zealand's coastline.

Major companies

Transpower Limited, Mighty River Power, Meridian Energy, Genesis Energy, Trustpower, Contact Energy, BP New Zealand, Dominion Oil Refining, Mobil Oil New Zealand, Caltex NZ

Transpower Limited: Level 7, Transpower House, 96 The Terrace, PO Box 1021, Wellington; (04) 495 7100; fax (04) 495 7100; www.transpower.co.nz

Mighty River Power: Level 19, 1 Queen Street, PO Box 90399, Auckland; (09) 308 8200; fax (09) 308 8209; www.mightyriverpower.co.nz

Meridian Energy Limited: PO Box 2128, Christchurch; (03) 353 9500 or free phone from within New Zealand 0800 496 496; fax (03) 353 9501; www.meridianenergy.co.nz

Genesis Energy: Cnr Woodward Street & The Terrace, PO Box 10568, The Terrace, Wellington; (07) 838 7863 or free phone from within New Zealand 0800 300 400; info@genesisenergy.co.nz; www.genesisenergy.co.nz

Trustpower: Private Bag 12023, Tauranga Mail Centre, Tauranga 3143; (07) 574 4754 or +64 7 574 4754 from overseas; www.trustpower.co.nz

Contact Energy: PO Box 10742, The Terrace, Wellington 6143; (04) 499 4001; fax (04) 499 4003; www.contactenergy.co.nz.

BP in New Zealand: Head Office 20 Customhouse Quay, PO Box 892, Wellington; (04) 495 5000; fax (04) 495 5400; GANZCustomerEnquiries@bp.com; www.bp.com – select New Zealand to be redirected to the appropriate section.

Mobil Oil New Zealand: PO Box 2497, Wellington; (04) 498 4000 or freephone from within New Zealand 0800 880 361; fax 0800 880 245; nzcustomer@exxonmobil.com; www.mobil.co.nz

Caltex New Zealand: www.caltex.com/nz

FACT

■ The engineering sector is set for particularly strong growth in the mechanical, automotive, chemical, civil and electrical areas.

Engineering and management services

The electronics industry is based mostly in Canterbury, as well as Auckland and Wellington, but engineering jobs are available throughout the country. Chemical engineering covers the production of consumer products from agricultural and forestry materials to food. Civil engineers are largely employed by private firms, but much of the growth in this area is affected by government funding and investment. Job growth for mechanical engineers is also set to continue, especially in the area of developing alternative fuel resources.

Fishing and aquaculture

The high quality coastal waters, along with the abundance of plankton, the number of sheltered harbours and inlets provide ideal conditions for shellfish aquaculture (the cultivation of fish, shellfish or aquatic plants in either natural or controlled water environments). New Zealand's aquaculture industry is currently dominated by Greenshell mussels, with King Salmon and Pacific oysters following. The farming of abalone (paua) is a growing industry. The most important area for farming mussels and salmon is the Marlborough Sounds, and other important sites are in Golden Bay, the Coromandel, Stewart Island and the far North for oysters.

Potential for future development looks positive with such species as turbot, eels, rock lobster, kingfish, geoduck clams, sea horses, and some seaweeds and sponges. Aquaculture production now employs nearly a third of New Zealand's total seafood industry workforce, and it has the potential to provide many more jobs for regional economies. The continuing careful management of precious coastal waters is essential.

Seafood is the country's fifth largest primary industry, contributing NZ$1.4billion towards GDP, and is the fourth largest export earner. About 90% of the annual seafood harvest is exported. Major export markets are Japan, the USA and Europe, as well as Australia and Hong Kong. More than 26,000 people are employed in the industry and in supporting jobs, and almost a third of the total seafood workforce is employed in the aquaculture sector. New Zealand's exclusive economic zone (EEZ), wherein the Ministry of Agriculture and Fisheries (MAF) controls all fishing, extends for 200 nautical miles from the coastline and is the fourth largest in the

FACT

■ New Zealand's clean waters provide fish of exceptional quality.

world, covering a total of 2.2million square miles. MAF runs a system of transferable quotas which has been in place since 1986, and more recent legislation has further tightened the procedures operated by the 'Quota Management System' (QMS). Quotas cover most major commercial species. Assessments are made about the size of the fishstock and the sustainable commercial catch for each species is estimated. The total catch is allocated between fishing companies through individual quotas, which companies can buy or sell. There are over 2000 quota holders, but the majority of quotas are held by seven leading fishing companies (listed below). 20% of quotas for new species are allocated to the Maori under a deal between the tribes and the government settled in 1992, and Maori stakeholders control one-third of the total quota through ownership of 50% of the largest fishing company, the Sealord Group. An organisation called Te Ohu Kai Moana focuses on furthering the interests of Maori in the fishing industry.

There is a small but growing crustacea and shellfish farming industry, which includes rock lobsters, scallops, oysters, clams, cockles and crabs. The main export products are Pacific oysters and green-lipped mussels. Increased diversity is expected in the next decade. Paua (a large New Zealand shellfish) farms and seaweed trial projects have already been established. This industry, like much of New Zealand's agricultural and horticultural output, is vulnerable to disease which can wipe out an entire season's crop, as happened in the summer of 1992/93 when toxic algae bloom resulted in shellfish harvesting being suspended. The other major threat to the seafood industry comes from trade barriers. About 85% of industry revenues come from exports, but most of the markets New Zealand trades with have volume restrictions (quotas) on imports. New Zealand currently has less two per cent of world seafood trade but there is definite potential for expansion.

The main commercial fishing areas are in the South Island and are run through Nelson, Lyttleton and Timaru ports. 80% of aquaculture exports come from the Marlborough Sounds. Other significant areas include Stewart Island, the Coromandel and Northland. Aquaculture now accounts for 20% of the total seafood industry income.

Major companies

Sealord Group, Sanford Group, Treaty of Waitangi Fisheries Commission, Amaltal Fishing Corporation, Vela Limited, Moana Pacific Fisheries, and Talley's Fisheries[AL]

Sealord Group – New Zealand: (09) 579 1659 or free phone from within New Zealand 0800 732 5673; fax (09) 525 32 89; inquiries@sealord.com; www.sealord.co.nz

Sanford Limited: 22 Jellicoe Street, Freemans Bay, PO Box 443, Auckland; (09) 379 4720; fax (09) 309 1190; info@sanford.co.nz; www.sanford.co.nz

Treaty of Waitangi Fisheries Commission (Te Ohu Kai Moana): PO Box 3277, Wellington; (04) 499 5199; fax (04) 499 5190; http://teohu.maori.nz

Amaltal Fishing Company Limited: Maitai Wharf, Port Nelson, PO Box 7064, Nelson; (03) 548 0109; fax (03) 548 2695; mail@amaltal.co.nz; http://home.xtra.co.nz/hosts/amaltal

Vela Fishing Limited: 12 Sir Tristram Avenue, Te Rapa, PO Box 10056, Hamilton; (07) 849 2376; fax (07) 849 4999; info@velafishing.co.nz; www.velafishing.co.nz

Moana Pacific Fisheries: 138 Halsey Street, PO Box 445, Auckland; (09) 302 1520; fax (09) 302 0872; enquiries@moana.co.nz; www.moanapacific.com

Talley's Group Ltd: PO Box 5, Motueka; (03) 528 2800; fax (03) 528 9298; inquiries@talleys.co.nz; www.talleys.co.nz

Health and social services

Between now and 2011 job growth in this industry is expected to rise by about 2.5% every year. As the population of New Zealand ages, more health and social services are needed. The government evaluates needs and funding for many jobs in this industry, and in recent years there has been high investment and spending in mental health services. Skills required vary, but prospective employees must provide evidence of their relevant clinical and medical training. Nurses, doctors, physiotherapists, pharmacists, etc., all have their own governing councils and bodies, and most working in this area must be certified annually as fit to practice. There is a current shortage of health professionals in New Zealand, and government initiatives and strategies are in place in increase the workforce in this area. The Ministry of Health provides national policy advice to the Government and also funds, supports and monitors the 21 District Health Boards around the country. The DHBs have overall responsibility for assessing health and disability support needs of communities in their regions and managing resources as best they can to meet those needs. District Health Boards divide the country into the following districts: Auckland, Bay of Plenty, Canterbury, Capital and Coast, Counties, Hawkes Bay, Hutt Valley, Lakes, MidCentral, Nelson-Marlborough, Northland, Otago, South Canterbury, Southland, Tairawhiti, Taranaki, Waikato, Wairarapa, Waitemata, Whanganui and the West Coast.

For more information, your first port of call should be the Ministry of Health website: www.moh.govt.nz. See also: www.centraltas.co.nz; www.nznurses.co.nz and www.zest4life.co.nz.

Manufacturing and production

Total manufacturing sales have increased significantly over the last few months. The highest levels of expansion were seen in the areas of meat and dairy production, and overall manufacturing volumes have increased. The recent rate of expansion within manufacturing conditions has slowed over recent years, hampered somewhat by labour shortages and the high New Zealand dollar.

Metal products, machinery and equipment

This includes assembling motor vehicles, electrical goods, electronic goods, machinery and metal goods. In 1989 New Zealand's import licences were removed and tariffs on imported vehicles were reduced, leading to a decline in the country's vehicle assembly industry and a quick increase in the number of imported Japanese cars. Most cars on the road have been imported from overseas. New Zealand motor assembling plants have developed successful production of vehicle componentry totalling NZ$400million, of which roughly NZ$150million comes from exports.

◣ Major companies
Ford NZ: 70 Plunket Avenue, Private Bag 76912, Manukau City; 0800 367 369; nzinfo@ford.com; www.ford.co.nz

Holden New Zealand: www.holden.co.nz
Toyota New Zealand: Roberts Line, PO Box 46, Palmerston North; 0800 869 682; www.toyota.co.nz.

Textiles, clothing, footwear and leather goods

This section of the industry is highly dependent on export markets, which provide a majority of the earnings. Although profitability is increasing, there are still a number of businesses in this area that are only marginally profitable and remain vulnerable to pressures such as further tariff reductions, which make imported goods cheaper. Growth is dependent on the ability of businesses to create new opportunities and develop new products. There is now less emphasis on sending raw products, such as wool, overseas and much of the industry is made up of small, owner-operated companies creating high-quality products for small niche export markets. Currently, although there is increased international interest in New Zealand's fashion designers, many clothing companies are small-scale and are losing orders because they are unable to meet demand. There is a shortage of people with production, pattern-making and machining skills. Increased on-the-job training and newly introduced cadetship programmes should help to redress this issue.

Steel and non-ferrous metals

Steel and aluminium are the only metals produced in any quantity in New Zealand. The New Zealand steel works at Glenbrook produces steel from the ironsands on the West Coast of the North Island by a unique direct reduction process. BHP New Zealand Steel remains the world's only producer of steel from ironsand, with a total production of around 700,000 tonnes. Unwrought aluminium from the Comalco smelter near Bluff is a major export earner using raw bauxite imported from Australia. Employment opportunities in this sector have decreased because of capital upgrades by firms to increase efficiency, and decreased demand from Asian countries cut export prices.

◼ Major Companies

BHP New Zealand Steel, Pacific Steel, Comalco-CHH Aluminium, Steel and Tube Holdings Limited, Superior Industries Ltd.New Zealand Steel: www.nzsteel.co.nz
Pacific Steel: www.pacificsteel.co.nz
Steel & Tube Holdings Limited: www.steelandtube.co.nz
Superior Industries Ltd: http://superior.co.nz

Electronics

Electronics is one of the success stories of the restructured New Zealand economy. Under the old regime of protected domestic industries the sector was predominantly involved in the manufacture of consumer electronics. Now most of these goods (TVs, videos, etc.) are imported from Asia where costs are cheaper. The major exception is the domestic whiteware industry ('whiteware' is the local term for fridges, dishwashers, ovens, etc.) where New Zealanders show a strong preference for long-established local brands such as Fisher and Paykel. The electronics industry, instead of declining with the reduction in tariffs, has diversified and found niche markets in high tech commercial and industrial products. For example, one Christchurch-

based company, Dynamic Controls, is the world's leading supplier of mobility control systems for power wheelchairs and scooters.

Software is another area where New Zealand firms have developed specialist markets. Big international firms such as Ericsson and IBM have introduced technological advancements and teamed up with companies like Synergy to develop cell phone and mobile internet software in New Zealand. Job prospects for skilled workers in the industry are good. There is currently a skills shortage from assembly workers through to engineers and software designers. The size of the New Zealand industry has limited the numbers being trained so that it has been unable to keep up with the current leap in demand for its products.

▉ Major Companies
Dynamic Controls: www.dynamicmobility.co.nz
Ericsson: www.ericsson.com/au
Fisher and Paykel Electronics: www.fisherpaykel.co.nz
IBM New Zealand: www.ibm.com/nz

Food and beverages
This is a major industry, contributing just under five per cent of the GDP and producing roughly one third of the country's exports. The largest sectors are dairy products and meat products. Meat processing remains an important employer in Southland and Manawatu-Wanganui. Dairy processing dominates in the Waikato, Taranaki and Canterbury. The three major dairy manufacturing companies are Fonterra, Westland and Tatua. Fonterra is the largest; it collects 96% of all milk

produced in the country and handles more than a third of the international dairy trade. Dairy production is expanding to cope with rising demand from new overseas markets such as Asia, and more land is being converted to dairy production as well as dairy herd sizes increasing, especially in Canterbury. 90–95% of New Zealand dairy products are exported.

Beverages for the domestic and export market include wine, soft drinks, fruit juice, spirits and beer, teas, fruit wines and water. The wine industry is an area of major growth, with wine exports expected to top NZ$1 billion by 2010. Marlborough is the biggest wine region, with 11,488 hectares currently in production, followed by Hawke's Bay (with 4,346 hectares), Gisborne (1,913), Otago (1,253) and the Wairarapa (777). Beer consumption is down, but sales of spirits are growing steadily. Sales of premixed drinks have nearly doubled over the last 6 years. There is an increased and continuing need for multi-skilled process operators with science and engineering knowledge. There is also concern that the current shortage of food technologists will hinder the country's success in turning agricultural products into the more diverse and value-added products required to keep up with consumer demand and appeal to new markets. However, the industry is expected to remain stable over the next two to three years, following a period of extensive restructuring.

Current trends for more ethnically-diverse foods have resulted in a wider variety of meats and cheeses in particular. Beverage companies are continuing to have success with popularity of energy drinks. Health or 'functional' foods are also being developed to meet the needs of consumers demanding low-sugar or low-fat options. Future growth in the food and beverage manufacturing industry will be influenced by factors such as the exchange rate, weather, international demand and the ability of manufacturers and exporters to establish and develop new markets.

■ Major companies

Bluebird Foods, DB Group, Cerebos Gregg, Goodman Fielder, Kraft General Foods, Nestle New Zealand, Lion Nathan, Abels, Fonterra, Westland, Tatua, Montana Wines, Villa Maria Wines.

Bluebird Foods: www.bluebird.co.nz
DB Breweries: www.dbbreweries.co.nz
Cerebos Gregg: www.cerebos.com.au
Fonterra: www.fonterra.com
Westland Milk Products: www.westland.co.nz
Tatua Foods: www.tatua.com
Goodman Fielder Corporate: www.goodmanfielder.com.au
Kraft Foods New Zealand: www.kraft.co.nz
Nestle New Zealand: www.nestle.co.nz
Lion Nathan: www.lion-nathan.com.au
Montana Wines: www.montana.co.nz
Villa Maria Wines: www.villamaria.co.nz

Tourism and hospitality

The tourism industry in New Zealand is made up of 10 major public-listed companies. Both directly and indirectly, tourism contributes around nine per cent of GDP and generates NZ$8.3billion per year in foreign exchange. There are between 13,500 and 18,000 small to medium-sized businesses in this area, and around 80% of these employ less than five people. The largest numbers of visitors come to New Zealand from Australia (33%), the UK (12%), the USA (10%) and Japan (7%). There are also a number of visitors from China and South Korea. Around 88% of international tourists say that they will visit New Zealand again in the future, and the Tourism Research Council estimates that international visitor numbers will reach 2.86 million arrivals within the next year. The most visited areas are Auckland, Christchurch, Rotorua, Queenstown, Wellington and Dunedin, and the highest proportion of hospitality enterprises are in the Auckland, Wellington, Canterbury and Waikato regions. The profile and visibility of New Zealand overseas has been enhanced by the use of the landscape in various productions such as the *Lord of the Rings* trilogy. Other contributors have included The America's Cup, Discovery Channel programmes, Billy Connolly's series and the Tourism NZ advertising campaign '100% Pure New Zealand'. Domestic tourism is also important, and accounts for 60% of the tourism industry. The main attractions for most are the clean environment and beautiful scenery, but a growing number of tourists are after more active holidays, skiing trips, jet-boat rides, white water rafting, black water rafting, even bungy jumping. This has led to the growth of a new type of tourism, called 'adventure tourism'. Another area that is beginning to take off is 'green tourism' or 'eco-tourism'. Often thought to be a contradiction in terms because the impact of visitors upon the environment is usually harmful, green tourism aims to combine sharing the environment with tourists and protecting it. Activities such as whale watching off the Kaikoura coast above Christchurch, and visiting bird sanctuary islands already attract many tourists and Kiwis alike.

International tourism was dramatically affected by world events such as the war in Iraq, the outbreak of SARS and the terrorist attacks on the USA and in tourist resorts around the world, but the rate of cancellations of travel to New Zealand was not particularly high. The country is still considered a highly desirable and safe destination, and once long-haul travel confidence returns the tourism industry is expected to recover any losses. The number of international travellers has a key role in determining demand for hotels and motels, but the majority of people making use of such places are domestic travellers. The hospitality industry is experiencing strong growth as the number of restaurants and cafés has increased. Employment and career opportunities are good, and the number of people entering the industry is expected to remain high.

There have been significant changes in New Zealand's travel industry over the last few years; an unsustainable oversupply of agencies resulted in a number of mergers and redundancies, and travellers are increasingly using the internet rather than agencies to make their own travel arrangements and bookings. In addition, the financial pressures many airlines have found themselves under have led to them reducing commission fees paid to agencies and enlarging call centres to increase direct sales. However, trade in services is the largest and fastest growing sector in the global economy and tourism is a significant component of this. The sector also has a direct impact on other sectors including accommodation, transport, retail, catering and financial services, and it benefits other sectors that provide supporting goods and services, including construction, printing and publishing, manufacturing and insurance.

FACT

▧ Tourism is one of the largest New Zealand industries, and it has a substantial role in job creation and export earnings.

FACT

▧ Tourism contributes NZ$18.6billion to the economy each year, and in the last year international travellers spent around NZ$8.3billion while visiting – this accounts for 19.2% of export earnings. Domestic visitors are a vital part of the industry, contributing about NZ$10.3billion to the economy each year.

Over 135,000 people are employed in the hospitality industry in New Zealand, and there has been unprecedented growth over the last five years, with a 20% increase in the number of employees compared to a 14% growth rate in the economy overall. During the same period 4,000 new hospitality businesses have been created in New Zealand, representing a 27% increase. Almost two-fifths of employees are aged 25 and under, and the shortage of skilled employees that has resulted in some reliance on new immigrants looks set to continue and perhaps increase.

By 2015 it is predicted that international visitor arrivals will have risen 3.4 million, with their expenditure totalling around NZ$12billion, while domestic expenditure will be around NZ$9.6billion.

For more information see www.hanz.org.nz, www.tourismnewzealand.com and www.newzealand.com. See also: www.tianz.org.nz and www.tourism.govt.nz.

Transport

As a small exporting economy at great distances from many of its markets, New Zealand is highly dependent on maintaining its external transportation links. Internal transportation networks are also important as its small population is spread over two islands nearly 2,000km in combined length. Early transport developments were largely the result of government investment. The rail network, harbours, and road building were all extensively developed under a programme of major public works during the 1870s. State ownership and investment was the pattern for transportation development over the next century. The government owned and ran the railways, a shipping line, and eventually the national airline. State ownership of transportation links diminished under the programme of state asset sales begun by the Labour government in the 1980s. Now private sector investment is behind most new transport projects, with the exception of road building, which remains the responsibility of Transit New Zealand, a government authority. Road transportation was deregulated during the 1980s as was public transport in most cities. New Zealand Rail was sold to a consortium made up of a Canadian, an American and a New Zealand company in 1993. Port authorities were set up as companies, largely owned by local authorities, with two partly privately owned.

Transport is very dependent on other areas of the economy, such as agriculture. Recent growth in logging, tourism and dairy, as well as production industry centralisation, means that there is currently increased demand for transport services and this is likely to continue. Bulk freight, such as steel, coal, and cargo including dairy products, is mainly transported by rail. The highest proportions of rail transport enterprises are in Wellington, Canterbury and Manawatu-Wanganui regions. International trade relies heavily on water transport, as almost 99% of all exports are carried by sea. The main ports are at Auckland, Wellington, Tauranga and Lyttleton. There are three main international airports – at Auckland, Wellington and Christchurch. There are two New Zealand airlines operating international flights; Air New Zealand and its subsidiary Freedom Air. Qantas Australia plans to enter the market, as does Virgin Blue. Such expansion would create many more employment opportunities.

◼ REGIONAL EMPLOYMENT GUIDE

The Upper North Island

Northland and Auckland

Major Cities: Auckland (pop. 404,658), Manukau (pop. 328,968), North Shore (pop. 205,608), Waitakere (pop. 186,444), Whangarei (pop. 74,463).

Newspapers: *The New Zealand Herald* (www.nzhearld.co.nz), *Northern Advocate.*

Chambers of Commerce: Auckland Regional Chamber of Commerce and Industry: 100 Mayoral Drive, PO Box 47, Auckland; (09) 309 6100; fax (09) 309 0081; akl@chamber.co.nz; www.chamber.co.nz. Northland Chamber of Commerce: 3–5 Hunt St, PO Box 1703, Whangarei; (09) 438 4771; fax (09) 438 4770; info@northchamber.co.nz; www.northchamber.co.nz.

Industry/Other Comments: The Auckland region is the main business and industrial centre and employs nearly one third of the total workforce. Around half are employed in the services sector, comprising wholesale, retail, community, social and personal services and also including tourism, film, television and sport. The Auckland region provides a wide range of job opportunities in manufacturing and distribution, boat building, construction, and business and financial services.

A significant number of companies in this area specialise in furniture, pharmaceutical and clothing manufacture, imports and exports. Auckland has a container port and an international airport. Employment prospects in the area are good and continue to improve; wholesale and manufacturing are two areas predicted to grow in the next couple of years. Much industry is based in southern Auckland areas, but the City Council has plans for business growth and maximising potential in the region which include developing and refurbishing several business precincts in areas such as Rosebank. Other proposals are in place to create a major business area around the University of Auckland. Business and office developments are already underway in other areas including the North Shore and Takapuna. The region is predicted to remain the leader in economic growth over the next few years and this is reflected in the number of businesses looking to expand their workforce.

Numbers of job advertisements continue to increase, and growth industries in the future are likely to be construction and service-based sectors. Outside the city and in surrounding areas, job prospects are likely to be associated with the growth of tourism and the expected improvement in agricultural export volumes, dairy farming and fruit growing, and ceramic clay and cement mining. There are also opportunities to work in areas such as marine engineering, tourism, forestry (exotic forest) and aquaculture for coastal shellfish farming. Northland has plenty of seasonal work opportunities, particularly picking and packing kiwifruit and citrus fruit (mostly from April to June), and winter pruning is another seasonal job to be considered. New Zealand's only crude oil refinery is located at Marsden Point, near Whangarei, on the east coast. South of Auckland, at Glenbrook, is the BHP New Zealand Steel factory that uses a unique production process based on the reduction

of local ironsand. West Coast beaches in New Zealand are characterised by the high proportion of iron ore in the sand, which results in black colouration. See: www. northlandnz.com and www.arc.govt.nz for more information.

The Central North Island

Waikato, Bay of Plenty, Gisborne and Hawke's Bay

Major Cities: Hamilton (pop. 129,249), Tauranga (pop. 101,200), Rotorua (pop. 55,100) New Plymouth (pop. 49,500), Gisborne (pop. 44,460), Hastings (pop. 73,400), Napier (pop. 56,700).

Newspapers: *The Waikato Times* (www.stuff.co.nz/stuff/waikatotimes), *Bay of Plenty Times* www.bayofplentytimes.co.nz), *Hawke's Bay Today* (www.hbtoday. co.nz).

Chambers of Commerce: Waikato Chamber of Commerce: 190 Collingwood Street, PO Box 1122, Hamilton; (07) 839 5895; fax (07) 839 4581; admin@waikatochamber. co.nz; www.waikatochamber.co.nz. Chamber of Commerce Tauranga Region: Smart Business Centre, Unit 3b, 65 Chapel Street, PO Box 414, Tauranga; (07) 577 9823; fax (07) 577 0364; chamber@tauranga.org.nz; www.tauranga.org.nz. Hawke's Bay Chamber of Commerce: 2 Market St South, Hastings; (06) 876 5938; fax (06) 876 3748; admin@hawkesbaychamber.co.nz; www.hawkesbaychamber.co.nz.

Industry/Other Comments: The Waikato is one of the main dairy farming regions in the country. Horticulture, particularly citrus fruit and kiwifruit, is the predominant industry in the Bay of Plenty on the East Coastcoast. There are also opportunities for expansion within the tourism, forestry and food processing industries. Hawkes Bay is a premium wine-making district, and has some of the oldest established wineries in the country; the Mission Vineyard, run by Catholic monks, first began producing wine in the 19th century. It is also a significant farming and fruit-growing region and there are many job and investment opportunities in agriculture, food processing and tourism.

Hamilton is home to a number of manufacturing enterprises, a university, and a large wholesale and retail sector. Most industry in the Waikato region is based on the processing of agricultural and forestry raw products, as well as dairy, technology, bloodstock, and education and research. The central region of the North Island is the main centre for the pulp and paper-making industry. Large plantation forests of radiata pine provide the raw materials for the production of newsprint, wood pulp, paper and paperboard. The Waikato is the largest coal-producing region in the country, with a number of mainly open cast mines producing over half the total annual sub-bitumous coal output of the country. Main industries on the East Coastcoast and in Gisborne are tourism, wine-making and forestry (there are large exotic forests with opportunities for further expansion).

Gas is the main product of the petro-chemical industry based on the Taranaki coast near New Plymouth. The Taranaki region supports many energy related industries, including specialised engineering, and is a major dairy area with value-added food processing opportunities. The region is also a tourist destination. Major attractions include the thermal region around Rotorua and the network of limestone caves near Waitomo. Economic prospects in the region are favourable particularly for horticulture and forestry, and associated industries.

The Lower North Island

Taranaki, Manawatu-Wanganui and Wellington

Major Cities: Wellington (pop. 179,463), Palmerston North (pop. 75,800), Wanganui (pop. 38,900).

Newspapers: *The Dominion* (www.stuff.co.nz/stuff/dominionpost), *Manawatu Standard* (www.stuff.co.nz/manawatustandard) *Wanganui Chronicle* (www.wanganuichronicle.co.nz).

Chambers of Commerce: Wellington Chamber of Commerce: Level 9, 109 Featherston St, Wellington; (04) 914 6500; fax (04) 914 6524; info@wgtn-chamber.co.nz; www.wgtn-chamber.co.nz. Wanganui Chamber of Commerce: Enterprise House, 187 Victoria Ave, PO Box 88, Wanganui; (06) 345 0080; fax (06) 348 8210; info@wanganuichamber.co.nz; www.wanganuichamber.co.nz. Taranaki Chamber of Commerce: 15 Young St, PO Box 2, New Plymouth; (06) 759 9080; fax (06) 759 9145; admin@taranakichamber.co.nz.

Industry/Other Comments: The capital city Wellington is the headquarters of central government. Most major law firms, accountants and management firms have their base in Wellington as well, although some firms prefer to have their head office in Auckland, reflecting that city's commercial dominance. Wellington is the centre of the performing arts, as the national orchestra and ballet are based there, and there is an abundance of dance companies, opera groups and professional theatres in the city. Wellington also hosts a biannual International Festival of the Performing Arts. Business, government and retail enterprises dominate the main urban area. Manufacturing industry is concentrated in the outlying suburbs and on the Petone seafront at the northern end of the Wellington harbour.

Growth industries in the Wellington region are information, communications, education and film. There are secondary processing opportunities in forestry, agriculture, horticulture and wine-making. Outside the urban area, to the north, the Wairarapa district is dairy and sheep farming country. The main industries in the Manawatu-Wanganui area are forestry, dairy, food processing, specialised engineering, intensive horticultural activities, education and agriculture technology, and research based on tertiary institutions and the area's strong farming base.

The population is growing quickly here (second-fastest in the country) and the region is the location for a wide range of national and international organisations and businesses, including: Toyota NZ, Ezibuy NZ, Jockey NZ, Click Clack NZ, NZ Pharmaceuticals, Food Manufacturing Australasia, Plumbing World, International Fine Foods Ltd, Wormald Technology Ltd, Kiwi Dairy Ltd, Van Globe Ltd and Fruehauf Traliers Ltd. Martinborough, north of Wellington, is one of the major players in wine production.

The Upper South Island

Nelson-Marlborough, West Coast and Canterbury

Major Cities: Christchurch (pop. 348,435), Nelson (pop. 60,500).

Newspapers: *The Christchurch Press* (www.stuff.co.nz/thepress/), *The Nelson Mail* (www.stuff.co.nz/nelsonmail/).

Chambers of Commerce: Canterbury Employers' Chamber of Commerce: 57 Kilmore St, PO Box 359, Christchurch; (03) 366 5096; fax (03) 379 5454; info@cecc.org.nz; www.cecc.org.nz. Nelson Chamber of Commerce, PO Box 1121, Nelson; (03) 548 1363; fax (03) 546 8373; office@commerce.org.nz; www.commerce.org.nz.

Industry/Other Comments: Marlborough is the largest wine-making region in New Zealand, and opportunities for expansion include wine-making, tourism, forestry and food processing. The Canterbury region is the largest sheep-farming region in the country. It has a container port nearby at Lyttleton and the second busiest international airport in the country. As well as agricultural industry, Christchurch is the largest region for manufacturing employment after Auckland. Canterbury has a number of high-tech electronic manufacturing and software firms, as well as wine-making, horticulture, floriculture, food processing businesses.

Tourism is a major source of economic activity in the region, thanks to the scenery and the skiing. Christchurch is only an hour away from the ski fields of Mount Hutt. Other important services here include education and research. Nelson is an important deep-sea fishing base and seafood processing location. West Coast industry is traditionally based on resource extraction – gold mining, coal mining and timber. This area is benefiting from its new deep water port, and the development of three new coal mines, which are expected to boost its already healthy coal exports. There is a coal mine in Stockton, from which exports go to Asia. Terrace Underground Mine now produces between 65,000 and 100,000 tonnes of coal per annum, which is a dramatic increase from the 25,000 tonnes produced back in 2000. The economy here is underpinned by increasing primary production levels of mining, dairy produce and tourism numbers, and there is an inevitable knock-on effect with secondary level industry such as manufacturing, service and retail, and general commerce. Skilled workers are required at all levels, especially tradespeople to cope with the demand for new housing, factory/commerce building and maintaining the region's infrastructure.

The Lower South Island

Southland and Otago

Major Cities: Dunedin (pop. 118,683), Invercargill (pop. 48,200).

Newspapers: *The Otago Daily Times* (www.odt.co.nz) *The Southland Times* (www.stuff.co.nz/ southlandtimes/).

Chambers of Commerce: Otago Chamber of Commerce and Industry Incorporated: Level 7, 106 George Street, Dunedin; (03) 479 0181; fax (03) 477 0341; office@otagochamber.co.nz; www.otagochamber.co.nz. Chamber of Commerce Southland Inc.: PO Box 856, Invercargill; (03) 218 7188; fax (03) 218 7927; office@commercesouth.com; www.commercesouth.com.

Industry/Other Comments: The strong agricultural base of the rural economy in Otago and Southland is mainly concentrated on sheep farming with smaller numbers of dairy and beef farms. Other important activities include food processing and tourism, as well as horticulture, particularly stonefruit. Vineyards are relatively new to the region. Until recently the climate was thought to be too cold for grape growing, but several local wineries have established an enviable reputation. There are ongoing vacancies in Southland for people with the right skills, mainly in the

FACT

■ The country's first legal casino opened in the former Christchurch railway station in 1994.

engineering, trades, health, road freight, tourism and agricultural sectors. There are specific needs for people in the following employment fields: trades – plumbers, electricians, carpenters; healthcare professionals, including midwives; engineering – fitters, turners, welders; education – maths and science teachers, primary and secondary; automotive – electricians, diesel mechanics; agriculture – skilled and experienced managers for sheep and dairy farms; engineers – civil/chemical/ mechanical/electrical; transport operators – digger/logging drivers. Main industries in Dunedin are education, tourism, food processing and niche manufacturing. Apart from Dunedin, manufacturing in the region is concentrated around Invercargill with the exception of the Comalco Aluminium smelter, which is located at Tiwai point near Bluff. Bluff is also known for its production of oysters.

■ DIRECTORY OF MAJOR EMPLOYERS

Accommodation and hospitality

Millenium and Copthorne Hotels: www.milleniumhotels.co.nz.
Restaurant Brands NZ Ltd: www.restaurantbrands.co.nz.

Accountancy

Gosling Chapman Chartered Accountants: Human Resources Manager, 51–53 Shortland Street, Auckland; PO Box 158, Auckland; (09) 303 4586; fax (09) 309 1198; mail@goslingchapman.com; www.gosling.co.nz.

Agriculture and forestry

Landcorp Farming Ltd: Lumley House, 3–11 Hunter Street, PO Box 5349, Wellington; (04) 471 0400; fax (04) 473 4966; enquiries@landcorp.co.nz; www.landcorp. co.nz.
Sanford Ltd: 22 Jellicoe St, Freemans Bay, Auckland; (09) 379 4720; fax (09) 309 1190; info@Sanford.co.nz; www.sanford.co.nz.

Banking, insurance and financial services

AMP Financial Services: www.amp.co.nz.
ASB Group Career Centre: www.asbbank.co.nz.
Bank of New Zealand: www.bnz.co.nz.
Deutsche Bank: Human Resources Manager, PO Box 6900, Wellesley Street, Auckland; (09) 351 1000; fax (09) 351 1001; www.deutschebank.co.nz.
KPMG: National Human Resources Manager, KPMG Centre, 18 Viaduct Harbour Avenue, Auckland; (09) 367 5800; fax (09) 367 5875; www.kpmg.co.nz.
Reserve Bank of New Zealand: HR Administrator, PO Box 2498, Wellington; (04) 472 2029; fax (04) 472 3759; recruitment@rbnz.govt.nz; www.rbnz.govt.nz.
Tower Limited: PO Box 590, Wellington; (04) 472 6059; fax (04) 473 2669; www. tower.co.nz.

The Treasury: HR Advisor, PO Box 3724, Wellington; human.resources@treasury.govt.nz; www.treasury.govt.nz.

Business and management services

AMP: www.amp.co.nz.
Ernst & Young: Recruitment and Retention Manager, PO Box 2146, Auckland; (09) 377 4790; fax (09) 309 8137; www.ey.com.

Construction and engineering

Beca Carter Hollings & Ferner Ltd: HR Advisor, PO Box 6345, Auckland; (09) 300 9000; fax (09) 300 9300; humanresources@beca.co.nz; www.beca.com.
Delta: Contract Services Manager, PO Box 1404, Dunedin; (03) 479 6693; fax (03) 479 6694; www.4delta.co.nz.
Fulton Hogan Limited: General Manager Southern, PO Box 39185, Christchurch; (03) 357 1400; fax (03) 357 1450; www.fhcareers.co.nz.
MWH Worldwide: www.bfound.net.
Opus: Recruitment, PO Box 12343, Wellington; (04) 471 7243; fax (04) 473 3017; cheryl.dudfield@opus.co.nz; www.opus.co.nz.

Cultural and recreational services

NZ Lotteries Commission: 54–56 Cambridge Terrace, PO Box 3145, Wellington; (04) 802 7000; fax (04) 385 2787; info@nzlc.co.nz; www.nzlotteries.co.nz.
NZ Totaliser Agency Board: 106-110 Jackson St, Petone, PO Box 38 899 Wellington Mail Centre; (04) 576 6999; fax (04) 576 6942; www.tab.co.nz.
Sky City Recruitment Centre: Level 6 Federal House, 86 Federal St, Auckland; (09) 363 6044; enquiries@skycity.co.nz; www.skycity.co.nz.
Sky Network Television Limited: 10 Panorama Rd, Mt Wellington, PO Box 9059, Newmarket, Auckland; (09) 579 9999; fax (09) 579 0910; www.skytelevision.co.nz.
Television New Zealand Limited: http://corporate.tvnz.co.nz and http://jobs.haineslink.co.nz/tvnz/.

Education

Open Polytechnic: www.openpolytechnic.ac.nz.
TeachNZ: www.teachnz.govt.nz/overseas-trained-teachers

Health

Auckland District Health Board: (09) 630 9900 or 0800 733 968; fax (09) 630 9927; recruit@adhb.govt.nz; www.adhb.govt.nz.
Auckland Health Careers: www.aucklandhealthcareers.co.nz.
District Health Boards New Zealand: PO Box 5535, Wellington; (04) 803 3940; fax (04) 803 3870; nationaloffice@dhbnz.org.nz; www.dhbnz.org.nz.
MidCentral District Health Board: www.midcentralhb.govt.nz.
Southern Cross Healthcare: Private Bag 999 34, Newmarket, Auckland; www.southerncross.co.nz.

South Auckland Health: HR, Middlemore Hospital, PO Box 93311, Otahuhu, Auckland; recruitment@middlemore.co.nz; www.sah.co.nz

Taranaki District Health Board: HR Advisor, Private Bag 2016, New Plymouth; (06) 753 6139; fax (06) 753 7770; hr@tdhb.org.nz; www.thcl.co.nz.

Waitemata District Health Board: 0800 472 284 or (09) 441 8953; fax (09) 489 0533; recruit@waitematadhb.govt.nz; www.waitematadhb.govt.nz.

Waikato District Health Board: PO Box 934, Hamilton; info@waikatodhb.govt.nz; www.waikatodhb.govt.nz.

West Coast District Health Board: Recruitment Co-ordinator, PO Box 387, Greymouth; (03) 768 0499; fax (03) 768 2791; www.westcoastdhb.org.nz.

Information Technology and telecommunications

Ernst & Young: Recruitment and Retention Manager, PO Box 2146, Auckland; (09) 377 4790; fax (09) 309 8137; www.ey.com.

Commsoft Group Ltd: www.commsoftnz.com.

Ericsson: www.ericsson.co.nz.

Fronde: Level 7, Synergy House, 131 Queen Street, PO Box 7445, Wellesley Street, Auckland; (09)377 2400; www.fronde.com

Gen-i: info@gen-i.co.nz; www.geni.co.nz

Inland Revenue (IT Dept): PO Box 2198, Wellington; (04) 382 7007; fax (04) 382 7054; hr.it@ird.govt.nz; www.ird.govt.nz.

JADE: Staff Development Manager, PO Box 20 152, Christchurch; (03) 365 2500; fax (03) 358 6050; js@jadeworld.com; www.jadeworld.com.

Meritec: HR Development Manager, PO Box 4142, Auckland; (09336 5376; fax (09) 379 1220; www.meritec.org.

Microsoft NZ: www.microsoft.com/nz/.

Oracle: HR, Oracle Tower, 56 Wakefield Street, Auckland; (09) 977 2100; fax (09) 977 2102; jobs_nz@oracle.com; www.oracle.com/global/nz.

SolNet Solutions Ltd: employment@solnetsolutions.co.nz; www.solnet.co.nz.

Telecom New Zealand: www.telecom.co.nz and www.telecom.co.nz/careers.

TelstraClear: www.telstraclear.co.nz.

Vodafone: www.vodafone.co.nz.

Law firms

Chapman Tripp: www.chapmantripp.co.nz.

Lane Neave: Meryll Waters, PO Box 13 149, Christchurch; (03) 379 3720;email@ laneneave.co.nz; www.laneneave.co.nz.

Morrison Kent: Level 5, 55–65 Shortland Street, Auckland; (09) 303 2164; Morrison Kent House, 105 The Terrace, Wellington; (04) 472 0020; www.morrisonkent.co.nz.

Russell McVeagh: National HR Manager, PO Box 8, Auckland; (09) 367 8000; fax (09) 367 8163; www.russellmcveagh.com.

Simpson Grierson: Lumley Centre, 88 Shortland Street, Private Bag 92518, Auckland; (09) 358 2222; fax (09) 307 0331; info@simpsongrierson.com; www.simpsongrierson.com.

Manufacturing and marketing

Pernod-Ricard New Zealand Limited: 4 Viaduct Harbour Avenue, Private Bag 92030, Auckland; (09) 336 8300; fax (09) 336 8301; information@pernod-ricard-nz.com; www.pernod-ricard-nz.com.

Alliance Group Ltd: 51 Don St, PO Box 845, Invercargill; (03) 214 2700; fax (03) 214 2708; www.alliance.co.nz.

Bendon Group Ltd: 8 Airpark Drive, Airport Oaks, PO Box 53042, Auckland Airport, Auckland; (09) 275 0000; fax (09) 257 1600; info@bendon.co.nz; www.bendon.co.nz.

Carter Holt Harvey Ltd: 173 Captain Springs Road, Te Papapa, Private Bag 92-106, Auckland; (09) 633 0600; fax (09) 633 0601; chhcontact@chh.com or careers@chh.co.nz; www.chh.co.nz.

Cavalier Bremworth Limited: 7 Grayson Avenue, Papatoetoe, PO Box 97-040, Auckland 1730; (09) 277 6000; fax (09) 278 7417; www.cavcorp.co.nz.

DB Group Ltd: www.db.co.nz and www.jobs.db.co.nz.

Dynamic Controls: www.dynamiccontrols.com.

Fairfax New Zealand Ltd: Level 3, 40 Boulcott Street, PO Box 2595, Wellington; (04) 496 9800; fax (04) 496 9841; www.fairfaxnz.co.nz.

Fisher & Paykel Healthcare Ltd: PO Box 14-348, Panmure, Auckland; (09) 574 0100; fax (09) 574 0136; http://careers.fisherpaykel.com/

Frucor Beverages Group Ltd: PO Box 76-202, Manukau City 1730; (09) 250 0100; fax (09) 250 0150; www.frucor.com.

Goodman Fielder NZ: www.goodmanfielder.com.au.

Methanex NZ Ltd: HR Advisor, Private Bag 2011, New Plymouth; (06) 754 97821; fax (06) 754 9701; nzpublicaffairs@methanex.com; www.methanex.com.

NZ Refining Company Ltd: Port Marsden highway, Ruakaka, Private Bag 9024, Whangarei; (09) 432 8311; fax (09) 432 8035; corporate@nzrc.co.nz; www.nzrc.co.nz.

Nuplex Industries Ltd: PO Box 12841, Penrose, Auckland; (09) 579 2029; nuplex@nuplex.co.nz; www.nuplex.co.nz.

PDL Holdings Ltd (Schneider Electric): Head Office: PO Box 15-355, New Lynn, Auckland; (09) 829 0490; fax (09) 829 0491; 14 Hazeldean Road, Addington, PO Box 1367, Christchurch; (03) 338 9059; fax (03) 338 9842; www.pdl.co.nz.

Powerware New Zealand: The Eaton Development Centre, 1 Barry Hogan Place, Addington; PO Box 111-88, Christchurch; (03) 343 3314; DC.info@eaton.com; www.powerware.com.

Steel and Tube Holdings Ltd: 15-17 Kings Crescent, PO Box 30 543, Lower Hutt, Hutt City 6315; (04) 570 5000; fax (04) 569 9622; www.steelandtube.co.nz.

Tait Radio Communications: Technical Recruitment Officer, 540 Wairakei Road, PO Box 1185, Christchurch; 0800 662 453; fax (03) 358 2029; www.taitworld.com.

ZESPRI International Limited: 400 Maunganui Road, Mt Maunganui 3002, PO Box 4043, Mt Maunganui South 3030; (07) 575 8864; fax (07) 575 1646; www.zespri.com or www.zespri.career.co.nz.

Mining

Newmont (Martha Mine): www.marthamine.co.nz
Solid Energy NZ Ltd: 2 Show Place, PO Box 1303, Christchurch; (03) 345 6000; fax (03) 345 6016; www.solidenergy.co.nz.

Science, research and development

ESR (Institute of Environmental Science and Research Limited): www.esr.cri.nz.
Hortresearch: www.hortresearch.co.nz
Industrial Research Limited: Gracefield Research Centre, Gracefield Road, PO Box 31-310, Lower Hutt, Wellington; (04) 931 3000; fax (04) 566 6004; info@irl.cri.nz; www.irl.cri.nz and www.irl.cri.nz/careers/vacancies/aspx.

Transport

Air New Zealand: (09) 336 3668 or 0800 747 500; careers@airnz.co.nz; www.airnz.co.nz.
Mainfreight: 2 Railway Lane, Otahuhu, Penrose, PO Box 14 038, Auckland; (09) 259 5500; www.mainfreightinternational.co.nz.
Transit New Zealand: Logical House, Level 8, 186-190 Willis Street, PO Box 27 477, Wellington; (04) 891 2580 fax (04) 801 2599; www.transit.govt.nz.

Utilities

Contact Energy Ltd: Level 1, Harbour City Tower, 29 Brandon St, PO Box 10742, Wellington; (04) 499 4001; fax (04) 499 4003; www.mycontact.co.nz.
Energy Online: Level 11, Newcall Tower, PO Box 8288, Symonds St, Auckland; ; www.energyonline.co.nz.
Genesis Energy: HR Advisor, Greenlane Office, Auckland; www.genesisenergy.co.nz.
Mercury Energy: Private Bag 92008, Auckland; www.mercury.co.nz.
LineLogix: info@linelogix.co.nz; www.linelogix.co.nz
Meridian Energy Ltd: www.meridianenergy.co.nz.
Mighty River Power Limited: Level 19, 1 Queen St, PO Box 90399, Auckland; (09) 308 8200; fax (09) 308 8209; email enquiries@mightyriver.co.nz; www.mightyriverpower.com.
OnGas: enquiries@ongas.co.nz; www.ongas.co.nz.
Transpower NZ Ltd: Level 7, Transpower House, 96 The Terrace, PO Box 1021, Wellington; (04) 495 7000; fax (04) 495 7100; keith.surgenor@transpower.co.nz; www.transpower.co.nz.
Trustpower Ltd: Private Bag 12023, Tauranga 3001; www.trustpower.co.nz.
United Networks Limited: 101 Carlton Gore Road, Newmarket, PO Box 99882, Auckland; fax (09) 978 7799; www.unitednetworks.co.nz.
Vector Networks: (09) 978 7788; fax (09) 978 7799; www.vectornetworks.co.nz.

■ RETIREMENT

Around 15% of New Zealand's population is aged 65 or older, and a significant number were born in other countries. Undoubtedly for many older people, the chance to be reunited with children who have already migrated to New Zealand is a major attraction. Having adult children in New Zealand also makes it easier to get permanent residency. Otherwise migration may be difficult for people of retirement age, as New Zealand's immigration policy is aimed at attracting people into the workforce.

Pros and cons of retiring to New Zealand

New Zealand offers many advantages for those considering a change of scenery for their retirement. The standard of living is high and the exchange rate is favourable, so your savings should go a long way. British and American retirees will not have to learn a new language and will find the culture reasonably familiar. The climate in most parts of New Zealand is warmer than Northern Europe. There are the attractions of living in a less crowded country, with, in general, fewer social problems and a lower crime rate. New Zealand's population is an ageing one, so there are many clubs and services that cater for older people's interests and needs. The drawbacks of emigrating have to be considered as well. You will be far away from friends and family in the northern hemisphere and you may find life a little lonely at first. Many retirees mention that one of the hardest aspects of their new life is not being able to afford to return home for family events such as weddings. New Zealand is 26 hours away from London by plane, and around 13 hours from the USA, and the trip is not cheap. Most migrants report that they find it easy to get to know New Zealanders, and although new friends are not a substitute for old, you need not fear being isolated for long in your new country – you just need to get out there and meet some new people.

Although doctors' visits cost about NZ$50 per consultation, hospital care is still free for New Zealanders and immigrants from countries with reciprocal social security agreements. On the other hand, certain types of specialist medical care may be better provided in America, the UK and European countries, simply because New Zealand is too small to have the range of expertise in these areas. In some situations, patients are being sent to Australia for certain types of treatment because of the overcrowded New Zealand waiting lists. Private health insurance is available though.

Residence and entry regulations

Because the general migration category is not open to people aged 55 or above, the most likely route to New Zealand residency for an older person is the family reunification or business development categories. Under the family reunification category, you are entitled to apply for residency if you have an adult child or children living in New Zealand and no adult children living in your own country. Alternatively, you can apply if you have children living in your home country but you have more children living in New Zealand than any other country including your own. If you are under the age of 65 and have sufficient capital you can apply under the business investment category. The minimum amount required is NZ$2million which you must agree to invest for a minimum of five years, and you must meet the pass mark (see Chapter Two: Moving to New Zealand: Before you go p.xx).

Applying for residence

To qualify for residency under the family reunification category, you will need to provide evidence of your family relationships, and the citizenship or residency status of your New Zealand children, and of your children living in other countries. You will need to submit birth and marriage certificates and copies of residency permits. Additionally, you will have to satisfy the health and character requirements outlined in Chapter Two: Moving to New Zealand: Before you go p.xx.

Possible retirement areas

Popular retirement areas are in the warmer regions on the East Coast of the North Island, and the north of the South Island. Many New Zealanders move to the coast when they retire, often to a beach house ('bach' or 'crib'). Some communities have a higher proportion of older people than others, which you may consider an advantage.

A popular retirement option for New Zealanders is the '10-acre block' or 'lifestyle block', a house in the country on a large section of land. 10 acres may be the size of farm in Europe, but by the standards of New Zealand farms these are just hobby plots for city folk who want to try the rural lifestyle. Some people cultivate their land or keep animals, while others just enjoy the extra space. See Chapter Three: Setting Up Home p.xx for more information and advice about Lifestyle Blocks.

Tauranga and the Bay of Plenty: On the East Coast of the North Island, the Bay of Plenty has a pleasant climate and is one of the main horticultural regions as a result. In the summer time, the sun, white sandy beaches and gentle waves of the beach at Mount Manganui attract many families. It is also a great place for walking and other outdoor recreational pursuits, and there are several new housing developments in this area. This area is enjoying a major growth spurt, and several of the outer Tauranga suburbs have shopping centres including Bayfair, Fraser Cover, Fashion Island and Palm Beach Plaza. The Bay of Plenty also hosts the annual National Jazz Festival. It is a wonderful area for gardening and growing all sorts of fruits and vegetables such as tangelos, avocadoes and kiwifruit. There are also a number of retirement villages in Tauranga and the surrounding area. For more general information about the area see: www.bayofplenty.com and www.tauranga.co.nz.

Hawke's Bay: Known for its pleasant climate and easy pace of life, Hawke's Bay is a popular retirement spot, and a great place for families. There is a wealth of orchards and vineyards here, and Hawke's Bay is one of the premier winemaking regions in the country. There are great opportunities for an outdoor lifestyle in Hawke's Bay, with plenty of places for cycling, golfing, walking, fishing, tramping and swimming.

FACT

One consideration to bear in mind is that in remoter areas you will certainly need to own a car or to live close to local services as public transport may not be convenient enough to rely on.

Over the summer, international cricket matches are often held at McLean Park Cricket Ground in Napier. Other annual events include New Year's Day Race Day, blues and jazz festivals, the Art Deco weekend, the Mission Estate Concert, the Hastings Blossom Festival, open-air cinema seasons and the Hawke's Bay A&P Show. Lovers of architecture will enjoy the buildings of Napier, the 'art deco capital of the world', which were built after the 1931 earthquake. A growing number of retired people live in Havelock North, a small town about twenty minutes from Napier. Hawke's Bay also boasts several beautiful beaches. For more information about the area see www.hawkesbaynz.com.

Kapiti Coast: Just north of Wellington, the West Coast of the North Island is a popular retirement destination for locals. It is dotted with small towns, from Paraparaumu up to Otaki, many made up largely of holiday homes that Wellingtonians use to escape for the weekends. There are a large number of permanent residents as well, many of retirement age. Transport networks are good, there is a commuter train service into Wellington city, as well as a local bus network. Driving to central Wellington takes about 40 minutes. The coast itself can be quite rough, but just down the coast the harbour provides more sheltered waters for boating or fishing. The Kapiti Coast is home to easily accessible nature and marine reserves, the country's top golf course, as well as the chance to enjoy outdoor activities and a range of shopping. For more information see www.kapiti.org.nz.

Banks Peninsula: Over the Port Hills to the south of Christchurch, the peninsula was called Bank's Island on the first map of New Zealand after Captain Cook's navigator, Joseph Banks, who thought its deep inlets cut it off from the mainland.

This is the life – Art Deco day in Napier

In contrast with the flat sweeping plains of Canterbury, the peninsula is all hills and valleys divided by deep harbours. Further east over the hills is Akaroa, with its echoes of the first French settlers. Streets are called 'Rues' and the building code specifies that new houses are to be built in the style of the homes of the original French settlers with steeply raked roofs. You would certainly need to be a car owner to live on the peninsula, as the bus service to Christchurch is infrequent and the remoter valleys lack local services. For more information see www.bankspeninsula.info.

Hobbies and interests

New Zealand offers many opportunities for using your new leisure time. The country is full of keen gardeners and the climate is well suited for those who like to spend time outdoors. If you are planning an active retirement, there is a lot of beautiful countryside to be explored. There are sporting opportunities to suit just about everybody. Golf is popular, and there are public golf courses outside most towns and cities. Lawn bowls and croquet are also popular with older people. If you are interested in cultural pursuits, you should consider settling near one of the main cities. Fortunately one of the advantages of living in New Zealand is that you can combine proximity to major cities with a semi-rural lifestyle if you so desire. Banks Peninsula, for example, is only 40 minutes away from the centre of Christchurch.

Every town has a senior citizens club, equally open to the recent immigrant as to the native New Zealander. These provide a chance to meet other older people as well as to make use of social facilities. Many older people use their new leisure time to return to study, either through night classes, through correspondence courses (such as those offered by the Open Polytech) or by enrolling in university part-time. Most New Zealand universities exempt mature students from formal entrance qualifications and instead will assess your ability to study and will enrol you at the appropriate level. A pre-degree certificate in liberal arts, which has less rigorous assessment procedures, may help you to get into (or back into) the swing of studying. Night classes are offered in a wide variety of subjects from foreign languages through to car maintenance and self-defence at local high schools or polytechnics.

Useful resources

Age Concern: Level 4, West Block, Education House, 178 Willis Street, Wellington; PO Box 10–688, Wellington 6143; (04) 801 9338; fax (04) 801 9336; national. office@ageconcern.org.nz; www.ageconcern.org.nz. There is a local Age Concern Council in all cities and most provincial centres around the country – see the website or telephone for more specific details of your closest office.

Auckland Bowls: (09) 524 4577; infoline: (09) 524 4566; fax (09) 630 3093; www.aucklandbowls.co.nz.

Bowls New Zealand: www.bowlsnz.co.nz.

British Pensioners Association (NZ) Inc: 6a Taikata Road, Te Atatu Peninsula, Auckland 1008; (09) 834 8559; fax (09) 834 8885. Provides information about rights, pensions, taxation, Community Services cards, etc.

Citizens Advice Bureau (National Office): www.cab.org.nz. Use the website to find contact details for a bureau near you. Citizens Advice have information about local social clubs and interest groups, and there are over 90 offices throughout New Zealand.

Grey Power: Aims to provide a voice for all older New Zealanders, and to advance, support and protect the wellbeing and welfare of older people. Provides information and advice about a wide range of issues. PO Box 2721719, Papakura 2244; (09) 299 2113; fax (09) 299 2118; fed-office@xtra.co.nz; www.greypower.co.nz. Also produces a quarterly magazine, *Grey Power Lifestyle Quarterly*: PO Box 9711, Newmarket, Auckland 1149; (09) 307 7061; fax (09) 307 7854.

New Zealand Golf Network: www.golf.co.nz

NZ-American Association (Wellington): PO Box 2957, Wellington; (04) 232 6053; NZAA@xtra.co.nz; www.nzaa.org.nz.

NZ Communities Development Trust: www.communities.co.nz. Online magazine contains information about sports, gardens to visit, hobbies and interests.

NZ Golf Association: Ground Floor, Exchange Place, 5–7 Willeston Street, Wellington; PO Box 11–842, Wellington 6142; (04) 471 0990; fax (04) 471 0991; nzgolf@nzgolf. org.nz; www.nzga.co.nz. The website also includes information about regional and national Seniors Golf tournaments and events.

Pension Service (UK): www.thepensionservice.gov.uk.

SeniorNet: toll free: 0800 SENIORNET (0800 736 467); www.seniornet.org.nz. There are 102 SeniorNet learning centres throughout the country, teaching older people about new communication and information technology. For those over the age of 55. See also: www.grownups.co.nz/community.

Women's Golf New Zealand: www.womensgolf.org.nz

New Zealand pensions

To qualify for New Zealand Superannuation, you must be 65 years of age or over, must be a New Zealand citizen or permanent resident and have lived in New Zealand for a total of at least 10 years since the age of 20, including at least five years since the age of 50. This is unless you have spent some of this time overseas having special medical or surgical treatment, doing special vocational training, working as a missionary, working with Volunteer Service Abroad, serving in one of the Commonwealth's armed forces or working on a New Zealand owned or registered ship trading to and from New Zealand. If you have been out of the country for any of these reasons, you must have been living in New Zealand before and after you were overseas in order to qualify. Equally, if you spent time in Australia, Britain, Jersey, Guernsey, Canada, Denmark, the Republic of Ireland, Greece or the Netherlands, that may also count as time towards your Superannuation.

National Superannuation currently pays a gross (before tax) fortnightly rate of NZ$673.30 for a single person living alone (which works out at NZ$554.12 after tax if you have no other income) and NZ$511.40 each a fortnight, before tax, for a married (or de facto or civil union) couple if both partners qualify. After tax this works out at NZ$426.24 per person if you have no other income. If only one partner qualifies, they will receive NZ$486.56 fortnightly (NZ$406.44 after tax) although this amount may be affected by other income you receive. If you are single, but live with other people, you will be entitled to NZ$619.32 a fortnight before tax. If you live alone, you may also qualify for a Living Alone Payment on top of your Superannuation.

If your partner doesn't already qualify for their own Superannuation, you can

Superannuation

Superannuation (as the state pension in New Zealand is known) has been a fraught issue for more than 30 years, and nearly every government since 1972 has introduced change, either to the structure of the scheme or to the levels of pension. 1898 saw the first state provision of retirement income, as the old age pension was introduced, payable at 65 and subject to income and asset tests and a residence qualification. In addition, in order to qualify, a person had to be of 'good moral character and sober habits'. There were several alterations to the scheme through the years, and in 1960 universal superannuation replaced the age benefit and the state-funded retirement pension for those over 65. Income-tested age benefit remained for those aged between 60 and 65. In 1977, a compulsory contributory scheme introduced in 1975 was replaced by a national superannuation, payable at 60 without regard to income and assets and with pension rates linked to average wages. In 1989 these rates were replaced by a combined wage price indexation that saw rates move in relation to price movements. The pension was renamed 'guaranteed retirement income' and there were indications that the qualifying age would shortly be increased to the age of 65. In 1990 a higher rate was introduced for unmarried recipients living alone. In 1992 the qualifying age was increased to 65. In 1998 the minimum level for a married couple relative to the average wage was lowered from 65% to 60%. In 2000, the superannuation rate was reinstated at 65% of the net average weekly wage. The New Zealand Superannuation Act 2001 provided for funding to be set aside to finance the pension in the future, when there will be a greater number of older people.

choose to 'include' them in your payments. Bear in mind though that any other income either of you earn could affect how much you receive. Receiving other income does not affect your Superannuation unless your partner is included in your payments. If they are, you can have other income of up to NZ$80 a week (before tax). If you earn more than this, 70c is taken off your payment for each dollar of income over this limit. Contact Work and Income for more information and to see if you qualify.

Your payments will usually start between one and two weeks after you qualify, providing that you apply at least two weeks before then. Remember that it is not possible to backdate your payments. If you want your partner 'included' it may take longer to arrange. Payments will be made directly into your bank account every two weeks.

New Zealand Superannuation is taxed before it is paid to you, but you still need to pay tax on any other income. If you do have other income, talk to Income Revenue about your tax rate to avoid an unwelcome tax bill at the end of the year.

Superannuation is administered by Work and Income New Zealand (WINZ), and you will need to meet with a representative to apply. Call 0800 552 002 for more information or to arrange a meeting. You must take the following items with you:

- Two documents each confirming your identity and New Zealand residency, and your partner's identity and residency. These should include: 1) birth certificate, passport or citizenship papers and 2) driver's licence or Community Services Card;
- Evidence of any name changes you or your partners have undergone, such as marriage certificate, civil union certificate or deed poll papers;
- Proof of your bank account number(s), ie your bank book or statement with account numbers;
- Evidence of IRD (tax) numbers for you and your partner in the form of letters or forms from Inland Revenue;
- Evidence of benefits or pensions from overseas, ie letters, statements or payslips showing payments;
- Proof of your housing costs: a rent book or letter from person you board with. If you own your own home bring details of your mortgage, rates, insurance, bills and home repair costs;
- Other items will probably be required – speak to WINZ before your appointment to ascertain exactly what these might be.

New Zealand currently has overseas social security arrangements with eight countries: the UK, Ireland, the Netherlands, Greece, Australia, the States of Jersey and Guernsey, Denmark and Canada. The general principle of these reciprocal arrangements is that people migrating from one country to the other are treated like citizens of their new country with regard to social security arrangements and are entitled to the same range of benefits. However, the particular arrangements differ between countries.

UK: A special banking option was introduced in April 1997 for UK pensioners living in New Zealand. People choosing this option agree to have their UK pension paid into a bank account accessible only by Work and Income. In return, these pensioners receive the full rate of New Zealand benefits or pensions. About 33,000 British pensioners live in New Zealand and roughly 23,000 of them have taken up this special banking option.

Republic of Ireland: Rates of payment vary according to the period of the person's residence in New Zealand, Irish pensions are paid to people living in New Zealand who have contributed to the Irish social security scheme. The agreement between the two countries is currently under review.

The Netherlands: Analogous Netherlands pensions are paid to people living in New Zealand who have contributed to the Netherlands pension scheme. Since July 2002 the same special banking option as was introduced for UK pensioners (see above) has been available to qualifying pensioners from the Netherlands living in New Zealand.

Greece: Greek pensions are paid to people living in New Zealand who have contributed to the Greek social security scheme.

Australia: The 1994 Social Security Agreement between New Zealand and Australia provided for Australians who have lived in New Zealand for more than ten years to receive New Zealand's pensions and income support services, subject to certain conditions. Australia reimbursed New Zealand for pensions and income support paid for residents with less than 10 years' residence in New Zealand. A revised agreement was implemented in 2002, meaning that Australia pays its entitlements directly in New Zealand.

Jersey and Guernsey: Rates of payment vary depending on the period of time that the person has been resident in New Zealand. Analogous Jersey and Guernsey pensions are paid to people living in New Zealand who have contributed to the Jersey and Guernsey social security schemes. The social security agreement between the countries is currently under review.

Denmark: Rates of payment vary depending on the period of time that the person has been resident in New Zealand. Analogous Danish pensions are paid to people living in New Zealand who have contributed to the Danish social security schemes.

Canada: Rates of payment vary depending on the period of time that the person has been resident in New Zealand. Analogous Canadian pensions are paid to people living in New Zealand who have contributed to the Canadian social security schemes.

UK citizens, if entitled to receive a British retirement pension, can continue to receive it in New Zealand. The level of the British pension is frozen from the point you leave the UK, and is not inflation adjusted. If you become eligible for the pension while in New Zealand, it will be paid at the rate that applies in the UK when you are first entitled to a pension. Under the reciprocal agreement, if you qualify for National Superannuation, the New Zealand government supplements the British pension so that it is at the same level as National Superannuation.

Emigrants who settle in New Zealand are entitled to a pension when they reach the qualifying age of 65. The amount of the pension is dependent on the number of years in paid employment, ie the amount you have contributed to the social security scheme in your country of origin. The pension can be directly credited to a New Zealand bank or building society account. When you become entitled to New Zealand Superannuation, you will receive the full New Zealand pension, made up of the pension plus the balance being paid by the New Zealand government. To apply for the UK pension, write to the the International Pension Centre. Any pension you receive from an overseas government is likely to be deducted from your New Zealand Superannuation. For more details, call 0800 552 002 (within New Zealand).

You may also be able to apply for extra assistance with your Superannuation, depending on your income and circumstances. Options may include the Community Services Card, which reduces the costs of prescriptions and visits to the doctor, or

 The International Pension Centre: Tyneview Park, Newcastle upon Tyne, NE98 1BA, UK; 0044 191 218 7777; fax 0044 191 218 7293; www. thepensionservice.gov.uk

the High Use Health Card, which you may be eligible for if you don't qualify for a Community Services Card (ask your doctor for information about this if you have to visit them regularly). If you and your family require a number of prescriptions every year, your pharmacist will be able to tell you whether you qualify for a Pharmaceutical Subsidy Card. If you are caring for dependent children, you can apply to Inland Revenue for Family Support. If you have a disability, you may be entitled to a disability allowance to help with any extra costs you have such as ongoing visits to the doctor or hospitals, medicines, extra clothes, travel, etc. There is also the possibility that you may qualify for an accommodation supplement, which contributes to the cost of renting, boarding or owning a home.

If you are not entitled to Superannuation, you may still qualify for another type of income support such as Domestic Purposes Benefit. There are also other types of income support available for widows, sole parents, people looking for work, and people who are unable to work due to sickness, injury or disability.

Useful resources

Age Concern: Level 4, West Block, Education House, 178 Willis Street, Wellington; PO Box 10-688, Wellington 6143; (04) 801 9338; fax (04) 801 9336; national. office@ageconcern.org.nz; www.ageconcern.org.nz. There is a local Age Concern Council in all cities and most provincial centres around the country – see the website or telephone for more specific details of your closest office. Promotes rights, quality of life and wellbeing for older people.

Britannia Financial Services Ltd: Unit 4, 106 Bush Road, Albany, PO Box 302–369, Auckland, New Zealand; (09) 414 4215; (09) 414 4219; 0800 857 367; alun@opt-ltd. co.nz; www.ukpensionstonz.com. New Zealand's largest pensions transfer service, specializing in transfers from the UK to New Zealand.

British High Commission: www.britishhighcommission.gov.uk. See the website for information about New Zealand pension entitlements, and contact details.

British Pensioners Association (NZ) Inc: 6a Taikata Road, Te Atatu Peninsula, Auckland 1008; (09) 834 8559; fax (09) 834 8885. Provides information about rights, pensions, taxation, Community Services cards, etc.

Citizens Advice Bureau (National Office): www.cab.org.nz. Use the website to find contact details for a bureau near you. Citizens Advice have information about local social clubs and interest groups, and there are over 90 offices throughout New Zealand.

Grey Power: Aims to provide a voice for all older New Zealanders, and to advance, support and protect the wellbeing and welfare of older people. Provides information and advice about a wide range of issues. PO Box 2721719, Papakura 2244; (09) 299 2113; fax (09) 299 2118; fed-office@xtra.co.nz; www. greypower.co.nz. Also produces a quarterly magazine, *Grey Power Lifestyle Quarterly*: PO Box 9711, Newmarket, Auckland 1149; (09) 307 7061; fax (09) 307 7854.

Inland Revenue (Superannuation): 0800 227 774; www.ird.govt.nz. Have your IRD number handy when you call. Depending on your circumstances, you may be able to apply to Inland Revenue for a lower tax rate.

Move My Pension: Provider of pension transfer services. 31 Balfour Crescent, P.O. Box 7139, Hamilton. freephone from within New Zealand 0800 485 736; info@ movemypension.co.nz; www.movemypension.co.nz. Free assessment of your situation is available through the contact form on the website.

The International Pension Centre: Tyneview Park, Newcastle upon Tyne, NE98 1BA, U K; 0044 191 218 7777; fax 0044 191 218 7293; www.thepensionservice. gov.uk

Retirement Commission: Level 3, 69–71 The Terrace, Wellington; PO Box 12-148, Wellington; (04) 499 7396; fax (04) 499 7397; office@retirement.org.nz; www. retirement.org.nz. This office is partly government funded, and has a range of activities aimed at raising public awareness and understanding of retirement income policies.

RSA Pensions Advice and Welfare Services: www.rsa.org.nz/pensions/

Work and Income (Ministry of Social Development): 0800 552 002 (call free to arrange a meeting); www.workandincome.govt.nz. This website contains a checklist of things you will need to take to a meeting to apply for New Zealand Superannuation. Items required include: your ID and New Zealand residency documents (two documents for each applicant), such as passports, birth certificates or citizenship papers; name change certificates (deed poll papers or marriage certificates); evidence of bank account and IRD numbers (forms, letters, statements, etc.); a letter/statement/payslip showing any benefits or pensions paid to you from overseas, evidence of your combined income from any source for the past 52 weeks (payslips, bank statements, etc.); and evidence of any income-earning assets owned by you or your partner (bank statements, share certificates, property valuations, etc.).

Receiving your pension abroad

Pension arrangements for expatriates vary. In some countries if you have established entitlement in your own country then you can continue to receive your pension in New Zealand. As noted above, some countries have reciprocal agreements with New Zealand, which entitle you to the same range of benefits as a local. You should contact your local Department of Social Security for further information. One New Zealand company that specialises in completing necessary documentation and liaising with overseas agencies is Britannia Financial Services Ltd.

Taxation

 Britannia Financial Services Ltd: Unit 4, 106 Bush Road, Albany; PO Box 302–369, Auckland, New Zealand; (09) 414 4215; (09) 414 4219; 0800 857 367; alun@opt-ltd.co.nz; www.ukpensionstonz.com

Once you are a New Zealand resident, you pay New Zealand income tax on your worldwide income, including income from any overseas-based pension schemes. Residency for taxation purposes has nothing to do with your immigration status. You are deemed to be New Zealand resident for tax purposes if you have a permanent place of abode in New Zealand, regardless of whether you also have one in another country. Having a permanent abode in New Zealand is not limited to owning a dwelling, the courts will also take into account social, personal, and financial ties as evidence of where your permanent abode is. If you are in New Zealand for more than 183 days in any 12-month period, you are regarded as a New Zealand resident for taxation purposes whether or not you have a permanent abode in New Zealand.

New Zealand has double tax treaties with 24 countries including the USA, Canada, the UK, France, Germany, and the Netherlands. These treaties limit the tax liability for citizens of one country resident in the other, so that an individual does not, in theory, pay tax twice on the same income.

Useful resources

Montfort International PLC: Home Farm, Shere Road, Albury, nr Guildford, Surrey GU5 9BL; 01483 202072; fax 01483 202073; info@miple.co.uk; www.miplc.co.uk. Provides expert tax planning and financial advice to migrants to maximise on opportunities and minimise any potential tax liabilities.

Community services cards

One of the drawbacks of the New Zealand healthcare system for a retired person is that although hospital care is free, doctor's visits are not, and neither are prescriptions. For those pensioners on low incomes from countries with reciprocal social security arrangements, the Community Services Card is available – this reduces the costs of health care. Your eligibility is means-tested, and if you are married, in a civil union or in a de facto relationship your application is based on your combined income.

Income limits are as follows: single person sharing accommodation – NZ$21.676; single person living alone – NZ$22,981; people in a married, civil union or de facto couple – NZ$34,328. If you are receiving New Zealand Superannuation and you also get a private pension, only half the pension is counted as income. You still need to put the full amount on your application form though. Permanent legal residents can apply to the National Community Services Card Centre (0800 999 999). Application forms can also be obtained from any Work and Income NZ centre, or your doctor or local pharmacy, or you can download them in PDF from from www.workandincome. govt.nz/get-assistance/csc/.

There is a cap on the total amount you will be charged annually for prescriptions, so if you need a lot of medication, you do not pay more than a certain amount. Your Community Services Card will be valid for between 12–24 months depending on your circumstances.

Private health insurance

Private medical insurance is one option to consider, to cover the additional costs of New Zealand health care. Private insurance will cover the cost of treatment in private hospitals, which will give you more choice about the timing of operations. But the annual cost of premiums is likely to make full private insurance costly unless you are a frequent user of primary health care services.

Wills and legal considerations

You should draw up a will in New Zealand if you are considering buying property and settling there. Dying intestate complicates matters sufficiently for one's heirs, without doing so in a foreign country. In the event that a non-New Zealander dies intestate, the laws of their own country will apply. As it is more likely that you will be a New Zealand citizen or at least domiciled there in the eyes of the law, New Zealand intestate laws would apply. Under New Zealand intestate laws, your estate would be divided between a surviving spouse and your children, with your spouse getting the major share. This would be the case even if you had separated from but not divorced your spouse.

In New Zealand, a will does not have to be drawn up by a lawyer. However, there are obvious advantages to having your will drawn up by a lawyer or trust company. If there are any mistakes in the way the will is drawn up they can invalidate it, and the lawyer or trust company chosen to draw up your will can administer your estate. This may be a good idea, particularly if you have no close relatives in the country. In some countries, people often nominate a relative or friend(s) as executor of the will. However, it is better to have a trust company or solicitor as your executor, and this also saves problems if your nominated executor predeceases you. Many New Zealand lawyers do not charge for drawing up wills, and if you nominated the solicitor or trust company that drew up your will, you will either pay no fee or a minimal fee for the execution of the will.

A living will is separate from the will you make about your assets. It expresses your wishes about your care and welfare before your death, in the event that you are unable to express such wishes yourself at the time. It contains directives for medical decisions, including how much care you wish to receive should you develop any terminal illness, and how vigorous such care should be. There is no legal basis for living wills, but Age Concern advises that they are viewed sympathetically. For further information contact your lawyer or a Community Law Centre.

Starting a Business

THE EMPLOYMENT MARKET

New Zealand is a very straightforward place to do business. It has an efficient market-oriented economy, stable and reasonably secure business environment and is relatively free from corruption. The workforce is, for the most part, highly educated and skilled, and the labour market is flexible and deregulated. The business scene is strong and flourishing. With one of the lowest tariff rates in the world, New Zealand companies are naturally competitive exporters. Comparative costs also make it a feasible place to set up a business – in cost-critical industries like call centres and back office business staffing costs will be up to 30% less than in Australia and up to 50% less than the USA. This is because there is no payroll tax, no social services tax and no superannuation tax. There is just a small levy for accident compensation. Property and energy costs are relatively low.

The prevailing attitude towards business ventures, whether started by New Zealanders or immigrants, is positive and helpful. To make a success of the venture requires, of course, the same blend of careful planning, energy and luck that you need in any country. More than anything, you need to research your chosen potential market or markets to ensure that the products or services you offer are geared to meet a real demand at an appropriate price. Much of your groundwork can be done in advance, but there is no substitute for visiting and seeing for yourself the environment in which you wish to try the venture. It may well be worth considering spending a reasonable amount of time living and working in New Zealand before making a final commitment to a particular enterprise.

In most cases, therefore, it is likely that you will have obtained New Zealand residency before setting up a business on your own.

Most New Zealand investment does not require approval. Only proposals involving international investment equity of a company of 25% or more, which have a value of NZ$50million or more, or are related to fishing quota or particular land purchases require the permission of the Overseas Investment Office Permission is dependent on the extent to which the projected business will contribute to the economy. However these restrictions will not affect most immigrants considering setting up a small business in New Zealand.

 Overseas Investment Office: 160 Lambton Quay, Private Box 5501, Wellington; (04) 462 4490; fax (04) 460 0111; oio@linz.govt.nz or info@linz.govt.nz; www.oio.linz.govt.nz

If you are organising your application for New Zealand residency with the intention of setting up a business there, you should note that a special scheme exists to attract business investors. (See the *Before you go* chapter p.XX.) The sums required to qualify for the Business Investment category are substantial, and in any case your investment funds are not yours to invest as you wish. This means that if you apply under this category you will need additional funds for your own business, to cover at least the first two years. If you do not have the necessary capital to qualify under this category, then you will need to apply under the Skilled Migrant or Family categories.

Brightly coloured restaurants – a good marketing tool

FACT

■ There are an increasing number of government agencies set up to help small businesses and the attitude towards entrepreneurs is positive.

In recent years, regulations governing setting up business in New Zealand have been relaxed. The Companies Act was substantially amended in 1994 to make the process of incorporating a company simpler. As part of encouraging individual initiative and competitive economic environment, the government is trying to cut down on the amount of red tape involved in doing business, and to encourage small businesses to set up and survive. The result is that it is a good time to be starting up a new business in New Zealand. This chapter will look at what is involved in buying a business in New Zealand or in starting your own.

■ PREPARATION

Choosing a business

Since in broad terms, New Zealanders engage in similar business, cultural and social activities to Europeans, there are similar potential markets for anyone contemplating setting up a new enterprise. The differences need to be borne in mind, however, not the least of which is that the comparatively small total population and its distribution will have a significant effect on the structure of potential markets. For example if you are considering setting up in the hospitality industry you will find that in the larger cities restaurants, cafés and wine bars abound; the market is pretty well saturated and thus very competitive. Such businesses are stretched to find some new competitive advantage and that is often manifested as gimmickry, which of course has a short-lived novelty appeal. In the rural areas, there are fewer restaurants and wine bars, but this is of course partly because there is less population to support them as New Zealand is not particularly densely populated. This may provide an opportunity, yes, but maybe

FACT

■ New Zealand business is characterised by the prevalence of small firms; the country has a high rate of entrepreneurship. 85% of firms employ five or fewer people.

one that requires a lot of 'up front' and sustained investment in marketing and publicity. Given that moving to a new country is going to be pretty challenging in itself, it may be wise to opt for a safer bet such as selecting an enterprise for which there is a known or an established market, or one in which you have particular skills and experience. Obviously there is an advantage in buying an already established business in this respect, however before you buy you should research the track record of your chosen enterprise. Remember that the majority of businesses succeed not on the uniqueness of the concept but on the application of sound and careful management techniques.

Researching your business

Research shows that most small firms either stay small or expire – few grow to significant sizes, so it is important to find a solid starting point for your business.

Whether it is your intention to buy a business or to set up from scratch, researching the potential market for your business is essential. The specific information that you need to determine whether there is a viable market will depend greatly upon the type of business, the services or the products you have in mind. There are companies specialising in market research in the major cities in New Zealand, which would be able to provide data on most aspects of the market or would offer to conduct specific enquiries, for a fee, in areas of the market which were less well researched. This type of service is usually beyond the budget of those setting up a small business. There are some companies offering research services specifically tailored for small businesses and you can do some of the research work yourself.

One of the first places to start looking for information is the local public library. Most public libraries run an information service for local businesses and for those intending to set up a business. They will have information on market trends, local suppliers, possible competitors, planning and development strategies. Some libraries offer a contract research service and will do a lot of the legwork by investigating the feasibility of a project for you. This may be a cost-effective option simply because they will be familiar with the sources of information and will be able to find out quickly what you need to know. Information on businesses and commerce in specific regions can be obtained from the local Chamber of Commerce. Chambers of Commerce in the main cities are listed below.

Statistics New Zealand (www.stats.govt.nz) runs a professional consultancy service for data on imports, prices, population, etc. They publish the *Quarterly Economic Survey* of various sectors of the economy. Predominantly this is income and expenditure data, although they also collect investment data. Each year this is gathered into the more detailed *Annual Enterprise Survey*. More general data on the New Zealand economy is published in the monthly *Key Statistics*. They also publish the *New Zealand Yearbook*, and have a detailed business and economy information menu on their website as well as several useful links (see below). If your business is involved in the export market, the Ministry of Foreign Affairs and Trade can help with economic and political information about your target markets. The New Zealand Immigration Service has established a section of its website to provide information for people coming to New Zealand to set up businesses (www.immigration.govt.nz – follow the 'Invest' link to the 'Starting a Business' page).

Researching market opportunities in New Zealand from overseas is naturally more difficult than doing the groundwork once you arrive. There are companies that offer an information-gathering service specifically for intending immigrants, in areas ranging from business opportunities to education prospects (see 'Business and Market Research Organisations' listed below). Another source of information is the *New Zealand Yearbook*, which provides a highly detailed picture of social, demographic, and economic trends in New Zealand. It is a useful introduction to the structure of the economy and the main business sectors. The disadvantage of the Yearbook is that the information is based on five-yearly census data, so while it is very detailed, it is not always up to date. The last census was in 2006. Copies of the Yearbook can be found in some libraries or from Statistics New Zealand, or bought at the Kiwifruits New Zealand Shop, which specialises in New Zealand products. New Zealand High Commissions and Embassy also have copies of the Yearbook as well as individual chapters on specific topics. Another excellent source of information is the New Zealand Institute of Economic Research which is a primary source of information about economics in New Zealand and provides independent consulting services to the public sector, industry and businesses. It also publishes the *Quarterly Survey of Business Opinion*, which surveys private sector enterprises with at least six employees in the manufacturing, building, distribution and services industries.

 Kiwifruits New Zealand Shop: 7 Royal Opera Arcade, London SW1Y 4UY; 0207 930 4587; theteam@kiwifruitsnzshop.com; www.kiwifruitsnzshop.com

 New Zealand Institute of Economic Research: (04) 472 1880; econ@nzier.org.nz; www.nzier.org.nz

Employment patterns are changing as New Zealand business develops; many new industries, such as biotechnology and wine-making, are based on agriculture, but there are a number of new and fast growing industries in other sectors. These include ICT, tourism and education services. In addition, there is a growing international appetite for creative industries, such as film and television, yacht design, fashion and art.

Chambers of commerce

New Zealand Chambers of Commerce: www.nzchamber.co.nz.
Northland Chamber of Commerce: 3–5 Hunt St, PO Box 1703, Whangarei; (09) 438 4771; fax (09) 438 4770; info@northchamber.co.nz; www.northchamber.co.nz.
Auckland Regional Chamber of Commerce and Industry: 100 Mayoral Drive, PO Box 47, Auckland; (09) 309 6100; fax (09) 309 0081; akl@chamber.co.nz; www.chamber.co.nz.
Waikato Chamber of Commerce: 190 Collingwood Street, PO Box 1122, Hamilton; (07) 839 5895; fax (07) 839 4581; admin@waikatochamber.co.nz; www.waikatochamber.co.nz.
Chamber of Commerce Tauranga Region: Smart Business Centre, Unit 3b, 65 Chapel Street, PO Box 414, Tauranga, (07) 577 9823; fax (07) 577 0364; chamber@tauranga.org.nz; www.tauranga.org.nz.

TIP
■ The fact that the economy is growing and diversifying means that business legislation is being revised constantly, so you will need to keep an eye on the latest legal aspects as you are researching your business ideas.

Hawke's Bay Chamber of Commerce: 2 Market St South, Hastings; (06) 876 5938; fax (06) 876 3748; admin@hawkesbaychamber.co.nz; www.hawkesbaychamber.co.nz.
Wanganui Chamber of Commerce: Enterprise House, 187 Victoria Ave, PO Box 88, Wanganui; (06) 345 0080; fax (06) 348 8210; info@wanganuichamber.co.nz; www.wanganuichamber.co.nz.
Taranaki Chamber of Commerce: 15 Young St, PO Box 2, New Plymouth; (06) 759 9080; fax (06) 759 9145; admin@taranakichamber.co.nz.
Wellington Chamber of Commerce: Level 9, 109 Featherston St, Wellington; (04) 914 6500; fax (04) 914 6524; email info@wgtn-chamber.co.nz; www.wgtn-chamber.co.nz.
Nelson Chamber of Commerce: PO Box 1121, Nelson; (03) 548 1363; fax (03) 546 8373; Office@commerce.org.nz; www.commerce.org.nz.
Canterbury Employers' Chamber of Commerce: 57 Kilmore St, PO Box 359, Christchurch; (03) 366 5096; fax (03) 379 5454; info@cecc.org.nz; www.cecc.org.nz.
Otago Chamber of Commerce and Industry Incorporated: Level 7, 106 George Street, Dunedin; (03) 479 0181; fax (03) 477 0341; office@otagochamber.co.nz; www.otagochamber.co.nz.
Chamber of Commerce Southland Inc.: PO Box 856, Invercargill; (03) 218 7188; fax (03) 218 7927; office@commercesouth.com; www.commercesouth.com.

Business and market research organisations

BERL (Business and Economic Research Ltd): Level 5, 108 The Terrace, PO Box 10277, Wellington; (04) 931 9200; fax (04) 931 9202; info@berl.co.nz; www.berl.co.nz.
Research New Zealand: Level 7, Forsyth Barr House, PO Box 10–617, Wellington; (04) 499 3088; fax (04) 499 3414; info@researchnz.com; www.researchnz.com
Business Information Service: Auckland City Library; (09) 307 7790; bis@aucklandcity.govt.nz. Fee-based information service, annual membership subscription costs NZ$180 excluding GST.
New Zealand Institute of Economic Research: 8 Halswell Street, Thorndon, PO Box 3479, Wellington; (04) 472 1880; fax (04) 472 1211; econ@nzier.org.nz.

Government departments

NZ Ministry of Foreign Affairs and Trade: 195 Lambton Quay, Private Bag 18 901, Wellington; (04) 439 8000; fax (04) 472 9596; enquiries@mfat.govt.nz; www.mft.govt.nz.
Statistics New Zealand (Head Office): Aorangi House, 85 Molesworth Street, PO Box 2922, Wellington; (04) 931 4600 or 0508 525 525 for the Information Centre; fax (04) 931 4610; info@stats.govt.nz, library@stats.govt.nz or publications@stats.govt.nz; www.stats.govt.nz.
Statistics New Zealand: Information Consultancy Groups:
Auckland: UniServices House, 70 Symonds Street, Private Bag, 920003, Auckland; (09) 920 9100; fax (09) 920 9198.
Christchurch: Dollan House, 401 Madras Street, Private Bag 4741, Christchurch; (03) 964 8700; fax (03) 964 8964.

Choosing an area

Having decided on your line of business, the next logical step is to decide where to locate it. Obviously the type of business will determine this in many cases; for example choosing where to site a horticultural enterprise will largely be determined by climate and crop suitability. The tourism industry was once concentrated in the geothermal area around Rotorua, and the South Island more generally, with most visitors staying in Christchurch or Queenstown. Auckland and areas to the north, such as the Bay of Islands, are attracting visitors for longer stays and are growing tourism areas. Another growing sector is adventure tourism, with the south of the Waikato region around Waitomo caves, Nelson and the West Coast likely to benefit. Export manufacturing is strongest in Auckland and Christchurch. Forestry, another export sector predicted to grow, is likely to benefit the region around the central North Island. Overall Auckland is likely to continue to enjoy the highest economic growth over the next few years, but the outlook is also positive for Canterbury and the Bay of Plenty.

Small and medium enterprises

New Zealand is an economy of small businesses, and 85% of registered New Zealand businesses employ fewer than five people. There are a number of community-based enterprise and employment centres involved with developing new employment and small business initiatives; contact your regional council for details. The Small Business Company also provides information, education and resources to owner-operators and managers, and offers online training and a free newsletter.

 The Small Business Company: Level 6, 138 Victoria Street, PO Box 25 159, Christchurch; (03) 365 4242; fax (03) 365 4243; info@tsbc.co.nz; www.tsbc.co.nz

If you employ fewer than 25 people and your business is less than six months old, you are eligible for a business mentor with the Business in the Community Mentoring Programme. The mentors are experienced and successful businesspeople who are willing to share their expertise to help you grow your business. You can apply online for a Business Mentor to assist you in developing your business (at www.businessmentor.org.nz), or contact the National Office of Business in the Community. The Policy Advice Division of the Inland Revenue Department (IRD) runs

 National Office of Business in the Community: PO Box 9043, Newmarket, Auckland 1149; 0800 103 400; fax (09) 525 0482; bmnz@bitc. co.nz; www.businessmentor.org.nz

 The Business Information Zone: 0800 424 946; fax (04) 499 8654; email through the website: www.business.govt.nz

a small business advisory service, which provides help with working out your tax obligations. It can be contacted through your local IRD offices, or see the website (www.taxpolicy.ird.govt.nz). The Business Information Zone (www.business. govt.nz) is a specialist business information service for individuals and small and medium enterprises; it will help you identify organisations, people, training programmes and resources to help develop your business. Biz produces a number of useful publications, based around the general themes of 'Considering Starting a Business', 'Starting a Business' and 'Growing a Business'. The website provides important regulatory information, including help with taxes, ACC, workplace safety and employing staff, information on training and a number of other useful resources. It also gives details about Business Incubators, which are facilities designed to assist businesses becoming established and profitable during start-up. The incubation period is normally between one and three years, and provides business with advice and services, networking, mentoring, managers and shared premises. The New Zealand Trade and Enterprise (NZTE) website provides information about Business Clusters, or groups of companies that collaborate to grow business using a collaborative team approach. NZTE provides tools, advice, facilitation and funding to businesses, regions, and groups of organisations (www.nzte.govt.nz).

There are 52 Small Business Enterprise Centres (www.sbecnz.org.nz) throughout New Zealand; these community-based organisations specialise in helping small

FACT
■ US statistics have shown that Business Incubators increase the success rate of start-ups from 20% to 87%.

businesses. They offer: practical business facilitation; referral to other help agencies; introductions to government departments, local businesses and consultants; business courses, seminars and workshops; and ongoing support and networks. They provide independent, confidential, competent and practical assistance to encourage economic enterprise and employment development. Some of these centres also provide specialist services for new migrants who want to start a business. See the website (www.sbecnz.org.nz) for more information about membership, products and services, links, resources and free information. For general enquiries, contact Sarah Anderson, a small business specialist.

 Sarah Anderson,small business specialist: PO Box 5157, Palmerston North; (06) 354 6900; fax (06) 350 1814

■ BUYING A BUSINESS VERSUS SETTING UP FROM SCRATCH

The decision between buying a business or setting up your own is basically about the degree of risk you are prepared to take and what kind of capital you can raise. Buying a business requires much more money, but on the other hand, you will be buying a going concern that will provide an immediate source of income. Setting up from scratch can be done on a shoestring, but if you underestimate your financial needs at the beginning, your enterprise may not last long. Your first years in business may be difficult in terms of cash flow and unanticipated expenses, so it is important not to miscalculate the size of the budget you can realistically manage on. You may also find that the stress of changing your country of abode is enough to cope with during your first years in New Zealand, and the move to set up your own operation may be easier after you have acclimatised to New Zealand in other ways. If you do decide to go ahead and buy an existing business, the place to start looking is the daily newspapers classified sections. Specialist business estate agencies can be found in your local Yellow Pages, or see www.nzbizbuysell.co.nz where you can view lists of NZ businesses currently for sale.

■ RUNNING A HOME BUSINESS

For some, working from home is a stepping stone to building up a bigger business, and for others it is a lifestyle choice. Depending on circumstances, the Inland Revenue Department may allow you to claim back a portion of your household expenses, and likewise if you use a private vehicle for business purposes you may claim a portion of running costs. You must keep careful records and retain invoices as for any other business expense you would claim, and household expenses you may claim a portion of include rates, insurance, power, mortgage interest and depreciation (if you own the house). You can only claim expenses that relate to the area of your house specifically set aside for business purposes. Work out the percentage of the work area compared to the total floor area of the house and then

FACT

■ Many successful Kiwi businesses started at home, and it is estimated that there are more than 200,000 home-based businesses in New Zealand.

apply this percentage to the total house expenses. You may also claim a deduction for telephone rental. If your home is the centre of operations or management for the business, you may claim a deduction of 50% of the telephone rental. Identify toll-calls that are business related – perhaps highlight them every month on your phone bill. If you have separate commercial and domestic line rental, you can claim the full cost of the commercial line for both income tax and GST, but none of the domestic rental. If you make any private calls on the business line you will have to make an adjustment for them. See www.ird.govt.nz for more information and to find out whether you fit the required criteria for compensation. The information provided will also show you how to use a logbook to document travel.

■ RAISING FINANCE

Banks and business plans

There are various sources of loans available for small businesses, the most common being the banks. However, any lender or giver of grants will expect some reassurance of serious commitment from the person or persons asking for help. This means, in most cases, evidence that they are committing a significant amount of their own capital to the venture. As was noted above, the major reason for small business failure is bad financial planning so, in order to convince a bank that you are a worthwhile investment you need to produce a detailed business plan. Some organisations, such as Biz, New Zealand Trade and Enterprise, and The Small Business Company, may be able to offer you some assistance (see contact details above). Without going into too much detail here, your business plan should include:

- A summary containing a broad outline of your vision of the business.
- A brief CV of each person involved in the business, highlighting skills, experience and expertise relevant to the scheme.
- A description of the main services or products that you intend to offer.
- Evidence that a viable market exists for your services or products.
- An outline of your marketing communication strategy (how you intend to contact your potential customers).

It should also include financial information:

- Expenditure
- Start-up costs
- Cash flow projections
- Salaries
- Running (operating) costs including materials, production, utilities, premises (rent), etc.
- Other expenses (remember to make a generous allowance for contingencies).
- Projected income – income from sales.

Remember that you are trying to present a positive case to your audience; the more professional and credible the plan, the more chance you have of success. Clarity and a realistic, rather than optimistic, view will enhance your proposal. If the realistic approach suggests that the idea is not sound, then you must review it or even come up with another idea.

A final comment on business plans: there are people who can offer advice on how to write your plan, and you should listen to that advice. There are also people who will write it for you, but if you prepare it yourself, then you will be that much closer to an understanding of your projected business and you will be that much better prepared to explain the details to those you may have to convince along the way.

Investment incentives

There are several investment incentive schemes available directly from central government. New Zealand Trade and Enterprise Development Grants are aimed at assisting companies to gain additional business skills and obtain external expertise and assistance in developing business projects – both start-ups and established businesses can apply. In addition, Enterprise Network Grants are available to assist

New Zealand Trade and Enterprise: 0800 555 888; www.nzte.org.nz; application forms should be emailed to edg@nzte.govt.nz

Biz: 0800 424 946; www.biz.org.nz

groups of businesses; contact NZTE to check whether you are eligible. NZTE also manages the Cluster Development Programme Fund, which is to facilitate clusters with significant growth potential. Biz provides free access to information about assistance available to businesses, including courses. If your idea involves practical environmental initiatives, the Ministry for the Environment Sustainable Management Fund (SMF) may be a possible source of funding. SMF will consider funding projects that fit under one of its four main topic areas: Freshwater Management Initiatives; 'Adopt A' Schemes; Urban Sustainability; and Community-level Climate Change. Contact the SMF for further details.

Ministry for the Environment Sustainable Management Fund: PO Box 10362, Wellington; (04) 917 7400; fax (04) 917 7523; information@mfe. govt.nz; www.smf.govt.nz

Technology NZ is a government-funded agency that provides a range of programmes to assist businesses with technology-based development projects. Guidelines and application forms on the TechNZ website provide a clear outline of the requirements for proposals, and you should use the Project Assessment Guide to focus your proposals. TechNZ Investment Managers will assist applicant companies to prepare a good proposal. Further assistance may be obtained from independent consultants, private sector research companies, Crown Research Institutes (CRI) and University business managers as well as accountants.

Crown Research Institutes: Level 11, Clear Centre, 15-17 Murphy Street, PO Box 12–240, Wellington; (04) 917 7800; fax (04) 917 7850; www.frst. govt.nz

If your business concept has an arts focus, Creative New Zealand is a worthwhile place to ask about funding possibilities.Creative New Zealand offers a range of contestable funding programmes, grants to one-off arts projects and support to professional arts organisations on an annual or 3-year basis.

 Creative New Zealand: National Office, Old Public Trust Building, 131–135 Lambton Quay, PO Box 3806, Wellington; (04) 473 0880; fax (04) 471 2865; info@creativenz.govt.nz; www.creativenz.govt.nz

For businesses with a community or social service focus, the New Zealand Lotteries Commission's Lottery Community Committees make grants for developmental or preventative projects, welfare and support services, and projects that help improve the well-being of people in the community. You can download a pamphlet entitled *Applying for Grants Online* in PDF format from www.dia.govt.nz.

 New Zealand Lotteries Commission's Lottery Community Committees: 0800 824 824; grantsonline@dia.govt.nz; www.cdgo. govt.nz

Addresses of New Zealand Trade and Enterprise Offices

Auckland: Level 11, ANZ Centre, 23-29 Albert St (cnr Albert, Federal and Swanson Streets), PO Box 8680, Symonds Street, Auckland; (09) 366 4768; fax (09) 366 4767.

Hamilton: 29 Liverpool Street; PO Box 9515, Hamilton; (07) 846 8490; fax (07) 846 8391.

Tauranga: 306 Cameron Road, PO Box 568, Tauranga; (07) 577 6199; fax (07) 577 6010.

Napier: 2nd Floor, Tourism House, Civic Court, 64 Dickens Street, Napier; (06) 835 6245; fax (06) 835 6247.

New Plymouth: 9 Robe Street, PO Box 670, New Plymouth; (06) 759 5165; fax (06) 759 5154.

Palmerston North: 1st Floor, 53-5 Queen Street, PO Box 12065, Palmerston North; (06) 354 1812; fax (06) 350 1804.

Wellington: Level 15, The Majestic Centre, 100 Willis Street, PO box 2878, Wellington; (04) 816 8100; fax (04) 816 8101.

Nelson: 39 Halifax Street, PO Box 840, Nelson; (03) 546 8084; fax (03) 546 7253.

Christchurch: Level 8, Price Waterhouse Centre, 119 Armagh Street, PO Box 468, Christchurch; (03) 962 3838; fax (03) 365 2555.
Dunedin: WestpacTrust Building, Level 2, 106 George Street, PO Box 5642, Dunedin; (03) 470 7309; fax (03) 470 7301.

◼ BUSINESS STRUCTURES AND REGISTRATION

Businesses in New Zealand can take various forms: Company, Partnership, Non-Profit or Sole Trader. The three most common forms for small businesses are sole trader, partnership or company. The form of your business determines not only who benefits from it but also who is liable should something go wrong. It is not uncommon for businesses to start up in one form then change into another as they expand, so you don't have to make a once-and-for-all decision before you start.

Sole trader

In this structure, you are the sole owner, controller and manager of your business, are personally entitled to all the profits and will be personally liable for all business taxes and debts. This is the simplest form of business structure to start up: you simply tell the IRD you are becoming self-employed and there are no formal or legal processes that must be followed. You may employ other people to help run the business. If your business has an annual turnover greater than NZ$40,000, excluding Goods and Services Tax (GST), you will also need to register for GST, but these are the only legal formalities required. GST registration is optional if your annual turnover is less than NZ$40,000. The disadvantage of the simple structure is that as a sole trader your personal assets can be taken as payment for any debts incurred by your business. See www.ird.govt.nz/gst.

Partnership

Partnerships are formed by private agreement between two or more people. Partnerships are quite flexible, dependent upon the terms of that agreement. Each partner shares the responsibility for running the business, shares in any profit or loss equally, unless the partnership agreement states otherwise, and is liable for any debt within the partnership. It is a good idea, although not legally necessary, to have a lawyer draw up or check your formal partnership agreement. Juliet Ashton, in her book *Your Successful Small Business*, suggests that the agreement should cover the following:

- the name of the partnership and the business;
- the date of the agreement;
- an indication of how long the partnership is intended to last;
- the amount of capital invested by each partner in the firm and the interest on it;
- how the profits will be split;
- who is responsible for management and control of the business;

- arrangements about holidays, illness, division of responsibilities; and
- what will happen if one of the partners dies.

There is a tendency to assume you will work things out as you go along, particularly if you are going into business with a friend. However, there are many potential pitfalls in this approach, and although it may seem legalistic it is a better idea to have written clearly who is responsible for what aspect of the business rather than put your partnership under strain by not having a clear understanding from the beginning. You should in any case think twice before going into business with a friend. You need to assess objectively their strengths and weaknesses as a potential businessperson, as well as how you will get along with them under pressure. As with a sole trader structure you are personally responsible for any debts incurred by your business, even if your partner made the decisions that led the business into difficulties. The partnership itself does not pay income tax; instead it distributes the partnership income to the partners and the partners then pay tax on their own share. In some cases, some partnership profits or losses are distributed to a relative or associated person. However, if IRD consider this distribution to be excessive or unreasonable, it may be reallocated.

Limited company

As distinct from partnerships and sole-trading operations, if you own a company you are not personally responsible for its debts. The company has a separate formal and legal existence and your liability is limited to the extent of your share ownership. However it is worth noting that if you have to borrow money to set up your company, banks will commonly require personal guarantees from the directors, so you will not be protected by the company's legal status. You can either buy a company off the shelf from one of the businesses that specialise in selling shelf companies (advertised in the Yellow Pages) or you can set one up yourself. Company incorporation in New Zealand was simplified under the Companies Act of 1993. There is now only one type of company and there is no longer any minimum or maximum number of directors or shareholders required. To set up a company you require the following:

- a name;
- at least one shareholder;
- at least one director;
- at least one share;
- a registered office; and
- an address.

The director and shareholder can be one and the same so in fact it only needs one person to set up a company. You begin by registering the name you have chosen with the Registrar of Companies. Obviously you have to pick a name that no-one else has used already. Once the name has been approved you can apply to have your company registered. Along with your application (which must state the company's name, registered office and address) you must include consents from all directors to act as such and certificates stating that they are not disqualified from acting, consents by shareholders to take the stated number of shares, notice from the Registrar reserving the company's name, and the constitution of the company

■ It is now possible to incorporate a company over the internet, by lodging incorporation documentation with the Companies Office (www.companies. govt.nz), which is a Business Unit in the Ministry of Economic Development (www. med.govt. nz). This process has made registering a company significantly cheaper and easier, as, theoretically, it can be done in a matter of minutes. The first step is to reserve your company's name online, which costs NZ$10. The second step is registering the company, which costs NZ$50. You will receive an electronic response from the Registrar of Companies and a certificate of incorporation, which you can print out.

if there is one. Providing certain conditions are met, directors and shareholders can elect that their company becomes a qualifying and/or loss attributing qualifying company, by completing an election form (IR436). Benefits can include the ability to make tax free capital distributions and offset company losses to shareholders.

■ IDEAS FOR NEW BUSINESSES

Most new immigrants will need a chance to look around once they arrive in New Zealand before deciding what line of business to take up. There are a lot of established avenues for the first-time businessperson, as you will see when looking at the 'Businesses For Sale' section in the papers. Should you want to consider trying something different, the following suggestions may give you some ideas.

Catering

Running a catering business from home, particularly if you are able to provide authentic ethnic foods or have a point of difference of some kind such as all organic foods, can be a good idea. However, it is not as easy as simply preparing food in your own home – you must consider food safety regulations if you want to work from home. In New Zealand all food preparation for sale or promotion must take place on approved premises. This means you must either register your food business with your local Council environmental health officers or have an approved food safety programme through the Ministry of Health. You must also make your business available for regular inspections to ensure food safety. Most local council websites should offer information. This is not always a commercially viable way of setting up your first small business, but other options might include offering your services to a local social club or ethnic group, provided their premised are registered for food preparation. Alternatively, you could provide your services as a caterer/chef rather than a commercial food supplier. In all likelihood, this would mean hiring your skills out on an hourly basis (maybe around NZ$25 an hour), but this does mean that you must undertake all food preparation in the customer's home. If you choose to work in this way, be aware that you are not allowed to sell any of the food you prepare commercially.

Accommodation

As long as the tourist boom continues, providing accommodation is likely to be a reasonably safe bet. B&Bs are not as common in New Zealand as they are in the UK, although the idea is beginning to catch on as an inexpensive accommodation option. However, you will need to research the potential market carefully. Many tourists arrive on package deals with accommodation organised through the large hotel chains. Another relatively undeveloped type of accommodation in New Zealand is the country house hotel. While there are a number of luxury country lodges at top prices, the market is by no means oversupplied at the high end.

Flower growers and exporters

Big increases are being expected for New Zealand's richly coloured exotic flowers. There has been a recent surge of interest in Europe and the USA, with Japan the most significant market. There are other markets that look promising, including France, Germany, Switzerland and East Asia. Exports of cut flowers and bulbs are currently worth about NZ$60million annually, but demand is growing steadily.

Investing in property

Buying residential property or holiday homes to rent out is one investment opportunity. Other options include investing in vineyards, orchards or farms. The best bargains these days are probably to be found in the South Island, but you should take your time and have a careful look around.

Farm-sharing

This is a new theme in New Zealand farming, and is gaining in popularity. Basically it involves clubbing together with other like-minded buyers. Owners may have differing degrees of ownership and responsibility for running the farm, or may have their farm/s run by professionals, while they carry on their primary homes and employment elsewhere. Lifestyle blocks are another solution, offering a similar chance to enjoy some of the space that New Zealand has to offer.

IT recruitment

Although there are several large specialist recruitment agencies in the IT area, there is still room for expansion, particularly if you target your business towards providing an avenue for employers to access a selection of IT specialists looking to immigrate to New Zealand. Technology skills shortages remain a serious issue for employers, and these jobs often pay more than those in any other sector. In late 2007 there was a distinct increase in the higher end of the remuneration range, indicating that employers are paying their staff, particularly top performers, more.

Gourmet foodstuffs

With such a wide variety of produce available, it's no wonder that special New Zealand-made gourmet products are proving hugely popular. Export markets present the greatest long-term growth opportunities. Fruit pastes and pates, to complement cheeses, and fruit vinegars, are an innovative manufacturing and export line that is reaping rewards. There are many opportunities to trade on New Zealand's 'clean and green' image by coming up with unique ideas in organic food and beverage manufacturing.

■ Olive oil is one of the country's newest and fastest-growing gourmet food industries, and the premium quality oil is gaining international attention. Excellent olives are produced in the Marlborough and Hawke's Bay regions. Some businesses are also beginning to manufacture avocado oil.

■ RUNNING A BUSINESS

Employing staff

You must register as an employer before you actually employ anyone. To register, you must fill in an IRD form, which you can do online (www.ird.govt.nz). You will need an IRD number to do this (see below).

As an employer you may negotiate individual contracts of employment with your staff, or a collective contract with some or all of your employees. Employees can either nominate a bargaining agent in the negotiations or represent themselves directly. While there is a lot of flexibility over negotiating terms and conditions relevant to your workplace, certain statutory protections remain for workers.

Important points for employers

- There is a legal minimum hourly wage of NZ$9.00 for workers aged 16–17 years and NZ$11.25 for employees aged 18 years and over.
- There are 11 paid public holidays. All employees are entitled to a paid day off on a public holiday if it would otherwise be a working day for them. These public holidays are separate from and additional to annual holidays. If the Christmas and New Year holidays fall on a weekend, and your employee doesn't normally work on the weekend, the holiday is transferred to the following Monday or Tuesday so that the employee still gets a paid day off if they normally work those days. Other public holidays are celebrated on the days on which they fall. In years where Waitangi Day or Anzac Day fall at the weekend, employees who do not normally work on the weekend have no entitlement to payment for the day.
- Under the Holidays Act 2003, all employees are entitled to a minimum of three weeks paid annual holidays. On 1 April 2007 this was increased, and employees are now entitled to four weeks annual holidays.

- Annual leave accrues after one year of service and two weeks' leave should be made available within the next six months.
- Annual leave is paid at the rate of average weekly earnings or not less than the ordinary rate of pay when leave began, whichever is greater.
- Anyone employed on a part-time basis may agree with the employer that holiday pay will be included in the hourly rate, although it must be shown as a separate amount.
- Untaken annual leave and lieu days must be paid out when employment terminates.
- There are provisions for special leave in the case of bereavement, sickness (of partners, children or dependent parents) and parental leave (both maternity and paternity, although new dads get less time off than new mums).

When you register as an employer, IRD will send you an information pack containing all the books and forms you need to get started, See chapter on Working Conditions for further details. For more information, contact Business New Zealand. Or see the Employment Relations Service website (www.ers.govt.nz), or call the ERS Infoline 0800 20 90 20 or +64 9 969 2950.

 Business New Zealand: Level 6, Lumley House, 3–11 Hunter Street, PO Box 1925, Wellington; (04) 496 6555; fax (04) 496 6550; admin@businessnz. org.nz; www.businessnz.org.nz

Contracts

Employment contracts must contain a section on dispute settlement, and there are standard procedures for dealing with personal grievance cases against employers for unjustified dismissal.

Wages and time record

You are required to keep a wages and time record for each employee. Wages must be paid in cash unless there is an agreement to pay by cheque or direct credit. All deductions must be agreed, unless required by law. Employees or their representatives are entitled to see their own wage and time record and to claim back any arrears or wrongly-made deductions.

Taxes

Your other legal obligations as an employer concern taxation. You are required to deduct payroll taxes (known as PAYE) from your employees' wages and make returns of the same to the Inland Revenue Department. Legally required taxes include: PAYE (including ACC earner premiums); levies; child support payments; and student loan repayments. Other tax deductions may include withholding tax (from payments to people who work for you on a contract-for-service basis), superannuation scheme contributions, etc. If you provide any perks for staff as part of their employment package, then you have to pay fringe benefit taxes on them. (See Taxation below for more details.) For more information about your tax obligations as an employer, contact the IRD.

Inland Revenue Department 0800 377 772; www.ird.govt.nz/businesses

Accountants

As has been noted, the major reason for small business failure is poor management, usually poor financial control. You would be well advised to consult an accountant who specialises in dealing with small businesses to help you look after this important area. You can find a list of local accountants through biz (www.biz.org.nz), through your local Small Business Enterprise Centre (www.sbecnz.org.nz), or through your local Chamber of Commerce. In the case of companies, there are certain statutory requirements you must fulfil with regard to financial reporting. Every company is required to keep a full, true and complete record of its affairs and transactions, including providing a Profit and Loss Account and a Balance Sheet. Accounting practice is regulated by the New Zealand Institute of Chartered Accountants which provides mandatory standards for company financial reporting called Statements of Standard Accounting Practice (SSAPs). Any material departure from these has to be disclosed in financial statements.

Taxation

The Inland Revenue Department publishes a guide for small businesses on their tax obligations. You can obtain copies from any IRD office or see the website (www.ird.govt.nz). They also run the Small Business Advisory Service which advises beginning business people on taxes they need to know about, what records to keep, how to complete tax returns and when to file returns and make payments. To get in touch with the service, you simply indicate when you register for GST or as a new employer that you would like an advisory consultation. You can either go into an IRD office for an appointment or an advisor will come and visit your office. Information about business income tax, getting an IRD number, provisional tax, depreciation, claiming expenses, records and tax on interest and dividends is also available from biz (www.biz.org.nz)

Applying for an IRD number

One of the first requirements of any type of business operation is an Inland Revenue Department (IRD) number. Your business must have its own IRD number if it is a partnership, company, non-profit organisation or trust/estate. Each person in a partnership must also have their own personal IRD number. If you are a sole trader, you may use your personal IRD number rather than obtaining a different one for your business. You will need a passport or birth certificate as identification for a personal IRD number. In the case of a partnership, you must provide the IRD numbers of the partners, and for a company IRD, a copy of the certificate of incorporation. If you are an individual in business you will need to fill in an IR595 form, or an IR596 if you are a partnership, trust, company or other organisation. Both types of forms can be downloaded as pdfs from the IRD website (www.ird.govt.nz/yoursituation-bus/starting/registrations/), or you can telephone the Business Income Tax and General Enquiries Line on 0800 377 774 (+64 4 978 0779 from overseas).

Types of tax

There are four major types of taxes which you will have to deal with when doing business in New Zealand; income tax and company tax, Goods and Services Tax (GST), Accident Compensation Levies and Fringe Benefit Tax.

■ Income tax and company tax

Income tax is payable by all persons or business entities. Individuals are taxed on a progressive rate system whereby 19.5% is payable on earnings up to NZ$38,000, 33% over NZ$38,001 and 39% over NZ$60,001. Resident companies are taxed at a flat rate of 33% on income earned, whereas non-resident companies are taxed at 38%. If your gross annual PAYE deductions are less than NZ$100,000 then you are classed as a small employer. PAYE deductions must be paid to the IRD monthly, by the 20th of the month following the payment they were deducted from.

Income tax is payable on the net profit from your business, which is all income that comes into your business, minus allowable business expenses. Business income is income earned from goods and services you sell (including invoices you've issued but have yet to receive payment for). If you have not been making tax payments during your first year in business, your tax will need to be paid by 7 February in the following year if you have a 31 March balance date (or by 7 April if you have an agent). If you want a balance date other than 31 March, you must apply in writing stating your reasons. After your first year in business you may be required to pay income tax in three instalments throughout the year. This is called provisional tax.

■ Goods and services tax (GST)

All businesses with an anticipated turnover greater than NZ$40,000 per annum are required to register for GST. GST is not a tax on your own business, it is a tax on sales to your customers (called 'taxable supplies') which you collect on behalf of the IRD. You must charge and account for GST of 12.5% on these supplies. Under the NZ$40,000 threshold you can choose whether or not to register. If you deal with other registered businesses it may be worthwhile because they will be charging you GST which you will not be able to claim back. You should be aware, however, of the extra accounting processes and time that will be required. You pay GST on all your business inputs, supplies, etc. You then add GST to all the sales you make. You make GST returns every six months. For more GST information contact the IRD (0800 377 776) or obtain the IR365 booklet (as a pdf from the website) and complete the attached IR360 registration form.

■ Fringe benefit tax and accident compensation

If you provide any extra benefits to your employees, such as a company car, then you must pay fringe benefit tax. This includes benefits provided through someone other than an employer. Even if you do not provide any perks, you must send in a yearly return. For an FBT guide, see www.ird.govt.nz/fringebenefittax/. ACC is a fixed levy on each member of your workforce, however, from June 1998, there is a provision for workplace accident insurance to be arranged through private insurance firms. ACC earner premiums are included in PAYE deductions.

Tax returns

Different returns will be required depending on whether you are a sole trader, a company or a partnership. The tax year runs from 1st April to 31 March, and although businesses can use different year-end dates for reporting purposes, the balance date will be related to the nearest 31st March for tax purposes. Sole traders, partnerships and companies must all complete different returns. Each company shareholder must also file an individual return. Included with each return must be a copy of the accounts. It is now possible to file monthly payroll details to the IRD online, using the ir-File Service. Large employers are obliged to do this, but small employers are encouraged to do so as well. For an interactive demonstration and registration instructions see the website (http://ir-file.ird.govt.nz) or telephone 0800 473 829. For more information about any aspect of taxation, contact your local Inland Revenue Office, see the website (www.ird.govt.nz) or phone the IRD General Inquiries line (0800 377 774).

For more general information about business in New Zealand, see www.business.govt.nz. You should seek professional advice as appropriate.

Useful websites

- www.business.govt.nz – General advice about starting or buying a business in New Zealand.
- www.ird.govt.nz/yoursituation-bus/starting/ – Taxation information for those starting a business, from the Inland Revenue Department.
- www2.careers.govt.nz/be_your_own_boss.html – Helping you find out about the type of skills you need to succeed in self-employment. Also includes links to sources of information about how to set up and run your own business.
- www.workandincome.govt.nz/documents/brochures/start-your-own-business.pdf – Information to help you decide whether starting your own business is the right decision for you, and provides ideas for places to turn for practical help and support, including information about the Enterprise Allowance and Business Training and Advice Grant.
- www.nzte.govt.nz/section/14189/12932.aspx – Business Steps: a practical guidebook for small business. Explains the basic requirements for being in business. Download is free.
- www.business.govt.nz – search for 'Your Business Plan' for information from a variety of sources about developing your business plan.
- www.companies.govt.nz/cms – Information about registering your company online, reserving a company name, and maintaining your company details online.
- www.ers.dol.govt.nz/audienceinfo/employers – Information for employers.
- www.businessmentor.org.nz – You are eligible to apply for a business mentor if your business has been trading for more than 12 months, employs fewer than 25 people and provides you with your primary source of income. There is an online application form, and you will have to pay a registration fee, but the mentors' services are volunteered free of charge.
- www.osh.dol.govt.nz – Information and publications about workplace health and safety.

Time Off

New Zealand's international reputation is for a clean, green, outdoor lifestyle, and there are unlimited opportunities for getting out there and enjoying some of the most beautiful scenery in the world. Whether you are an adrenaline junkie or prefer a gentle ramble towards a picnic spot, you will discover many lovely locations to enjoy your outdoor leisure activity of choice. If cultural activities, café society, or culinary pursuits and wine-based explorations are more your thing, you will also find plenty to keep you busy in New Zealand. The country is home to numerous established and experimental theatre groups, a thriving and innovative music industry, many interesting film-makers, craftspeople and artists, as well as a wonderful selection of restaurants, boutique food-producers, established and developing vineyards and talented wine-makers.

Sporting and fitness activities abound all around the country, and popular sports include: walking, tramping, cycling, mountain-biking, climbing, fishing, running, swimming, surfing, skiing, kayaking, canoeing, rafting, sailing, golf, snowboarding, hunting, rugby, rugby league, cricket, squash and tennis. Organised activities range from local sports teams and fitness training groups to such high-profile events as the famous annual Speights Coast-to-Coast Multisports Race in the South Island, which covers a gruelling course of 243 km across the Southern Alps. Most New Zealand sports, leisure and interest magazines can be obtained from: www. isubscribe.co.nz.

■ SPORT AND FITNESS

Cricket runs a close second to rugby in the interest of New Zealanders, although most New Zealanders bemoan the poor performance of their national team. However, test matches are followed closely on the television, even when broadcast from the other hemisphere in the middle of the night. In fact, television news bulletins always cover cricket and rugby – from watching New Zealand TV, you could be mistaken for thinking there are only two sports played in the

Taking it seriously

What can you say about a country where a former Prime Minister gets involved with the choice over the coach of the rugby team? New Zealanders are intensely nationalistic when it comes to identifying with the successes of their national teams, particularly the All Blacks rugby team. Losing a rugby match can cast a gloom over the entire nation. It is about more than just losing a game. New Zealand is such a small player in the international political and economic order, that the fact that the country's elite sports teams are capable of taking on the big guys and winning becomes a matter of national pride.

country. Much less coverage is given to the Silver Ferns, the women's netball team, although they are more consistently successful on the world stage. For a brief and glorious period the soccer team (the 'All Whites') were in the limelight when they qualified for the World Cup.

New Zealanders are not just enthusiastic about watching sport. A large number of people participate in their spare time. Nearly 50% of the population belongs to some kind of sport, fitness or leisure club. The most popular activities are aquatic sports such as swimming, diving, rowing, or water polo. As well as team sports such as hockey, netball, rugby and soccer, an increasing number of New Zealanders are involved in individual sports like surfing, snowboarding, mountain biking, rock climbing, skateboarding, tramping, triathlon competitions, or motorcross. Adrenaline sports are on the increase in the country, as thrill seekers face the challenges presented by the mountains and rivers around them. From the birthplace of bungy jumping, adventures such as black water rafting (rafting in caves) rap jumping (abseiling face-down on a building) and river sledding (going down white water rapids on a boogie board) are on offer for large sums of money. New and more terrifying sports emerge each year. But if you do not count yourself among the adrenaline junkies there are plenty of more rational and relaxing sports and outdoor activities available including scuba diving, whale watching and swimming with dolphins in the open sea.

The New Zealand Adventure Company specialises in customised travel and activity packages in New Zealand, arranging activities, car rental and accommodation tailored to your requirements, or you can choose from one of their carefully constructed packages. For further information, see: www.nzadventureco.com or email: info@nzadventureco.com.

Recreational fishing restrictions

Fishing is a popular sport in New Zealand, and there is an abundance of clean rivers, lakes and fish life. However, there are regulations concerning New Zealand fishing in order to protect the resource. Amateur fishermen are not allowed to take more than the daily limit, sell or trade what they caught, or catch undersized fish. There

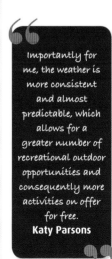
Importantly for me, the weather is more consistent and almost predictable, which allows for a greater number of recreational outdoor opportunities and consequently more activities on offer for free.
Katy Parsons

MAF Information Bureau: ASB Bank House, 101–103 The Terrace, PO Box 2526, Wellington; (04) 474 4100; fax (04) 474 4111; www.maf.govt.nz/mafnet (there is an online enquiries form)

are also restrictions on the minimum size of shellfish and lobsters. Fishermen who operate commercially are required to have a fishing permit. For more information, contact the Ministry of Agriculture and Forestry Information Bureau. For great guided troutfishing trips in Hawkes Bay, see www.jacktrout.co.nz, email troutfishing@jacktrout.co.nz, or telephone (06) 877 7642.

Useful sports and fitness websites

- www.activenewzealand.com
- www.alpinehunting.com
- www.canoeandkayak.co.nz
- www.coastalkayakers.co.nz
- www.coasttocoast.co.nz
- www.coolrunning.co.nz
- www.cyclechallenge.com
- www.cyclingnz.com
- www.fergskayaks.co.nz
- www.fishnhunt.co.nz

- www.fourcorners.co.nz/new-zealand/skiing/
- www.hunting-fishing.co.nz
- www.huntingnewzealand.info
- www.jacktrout.co.nz
- www.mountainrunning.org.nz
- www.natureshighway.co.nz
- www.nzclubrugby.co.nz
- www.rugby.co.nz
- www.snow.co.nz
- www.snowreports.co.nz
- www.troutntrophy.co.nz

■ ENTERTAINMENT AND CULTURE

New Zealand may not be as well known overseas for its musicians and artists (pop band Crowded House and opera diva Dame Kiri Te Kanawa excepted) as it is for its sports men and women, but in fact there is a lively local cultural scene. Increasingly, performers from New Zealand are succeeding internationally. Kiri Te Kanawa is respected throughout New Zealand, not so much because every household worships opera, but because like the All Blacks she is a New Zealander succeeding internationally. She attracts huge audiences when she returns home to perform. Amongst younger generations, musicians such as Bic Runga and Holly Smith, and bands such as Fat Freddy's Drop, The Black Seeds, The Mint Chicks and The Datsuns are also achieving some level of international success and are increasingly touring and being promoted overseas, mainly in the UK and the USA.

There are three fully professional orchestra companies, based in Auckland, Wellington and Christchurch, and there are a number of semi-professional and amateur regional orchestras. International soloists and chamber groups visit frequently, and every two years the Wellington Festival of the Performing Arts attracts some highly regarded orchestras and ensembles from all over the world.

Other types of performing arts thrive, particularly in Wellington where there are a number of professional theatres, the Royal New Zealand Ballet, several contemporary dance companies and the New Zealand Symphony Orchestra.

The New Zealand film scene has enjoyed much success both at home and overseas. *The Piano*, made by New Zealander Jane Campion, is one of line of internationally acclaimed films which includes *Heavenly Creatures*, *Once Were Warriors*, and *Angel at my Table*. There is much current international interest in New Zealand film makers, as director Peter Jackson's trilogy of *The Lord of the Rings* has had tremendous international success since the first film was released in 2001.

New Zealand visual arts are on display all over the country, with fine art galleries and public spaces in many different centres. Famous homegrown fine artists include Frances Hodgkin and Colin McCahon. The main arts centres are Auckland, Wellington, Christchurch and Dunedin, and the public galleries house regular exhibitions as well as regular displays. Craft traditions are strong in New Zealand, and the work of studio jewellers, printmakers, glass artists and ceramicists can be found in many galleries and art outlets, particularly in the larger centres.

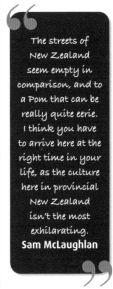

" The streets of New Zealand seem empty in comparison, and to a Pom that can be really quite eerie. I think you have to arrive here at the right time in your life, as the culture here in provincial New Zealand isn't the most exhilarating.
Sam McLaughlan

Useful websites

- www.amplifier.co.nz – New Zealand's premier site for listening to, downloading and purchasing New Zealand music.
- www.aucklandartgallery.govt.nz – The most extensive collection of national and international art in New Zealand; also hosts visiting international exhibitions.
- www.christhurchartgallery.org.nz – Hosts touring exhibitions, and holds a permanent collection of New Zealand painting. Also home to a sculpture garden.
- www.citygallery.org.nz – Holds well-curated and interesting exhibitions in great spaces. Located in the heart of Wellington.
- www.dunedin.art.museum/ – Dunedin Public Art Gallery, located in the middle of Dunedin. Interesting programme combining special exhibitions with informative tours and a good permanent collection.
- www.danz.org.nz – Contemporary dance organization, based in the Wellington Arts Centre and in Tamaki.
- www.eventfinder.co.nz – Tickets and booking information for music, dance, cinema, musicals, pop concerts, and community events around the country.
- www.fingers.co.nz – Contemporary studio jewellery from New Zealand makers, in Auckland.
- www.loveart.co.nz – Original NZ art, sculpture and contemporary jewellery for sale.
- www.nzballet.org.nz – The Royal New Zealand Ballet.
- www.nzcinema.co.nz. Independent guide to NZ cinema scene, including listings and a cinema finder.
- www.nzso.co.nz – The New Zealand Symphony Orchestra.
- www.statementsgallery.co.nz – Napier gallery that exhibits and sells quality original contemporary paintings, sculpture, studio glass, ceramics and jewellery.

ACTIVITIES FOR CHILDREN

Children are well catered for in New Zealand, and are generally welcome everywhere apart from pubs, bars clubs and other obviously adults-only venues. Most residential areas have public parks and reserves fairly close by, and these often include children's play areas such as swings, slides and sometimes skateboard facilities. In the suburbs or within the cities, there are public places for older children to go and amuse themselves with their friends. Many towns have public swimming pools, which are not expensive to visit and have lifeguards on duty so that you can be sure your swimmers are safe.

Public libraries are another great resource for children and adults alike, and many libraries host events such as 'storytimes' and readings by visiting or local authors specifically tailored for children, especially during school holidays. Some of the most popular extra-curricular activities with New

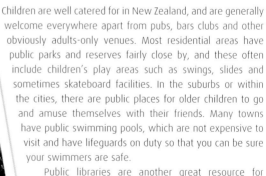

Zealand children include sports teams and dancing
classes, swimming instruction and music lessons. Ask
your new friends in the local area to recommend the
best instructors/classes for your child, or visit venues for
more information. Great family activities with children
include bush-walks, tramping, going to the beach
(make sure they swim only between the flags though
and keep your eyes on them at all times), fishing,
cycling, visits to the local zoo or wildlife parks, local
museums, mini-golf, go-karts.

■ SOCIALISING

Meeting people and making friends

Kiwis have similar values and a similar way of life to people in many Western
countries, but there are unique features to Kiwi social values. New Zealand does
not have a strong class system, or major social tensions compared to many other
countries around the world. Needless formality is generally disliked and regarded
as being old fashioned, a bit stuffy, or (the worst of all) a sign of 'putting on airs';
people tend to see each other as equals. It is considered quite normal to call round
to see friends or neighbours without a specific invitation, and most Kiwis want
you to feel comfortable visiting them in their homes. Again, excessive 'guest-and-
host' formality will be frowned on and while your hosts will probably go out of
their way to offer refreshments of one sort or another they will often expect you
to just make yourself at home and say if there is anything you need or want. There
is no English-style 'front room' rule to be adhered to and it is perfectly acceptable
to request a 'grand tour' of a new friend's house when you visit. Neighbours will
often drop in and introduce themselves to new people moving in, and perhaps
take them some baking.

For all the immediate friendliness, New Zealanders can be quite reserved in some respects. They are not likely to tell you much about their feelings or values until you get to know them well.

What's acceptable

Kiwis can also be very politically correct, particularly in the larger cities; derogatory, patronising or sexually-motivated remarks, relating particularly to gender or race, may be deemed wholly unacceptable. Such comments are unlikely to go unchallenged and may land you in hot water. Younger generations tend to be especially passionate about egalitarian social values. However, in more rural, 'blokey' settings, or among older generations you may find the exact opposite is true! As with so many situations, it is best to look before you leap.

Gay, lesbian, bisexual and transgendered New Zealand

New Zealanders are typically quite laid-back and non-judgmental about the choices of others, but as is true everywhere people in the big cities are usually more accepting and understanding in their attitudes. Auckland and Wellington have the most open and varied gay and lesbian communities. New Zealand does not have specific anti-discrimination laws tailored to the transgender communities, although it is generally assumed that the general anti-discrimination laws cover all transgendered people under the 'sex discrimination' of the Human Rights Act. Post-operative transsexuals have the right to marry as their new sex. The Property (Relationships) Act of 2000 gives de facto couples, whether of opposite or the same sex, the same property rights as married couples on the break-up of a relationship. The Civil Union Act (2004) established the institution of Civil Union for same-sex and opposite-sex couples. Government agencies, including the Royal New Zealand Navy and the police have 'gay-friendly' policies. There are no specific barriers to gay individuals adopting children, aside from the fact that men cannot adopt female children and gay couples cannot adopt as couples. There are a number of gay and lesbian Members of Parliament, including Chris Carter, Tim Barnett, Chris Finlayson, Charles Chauvel, Maryan Street and Marilyn Waring. Georgina Beyer became the world's first transsexual mayor in 1995, when she became mayor of Carterton.

FACT

Homosexual sex was officially decriminalised in New Zealand only in 1986, with the Homosexual Law Reform Act.

The Hero Festival, held in Auckland every summer, is the biggest celebration for gay, lesbian, bisexual and transgendered people in New Zealand, and the social and events calendar is packed for a fortnight. The programme includes the Big Gay Out, Heroic Gardens, parties, fashion parades, art exhibitions and sporting events. For more information and a festival programme see www.hero.org.nz. Gay Ski Week is held in Queenstown at the end of the winter, and incorporates a Dyke Hike as well as non-ski events such as other adventure activities for those who wish to attend but not to ski. For detailed information see www.gayskiweeknz.com.

The Auckland PRIDE Centre is an umbrella organisation for LGBT groups in Auckland, founded in 1988. It maintains the largest computer database of LGBT information for the whole of New Zealand. PRIDE publishes newsletters and provides a lending library of books, magazines and newspapers for members and also supplies a LGBT map of Auckland showing the locations and giving contact details for venues, services and organizations around the city. For more information see www.pride.org.nz.

Useful websites

- www.dorothyssister.co.nz - Friendly café and bar at Three Lamps on Ponsonby Road in Auckland.
- www.gay.co.nz – Free gay, lesbian, bisexual and transgendered personals.
- www.gaynz.com – News and events website for the gay and lesbian communities.
- www.gaystaynewzealand.com – An online reservation system listing a comprehensive range of gay men's and lesbian owned, established 'gay and lesbian friendly' and Rainbow Tourism Accredited homestays, B&Bs, guest houses, hotels, luxury lodges and inns around the country.
- www.gaytravel.net.nz – A Rainbow Tourism Accredited site with tourism, accommodation and package tour information. Also includes links to gay and lesbian venues, restaurants, bars and nightclubs, as well as saunas and cruise clubs.
- www.gaywellington.org – Originally known as the Wellington Gay Welfare Group, established over 25 years ago. Useful listings, events, support and information.
- www.urgebar.co.nz – Friendly venue, Auckland's longest running gay men's bar. Open late. 490 Karangahape Road, Auckland.
- www.wellington.lesbian.net.nz – Events, groups and general information fro lesbians in the Wellington area.

■ SOCIAL ATTITUDES

Perhaps as a result of their pioneering forebears, New Zealanders are an independent people. There is a great tradition of self-reliance, whether it comes to building an extension on the back of the house, or cutting off ties with the rest of the Western alliance during the Cold War period by refusing American nuclear armed ships access to New Zealand ports. Innovation is respected. Finding an ingenious, low-cost solution to a problem was obviously an asset in pioneering days. There is even a phrase for it, 'Kiwi ingenuity', which describes a pragmatic, imaginative approach to problem solving.

Despite approving of innovative and non-traditional approaches to problem solving, rural New Zealand remains quite conservative in outlook. Innovative or alternative lifestyles are not widely approved of. However tolerance is also a New Zealand characteristic, perhaps because the independent streak in the average New Zealander leads them to respect the rights of others to live their lives as they choose. Urban New Zealand is more liberal in outlook. Green issues receive quite a lot of support, perhaps because New Zealanders are aware they live in one of the last largely unspoilt wilderness areas in the world and they have some responsibility to hand it on to their children without ruining it. There is strong support for biculturalism and multiculturalism in theory. However *Pakeha* (Europeans) New Zealanders can sometimes be heard complaining that government treats the Maori more favourably. In fact positive discrimination programmes of the type common in the USA are more perceived than actual. There are, however, special grants for Maori business and for educational purposes. Few institutions

Kiwi identity

Like the Welsh and the Scots before them, New Zealanders feel the need to assert their own identity to prove that they are different from the English and the colonial power which shaped the early period of settlement, and hence became the original model for New Zealand culture. The need to assert themselves usually manifests itself as a fairly critical attitude towards English life, attitudes, culture and climate, on the part of those who have visited that country and even by some that have not. This criticism is usually not intended to be rude or offensive, rather it functions as a form of commiseration for the English for having had the misfortune to have been born there rather than in New Zealand. Reciprocal ruthless honesty about the drawbacks of living in New Zealand is unlikely to be welcomed however. In fact these kinds of Kiwis tend to be defensive about New Zealand, even though they think its merits ought to be self-evident.

A country pub

run a formal quota system although all are required to have an equal employment policy. Maori leaders acknowledge that Maori society is increasingly dependent on welfare benefits and Maori workers are more likely to be unemployed than *Pakeha*.

Smoking

Smoking is a lot less socially acceptable in New Zealand than it is in Europe. All forms of tobacco promotion, advertising and sponsorship are banned. Public buildings, including shopping malls, are smoke-free zones by law, and all workplaces are legally required to have smoke-free areas, and these areas must include shared space. The basis of government policy is that those who do not smoke should not be exposed to other people's smoke. Some employers do have smoking rooms, but these are increasingly rare. Smoking has recently been banned in bars, pubs or nightclubs, and many Kiwis are strongly in favour of this. If you are visiting a New Zealand home, it is perfectly acceptable for your host to request that you only smoke outside or in a particular place, and of course you should always ask permission before lighting up in someone else's house! Bear in mind that even a large number of Kiwi smokers don't smoke inside their own homes.

■ EATING OUT

Eating out isn't the letdown it once was, now that the country is no longer all that interested in 'traditional' British cooking. The quality of restaurants in the main cities is very high, as is the range of different international food styles on offer. Restaurants

FACT

■ Within the New Zealand population, roughly around 20% of Europeans and 50% of Maori smoke.

are constantly seeking to define a distinctive 'New Zealand cuisine', and come up with delicious combinations of fresh fruits, vegetables and meat.

The traditional New Zealand European diet was mostly derived from the 'meat-and-three-veg' eating patterns of British immigrants, influenced by the relative abundance of dairy products and cheap mutton and beef. New Zealanders still tend to consume too much cholesterol and saturated fat and as a result have one of the highest rates of heart disease in the western world. This is changing slowly as a result of government campaigns promoting healthier eating styles and a new interest in the diet and food of Asian countries. During the week the main meal is usually in the evening, which many New Zealanders call 'tea' or 'dinner'.

There is a range of fast-food options in New Zealand, ranging from hot pies, quick kebabs and the ubiquitous fish and chips to higher-priced takeaways from chains such as Hell Pizza, Burger Wisconsin and Burger Fuel. The usual inescapable international burger and chicken chains can be found in New Zealand as well but apart from these places quality is generally high, with meals based on interesting combinations of fresh ingredients. Food halls are popular in the main urban centres, and these will typically include Thai, Chinese, Indian, Malaysian and Japanese outlets.

The improvement in the domestic wine industry has helped to turn New Zealanders into more discerning gastronomes. There is a lot of interest in European food trends. Many New Zealand restaurants have what is called a BYO (Bring Your Own) licence. They are not allowed to sell alcoholic beverages; instead the customer brings their own wine, which the restaurant opens. They usually make a small charge called corkage for this (about NZ$5). The advantage of BYO establishments is that you avoid the huge mark up restaurants usually put on wine and you have a much wider choice of what to drink. BYO restaurants tend to be cheaper than fully licensed places, at around NZ$50 to NZ$95 a head for a three-course meal, not

TIP

Ask locals for their recommendations when you are looking for restaurants, as community favourites usually enjoy well-deserved good reputations and customer loyalty.

including what was paid for the wine. A three course meal at a licensed restaurant is more likely to be in the NZ$70 to NZ$150 range, including the cost of wine. The cheapest and often the most interesting food can be found at fashionable cafés, which have mushroomed in the big cities. You can usually eat well in these sorts of places for less than NZ$20.

Although there are world-class culinary offerings to be sampled around the country, particularly in the cities, the situation in small towns can be grim and 'greasies', such as Chinese takeaways or fish and chips, might be your best bet.

You will often see 'tea rooms' in the smaller towns as you pass through, and many of these will provide a selection of solid stodge along the 'pies and toasted sandwiches' line to heavily fortify you for another leg of your journey. Of course, there are many good local restaurants in small towns but these may not be immediately obvious or easy to find, so it is worth stopping to ask someone who looks like they might know where you can get a decent meal.

Vineyards open to the public sometimes include a restaurant, particularly in areas such as Marlborough, Martinborough and Hawkes Bay, but these may operate quite strict service hours so it is best to know where you are going ahead of time rather than just taking your chances. Indian restaurants are less common than in other countries, but other Asian food establishments, especially Japanese, Thai and Malaysian, are becoming more prolific. The fish and chips in takeaways are usually fresh and tasty, as instead of frying chips and other goodies in advance and letting them dry out under hot lamps, they fry your order up individually. Fish and chips still come wrapped in newspaper in most places too, with no European health regulations to interfere. No one has yet died in New Zealand of newsprint poisoning.

Tipping and service charges

Gratuities are not necessary in New Zealand, and service charges are not added onto hotel or restaurant bills. However, a tip as recognition of extra service or consideration would be appreciated.

◼ PUBLIC LIBRARIES

Public libraries in New Zealand are excellent quality facilities, and are amongst the most heavily-used of public libraries anywhere in the world. They are provided by local government, and are funded by people living in the local area. They offer browsing, studying and borrowing facilities as well as local history collections, reference materials and newspapers for use in the library. Most services are provided free of charge, although there may be fees for borrowing certain items such as music and DVDs. Local libraries usually offer computer and internet facilities,

South Christchurch library

as well as story reading and holiday programmes for children, and in some cases evening classes and other community groups for adults as well. In larger centres, a main central library will maintain a network of suburban libraries, and may also provide mobile library services. Many libraries offer online accounts for borrowers, allowing the reservation of popular titles and a messaging service alerting you when your books are ready for collection.

See: www.nzlibraries.com for further information and for details of your local public library.

■ MARRIAGE

Anybody can marry in New Zealand, as long as they are legally free to marry. Under New Zealand law this means:

■ They are not married already and if either person has been married, the marriage has been dissolved by a court of law;

■ They are old enough. The parties must be over 16, although consent is required if either party is under 20 years old;

■ They are not closely related by blood, marriage or adoption. Details of these "prohibited" relationships appear on the form Notice of Intended Marriage, which is used to apply for a marriage licence.

Marriage FAQs

Do I need to apply for a marriage licence before I get to New Zealand?

No. However, if you are arriving in New Zealand with very little time before your planned nuptials it may be in your interest to submit a completed Notice of Intended Marriage (BDM58) to New Zealand's Office of Births, Deaths and Marriages (www.bdm.govt.nz) before you go. It is easiest to sort it out once you arrive in New Zealand though – you simply need to be sure that you are arriving in time to apply for the licence and then leave a minimum of 3 working days before you need to collect it. Remember to bring your paperwork with you – details of your intended marriage location, the name and contact details of your celebrant, your birth certificates or passports, and importantly proof of dissolution of any previous marriages in the form of your decree absolute.

What is the minimum required period of notice?

Three working days.

If I choose to complete the Notice of Intended Marriage and send it to New Zealand ahead of my arrival, who can witness this document for me?

The marriage registrars in New Zealand will only accept witnessing by an authorised person at a New Zealand High Commission or Embassy, or by any approved Commonwealth representative. A solicitor or Justice of the Peace signature will not suffice.

Where can I go to have the Notice of Intended Marriage document witnessed in the UK and how much will it cost?

There are no fees for this service but you will need to visit New Zealand House, London to have the Notice of Intended Marriage witnessed by the Commonwealth Representative.

You will need to produce your passports for both parties and if either or both parties have been married before, then the original divorce papers issued by the court. If you are in another part of the world, contact your local New Zealand Embassy or High Commission to find out what you need to do.

Can the form be lodged with one Registrar and the Marriage Licence collected from another Registrar's Office?

No.

Do I send the Notice of Intended Marriage straight to the Registrar in New Zealand?

Yes, the forms must be received by the Registrar in New Zealand within three months of your signature being witnessed. The Marriage Licence is then valid for three months once it is issued.

Do either of the people marrying have to produce any other documentation?

Yes, if there has been a previous marriage then you must produce the original

 It is necessary to make an appointment ahead of time, for this witnessing to take place. To make an appointment email londonpassportenquiries@dia.govt.nz.

The Department of Internal Affairs office is located at New Zealand House, 80 Haymarket, London SW1Y 4TQ.

copies of your divorce papers. If you are marrying in a church there may be other paperwork you need to provide. The minister will be able to advise you of this.

How do I find a Marriage Registrar in New Zealand?

There are registrars in most major towns in New Zealand. These can be located in the New Zealand telephone directory (www.whitepages.co.nz).

 New Zealand Births, Deaths and Marriages [www.bdm.govt.nz] is also able to assist you in finding a Registrar and a celebrant. The National Office in Lower Hutt can be contacted at:

> Registrar of Marriages
> Central Registry BDM
> PO Box 31 115
> Lower Hutt
> New Zealand
> Tel: 0064 4 5706300
> Fax: 0064 4 5665311
> E-mail: bdm.nz@dia.govt.nz
> Website: www.bdm.govt.nz

Public Holidays

1 January	New Year's Day
2 January	Day after New Year's Day
6 February	Waitangi Day
April	Good Friday
April	Easter Monday
25 April	ANZAC Day
June	Queen's Birthday
October	Labour Day
25 December	Christmas Day
26 December	Boxing Day

However, the only days that almost all shops are closed on are Good Friday, Easter Sunday, ANZAC Day and Christmas Day.

About New Zealand

■ THE PEOPLE

Kiwi demeanour

- New Zealanders are friendly, outgoing, somewhat reserved initially yet polite, and enjoy extending hospitality.
- They are quite easy to get to know as they say hello to strangers and will offer assistance without being asked.
- Because they do not stand on ceremony and are egalitarian, they move to a first name basis quickly and generally shun the use of titles.
- Kiwis dress casually, but neatly. It is not at all unacceptable to go barefoot.
- Most restaurants do not have dress codes and except in business, dress is decidedly casual.
- Business dress is conservative, although jackets may be removed and shirtsleeves rolled up when working.

Environmentalism

- Kiwis are environmentally concerned and have a strong desire to preserve their country's beauty.
- One of the major local issues is the importing of predators, and most Kiwis are also fairy strict about recycling.

To the beach – Smugglers Cave Whangarei Heights

- Border controls are very tight and there are huge fines for importing food or other natural products such as wood, cane, etc.
- The local attitude towards the environment is largely influenced by the viewpoint of the indigenous population, the Maori, who traditionally believe that all things have a 'mauri' – a life force. Damage to this life force, or human attempts to dominate it, result in the mauri losing its energy and vitality, which affects the lives of people as well as the resilience of ecosystems. Maintaining the mauri of the environment and ecosystem resilience are equally important for sustainable development.

Egalitarianism

- The country has no formal class structure.
- Wealth and social status are not important to Kiwis.
- They take pride in individual achievements and believe that opportunities are available to all.
- As a 'welfare state' unemployment benefits, housing and access to health is all available free of charge to those who can't afford it

Meeting and greeting

- Greetings are casual, often consisting simply of a handshake and a smile.
- Never underestimate the value of the smile as it indicates pleasure at meeting the other person.
- Although New Zealanders generally prefer the use of first names rather than honorific titles and surnames, unless they are very advanced in years or occupy a particularly elevated social position.

Gift-giving etiquette

- If invited to a Kiwi's home, bring a small gift such as home baking, a bottle of wine, beer, flowers, chocolates, or a book about your home country to the hosts. If you are coming for a specific event, such as a barbeque, ask whether there is anything your hosts would like you to contribute, such as a salad or pudding.
- Gifts should not be lavish, but they should be thoughtful.
- Gifts are opened when received.

Dining etiquette

- New Zealanders are casual as is reflected in their table manners.
- The more formal the occasion, the more strict the protocol.
- Wait to be told where to sit.
- Meals are often served family-style.
- Keep your elbows off the table and your hands above the table when eating.
- Table manners are Continental – hold the fork in the left hand and the knife in the right while eating. They will not look askance, however, if you adopt American table manners.
- Indicate you have finished eating by laying your knife and fork parallel on your plate with the handles facing to the right.

Kiwi Slang

Aggro	Aggressive
Arvo	Afternoon
Aussie	Australian
Bach	Pronounced 'batch', holiday home (called a 'crib' in the South Island)
Banger	Sausage
Barney	Argument
Basin	Bathroom sink
Bassinet	Baby cradle
Bench	Kitchen counter, worktop
Biscuit	Cookie
Bloke	Man
Blotto	Drunk
Bludger	Someone who takes something for nothing, lives of others rather than supporting themselves.
Bonnet	Car hood
Boot	Car trunk

Kiwi Slang

Brassed off	Annoyed, disappointed, cross
Bugger	Used a lot, as a fairly gentle expression of annoyance, in a similar way to 'damn' in other places. 'Bugger all' means 'nothing' and 'buggered' means exhausted'.
Bush	Native forest
Carked it	Died
Chemist	Pharmacy, drugstore
Cheerio	Informal cheerful goodbye, also the name of a small cocktail sausage.
Chilly bin	Cooler, coolbox, called an 'eskie' in Australia.
Chips	Fries, hot fried potato chips
Chippies	Crisps, potato chips
Chocolate fish	A fish-shaped marshmallow sweet, covered in chocolate
Chook	Chicken
Chrissy	Christmas
Chunder	Vomit
College	High school not university
Creek	Small stream
Crook	Sick, ill, poorly
Dag	Hard case, especially a man, who tells tall tales or has a dry blokey sense of humour
Dairy	Corner store (not always on a corner!), selling bread, milk, newspapers, sweets, some groceries, etc
Dear	Expensive high school student in final academic year
Dole	Unemployment benefit
Dux	Top
Eh	Pronounced 'ay'. Turns a statement into a question, or instead of saying 'what?'
Fair go	An appeal for 'fair play', reasonableness.
Flicks	Movies, films
G'day	Universal greeting
Going bush	Taking a break on your own for a while
Good on ya	Congratulations, well done
Greasies	Takeaways, fish and chips
Gumboots	Wellington boots, rubber boots for outdoors
Guts for garters	'I'll have your guts for garters' means 'I'll get you for this' or 'You're in trouble with me'.
Heaps	A lot, 'I've got heaps of gardening to do'.
Hollywood	To fake or feign an injury, especially in sports
Hottie	Hot water bottle

(Continued on following page)

Kiwi Slang

How's it going?	Universal greeting
Iceblock	Ice lolly, popsicle
Jandals	Flip-flops, thongs
Jumper	Sweater, jersey
Kai	Food
Kick the bucket	Die
Laughing gear	Mouth. 'Wrap your laughing gear round that' means 'eat that'.
Lollipop	Sweet, candy on a stick
Lolly	Sweet, candy
Metal road	Gravel road
Mountain oysters	Lamb's testicles
Nana	Female grandparent
Nappy	Diaper
OE	Overseas experience
Pack a sad	Sulk
Pav	Pavlova
Piece of piss	Easy
Pikelet	Small pancake, Scotch pancake, griddle scone
Piss	Alcohol
Prang	Car accident
Pressies	Presents
Rattle your dags	Hurry up
Rellies	Relatives
Root	Engage in sexual intercourse
Rough as guts	Unpolished, uncultured
Sarky	Sarcastic
Sav	Saveloy sausage.
Scull	Drink quickly
She'll be right	Everything will be OK
Shoot through	Leave suddenly
Shout	Round, 'my shout' means 'I'm paying'. If you are told that 'smoko' is 'your shout' you will be expected to provide cakes or biscuits to go with cups of tea.
Smoko	Morning or afternoon tea break, especially from physical labour
Sook	Timid or 'soft' person
Sparkie	Electrician
Spuds	Potatoes
Stirrer	Trouble-maker

Kiwi Slang	
Take a hike	Go away
Tea	Dinner/evening meal
Tiki tour	Scenic tour, the roundabout way
Tinny	Lucky
Togs	Swimsuit, bathing costume
Tramping	Hiking, bush-walking
Ute	Small pickup truck, utility vehicle
Waikikamukau	Mythical remote country town, the essence of 'hickness', pronounced 'Why-kick-a-moo-cow'.
Wally	Silly person, idiot, but usually affectionate
Whinge	Complain
Wobbly	Tantrum, 'he threw a wobbly'
Wop-wops	The back of beyond, remote rural area
Yonks ago	A long time ago

◼ MAORI CULTURE

The Maori have been in Aotearoa (New Zealand) for approximately 1,000 years, a long time compared to the 150 years of Pakeha (European) settlement. Maori culture remains distinct from the rest of New Zealand culture, although each invariably influences the other.

Maori social customs

The Marae

The distinctive and central focus of Maori culture is the marae or meeting place. A *marae* consists of a *wharenui* (meeting house), a *wharekai* (eating house) and *wharepaku* (ablution block). To the Maori however, it is not the presence of the buildings that is significant, but the spiritual importance of the location, the discussions and exchanges between people and events ranging from marriages to funerals that take place on the *marae*. It is customary to welcome visitors onto the *marae* in a ceremony called a *powhiri* (welcome).

The Powhiri

Visitors (called the *manuhiri*) will gather outside the gate of the *marae*. It is considered improper to walk onto the *marae* uninvited. The visitors will be 'called on' by the host people (the *tangata whenua*). This is called the *karanga* and is usually performed by a woman from the host side. The *manuhiri* will proceed slowly onto the *marae* as one group. Usually the women are to the front of the group. One of these women will answer the welcoming call with a *karanga* of her own. The group will pause in silence to *tangi* (remember the dead) and then will move slowly to the seating provided. The front row of seating is reserved for those men who wish to *whaikorero* (speak). Traditionally, women do not have this right.

Whaikorero (speeches) are to welcome *manuhiri*, to remember those who have died, to thank *tangata whenua* and always mention the reason for the visit. Each speech is followed by a *waiata* (song), sung by the speaker's group to show their support of him. The final speaker for the *manuhiri* will lay down the *koha* (gift). Today *koha* are mostly monetary contributions towards the cost of the *hui* (gathering). The final speech is usually made by the host side.

At the conclusion of the *whaikorero* it is customary for the visitors and the hosts to *hongi* (press noses). This is usually done by shaking right hands, bracing your left hand on the other person's right arm and pressing your nose into theirs twice whilst looking them in the eye. Today some people will shake hands instead. It is best to follow the lead of the *tangata whenua*. After the formalities, hosts and guests share a meal together. It is at this point that the *manuhiri* become *tangata whenua* and the *powhiri* is concluded.

Points to remember

The *wharenui* is for gatherings and for sleeping. You should always remove your shoes before entering the *wharenui*. Never walk on mattresses or sit on pillows. Certain places are reserved for the elders (*kaumatua*) to sit and sleep in. You should never eat in the *wharenui*.

In the *wharekai* (eating house) be careful not to put hair clips, scarves, combs, glasses or anything to do with the head on the table. This is because the head is sacred (*tapu*). Tables are also *tapu*, so you must never sit or put your feet on any tables. A *hangi* is a delicious feast of food that has been cooked in the ground. Rocks heated by fire are placed in a hole in the ground, and the food baskets are filled with vegetables and meat and placed on the rocks and are then covered over with earth. When serving yourself, it is polite to take small helpings (and quite acceptable to have several of them) rather than one large plateful. Before meals there will usually be grace. It is good manners to allow the *kaumatua* to eat first, and after the first meal, once you have become part of the *tangata whenua*, to offer to help with the dishes or preparation of the next meal.

Do not smoke in any of the buildings on the *marae* and do not use cameras or tape recorders unless given permission. Never be afraid to ask what protocol you should be following. Part of Maori culture emphasises the importance of welcoming guests and making them feel at home, so if you are prepared to be respectful of the culture and traditions, then nobody will mind explaining points of protocol to you. A useful book on Maori culture is *Te Marae – A Guide to Customs and Protocols* (Hiwi and Pat Tauroa, Heinemann Reed, 1986). If you want to find out more about Maori culture during a visit to New Zealand, the New Zealand Tourism Board publishes a leaflet called *New Zealand Maori Cultural Heritage Guide* which lists a number of tourism operators who provide visits to *marae* and other cultural experiences. The New Zealand Immigration Service publishes a leaflet called *The Treaty of Waitangi* which explains the relevance of the Treaty to new immigrants.

Maori carving guarding Omaha Beach

Maori Greetings

Formal Greetings

Greetings beginning with 'tena' are used during important occasions or when addressing elders.

Tena koe	Formal greeting to one person
Tena korua	...to two people
Tena koutou	...to two or more people
Tena tatou	Formal inclusive greeting to everybody present, including yourself.

Informal Greetings

'Kia ora' is the most used informal greeting; it literally means 'be well'.

Kia ora	Hello, thank you, good luck, good luck, goodbye to any number of people.
Kia ora koe	Informal greeting to one person
Kia ora korua	...to two people
Kia ora koutou	...to two or more people

(Continued on following page)

Maori Greetings

Kia ora tatou	Informal inclusive greeting to everybody present including yourself.

General Greetings

Morena	Good morning
Ata marie	Good and peaceful morning
Ahiahi marie	Good and peaceful afternoon
Po marie	Good and peaceful evening
E noho ra	Goodbye (from person leaving to person staying)
E haere ra	Goodbye (from person staying to person leaving)
Hei kona ra	Goodbye (less formal).

Source: Information on Maori language can be found at www.korero.co.nz

 POPULATION

The population of New Zealand has changed dramatically over the last century. A hundred years ago the population was just 800,000, children (under 15 years old) outnumbered older people (over 64 years old) by eight to one, and life expectancy was about 60 years. Five percent of the population was Maori, immigrants mostly came from the UK and made up one-third of population growth, and more people lived in rural areas than in the cities and towns. At the time of writing the population is 4,260,674, children outnumber older people by just two to one, and life expectancy for a newborn child is around 80 years. Maori currently make up almost 15% of the population, and, although migration still accounts for roughly a third of population growth, immigrants now come from a wider range of countries and the ethnic mix is very much richer.

The vast majority of people (86%) now live in urban areas; over 70% of New Zealanders live in cities with populations of 30,000 or more.

New Zealand experienced steady population growth through the 20th century, with numbers reaching one million in 1908, two million in 1952 and three million in 1973. The highest growth was in the period 1946 to 1976. The total population is projected to grow to 5.09 million by 2031 and 5.57 million by 2061, then fall back slightly by 2101.

Maori, Pacific and Asian populations are all projected to grow at a faster rate than the New Zealand population as a whole. It is expected that the Maori population will roughly double to nearly one million by 2051, with the Pacific population almost trebling within the same timeframe to reach around 600,000. It is also predicted that the Asian population will reach 370,000 by 2016, which is about double what it was in 1996.

Infant mortality has fallen to low levels, and in September 2007 births exceeded deaths by 34,220 – the highest natural increase since 1991. Over the next century, however, it is expected that the population will reach a new stable age structure with a much higher average age. A return to higher fertility is unlikely, as the trend across all groups is towards smaller families. New Zealand's total fertility rate is similar to that of the USA, but is higher than most developed nations due largely to higher fertility amongst Maori and Pacific groups. The trend now is for the age of mothers giving birth to rise; currently the average age is 28 years. Women also tend to have fewer children now than in the past, and a growing number of women remain childless. Fertility is currently around replacement levels and it is predicted that it will fall further towards the levels of other industrialised countries. Growth in the proportion of older New Zealanders will quicken after 2011, as the generations born in the 1950s, 1960s and 1970s start to hit the 60+ age bracket.

There are concerns about an older population, most importantly the increases in old age dependency, the possibility of falling living standards for older people, and slower economic growth as output from workers will have to be shared among a larger non-working population. At the moment it seems increasingly likely that a higher retirement age may be brought into effect in the future. Deaths are projected to outnumber births from 2042.

■ HISTORY

The original inhabitants of New Zealand were the Maori, Polynesian settlers who arrived by canoe from the central Pacific in about the 10th century. They lived a nomadic lifestyle initially dependent on hunting a large flightless bird called the moa (now extinct), but by the 12th century there were settlements scattered along the coastline. Permanent settlements were based on cultivating the kumara, a type of sweet potato, and harvesting seafood.

By the time the first Europeans arrived in the 18th and 19th centuries, the Maori had settled throughout the warmer North Island. The Maori are a tribal people, with 79 traditional tribal bases throughout New Zealand. Their *whanau* (extended-family)-based society has always had a complex oral tradition and maintains a strong spiritual attachment to their customs and the land. The Maori were skilled craftspeople, particularly in woodcarving and weaving (which some still practise), and also in warfare. War between tribes was common at this time, as part of the competition for status and authority.

Among the first European visitors to New Zealand were members of a Dutch East Indies Company ship led by the explorer Abel Janzoon Tasman. They briefly anchored off the coast of the North Island in 1642, at a place they called Murderer's Bay because local Maori killed four of their crew there. Tasman named the country after Zeeland, a Dutch province in the North Sea. The Maori name for the country is 'Aotearoa', meaning 'the Land of the Long White Cloud'. Other explorers followed Tasman's lead. Englishman James Cook arrived in 1769 and returned again twice in the 1770s. Members of his second expedition were the first Europeans to make landfall in New Zealand and to explore the coastline thoroughly. As with Tasman's first contact with local tribes, there were

FACT

■ The capital of New Zealand is Wellington; the largest city and leading port is Auckland.

misunderstandings at first, the Maori interpreting the arrival of the strangers as a hostile force. Ten of Cook's men were killed in one incident. Other meetings were more favourable for the visitors, local Maori for the most part being curious to meet the strangers and keen to trade.

Trade and commerce provided the impetus for the first semi-permanent European settlements. Whalers and sealers arrived in the 1790s. They set up bases along the coasts but generally did not make permanent homes in the new country. Next to arrive, in the early 1800s, were Christian missionaries, who established stations around the Bay of Islands, on the north east of the North Island. They began preaching their faith amongst the tribes as well as introducing European cultivation techniques, literacy and other skills. They were the first to write down the Maori language so that they could translate the scriptures into Maori. Other settlers with more worldly ambitions soon arrived. They were interested in exploiting natural resources such as timber and flax. Local Maori tribes began cultivating wheat and maize to trade with the new arrivals. New Zealand's export trade in agricultural produce began in the 1840s with the export of potatoes, wheat and pigs to Australia. Maori farmers grew the bulk of the produce. Contact between Europeans and local tribes was confined to the small areas around the settlements, the whaling bases around the coasts of the South Island and the lower North Island, the mission stations in the north and the trading settlements at various points. For most of the first half of the 19th century, the balance of power between the settlers and the tribes was still very much in favour of the Maori, as the early settlements were dependent upon the goodwill of local tribes for their survival. However this was about to change. The Maori population was declining as a result of the spread of foreign diseases (such as influenza and smallpox) against which they had no immunity, and the introduction of firearms, which had transformed the formerly ritualised inter-tribal wars into massacres.

By 1840, a balance of firepower had led to a virtual halt in inter-tribal warfare, the cost in lives being too high. The legacy of the warring period was large-scale loss of life, disruption of land tenure and social dislocation. The decline in the Maori population alarmed the missionaries. They were also concerned about the rough, lawless lifestyle of the early settlements. Accordingly, back in Britain, the Church Missionary Society put pressure on the British Government to annex New Zealand as a Crown Colony, and to establish the rule of law.

In 1840, New Zealand was made a part of the British Empire. A treaty was signed at Waitangi, a little settlement in the Bay of Islands, between the new Lieutenant Governor Captain William Hobson and representatives of local Maori tribes. Hobson then sent copies of the Treaty around the country for other tribes to agree to, but some important chiefs refused or failed to sign. The terms, significance and validity of the Treaty of Waitangi have been a source of controversy ever since. Under the English text, the tribes ceded sovereignty to the British Crown and gained the rights of British citizens. The Maori text, hastily translated by local missionary, Henry Williams, is considerably vaguer in its terms. In particular, Williams used the unfamiliar term *'kawanatanga'*, a transliteration of the English word 'governorship', to express the concept of sovereignty. It is doubtful that the first signatories understood that they were handing over rule of the land to the newcomers.

During the late 1830s plans for widespread colonisation were developed under the auspices of Edward Gibbon Wakefield's New Zealand Company. Wakefield intended the settlements to mimic the pre-industrial class structure of England but the actual settlements bore little resemblance to his plans. Street plans formally laid out in Britain did not necessarily take into account the geographical vagaries of the mountainous land in New Zealand.

Prospective immigrants attracted by the promise of cheap land may not have been aware that the Company and its agents did not always acquire the land legitimately from the tribes, especially as the pressure to provide more land increased. Maori land tenure is complex as land is not owned by individuals but by the tribe as a whole. Company agents were not particularly scrupulous about whose signatures they obtained on sale documents and, as the increasing numbers of new settlers demanding land put pressure on them to provide it, their methods undoubtedly became more dubious.

New Zealand was directly governed by the British Crown between 1840 and 1852. After pressure from the settlers, self-government was granted in 1852. As European settlers increased in numbers and demand for land grew, conflicts occurred with the Maori people over land tenure. The tribes disputed a number of deals undertaken by New Zealand Company agents and resistance movements to further land sales developed.

The settler government ignored its responsibilities to protect Maori rights under the Treaty. Skirmishes between the government and the tribes began in the 1860s and full-scale war developed. It took nearly 15 years for the forces of the government, reinforced by troops from Britain, to defeat Maori opposition. Even at the end of hostilities in the 1870s, Maori tribes in the centre of North Island still held

Involvement in wars

New Zealand was involved in both World Wars as a British ally. The disastrous Great War campaign at Gallipoli in Turkey in 1915 proved to be one of the defining moments in forming a separate national identity. New Zealand lost more soldiers as a proportion of its population than any other allied country; nearly one in three men between the ages of 20 and 40 were killed or wounded. The interwar years brought the election of the first Labour government, which continued the tradition of pioneering social policy programmes started by the Liberals. The 1938 Social Security Act established a time national health service and a universal social security system. Public education to secondary level was free to all. The Second World War saw New Zealand participating again as a British ally, but in the post-war years it began to rely less on Britain for defence and to form closer relations with Australia and the USA. Britain's entry into the Common Market in the 1970s confirmed the loosening of colonial ties. At the same closer links were being developed with other countries in the Asia-Pacific region.

out against government control. The wars exacerbated the decimation of the Maori population and resulted in the confiscation of the land of the 'rebellious' and 'loyal' tribes alike. The loss of land and the resulting social breakdown probably contributed more than any other factor to the decline in the Maori population at the end of the 19th century.

Meanwhile European settler numbers were increasing, spurred on by the discovery of gold in the South Island in the 1870s, and the invention of refrigerated shipping in the 1880s which made the export of meat and dairy products to Europe viable. The gold deposits were soon mined out but the agrarian economy founded in the late 19th century has remained the basis of New Zealand's economic prosperity. Economic security brought on social reform, at least for the European population. First the extension of the vote to women (1893), then a new system of industrial relations, based on minimum wage rates for every industry (1894) and one of the earliest pension schemes (1898). Maori were legally equally able to vote but the property owning rule (which was based on European patterns of individual tenure, rather than an understanding of Maori communal tenure) effectively disbarred many of them until its abolition in the late 19th century.

Economic restructuring resulting from the increasingly poor performance of the economy since the late 1970s and race relations have been the major policy issues over the last three decades. The prevailing belief that relations between the races were harmonious was challenged by a number of Maori political movements during the last 30 years, ranging from radical groups calling for the restoration of Maori sovereignty to tribal leaders taking a more conciliatory stance. Two common concerns unite the diverse strands of Maori protest movements: a call upon the government to honour the terms of its original treaty with the Maori people and a concern with the inequality between Maori and European living standards. Income, life expectancy, health, and education standards differ markedly between the two groups. The Treaty has become central to government policy towards the Maori and in 1985 the Waitangi Tribunal was given power to hear grievances relating to Maori land. The government's obligations towards the Maori as an equal partner under the Treaty were acknowledged. Tensions remain between the Maori and the Government over historical injustices, particularly the large scale acquisition of Maori land by Europeans in the 19th century through confiscation, extortion, blackmail and theft, and the Government's neglect of its duty to protect Maori rights under the Treaty.

FACT

■ Maori people did not identify themselves by this collective name until the arrival of European people in New Zealand.

New Zealand History Timeline	
1300 (approx)	East Polynesian (now known as Maori) people arrive in NZ.
1642	Abel Tasman is the first European to see New Zealand.
1769	Captain James Cook arrives in New Zealand and claims it for Great Britain (the North Island in 1769, the South Island in 1770).
1840	Treaty of Waitangi signed.

New Zealand History Timeline

1891	Liberal Government embarks on significant social and infrastructure reforms.
1893	Women given the vote.
1907	New Zealand becomes a dominion.
1908	New Zealand population reaches 1 million.
1933	New Zealand adopts its own currency.
1947	New Zealand Parliament adopts the Statute of Westminster (1931) and becomes independent from Great Britain.
1952	New Zealand population reaches 2 million.
1981	Highly controversial tour of New Zealand by Springbok rugby team.
1983	Closer Economic Relations (CER) agreement signed with Australia.
1985	Waitangi Tribunal given power to hear historic Maori land grievances going back to 1840.
1987	Maori declared as an official language alongside English.
1987	New Zealand becomes nuclear free.
2003	New Zealand population reaches 4 million.

◼ ECONOMY

New Zealand has a worldwide reputation as an agricultural producer with increasingly efficient and innovative methods. The country has a mixed economy that operates on free market principles and is strongly trade oriented, with exports of goods and services accounting for about 33% of total output.

Since 1984 the government has undertaken some major restructuring and transformed New Zealand from an agrarian economy largely dependent on Britain to a more industrialised and globally competitive free market economy. Technology and research have played a major part in this transformation. The temperate climate is ideal for growing grass suitable for rearing farm animals cheaply, but it took a century and a half of effort to cultivate the ten million hectares of arable land currently in production. Modern machinery and efficient soil, stock and pasture management have played an important role. Much of the land was initially unsuitable for agriculture, being heavily forested, while the mountainous terrain has provided a challenge to develop alternative cultivation techniques. Nearly two-thirds of farmland is too rugged to be fertilised and sown by tractor. Instead New Zealand farmers pioneered the use of light aircraft to spread fertiliser and seed.

New Zealand was able to exploit its agricultural potential with the development of refrigerated transportation in the 1880s. Meat and dairy products joined wool as the basis of exports to Europe. At the end of the 19th century, New Zealand was one of the richest countries in the world. As a former colony, it enjoyed close cultural and economic links with the UK. For most of the following century, three-quarters of New Zealand's exports went to the UK. Britain was also the major source of imports.

FACT

◼ Maori became an official language in 1987 (English being the other) and knowledge of Maori culture and language is increasingly a prerequisite for employment in areas of public service departments and is stressed as equally important as cultural heritage.

By the 1950s New Zealand was an efficient producer of wool, meat and dairy products and could compete successfully in northern hemisphere markets. The success of the export industry allowed New Zealanders to enjoy a similar standard of living to the industrialised countries of Europe and America. The relatively high standard of living attracted a constant inflow of immigrants. In the early 1960s, as a result of a worldwide boom in commodity prices, it enjoyed amongst the highest living standards in the Organisation for Economic Co-operation and Development (OECD). However, even during this relatively prosperous period, it was recognised that future economic security depended on diversifying the export base, both in terms of markets and of the range of goods being exported. New Zealand's traditional market, Britain, was not growing as fast as other countries and there was the possibility throughout the 1960s that it would eventually join the European Economic Community (now the EU).

The golden years ended in the 1970s. Several factors were influential such as the entry of Britain into the EEC in 1973 and the first oil price-shock in the same year. Britain's entry into the EEC led to the restriction of access for New Zealand exports and this coincided with the rise in the price of oil which had a severe effect on the New Zealand economy, as it was extremely dependent on importing oil to meet its energy needs. There was a sudden decline in economic performance. The cost of imports rose sharply while exports receipts dropped and the Balance of Payments deficit plummeted to 14% of Gross Domestic Product (GDP). Arguably however the effect of these two events only exposed the underlying weakness of New Zealand's economy rather than causing the economic decline. The government of the time decided that the best solution to the problem of New Zealand's dependency on fuel imports was to embark upon a series of major investment projects to develop domestic energy sources. Unfortunately the viability of these projects was based on the price of oil continuing to rise more than it did. Most of the so-called 'Think Big' projects turned out to be expensive white elephants.

By the early 1980s, the economy was performing badly. Inflation was high, and at the same time, unemployment was rising rapidly. Subsidies protected inefficient sectors of the economy and discouraged innovation. Years of borrowing to cover the trade deficit and the cost of the 'Think Big' experiment had increased New Zealand's foreign debt. The National government tried to control inflation by imposing a price and wage freeze in 1982. The freeze succeeded in controlling inflation, but money supply continued to grow throughout the 2.5 years it was in place. In 1984 a Labour government was elected. At the time of the election there was no indication that the new administration would introduce a period of radical economic reform. The Labour Party manifesto made no mention of many of the central policy changes they enacted. The programme of economic liberalisation included removal of price and wage controls, deregulation of financial markets, the floating of the dollar, the introduction of a sales tax, the reduction of agricultural and industrial subsidies, the removal of employment protection, and the weakening of the collective bargaining power of unions. This was accompanied by tight monetary policy and the selling of a number of state assets, including the railways, forests, the national airline and the telecommunications section of the post office.

During the mid-to-late 1980s the economy stagnated somewhat, entering a recession in the early 1990s. Output recovered in the mid-1990s, only to be hit by the slowdown of the economies of key Asian trading partners in 1997 and 1998. The droughts of 1997/98 and 1998/99 affected large parts of the country and had an obvious impact on economic activity; in combination with an already-slowing economy, these factors contributed to a contraction of the economy in 1998.

Against the above mentioned short-term swings in government economic policy, a longer-term process of economic adjustment has also been occurring. New Zealand's export industry has diversified both in product and export markets, and the economy is still heavily dependent on overseas trade. The agriculture and manufacturing industries have been developed to suit the needs of niche markets. A free trade agreement was signed in 1982 with Australia, which is now New Zealand's main trading partner. The development of new markets in Asia has been a significant development during recent years. Japan is the third largest source of overseas merchandise export income (accounting for NZ$3,554 million) after Australia (NZ$7,172 million) and the USA (NZ$4,594 million). The People's Republic of China provides export income worth NZ$1,867 million, The Republic of Korea accounts for NZ$1,438 million, Taiwan NZ$790 million, Indonesia NZ$664 million, Hong Kong (SAR) NZ$581 million, The Philippines NZ$568 million, Malaysia NZ$562 million and Singapore accounts for NZ$523 million. Europe, which in the late 1960s provided two-thirds of New Zealand's export revenue, now accounts for much smaller figures. The UK is only New Zealand's fifth largest export market, accounting for (NZ$1,704 million). Export income from Germany amounts to NZ$809 million, from Belgium NZ$519 million, and Italy NZ$500 million. Total exports generate an income of NZ$35,202 billion.

New Zealand's Top 15 Export Commodities	
Commodity	NZ$ million
Milk powder, butter and cheese	5,669
Meat and edible offal	4,426
Logs, wood and wood articles	1,932
Mechanical machinery, equipment	1,776
Aluminium and aluminium articles	1,213
Fruit	1,184
Fish, crustaceans and molluscs	1,149
Electrical machinery and equipment	1,104
Iron and steel	713
Wool	681
Textiles and textile articles	651
Casein and caseinates	645
Beverages, spirits and vinegar	640
Miscellaneous edible preparations	612
Wood pulp and waste paper	503

Source: Statistics New Zealand 2008 and Investment New Zealand

The range of exports has diversified to include horticulture and wine, and fishing and tourism have become more significant. Dairy, meat and wood exports still make a large contribution to the economy, although wool has declined, while forestry and manufacturing exports have become increasingly important. In the 1960s, the dairy, meat and wool sectors accounted for over 80% of export revenue; they now make up less than 50%. However, although the range of products has diversified, the economy as a whole is still reliant upon exporting agricultural and horticultural commodities. This heavy dependence on trade leaves growth vulnerable to changes in economic performance, particularly in Asia, the USA and Europe. New Zealand's growth prospects are also vulnerable to climatic and environmental factors.

Gross Domestic Product (GDP)	
Industry Sector	Total
Agriculture	4.6%
Fishing, forestry and mining	2.1%
Manufacturing	14.4%
Utilities	1.9%
Construction	4.7%
Wholesale trade	8.2%
Retail	7.9%
Transport and communications	10.6%
Finance	25.9%
Government	4.6%
Community services	12.1%
Other	2.9%

Source: Statistics New Zealand 2008 and Investment New Zealand

The adjustment process to the restructuring has been long and difficult. Unemployment rose from under 4% in 1985 to over 10% in 1990, levels not seen since the Depression years, as economic activity declined due to tight monetary policy. Farmers' gross incomes dropped by nearly half when government subsidies were removed. A large number of manufacturing industries went to the wall, unable to compete with cheap imports once tariffs were removed. The abolition of financial controls caused a brief speculative boom in the mid-1980s but the stock market crash in 1987 exposed much of the increased activity as paper wealth. The NZ dollar rose as high interest rates attracted overseas investment, which reduced returns from exports, critical to the overall health of the economy.

Whether the social costs of economic restructuring outweigh the efficiency gains is still being debated. Some sectors of the economy have adjusted better to deregulation than others. Despite predictions that many farms would not survive the removal of agricultural price supports, there were only a few casualties. The agricultural sector has become more efficient. Manufacturing has not been as fortunate and the shedding of jobs in this sector along with the restructuring of previously inefficient government industries largely accounted for the rise in unemployment. Unemployment has now dropped to 3.5% – the lowest rate for 23 years. However, the gap between high- and low-income earners has grown and poverty has emerged for the first time since the war as a visible social problem. The gap between rich and poor continues to widen and the government has been forced to introduce updated income support measures to ensure a reasonable standard of living for low-income families in work (as distinct from beneficiaries). For a country that used to pride itself on its egalitarian ethos and comprehensive social welfare system, these developments have caused much public concern.

Taxation remains a topic for disagreement and discussion. Fiscal surpluses have been substantial in recent years and there has been resulting and increasing pressure on the government to reduce personal taxes. The government maintains that these surpluses are better used by it in superannuation, while opposition parties argue that the rates of tax for both businesses and individuals should be reduced. With increasing interaction between New Zealand and Australia, it is argued by business organisations that the rates of company tax in both countries (currently 33% in New Zealand and 30% in Australia) should be harmonised so that New Zealand companies are able to compete on a more even playing field. Public debt has fallen to 19.2%, and net debt is non-existent once the government's Superannuation Fund is taken into account. Annual average GDP growth is forecast to be 2.9% for 2008–09, largely based on considerable confidence in both export markets and domestic demand. It is expected that fiscal policy will become increasingly expansionary over the next 4 years, following the September 2008 election, and both the National Party and the Labour Party promise tax cuts as part of their election campaigns. The government is expected to shift policy focus from attracting inward foreign investment more towards encouraging New Zealand owned businesses to establish and expand foreign operations, looking outward for business operations rather than encouraging outsiders to look towards New Zealand.

The exchange rate for the New Zealand dollar has strengthened in recent years, and now stands higher than it has for some time against the US dollar, the Australian dollar, and GBP sterling. While this makes the cost of imports cheaper, it also has the effect of making exports dearer and therefore possibly less desirable in some of New Zealand's markets. Deregulation of the economy since the 1980s has meant that most protections for local and primary manufacturing industries have gone, resulting in, for example, significant sections of the clothing and footwear industries going out of business because they are unable to compete with cheaper imported goods. The small size of the New Zealand market has meant that other industries have suffered as well; motor vehicle assembly, for example, no longer

New Zealand's Top 15 Import Commodities	
Commodity	NZ$ million
Petroleum and products	5,722
Mechanical machinery and equipment	5,234
Vehicles, parts and accessories	4,831
Electrical machinery and equipment	3,694
Textiles and textile articles	1,888

(Continued on following page)

New Zealand's Top 15 Import Commodities (contd)	
Plastics and plastic articles	1,571
Iron and steel and articles	1,494
Aircraft and parts	1,227
Optical, medical and measuring equipment	1,192
Paper and paperboard articles	1,004
Pharmaceutical products	998
Furniture, furnishings and light fittings	608
Inorganic chemicals	573
Rubber and rubber articles	477
Other chemical products	469

Source: Statistics New Zealand 2008 and Investment New Zealand.

exists as an industry in the country, and vehicles are these days imported fully built up from Australia, America, the UK and Asia. However, as the unemployment figures demonstrate, the economy has adapted to these downturns and employment is expanding in other, less traditional, areas.

Despite all the problems, the high growth of the past three years makes this one of the best periods in New Zealand for the last 25 years; nominal GDP growth in 2007 was 4.5%, with real GDP growth at 1.2%. Domestic demand has continued to drive growth, with consumption and investment growing strongly. Exports are still recovering from their mid-2003 slump, returning to high growth, and all industries have grown recently, most by a fairly significant amount. Such strong economic growth has meant an improvement in labour market conditions, and further contributions to growth have been made by high job growth and a strong labour market, growth in labour productivity and a fall in unemployment.

The economy grew by 2.2% and inflation by 2.7% in the year ending June 2007. Over the previous few years, growth has been curtailed by the high Kiwi dollar, which has limited net exports, and by rising interest rates. In the second half of 2007 growth rebounded a little, in part due to the commodity market experiencing a boom in prices. The high dollar has caused problems for non-dairy exporters however, and in July 2007 the Kiwi dollar reached its highest point in 22 years. The boost in the value of the dollar is partly due to overseas capital which has been attracted to these high interest rates.

Domestic demand as well as the strong currency have also peaked growth in the current deficit, and this hit 9.7% of GDP in September 2006 but by September 2007 had dropped back a little to 8.2% of GDP. Annual inflation has steadied at 1.8% as domestic growth, especially in the property market, has slowed and also because of the strength of the dollar.

GEOGRAPHY AND CLIMATE

Located in the southwest Pacific Ocean, midway between the equator and the South Pole, New Zealand is an island chain on the south edge of the 'Pacific Rim of Fire', an

Arthur's Pass, South Island

area characterised by volcanic activity and frequent earthquakes. It is approximately 1600km east of Australia and the closest countries to the north are Fiji, Tonga and New Caledonia.

Consisting of two major islands (North and South) and a number of smaller ones, New Zealand has a total land area of 270,534 sq km (103,515 sq miles). This makes it about the size of Japan, Italy, or Colorado, and slightly larger than the United Kingdom. It is nearly 1600km long, stretching across 13 degrees latitude from 34 degrees S to 47 degrees S, only 420km wide at its widest point. The two main islands are separated by Cook Strait, which is 32km across at its narrowest point. Most of the country is mountainous.

The snow-capped Southern Alps form the backbone of the South Island, from one end to the other, dividing the land between the rainforests of the West Coastand the dry pasture lands of the Canterbury, Marlborough and Otago.

The Alps include 18 peaks reaching higher than 3,000 metres, including Mount Cook which is the tallest at 3,754 metres. The Maori name for Mount Cook is *Aoraki*, meaning 'cloud piercer'. Over 360 glaciers, which carry snow and ice down from the Alps, feed the major rivers on both sides of the island. Fiordland, the south-west corner of the South Island, is almost all national park and as its name suggests consists of deep sounds or fiords carved into the bush-covered mountains. Mountains in the North Island include several volcanic cones, such as Ruapehu, Tongariro, Taranaki and Ngauruhoe. The chain of occasionally active volcanoes runs from White Island (sending up clouds of steam off the east coast) through the central volcanic zone (where snow exists alongside hot springs and steam vents) to Mount Taranaki on the West Coast.There are active thermal areas where mud pools literally bubble and geysers send up streams of boiling water. There are many lakes throughout the country. In the South Island the major lakes originate from glaciers, while in the North Island the larger lakes lie on the central volcanic plateau. No point on either of the main islands is further than 120 km from the coast.

National parks

Roughly 30% of New Zealand's land area is in protected conservation sites, in a network of national, maritime and forest parks. Many of these wilderness areas are untouched by human habitation, although unfortunately the effect of the animals introduced with the arrival of humans has been harder to control. The Department of Conservation (which looks after the parks) aims to preserve the flora and fauna as far as possible, while allowing people recreational access. They look after an extensive network of tracks and huts for hikers (known in New Zealand as trampers). There is usually a small fee for using the huts. The walking tracks vary in difficulty from family strolls of less than half a day to serious two- or three-day hikes. Most New Zealanders go tramping at some point in their lives, whether they are dragged reluctantly along on a school trip or are keen walkers every weekend.

Bear in mind, however, that although the New Zealand bush looks welcoming on a warm day, it can be a very hostile environment. The weather can change unexpectedly and, in some areas of New Zealand's national parks, you can be far away from any inhabited areas if something goes wrong.

Climate

New Zealand has a complex oceanic climate, without extremes of hot or cold except for isolated areas of the central South Island. It is temperate, but with sharp regional contrasts. Mean annual temperatures range from 10°C in the south to 16°C in the north. Most areas enjoy ample sunshine, wind and rainfall. The seasons are not as varied as in the USA and Britain, and are the opposite of the northern hemisphere. January and February are the warmest months, and July is the coolest. In the summer, temperatures can reach the 30s (C) in eastern and inland regions. There are relatively small variations between the summer and winter temperatures, but the variation will be greater inland and to the east of the mountain ranges. Sunshine hours are higher in areas that are sheltered from the west, and on average, most of the country would have at least 2,000 sunshine hours every year.

New Zealand's long thin shape results in the considerable climatic variation between regions. The far north of the country has an almost subtropical climate, with mild winters and hot summers. In the south of the South Island, the country can be frozen over for 3 months during the winter and the summers are hot and dry. During the winter there is extensive snowfall on the Southern Alps, and the central North Island mountains. The mountain chains extend the length of the country providing a barrier for the westerly winds, and they also divide the country into its climatically different regions. Snow does not often fall at lower levels, and when it does it is only in the southern parts of the South Island. Snow falls only very rarely in the coastal areas of the North Island and the west of the South Island, although the east and south of the South Island may see some snow in winter. Frosts occur all over New Zealand, and are most common on clear, cold nights with little wind. Throughout the country, rainfall varies widely. Rainfall tends to be lowest in summer for most of the North Island and for the north of the South Island. But in inland Otago, Canterbury and Southland, and particularly on the West Coast of the South Island, rainfall seems to be lower during the winter months. The area just over 100km to the east of the mountains in the South Island tends to be the driest area of the country. Most areas of New Zealand have rainfall of between 600 and 1600 mm spread throughout the year, with a dry period in the summer. In the northern and central areas rainfall can be higher in winter than in summer; conversely the winter in the South Island sees less rainfall than the summer. The sun is strong in the southern hemisphere, and unfortunately the ozone hole over the Antarctic has a tendency to drift north over New Zealand during December, which heightens the risk of burning even further. The UVI (midday summer solar radiation index) is often extremely high, especially in northern New Zealand and the mountainous areas. The UVI in most areas can also be high during autumn and spring. During the summer, a 'burn time' rating is included with television and radio weather reports to warn people of the time it takes to burn during the hottest hours of the day. This can sometimes take as few as 12 minutes. The application of sunblock should be incorporated into your daily grooming routine, and many Kiwis apply it to the backs of their necks, hands, arms and legs as well as their faces even just for going into town during the summer. Along with Australians, New Zealanders have one of the highest rates of skin cancer in the world. It goes without saying that roasting your body on the beach like a Sunday leg of lamb in the oven is not recommended, and you can still be burnt if you are in the water. For more information about skin cancer in New Zealand and recommended protection see the New Zealand Cancer Society website: www.cancernz.org.nz.

The North Island

Northern New Zealand, including Kaitaia, Whagarei, Auckland and Tauranga is a subtropical climate zone, which enjoys mild winters and warm summers with relatively high humidity and frequent sea breezes. During the summer, average daytime maximum temperatures range from 22°C–26°C and will only infrequently exceed 30°C. Annual sunshine hours average about 2,000 hours, with at least 2,200 hours in Tauranga.

During the winter, temperatures range from 12°C to 17°C and there is more rain with the weather generally being more unsettled. Summer and autumn often bring storms from the tropics, with high winds and heavy rainfall from the north or north-east.

The Eastern North Island, including Gisborne, Napier, Hastings and Masterton, is largely sheltered by the high country to the west and as a result enjoys a dry and sunny climate with predominantly dry, warm and settled summer weather. In the summer, typical daytime temperatures range from 20°C to 28°C and occasionally exceed 30°C. High temperatures are common during the summer and may be

Waterfall on the Napier – Taupo Road

exacerbated by the strong dry winds which sweep in from the north-east. There are often sea breezes in coastal areas on the warmer summer days. Temperatures of up to 39°C have been recorded in this area. Winter is very mild in the more northern parts of this region and cooler to the south, with winter temperatures during the daytime ranging from 10°C–16°C. Heavy rainfall more commonly comes from the east or south-east. Average annual hours of bright sunshine in Napier and Gisborne number about 2,200.

The Central North Island region covers Hamilton, Taupo and Rotorua. The high country to the south and east of this inland area shelters it somewhat, and consequently it experiences less wind than many other regions but still has a wide range of temperatures. Winters are cool and the weather at this time of year is more unsettled unusually than other seasons. Typical temperatures during winter days range from 10°C–14°C, with frosts occurring during clear and calm winter conditions. Summer sees mainly settled, dry and warm weather dominating, with maximum temperatures ranging from 21°C to 26°C and rarely exceeding 30°C. Sunshine averages between 2,000–2,100 hours every year in most places, and both Taupo and Rotorua often experience lake breezes during the warmth of summer.

The south-west of the North Island includes the areas of New Plymouth, Wanganui, Palmerston North and Wellington. This region is very exposed to the disturbed weather systems from the Tasman Sea, and often experiences high winds but few climate extremes. Summers are warm, and share with autumn the most settled weather through the year. Summer temperatures typically reach between 19°C and 24°C, and only very rarely exceed 30°C, with occasional sea breezes along the coast. New Plymouth and Wanganui enjoy relatively mild winters, but Palmerston North and Wellington winter weather is definitely cooler and more unsettled. Winter daytime temperatures range from 10°C–14°C, with calm and clear winter conditions bringing inland frosts. Inland, Palmerston North is much cloudier than other areas in this region, but annual sunshine hours average about 2,000 for other places.

The South Island

The northern South Island includes Nelson and Blenheim and is largely sheltered from winds and unsettled weather by the high country to the west, south and in some cases east. The weather here is predominantly warm, settled, and dry during summers, and winter generally brings mild days preceded by frosts. Summer temperatures during the daytime average between 20°C and 26°C but can rise above 30°C on occasion. The least settled weather occurs during early spring and late winter, with average winter temperatures between 10°C–15°C. Annual hours of sunshine average at least 2,300 hours, with prevailing winds coming from the north-north-east in Nelson and from the south-west in Blenheim. Nelson's temperatures are often evened out by sea breezes, but it has less wind than the other urban centres, and Blenheim has more frequent high temperatures.

The western South Island covers the areas of Westport, Milford Sound, and Hokitika, amongst others, and this region experiences very high mean annual rainfall generally from the north-west. The climate here is very influenced by the Tasman Sea weather systems, from which is has no protection, and by the Southern Alps to the east. Dry spells occur in late summer and in winter, with mild summers and frosts beginning winter days. Summer daytime temperatures typically range from 17°C–22°C, only seldom topping 25°C, and daytime winter temperatures range from 10°C-14°C. North-north-east winds are common in Westport and Hokitika, along the coast, while prevailing winds further south in coastal areas are more usually south-easterly.

The eastern South Island, including Kaikoura, Christchurch and Timaru, has warm summer temperatures ranging from 18°C–26°C with the highest temperatures (sometimes over 30°C) resulting when the hot, dry north-westerlies blow over the plains and Alps. Christchurch once recorded a summer temperature of 42°C, but this would be remarkable. The climate here is very dependent on the Southern Alps, which lie to the west. Mean annual rainfall is quite low, with long, dry spells especially during the summer when temperatures are cooled by north-easterly sea breezes. Winters are cold with frequent frosts, and nights throughout the year are cool. Typical winter daytime temperatures range from 7°C to 14°C, with south-westerly winds more frequent during winter but north-easterly winds prevailing about the coast for the majority of the year.

Inland South Island, covering Lake Tekapo, Queenstown, Alexandra and Manapouri, is largely sheltered by high country to the south and east, but the climate is also influenced by the Southern Alps to the west. Summers see long dry spells, with very warm afternoons and low mean rainfall. High temperatures particularly result from the dry, hot north-westerly winds that blow over the Alps. During summer days, temperatures are usually between 20°C-26°C and sometimes over 30°C. Snow falls occasionally in the winters, which are very cold with severe frosts, and the snow may stick on the ground for days at a time. During the winter, temperatures during the days range from 3°C through to 11°C. Winds really do depend on exact location, but the strongest winds flow through from the north-west.

Southern New Zealand includes the areas of Dunedin and Invercargill. Cool coastal breezes are typical of this region, and there is little to shelter the country here from unsettled weather that moves in over the sea. Sometimes there are high summer temperatures, brought by hot winds from the north-west, ranging from about 16°C to 23°C and rising occasionally over 30°C. Sunshine hours are often affected by low coastal cloud or high cloud, and average about 1,600 hours annually. Prevailing winds come from the south-west around Southland, and more usually from the north-east around the north of Dunedin.

Average Maximum Temperature, Sunshine and Rainfall

City	Mean Daily Maximum Temperature		Mean Annual Total Bright sunshine hours	Max Annual Rainfall (mm)
	February (°C)	Jul (°C)		
Kaitaia	24.5	15.6	2070	1334
Whangarei	24.2	15.1	1973	1490
Auckland	23.7	14.5	2060	1240
Tauranga	23.3	14.3	2260	1198
Hamilton	24.3	13.6	2009	1190
Rotorua	23	12.1	2117	1401

(Continued on following page)

Average Maximum Temperature, Sunshine and Rainfall (contd)				
	Mean Daily Maximum Temperature		Mean Annual Total Bright	Max Annual Rainfall
City	February (°C)	Jul (°C)	sunshine hours	(mm)
Gisbourne	24.9	14.1	2180	1051
Taupo	23.3	11.2	1965	1102
New Plymouth	22.3	13.3	2182	1432
Napier	24.1	14.1	2188	803
Wanganui	22.7	13.2	2043	882
Palmerston North	22.9	12.5	1733	967
Masterton	23.9	12	1915	979
Wellington	20.6	11.4	2065	1249
Nelson	22.4	12.4	2405	970
Blenheim	23.6	12.8	2409	655
Westport	20.4	12.6	1838	2274
Kaikoura	20	10.9	2090	844
Hokitika	20	12	1860	2875
Christchurch	22.2	11.3	2100	648
Mt Cook	20.8	6.4	1532	4293
Lake Tekapo	21.6	5.9	2180	600
Timaru	20.9	10.1	1826	573
Milford Sound	19.5	9.1	1800	6749
Queenstown	22.7	8.2	1921	913
Alexandra	23.8	7.9	2025	360
Manapouri	20.8	9.8	1700	1164
Dunedin	18.7	9.8	1585	812
Invercargill	18.8	9.5	1614	1112
Chatham Islands	18.1	10.4	1415	855

Mean monthly average since 1971.

Source: National Institute of Water and Atmospheric Research Ltd.

■ POLITICS AND THE SYSTEM OF GOVERNMENT

Government

New Zealand is an independent parliamentary democracy within the British Commonwealth. Queen Elizabeth II is the titular head of state, represented in New Zealand by the Governor-General. The current inhabitant of Government House is His

Excellency Anand Satyanand. The Prime Minister is the head of government, supported by a Cabinet of Ministers chosen from the elected Members of Parliament.

While levels of local government exist in New Zealand, they do not provide a countervailing force as their powers and responsibilities are comparatively weak. Local government bodies are funded largely by rates (property taxes), and exist in the form of regional councils, community boards, special authorities and territorial authorities. The Parliament is unicameral in that it comprises only a single 'house', and 'royal assent' of legislation and government decisions by the monarch's agent, the Governor-General, is simply a formality.

Until the introduction of a proportional electoral system in 1996 (see below) radical policy programmes could be introduced relatively quickly as was demonstrated by the fourth Labour government, which transformed the country between 1984 and 1990. A former Prime Minister from the period, Sir Geoffrey Palmer, dubbed the New Zealand political system as an 'elected dictatorship'.

The electorate has not universally welcomed change as was demonstrated by the electoral backlash against both the major parties in the 1993 election. Neither of the big parties gained the confidence of the electorate, and small parties got a record number of seats. The result on the night was a hung parliament, but a recount in some of the most marginal seats resulted in a narrow victory for the ruling National party. Today the public remain wary of radical reform and the introduction of the proportional electoral system was a response to the policy 'lurches' of successive administrations.

All New Zealanders over the age of 18 have the right to vote. Parliament is elected every three years by Mixed Member Proportional Representation (MMP); this system has now been in place for 11 years. The electorate continues to be polarised on the merits of MMP. It has the benefit, however, of allowing significant minority votes to be recognised and of providing the chance for those voters to have a seat in parliament. Two of the parties in the present parliament are represented without having won an electoral seat.

Under the MMP system, voters have two votes; the first for the political party ('party vote') that enables them to choose which party they would like to see in Parliament, and the second, an 'electorate vote' is for the MP they want to represent their local area electorate. As an almost fully proportional system, MMP is a system that makes it difficult for a party to win a majority of parliamentary seats and govern in its own right. This means that coalition or minority government is the most likely form of government, as has been the case since 1996.

Parliament is usually made up of 120 MPs (although 121 at present), and the proportion of each party is dependent upon the outcome of the party vote. A total of 62 electoral representatives are chosen from the 46 general electorates in the North Island and 16 in the South Island, as well as the seven Maori electorates that cover the whole country. Voters of Maori descent may choose whether to register on the general or the Maori electoral roll. The remaining 51 MPs are called 'Party list MPs', and win their places in Parliament by making up the proportion of their party according to the 'party vote'. Party lists are the pecking order of MPs for that party. As well as pitting MPs in the same party against each other in the undignified struggle for selection, MMP makes it much easier for small parties to gain representation than was previously the case.

The main party in the present government, Labour, does not command a majority of seats and is reliant upon agreements with several minor parties to cobble together

"

Though the New Zealand government may have its fingers in some interesting pies, for the most part it keeps its nose out of other people's business. This is what makes it the laid-back country that it is.
Sam McLaughlan

"

majorities for specific policies. The system means that, ideally, parties are required to tailor policies to reflect wider interest than simply their own.

MMP has also resulted in increased numbers of Maori and ethnic minority politicians, as well as women, in Parliament. In 2007 39 women, 21 Maori, four Pacific Islanders, and two Asian MPs were among the 121 MPs, as well as numerous openly gay and lesbian politicians, a transsexual and a Rastafarian.

Apart from the Greens, the minor parties formed under MMP have all sprung up from the two parties that had previously dominated New Zealand politics since the 1930s– National and Labour. Three MPs in particular decided that the best way to get on the new world of MMP was leave the big parties to found a party in their own image. Former National MP Winston Peters created the New Zealand First Party, former Labour Cabinet minister Peter Dunne founded the United Party, and Jim Anderton, a former Labour MP and party president, established the Alliance Party, which later became the Progressives. More information concerning MMP can be obtained from The Electoral Commission.

 The Electoral Commission: Level 6, Greenock House, 39 The Terrace, Wellington; (04) 474 0670; fax (04) 474 0674; info@elections.govt.nz; www.elections.org.nz

Political parties

Having been colonised by migrants seeking a more fair and prosperous society from the hardships of 19th-century life in the Northern Hemisphere, New Zealand has a history of progressive governments and political movements. The colonial government was founded on the 1840 Treaty of Waitangi which set out the rights of Maori and settlers under British rule, providing protections to the indigenous population that were world-leading and still exercised today.

In 1896 New Zealand was the first significant democracy to extend the right to vote to women. In the early half of the 20th century New Zealand adopted pioneering publicly funded health, welfare and housing programmes. Opposition to sporting ties with apartheid South Africa was a defining issue in New Zealand politics, culminating in the 1981 Springbok rugby tour that divided the nation. The 1986 Homosexual Law Reform Act, legalising gay sex, was equally polarising but now seems enlightened for its time.

For most of the second half of the 20th century, the New Zealand political scene has been dominated by two major parties, National and Labour. National is a conservative party, traditionally the party of farmers and business people. It has been the dominant political party in New Zealand politics, holding office for the majority of the post-war period. The Labour Party arose out of the labour movement, but has subsequently had relative independence from the trade unions. It has often been the innovator of radical social policies, even when these have gone against its own political traditions.

The fourth Labour Government, which held power from 1984 to 1990, was responsible for introducing anti-nuclear legislation that stopped American warships from entering New Zealand ports. It also deregulated the economy, ran a tight monetary policy along Thatcherite lines and sold off a number of state assets – not exactly socialist policies.

The current fifth Labour Government has enjoyed strong economic performance since entering office in 1999 and has used this window to build a modern social democratic state. This government has increased subsidies on health and education services, re-purchased the national airline and railways, re-instated a state-owned bank, lifted pay and conditions for low income workers, introduced paid parental leave and tax credits for families, while continuing an open, market-based economy. As an export-dependent economy mainly focused on primary products, such as meat, dairy, fish and fibre, New Zealand continues to lead the world in the trade liberalisation agenda. More recently environmental causes have been popular, with the current government recently enacting an economy-wide emissions trading regime to cover all gases in all sectors, another world first.

Until 1996, smaller parties were kept out of power by the First Past the Post electoral system. Parties were able to gain power holding less than a majority of votes, and small parties whose supporters were spread around the country would not even gain sufficient votes in any one electorate to elect an MP to Parliament, even though their overall share of the vote could be substantial. One of the results of MMP is that the minor party in the government can now be quite an influence on governmental policy.

There are eight parties represented in the present Parliament: Labour, Progressives (the governing coalition), National, New Zealand First, ACT, United Future, the Greens and the Maori Party. Helen Clark is the leader of the Labour Party and has been Prime Minister since 1999. The National Party elected John Key, a former currency trader, its leader in 2006. The most right-wing party, ACT, which was formed from the ashes of the 1984–1990 market reforms, is led by Rodney Hide. New Zealand First has had only one leader, Winston Peters, since it was formed, and despite the party's nationalist platform its leader is the current Foreign Minister. The Progressives was formed after a split in the left-leaning Alliance Party before the 2002 election. Both the Greens and the Maori Party subscribe to a co-leader philosophy, and advocate environmentalism and Maori self-determination respectively. United Future sees itself as a family-oriented, Christian values party. Its leader, Peter Dunne, is a former Labour government minister.

Evangelical Christians are taking an interest in politics, with one sect (The Destiny Church) proposing to contest over 30 seats in the next election. The Exclusive Brethren Sect tried to influence the 1995 election by taking out anonymous advertising discrediting liberal candidates. Church leaders have been prompted to take this stance because of what they choose to call a decline in the protection of 'family values' with the legalizing of prostitution, the introduction of civil unions legislation and the recognition of same-sex (and de facto) relationships by the present parliament.

Local government

Local government in New Zealand is very much subordinate to central government. Its powers and functions are set by parliament. Local government is the system of locally-elected members representing their communities and making decisions on their behalf. Its function is to ensure the functioning and sustainable well-being of the local community, as local factors (such as environment, health and social services, geography and economic opportunities) are best taken care of by locally-elected councils with the wellbeing of the local community at heart.

There are two levels of local government. Regional councils have broad responsibilities relating to the environment and land use, including control of pests and noxious plants. They also have some responsibilities over civil defence in the case of flood or earthquake. At the next level are territorial or local councils. Both are directly elected, and have the power to set rates. They mostly provide services such as rubbish collection and disposal, parks, swimming pools, cemeteries and libraries. They are responsible for a variety of regulatory measures, for example, building consent, health inspection and control of noise, pollution and parking.

New Zealand's local councils, and their contact telephone numbers, are as follows:

Northland

Northland Regional Council: (09) 438 4639
Kaipara District Council: (09) 439 7059
Far North District Council: (09) 405 2750
Whangarei District Council: 0800 932 463

Auckland

Auckland Regional Council: (09) 366 2000
Waitakere City Council: (09) 839 0400
Manukau City Council: (09) 263 7100
Auckland City Council: (09) 379 2020
North Shore City Council: (09) 486 8600
Franklin District Council: (09) 237 1300
Rodney District Council: 0800 426 5169
Papakura District Council: (09) 295 1300

Bay of Plenty

Bay of Plenty Regional Council: 0800 368 267
Tauranga City Council: (07) 577 7000
Opotiki District Council: (07) 315 3030
Whakatane District Council: (07) 306 0500
Kawerau District Council: (07) 323 8779
Rotorua District Council: (07) 348 4199
Western Bay of Plenty District Council: (07) 571 8008
Taupo District Council: (07) 376 0899

Waikato

Waikato Regional Council: 0800 800 401
Hamilton City Council: (07) 838 6699
Franklin District Council: (09) 237 1300
Hauraki District Council: (07) 862 8609
Waikato District Council: (07) 824 8633
Otorohanga District Council: (07) 873 8199
Waipa District Council: (07) 872 0030
South Waikato District Council: (07) 885 0340

Matamata-Piako District Council: (07) 884 0060
Rotorua District Council: (07) 348 4199
Thames-Coromandel District Council: (07) 868 0200
Waitomo District Council: (07) 878 8801
Taupo District Council: (07) 376 0899

Gisborne

Gisborne District Council: (06) 867 2049

Taranaki

Taranaki Regional Council: (06) 765 7127
South Taranaki District Council: 0800 111 323
New Plymouth District Council: (06) 759 6060
Stratford District Council: (06) 765 6099

Hawke's Bay

Hawke's Bay Regional Council: (06) 835 9200
Napier City Council: (06) 835 7579
Hastings District Council: (06) 878 0500
Rangitikei District Council: 0800 422 522
Wairoa District Council: (06) 838 7309
Central Hawke's Bay District Council: (06) 857 8060
Taupo District Council: (07) 376 0899

Manawatu-Wanganui

Manawatu-Wanganui Regional Council: (06) 952 2800
Palmerston North City Council: (06) 356 8199
Rangitikei District Council: 0800 422 522
Horowhenua District Council: (06) 949 4949
Stratford District Council: (06) 765 6099
Waitomo District Council: (07) 878 8801
Tararua District Council: (06) 374 4080
Manawatu District Council: (06) 323 0000
Ruapehu District Council: (07) 895 8188
Wanganui District Council: (06) 349 0001
Taupo District Council: (07) 376 0899

Wellington

Wellington Regional Council: 0800 496 734
Upper Hutt City Council: (04) 527 2169
Hutt City Council: (04) 570 6666
Wellington City Council: (04) 499 4444
Porirua City Council: (04) 237 5089
Masterton District Council: (06) 378 9666
Carterton District Council: (06) 379 6626
Kapiti Coast District Council: (04) 904 5700
South Wairarapa District Council: (06) 306 9611

Tasman
Tasman Disctrict Council: (03) 543 8400

Nelson
Nelson City Council: (03) 546 0239

Marlborough
Marlborough District Council: (03) 578 5249

West Coast
West Coast Regional Council: (03) 768 0466
Westland District Council: (03) 755 8321
Buller District Council: (03) 788 9111
Grey District Council: (03) 768 1700

Canterbury
Canterbury Regional Council: (03) 353 9007
Christchurch City Council: (03) 941 8999
Banks Peninsula District Council: (03) 941 8999
Waimate District Council: (03) 689 8079
Waimakariri District Council: (03) 313 6136
Waitaki District Council: (03) 434 8060
Timaru District Council: (03) 687 7200
Mackenzie District Council: (03) 685 8514
Ashburton District Council: (03) 307 7700
Hurunui District Council: (03) 314 8816
Selwyn District Council: (03) 324 8080
Kaikoura District Council: (03) 319 5026

Chatham Islands
Chatham Islands Council: (03) 305 0033

Otago
Otago Regional Council: (03) 474 0827
Dunedin City Council: (03) 477 4000
Central Otago District Council: (03) 448 6979
Clutha District Council: (03) 419 0200
Queenstown-Lakes District Council: (03) 441 0499
Waitaki District Council: (03) 434 8060

Southland
Southland Regional Council: (03) 211 5115
Invercargill City Council: (03) 211 1777
Gore District Council: (03) 209 0330
Southland District Council: (03) 218 7259

For more information about how local government functions, see www.lgnz.co.nz and www.localcouncils.govt.nz.

■ OFFICIAL INFORMATION

Information held by the government and its ministries, education and health institutions, State Owned Enterprises and local government is called official information. There is legislation governing the availability of this material, and members of the public can write in to the organisation concerned to find out certain facts and figures. To find out more, see www.justice.govt.nz and search for 'official information'. For instructions about how to make a request for official information, see www.ombudsmen.govt.nz. Your request does not have to be in writing, or in legal language, but there may be a charge for the information depending on the rules of the particular agency in question.

■ RELIGION

Just over two million Kiwis currently living in New Zealand are Christian, including Maori Christian, and under this umbrella the main groups are Catholic, Methodist, Anglican, Presbyterian, Congregation and Reformed denominations. This total figure represents 55.6% of the people who answered the religious affiliation question in the 2006 census, compared to 60.6% who answered the same question in 2001. The 2006 results saw an increase in the numbers of people identifying themselves as Catholic or Methodist, but decreases in the number of people who list themselves as belonging to the Anglican, Presbyterian, Congregation and Reformed denominations. Affiliations with other denominations increased between 2001 and 2006; the number of people identifying themselves as Orthodox Christians increased by 37.8%, affiliation with Evangelical, Born Again and Fundamentalist religions increased by 25.6, and the number belonging to Pentecostal religions increased by 17.8%. Over 80% of Pacific peoples living in New Zealand identify themselves as belonging to Christian religions. Of the Maori respondents, 11.1% identified with a Maori Christian religion such as Ratana and Ringatu.

Corresponding with the small decrease in the number of people identifying with Christian religions from 2001 to 2006 there was an increase in the numbers of people affiliating with non-Christian religions. The number of people listed as Sikh increased from 5,196 to 9,507 (an increase of 83%), and people affiliated with Hinduism or Islam increased by 61.8 % and 52.6 % respectively (Hinduism increased from 39,798 to 64,392 and Islam increased from 23,631 to 36,072). These increasing numbers can be mainly attributed to migrants, particularly those from Asia. In total 78.8% of those affiliated with the Hindu religions were from abroad, mainly from Southern Asia and the Pacific Islands. Seventy-seven per cent of those affiliating with Islam were born in the Middle East or Southern Asia, and the majority of those affiliating with Buddhism (34,422 from a total number of 37,590) were born in Asia. Of those born outside New Zealand and identifying themselves as Hindu or Muslim, almost half had arrived in New Zealand less than five years ago; just over one third of Buddhists born abroad had arrived less than five years ago.

In 2006 34.7% of Kiwis stated that they had no religion at all, compared with 29.6% stating the same in 2001. Forty-three per cent of children aged 14 years or younger were listed as having no religion, and overall younger people were more

FACT

■ Most New Zealanders live in the North Island, one third of them in the greater Auckland region.

The skyscrapers in downtown Aukland

likely to be recorded as having no religion compared with 11.8% of those aged 65 years or over. Out of the ethnic groups, those stating they had no religion were most likely to be either 'New Zealanders' (37.6%) or 'Europeans' (37.7%). Those most unlikely to record themselves as 'no religion' were people from the ethic groupings Middle Eastern, Latin American and African (only 11%).

■ REGIONAL GUIDE

The two major North Island cities, Auckland, the largest city, and Wellington, the capital, provide the closest New Zealand equivalent to the culture and lifestyle of big cities in the rest of the world. Wellington takes itself more seriously as befits a capital city. It is the headquarters of most national cultural institutions, such as the Royal New Zealand Ballet and New Zealand Symphony Orchestra, home to many thriving theatre companies, and the seat of government.

The South Island is more sparsely populated but attracts more foreign visitors than the North Island because of the splendours of the scenery. Christchurch, the biggest city in the south, is very English in appearance and has a rather staid, conservative

FACT

■ There is amicable rivalry between Auckland and Wellington, Auckland being bigger, brasher and more commercial – Sydney for beginners according to some people.

Demographics	
Main Urban Areas	Total Populations (2007)
Whangarei	50,900
Auckland	1,294,000
Tauranga	114,200
Rotorua	55,500

Demographics	
Main Urban Areas	**Total Populations (2007)**
Hamilton	163,900
Napier-Hastings	122,500
Gisborne	33,600
Wanganui	39,800
New Plymouth	51,000
Palmerston North	79,300
Wellington	379,000
Nelson	58,300
Christchurch	378,700
Dunedin	114,600
Invercargill	47,900

feel, perhaps because of the architecture. Groups of new immigrants often used to settle in particular regions. The area just north of Auckland is full of family vineyards run by Dalmatian immigrants who arrived last century from what is now the country of Croatia. Danes settled in the Wairarapa, the area just north of Wellington.

Information facilities

The New Zealand Tourism Board runs a network of i-SITE Visitor Information Centres throughout the country, where you can obtain maps of the area, information, public transport timetables, and answers to your questions. Information Centres

New Zealand Tourism Board: Level 16, 80 The Terrace, PO Box 95, Wellington; (04) 917 5400; fax (04) 915 3817; www.newzealand.com

can be found in most large towns. For the listing of the offices you want, go to www.newzealand.com/travel/vins and choose your destination. There are offices in Wellington, Christchurch and Auckland. Other useful websites for a general overview include the AA New Zealand Guide (www.aaguides.co.nz), Pure New Zealand (www.purenz.co.nz), the New Zealand Information Network (www.newzealandnz.co.nz) and Jasons Travel Channel (www.jasons.co.nz).

Regional divisions and main towns

Regional divisions:	Main Cities:
North Island: Northland, Auckland, Waikato, Bay of Plenty, Gisborne/Hawke's Bay, Taranaki, Manawatu/Wanganui, Wellington. **South Island:** Nelson/Marlborough/Tasman, West Coast, Canterbury, Southland and Otago	**North Island:** Auckland, Wellington and Hamilton. **South Island:** Christchurch and Dunedin.

The following regions correspond to the territorial divisions of local government, with the exception of some of the smaller districts such as Gisborne, which have been grouped with larger neighbours.

Northland

Main city: Whangarei ('wh' in Maori is pronounced as 'f').

Northland stretches from north of Auckland to the very tip of the North Island, Cape Reinga, where according to Maori legend, departing souls in the form of birds pause on the tree at the very end of the land before setting off for the oceans. Northland has a semi-tropical climate, miles of diverse and stunning coastline, enormous tracts of forest (home to the ancient Kauri tree) and plentiful birdlife. The legendary Maori adventurer Kupe and his crew made their first landfall in Hokianga Harbour and the Bay of Islands on the East Coast was one of the earliest sites of European settlement. The Treaty of Waitangi, under which the British Crown gained sovereignty over New Zealand, was signed at Waitangi on one side of the Bay of Islands. On the opposite side of the bay is Russell, which was the capital of New Zealand for the first 20 years of British rule. These days one of the main areas of economic activity is tourism. Northland is also a renowned grape-growing region, producing some award-winning wines. The beautiful and distinctive scenery, wonderful beaches, historical aspects and the warm climate make Northland a popular destination for visitors from both New Zealand and overseas. Aside from the historical attractions, it is a centre for big game fishing enthusiasts, sailors and divers.

Auckland

Main city: Auckland.
Major regions: Auckland City; Franklin District; Manukau City; North Shore City; Papakura District; Rodney District; Waitakere City.

FACT

■ The Auckland region is dominated by the city from which it takes its name, the largest in the country with a population of almost 1.3 million people.

The Auckland region stretches from the West Coast, through the city (sometimes known as 'The City of Sails', thanks to the huge number of yachts in the harbour), to the East Coast and out to the islands of the Hauraki Gulf. Two natural harbours, one on the Pacific coast, the other on the Tasman, bite deep into the land forming an isthmus, and the island consequently is narrow at this point. The city covers the width of the island between the harbours.

Auckland is the financial and manufacturing centre of the country, and the major industries represented here are technology, biotechnology, marine, film/TV production and engineering. Although Auckland has the highest population concentration in the country, it is not densely populated by the standards of other cities around the world. Most Aucklanders live in detached single storey dwellings in the suburbs, which creep further into the surrounding countryside each year. The city centre is situated beside the Waitemata Harbour and although it has a number of modestly tall high-rise buildings, it's not exactly Manhattan. In fact one of Auckland's most attractive aspects is the parks and reserves that are dotted throughout the urban area. Many of these reserves are volcanic hills, such as Mount Eden; there are in fact 48 extinct volcanic cones in the area. Another attractive feature is the beaches within walking distance of the city centre.

Anti-Aukland

The remainder of the country sometimes resents Auckland as it dominates New Zealand through its size and concentration of economic activity. There is also a general feeling (sometimes justified, admittedly) that Aucklanders don't think there is anything worthwhile 'south of the Bombay Hills' (the cluster of hills that marks the division between Auckland and Waikato).

Auckland has an ethnically diverse population, and Maori, Polynesian, European and Asian cultures all have a strong presence here. Different ethnic influences are evident in the thriving art and music scenes, and also through the plentiful mix of cuisines on offer. Over 70% of all New Zealand's immigrants choose to make Auckland their home, as do a large proportion of New Zealanders returning from living overseas. All in all, nearly one third of New Zealand's population lives in the greater Auckland region and this is likely to continue as the fastest growing area of economic activity for some time to come.

Waikato and Maoris

The Waikato is the headquarters of the King movement, one of the Maori cultural and political movements responsible for the renaissance of Maoridom in the 20th century. The King movement is based at Turangawaewae marae (Maori meeting place and cultural centre) at Ngaruawahia, the home of the Maori king.

Waikato

Main city: Hamilton.

The Waikato region stretches from the Bombay Hills south of Auckland to Lake Taupo in the centre of the North Island. The lake has an area of 60,606 hectares (234 sq. miles) and is the source of the river for which the region is named. The Waikato River is the longest in New Zealand. Along its 425km (264 mile) length there are eight dams and nine hydro-electric power stations which provide a large part of the North Island's electricity requirements. The first electric power station was built at Horahora to supply electricity for the Marth gold mines and Waihi. These power schemes generate roughly 4000 GWh of electricity, which is about 13% of the whole country's total electrical generating capacity.

New Zealand's dairy industry is centred in Hamilton, the largest city, and there is a strong technological-based research and development presence as well. There are several research facilities located in and around the city, including Landcare Research, AgResearch and Dairying Research Corporation. The University of Waikato and Waikato Polytechnic are also in Hamilton.

The Coromandel Peninsula, in the north-east corner of the region, is a centre for forestry production. The Coromandel is a popular holiday destination and many families own second homes there. Its rugged bush-clad mountains protect almost deserted beaches. Other attractions include the thermal regions around Wairakei, where steam is harnessed to drive turbines producing electricity, and the limestone caves at Waitomo.

Bay of Plenty

Main towns: Tauranga, Rotorua.

The Bay of Plenty is one of the main horticultural regions in the country and has a population of growing at five times the national average. Currently the economy is the fastest growing in the country, and the Port of Tauranga is New Zealand's largest port. The Bay of Plenty is located on the east coast of the North Island above East Cape. The area around Te Puke is the kiwifruit-growing capital of the

The Ratorua Museum

country. If you are fond of the small, furry, brown fruit, you can find them on sale at roadside stalls at ridiculously cheap prices during the season; sometimes when export cargoes are held up for any reason, growers practically give them away. The Bay of Plenty region is a good place for finding casual fruit picking work in season, although students increasingly snap up such jobs.

Rotorua is famous for its geysers, mudpools, steam rising from the street drains, and distinctive sulphuric smell of the thermal activity, reminiscent of rotten eggs. People who live here will tell you that it has the highest sunshine hours and the best climate in the country. The beaches around Tauranga and Mount Maunganui are very picturesque and attract crowds (by New Zealand standards) of families and young people during the summer months.

Hawke's Bay/Gisborne

Main towns: Napier, Hastings, Gisborne.

The East Cape region is very sparsely populated, and over three-quarters of the inhabitants live in the main town of Gisborne. The Gisborne District has a population of about 45,000, with 32,700 of these living in Gisborne city. Dairy and sheep farming are the dominant industries, although wine-making is small but growing activity. Gisborne generally has warm summers and mild winters – temperatures as high as 38°C have been recorded during summer months – and it is the first city in the world to see the sun each day. Gisborne has a busy city port and golden beaches with good surf. Along here the early Maori voyaging canoes made their first landings after sailing south from the islands of the central Pacific. This is also where the Captain James Cook made his first New Zealand landfall in 1769. European settlement was established in 1831.

Hawke's Bay, located south of the East Cape, is another primarily agricultural and horticultural region and has a population of about 148,500. It has a mild climate with long sunshine hours and low rainfall. The area around Napier and Hastings is particularly known for its vineyards, and is maturing into one of the country's leading wine-producing regions. There is also a heavy focus on primary food processing, and other strong industrial sectors include forestry and wood processing, engineering and technologies, finance and business services, retailing, and rapidly growing tourism. Napier boasts some of the most striking architecture in New Zealand. Totally flattened by an earthquake in 1931, the city was rebuilt in the art deco style then fashionable around the world. Most of the original buildings survive undwarfed by modern tower blocks.

Taranaki

Main city: New Plymouth.

The dominant feature of the Taranaki landscape is Mount Taranaki, a perfect volcanic cone, topped year-round with snow.

Taranaki is dairy country and is also the centre of the petrochemical industry. Aside from these, the major industries are engineering, tourism, exports and horticulture. Sunshine hours are reportedly 2,182 per year, with an annual average of 1,432 mm of rain. The population of approximately 103,000 is largely European, with about 15% Maori and a small proportion of Asian and Pacific Island peoples. The region around Mount Taranaki is a national park and there are a number of tramping paths on the mountain and surrounding area. Climbing to the summit is a popular summer activity, and the proximity of mountains to sea makes this an ideal area for outdoor people; you can quite literally spend the morning on the mountain and the afternoon at the beach.

Manawatu/Wanganui

Main cities/towns: Palmerston North, Wanganui, Fielding.

The Manawatu-Wanganui region stretches from Himatangi Beach, just above Wellington up to Rangiwahia in the centre of the North Island's central volcanic plateau, and the population is 222,423. The main river in the region is the Wanganui, which is the same name as the town situated on its banks. They should both correctly be known as Whanganui, but established usage prevails. The town was one of the earliest established by European settlers who recognised the navigable properties of the river. While other cities have expanded, Wanganui has retained the atmosphere of a quiet country town. Tourist attractions include jet boat rides on the Wanganui river.

The main industry is sheep and dairy farming. Tongariro National Park, in the north of the region, has within its bounds the highest points in the North Island, the snow-capped volcanoes, Mount Ruapehu (2,797 metres), Mount Ngaruahoe (2,287 metres) and the shortest of the three, Mount Tongariro (1,967 metres).

Skiing on the North Island

Mount Ruapehu is the main North Island skiing destination, although it is still an active volcano and the eruptions that occurred inconveniently in the winters of 1995 and 1996 wreaked havoc on following ski seasons. It was feared for some time that some ski-fields would have to close, as they had lost so much income, but during recent seasons the snow and business have improved. There have been further eruptions in October 2006 and September 2007.

FACT

■ The cost of living in Manawatu is amongst the lowest for any city in New Zealand.

The whole area is a popular centre for outdoor activities, from climbing and bridge swinging to jet boating and fly-fishing. In the thermal region nearby there are hot springs, and a dip in a naturally heated pool is a popular end to a day's skiing. The largest town, Palmerston North, is towards the south of the region. It has a population of 76,400, and is the home of Massey University, originally one of two specialist agricultural colleges in the country. The major industries are agriculture, science and research, education, distribution and manufacturing. Manawatu has the highest ratio of scientists per head of population in the country, and contract research activity in the region is worth more than NZ$115 million per year.

Wellington

Main cities: Wellington City, Porirua City, Lower Hutt City, Upper Hutt.

The Wellington region covers the southern tip of the North Island and has a population of 448,959. It is named for its largest city, Wellington, which is the political, financial and cultural capital of New Zealand and is home to a multicultural society of 163,824 people. The ethnic composition is roughly 80% European, 12% Maori and 8% Pacific Island. Parliament is usually housed in the distinctive circular building nicknamed 'the Beehive'. The city spreads across steep hills overlooking a harbour shaped like a natural amphitheatre. A favourite cheap thrill amongst inhabitants is watching aeroplanes attempt to battle their way into Wellington airport on a blustery day. Being a passenger on a plane trying to land at Wellington is less fun, as the landing strip is situated on a narrow strip between the harbour and the sea, and sometimes planes abort their takeoff or landing due to high winds and fly to nearby Palmerston North.

The city itself is quite compact, but despite its size it is cosmopolitan, lively and energetic. There are a host of late night cafés and bars, many of which feature local bands and DJs, a thriving theatre scene, a tremendous range of excellent restaurants and several independent cinemas. As a trustee, *Lord of the Rings* director Peter Jackson has helped drive the NZ$4.5million renovations of the Embassy Theatre, a grand old-style cinema on Kent Terrace, at the end of Courtenay Place. Wellington

FACT

■ Wellington is infamous for its winds, which must easily rival those of that other windy city, Chicago.

hosts a biannual arts festival, and this attracts international musicians and performing artists as well as local performers. There is also a newly completed stadium, clearly visible as you enter the city along the motorway, and this was built to host concerts as well as sporting events.

Most of the other towns in the region provide commuter fodder for Wellington. There are some fascinating little towns along the edge of the harbour opposite Wellington, all with their own distinct personalities and tight communities. Most of these are scarcely more than villages as the steep hills drop almost into the sea at this point leaving only a narrow strip of land to build on. A regular ferry service takes about 25 minutes to cross the harbour to Wellington from Days Bay.

Wellington is also a thriving and creative business centre, recognised for the wide variety of innovative and unique products and services it produces. The major industries in this area include property and business services, finance and insurance, general communication services, social and political research, and manufacturing. Comprising several cities, the Wellington region offers a wide range of business, investment, employment and lifestyle opportunities.

Marlborough/Tasman

Main cities: Nelson, Blenheim.

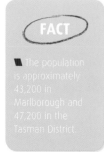

FACT

■ The population is approximately 43,200 in Marlborough and 47,200 in the Tasman District.

The Marlborough and Tasman districts cover the top of the South Island and Marlborough produces a significant proportion of the country's wine exports. Other major industries here include tourism, aquaculture, forestry, traditional pastoral farming and general horticulture and fishing. The climate is pleasant, hot without being as humid as northern parts, with more sunny days and less rain than Auckland. Marlborough enjoys more sunshine hours than any other region in New Zealand, with an average of 2,395 hours per annum with annual rainfall varying from 650mm in the east to over 2,000mm in the west. The Tasman District covers 9,786 km of mountains, lakes, parks, rivers, valleys, plains and coastline and boasts a host of special geographical features and attractions. Some of these include the Abel Tasman and Kahurangi National Parks, Farewell Spit, Lake Rotoiti and golden and white sandy beaches.

The Tasman District is a popular place to retire, with many older people choosing to make their homes in the more populated areas of Richmond, Motueka, Waimea and Golden Bay. The area around Nelson is a centre for artisans and craftspeople, particularly potters, which may account for the slightly alternative feel to the town. It is a relaxed, laid-back place (as are most South Island towns) with a warm and welcoming community and easy access to some beautiful wilderness areas and beaches. Over the Takaka hills to the west lies the aptly named Golden Bay. There are a number of national parks in the Tasman district. The Marlborough district lies east of the city of Nelson and boasts the spectacular Marlborough Sounds, a popular yachting and holiday destination. In this area, along the water, there are many small houses accessible only by boat. Blenheim is the main town in the region.

West Coast

Main towns: Greymouth, Westport.

The West Coast is a wet and wild part of the South Island with its own distinctive breed of New Zealanders. It has the smallest population of the country, with approximately 31,000 permanent residents spread along 600km of rugged coastline. There are about 6,000 people living in Westport, about 1,000 in Reefton and 13,221 in Greymouth (that makes up 42% of the inhabitants of the entire West Coast), and the majority of people living in these areas are of European origin. The Coast is the most isolated part of New Zealand, and there are only four passes available for road travel. These climb up the Alps in a series of hairpin bends through lush grasslands and spectacular scenery. The routes through the centre of the island are occasionally cut off by weather, which may account for the remote feeling of the Coast.

Early settlers spurned the West Coast due to the lack of good farming land, and there had not even been an extensive population of Maori prior to European arrival. Maori activity in this region had been largely restricted to sourcing food and *pounamu* (New Zealand jade or 'greenstone') to trade on the East Coast.

However, in 1864 European explorers discovered gold and coal and the West Coast was suddenly humming with men desperate to make their fortunes. By the 1870s, the West Coast was a hub of the colony's economy, albeit briefly. The legendary rugged independence of its inhabitants may result from the area's historical legacy. In addition to mining, gum digging and possum trapping were the main industries for much of the last two centuries – all fairly solitary occupations. Consequently 'West Coasters' are renowned for their 'Man Alone' strength of character and their sincere hospitality.

There are so few cars on the road that, if driving, you end up waving to every car you pass! Popular tourist industries are as diverse as walking on the Fox and Franz Joseph Glaciers, eco-tourism and wildlife tours, to watching glass blowing, stone carving and gem stone manufacture or going to the local rodeo. The geography of this region is dramatic, from the 'Pancake Rocks' and blowholes on the coast in the north, to the spectacular glaciers and mountains in the south. Aoraki/Mount Cook, at 3,754 metres, is New Zealand's highest mountain, but its stature was reduced 10.5 metres in 1991 when the top of the mountain fell off in a landslide. It is a region of extremes; the rainfall is very high and the sandflies can be diabolical.

Canterbury

Main city: Christchurch.

The Canterbury region is mostly sheep farming country, miles of pastureland stretching from the foothills of the Southern Alps to the coast. The population of the whole Canterbury province numbers around 533,200. The main city, Christchurch, is the largest in the South Island with a population of almost 360,000. Founded by an idealistic bunch of Oxford University graduates, it was named for their old college. These days it is known as the Garden City, for its botanic parks, trees and green spaces. It is set on the Avon river and is a popular destination for many tourists who like the slightly English flavour Christchurch retains. The skyline is dominated to the east by the Port Hills, and to the west by the Southern Alps. Mount Hutt, a major ski resort, is only an hour's drive from the city.

East of Christchurch is Banks Peninsula, a collection of bays and hills jutting out into the Pacific. Lyttleton Harbour is the deep water port for the city of Christchurch and is connected to the city by a 1.6km tunnel running through the Port Hills. Akaroa, the main settlement on the Peninsula, was originally founded by the French, who had ambitions to colonise New Zealand but were beaten to it by the British. These days the French influence does not extend much beyond the street names and the architecture. The Canterbury plains are prime crop-growing land. Further west on the foothills of the Alps, the land is mostly used for sheep farming.

Despite the large focus on agriculture, the Canterbury region is now also an important centre for electronics, telecommunications, software development, light engineering and niche-market manufacturing, and in addition boasts a number of high-quality education and research facilities.

Otago

Main city: Dunedin.

The Otago region covers the south-eastern part of the South Island, and is home to just 5% of the New Zealand population. Land is used mostly for dairy farming and crop growing. The central Otago basin enjoys surprisingly hot, dry summers despite its latitude, and is a centre for horticulture, particularly stone-fruit orchards. The southerlymost city, Dunedin, was founded by Scottish settlers and now has a population of about 122,000. As well as a vibrant restaurant and café scene, there are a number of well-connected art galleries and museums (which sometimes host international exhibitions not touring any other parts of the country), professional and amateur theatre, sports training and leisure facilities, and a rich heritage of Edwardian and Victorian architecture. Perhaps the most characteristic buildings are those of Otago University, which reflect the importance of education to the early settlers; founded in 1869, it is the oldest university in New Zealand.

The discovery of gold brought a temporary economic boom in the mid-1800s, and Dunedin grew to be one of biggest and most prosperous towns in colonial New Zealand. However, the gold largely ran out after the initial boom, and Dunedin's growth rate fell behind the northern cities. It has remained much the same size since the early days of the 20th century, and many of its historic buildings have been preserved as a result. It has also retained the somewhat austere character of its Presbyterian forefathers, although every year a new intake of students at Otago University tries to reverse this.

Otago offers the opportunity to participate in a wide range of outdoors activities. Just by driving minutes from the Dunedin city centre you can reach miles of white sandy beaches, walking tracks, golf courses and fishing areas. Winter skiing and snowboarding, lakes and vineyards are only a few hours away and are perfect options for a day out or an exciting weekend away.

Studentville

Otago is the only truly 'student' town in the country, university life dominating the town during term time while the students (or 'scarfies' as they are known in this part of the country) provide much needed revenue for local businesses. The tertiary student population is roughly 25,000, and the city is noticeably emptier when the students are away! As in other places where student life dominates society, such as Oxford or Cambridge in the UK, there can be a clearly noticeable divide between 'town' and 'gown'.

Three and a half hours inland from Dunedin lies Queenstown, a major tourist area. Set on Lake Wakatipu against a spectacular mountain backdrop, it is close to ski resorts and the home of adrenaline activities. Try the 71-metre Skipper's Canyon bungy jump if you dare.

Southland

Main towns: Invercargill, Gore.

Southland, as the name suggests, is the southernmost region of the South Island and about 93,000 people call it home. It is the largest province in New Zealand, at 3.6 million hectares, and major focuses here include farming of sheep, beef and dairy animals, a variety of crops, and forestry. Off the coast, fishermen make a living from crayfish, blue cod, oysters and abalone, as well as farming salmon and abalone. Stewart Island, at the very bottom of the South Island, is the southernmost inhabited point of the country. It is off the coast of Southland, below Invercargill, the largest town in the region.

At Bluff near Invercargill is the country's only aluminium smelter, powered by locally produced hydro-electricity. In the western part of the region is Fiordland National Park. It contains some truly awe-inspiring scenery, with fiords or sounds carved out by glaciers, cutting deep channels into the land. The surrounding cliffs are covered in bush and traced by waterfalls. One of the best-known parts of Fiordland is Milford Sound, the destination of the Milford Track, a popular walking trip for tourists and Kiwis alike. On the eastern coast of Southland lies the Catlins area, which features abundant wildlife (seals, sea lions, and Hector's dolphins), native forests, waterfalls and caves. The spectacular Cathedral Caves are only accessible at low tide.

Stewart Island

Stewart Island is the third largest island of New Zealand, with a small population of only 400. Most of the population lives in the only town of Oban. Stewart Island is 30km south of the South Island across Foveaux Strait. The Rakiura National Park covers 85% of the island, and access to the mainland is by ferry or helicopter. It is a largely undiscovered eco-tourism and holiday destination, and is generally hilly, wooded and windswept with a 164-km coastline. The island is roughly triangular, measuring approximately 70 x 40km, and has a total land area of 1,746 square km.

Appendices

USEFUL BOOKS

General

Accounting for Small Business: by Sari Hodgson, (Tandem Press, 2000).

Basic Marketing: Marketing in the Third Millenium (6th ed.): by P. Rose (Dunmore Press, 2004).

Business and New Zealand Society: by P. Longman, (1994).

Cultural Studies in Aotearoa New Zealand: Identity, Space and Place: by Claudia Bell and Steve Matthewman (Oxford University Press, Melbourne, 2004).

Foundations for Growth: A New Zealand Guide to Business Improvement: New Zealand Trade & Enterprise (September 2004).

Growing Tall Poppies: *by Michele Cox.*

New Zealand: Business Law Handbook; USA: (International Business Publications, 2002).

New Zealand: Investment and Business Guide; USA: (International Business Publications, 2002).

New Zealand Dictionary of Business Terms: by M. Lawrence and K. Switzer, (Dunmore Press).

New Zealand for Free: by L. Duncan and S. Roberts; www.steeleroberts.co.nz

Penguin New Zealand Small Business Guide (3rd ed.): Higham and Williams (Penguin, 1999).

Planning for Success: New Zealand Trade & Enterprise, 0800 555 888; www.nzte. govt.nz (updated January 2004).

Political Expression and Ethnicity: Statecraft and Mobilization in the Maori World: by Kayleen M. Hazlehurst (Praeger Publishers, Westport, Connecticut, 1993).

Property Investment in New Zealand: A Strategy for Wealth: by M. Hawes (2001).

Small and Medium Sized Enterprises: A New Zealand Perspective: by A. Cameron and C. Massey (Pearson Education New Zealand Ltd,1999).

Small Business Survival Tactics: by G. Senior, S. Glen and I. McBride (Enterprise Pub, 2000).

The Penguin History of New Zealand: by Michael King (Penguin Books, Auckland, 2003).

The Small Business Book: by L. Oliver and J. English (Bridget Williams Books, 2002).

Where to Live in Auckland: The Essential Homebuyers' Guide: by Stephen Hart (Barbican Publishing, New Zealand, 2008).

Winning Legal Strategies: Doing Business in New Zealand: In-Depth Analysis of Regulations, Corporate Climate and Other Critical Issues Every Company Needs to Know About: by D. Quigg, J. Horner and M. Quigg (Aspatore Books, Boston, 2004).

Your Successful Small Business: A New Zealand Guide to Starting Out and Staying In Business: by J. Ashton (Viking Pacific, 1992).

8 Secrets of Investment Success: by M. Hawes (Penguin).

Lifestyle books

Carnachan, H., 2003. 'The Lifestyle Block Boom'; *Investigate*; June; www. investigatemagazine.com/jun03life.htm.

Fairweather, J.; 1993. 'Smallholder Perceptions of the Rural Lifestyle. Agribusiness and Economics Research Unit'; Research Report No. 220; Lincoln University, Canterbury.

Fairweather, J., 1996. 'We Don't Want to See Our Neighbours' Washing: Rural Lifestyle Ambitions and Constraints Around Christchurch'; *New Zealand Geographer*, 52(2), 76–83.

Fairweather, J. and Robertson. N., 2000. 'Smallholders in Canterbury: Characteristics, Motivations, Land Use and Intentions to Move'; Agribusiness and Economics Research Unit, Research Report No. 245 Lincoln University, Canterbury.

Grant, I., 2000. 'Looking for the Good Life'; *New Zealand Geographic*, 45, 34–55.

The Smallfarming Revolution: New Beginnings in Rural New Zealand: by I. Grant and D. Grant (Penguin Books, Auckland 1998).

Ministry of Agriculture and Forestry, 2005; 'Key Facts.' http://www.maf.govt.nz/mafnet/rural-nz/agriculture-forestry-horticulture-in-brief/2005/key-facts-01.htm (accessed July 2005).

New Zealand Herald, 1999. 'Lifestyle Blocks Often Domains of the Rich.' 5 April, A11.

Paterson, John, 2001. 'Resistance to the Agriculture of Modernity: The Old Order Amish, Biodynamic Agriculture, and Smallfarming in New Zealand'; Occasional Paper No. 2, Department of Sociology and Social Policy, University of Waikato.

Payne, W.G., 1978. 'Taxation and the Smallfarmer'; *The Smallfarmer*, 3:2–3.

Phillips, Martin, 1993. 'Rural Gentrification and the Processes of Class Colonisation.' *Journal of Rural Studies*, 9(2), 123-140.

Sanson, Robert, Andrew Cook and John Fairweather, 2004. 'A Study of Smallholdings and Their Owners'; Prepared for MAF Policy; MAF Information Paper No. 53.

Sellers, Beverley, 1999. 'Shear Beauty'; *Next*, 102, September, 40–49.

Slater, T., Curran, W. and Lees, L., 2004. 'Guest Editorial: Gentrification Research: New Directions and Critical Scholarship'; *Environment and Planning A*, 36, 1141–1150.

The Best of Both Worlds: A Guide to a Semi-Rural Life-Style: by D. Verex (GP Books, Wellington, 1998).

▌ USEFUL WEBSITES AND CONTACTS
Settlement Support New Zealand

Auckland Regional Migrant Centre (ARMS) www.arms-mrc.org.nz
Three Kings: 09 625 2440; reception@arms-mrc.org.nz
Manukau: 09 263 5490; manukau@armsmrc.org.nz
Dunedin: 03 474 3332; fmcay@dcc.govt.nz
Tauranga: 07 578 9272; ssnz@ymcatauranga.org.nz
Whangarei: 09 430 420 ext.8356; ellena@adc.govt.nz
Taranaki: 06 759 1088; ssnp@xtra.co.nz
Rotorua/Taupo:07 348 4199; heather.mcalllister @rdc.govt.nz; www.rotorua-living.com
Southland: 03 211 1803; sue@venturesouthland.co.nz
Nelson/Tasman: 03 546 0289
Napier/Hastings: 06 835 2723; ninas@napier.govt.nz

The New Zealand High Commission in London
The New Zealand High Commission is an overseas post of the New Zealand Ministry of Foreign Affairs and Trade [www.mfat.govt.nz].

The High Commissioner to London, the Right Honorable Jonathan Hunt, ONZ is also New Zealand's Ambassador to Ireland and is accredited to Nigeria. The Deputy High Commissioner is Bronwen Chang.

The High Commission is staffed by a team of 20 diplomats and local staff. The focus of the High Commission's work is managing New Zealand's political, economic and trade relations with the United Kingdom and Ireland.

New Zealand High Commission
New Zealand House
80 Haymarket
London SW1Y 4TQ
United Kingdom
Tel: 0044 20 7930 8422
Fax: 0044 20 7839 4580
aboutnz@newzealandhc.org.uk

Information Office
The New Zealand High Commission has an Information Office which answers enquiries relating to New Zealand government services (but not Immigration New Zealand) on telephone 0207 316 8989 or via email aboutnz@newzealandhc.org.uk.

The New Zealand High Commission Information Office will not respond to emails or telephone calls regarding visas, work permits or residency applications for New Zealand.

For all immigration matters refer to www.immigration.govt.nz (details below) or: telephone (within the UK): 09069 100100 (national callers please note: calls cost £1.00 per minute)
From outside the UK telephone: +44 1344 71 61 99 (normal toll charges apply)

Immigration New Zealand offshore branches

See: www. http://www.immigration.govt.nz/migrant/general/aboutnzis/contactus/ for details of offices in Apia, Beijing, Bangkok, Dubai, Hong Kong, Jakarta, London, Los Angeles, Manila, Moscow, New Delhi, Nuku'alofa, Shanghai, Singapore, Suva, Sydney, Taipei, Tarawa, The Hague and Washington. There are other offshore receiving offices in Africa, the Americas, Asia, Europe, the Pacific and the Middle East, and their details are also listed here.

Land Transport New Zealand

www.ltsa.govt.nz. For the roadcode, see www.ltsa.govt.nz/roadcode/.

▌WEIGHTS AND MEASURES

New Zealand uses the metric measuring system for distances, weights and measures, with a few imperial hangovers. Beer, for example, is usually sold by the pint. People still talk about a pint of milk or a pound of butter, although these products are packaged in metric measurements. Road signs are all in kilometres, as are speed limits. Temperatures are in degrees Celsius. As a rough guide, convert to Fahrenheit, double the degrees and add 30.

■ PUBLIC TRANSPORT INFORMATION FOR WELLINGTON, AUCKLAND AND CHRISTCHURCH

Wellington

For up-to-the-minute timetable and fare information for bus, train and harbour ferry services covering Wellington City and Greater Wellington – which includes the Kapiti Coast, Porirua, the Hutt Valley and Wairarapa – see www.metlink.org.nz. The site also contains a journey planner and school bus route information for all the Wellington schools. If you don't have access to the internet, you can phone the Metlink Service Centre for information on 0800 801 700.

Auckland

For bus, train, ferry and even cycle information in the Auckland regional area, see Maxx Regional Transport: www.maxx.co.nz. It provides all the very latest travel, route amendments and road closure updates, revised services, timetables, ticket and fare information, and a quick search journey planner. You can contact MAXX on (09) 366 6400 or email on: MAXXenquiry@maxx.co.nz. If you want to speak to someone in person, or for printed timetables and other material visit the Britomart Information Kiosk. It is located in Britomart, on the ground floor, next to the ticketing counters. It is open every day except Christmas Day, and the opening hours are Monday to Friday from 7.30am to 6.30pm, and Saturday, Sunday and public holidays from 8.00am to 3.30pm. For further information you can see the Auckland Regional Transport Authority (ARTA) website: www.arta.co.nz. Established in 2004, ARTA is focused on developing and implementing more efficient transport solutions for the Auckland region as its population continues to swell.

Christchurch

For comprehensive city/suburban bus service information, and also information about the free city shuttle service, see the Metroinfo website: www.metroinfo. org.nz. This site includes a journey planner, all timetables, maps, and information about fares and the Metrocard. You can contact the Metroinfo Team by emailing metroinfo@ecan.govt.nz, in Christchurch by telephoning 366 8855 or in Timaru by telephoning 688 5544. The phone lines are open Monday to Saturday from 6.30am to 10.30pm and on Sunday from 9.00am to 9.00pm. To visit in person, go to the Metroinfo Counter at the Bus Exchange on the corner of Colombo and Lichfield Streets in Christchurch, or to i-Site in Timaru at 2 George Street.

▮ INDEX

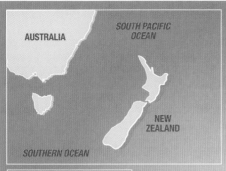

AUSTRALIA

SOUTH PACIFIC
OCEAN

NEW
ZEALAND

SOUTHERN OCEAN

KEY

✈ Airports

▬▬▬▬ Major roads

▬▬▬▬ Railroads

🚢 Ferry routes

NORTH

TRANSPORT**OF**NEW ZEALAND

SOUTH PACIFIC
OCEAN

Paihia
Whangarei

Great Barrier Island

AUCKLAND ✈

Hamilton   Tauranga
Rotorua
Gisborne

New Plymouth

Napier

Palmerston North

TASMAN SEA

Nelson
✈

Greymouth

WELLINGTON

Wellington to Picton (South Island) 🚢

Kaikoura

Harihari

CHRISTCHURCH ✈

Timaru

SOUTH PACIFIC
OCEAN

Queenstown

Te Anau   Dunedin

Invercargill

Stewart Island

🚢 Bluff to Stewart Island

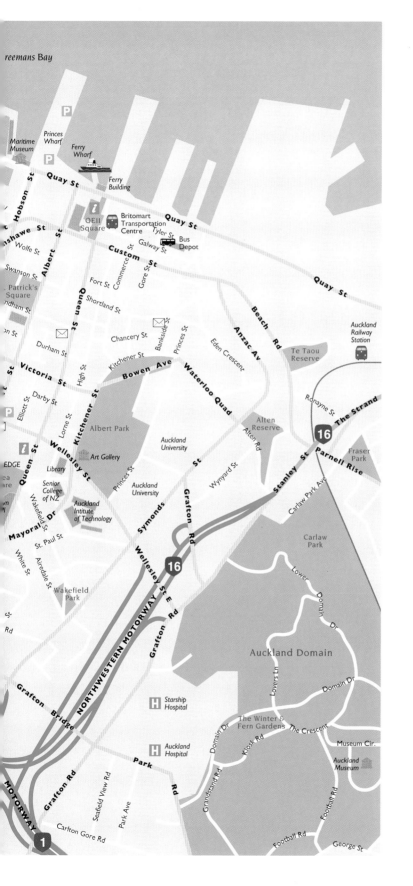

Essential Phone Numbers

Emergency Services

Fire service	**111**
Police	**111**
Ambulance	**111**
Coastguard	**500**

Hospitals
Auckland City Hospital	**09 367 0000**
Christchurch Hospital	**03 364 0640**
Wellington Hospital	**04 385 5999**

Phone information
Directory enquiries	**018**
Operator (international)	**0170**
(national)	**010**
International access code	**0064**

Travel
Auckland Airport	**09 275 0789**
Christchurch Airport	**03 358 5029**
Wellington Airport	**04 385 5100**

Embassies
Australia: *Wellington*	**04 473 6411**
Canada: *Wellington*	**04 473 9577**
India: *Wellington*	**04 473 6390**
Ireland: *Auckland*	**09 977 2252**
China: *Wellington*	**04 472 1382**
South Africa: *Wellington*	**04 234 8006**
United Kingdom: *Wellington*	**04 924 2888**
United States: *Auckland*	**09 303 2724**